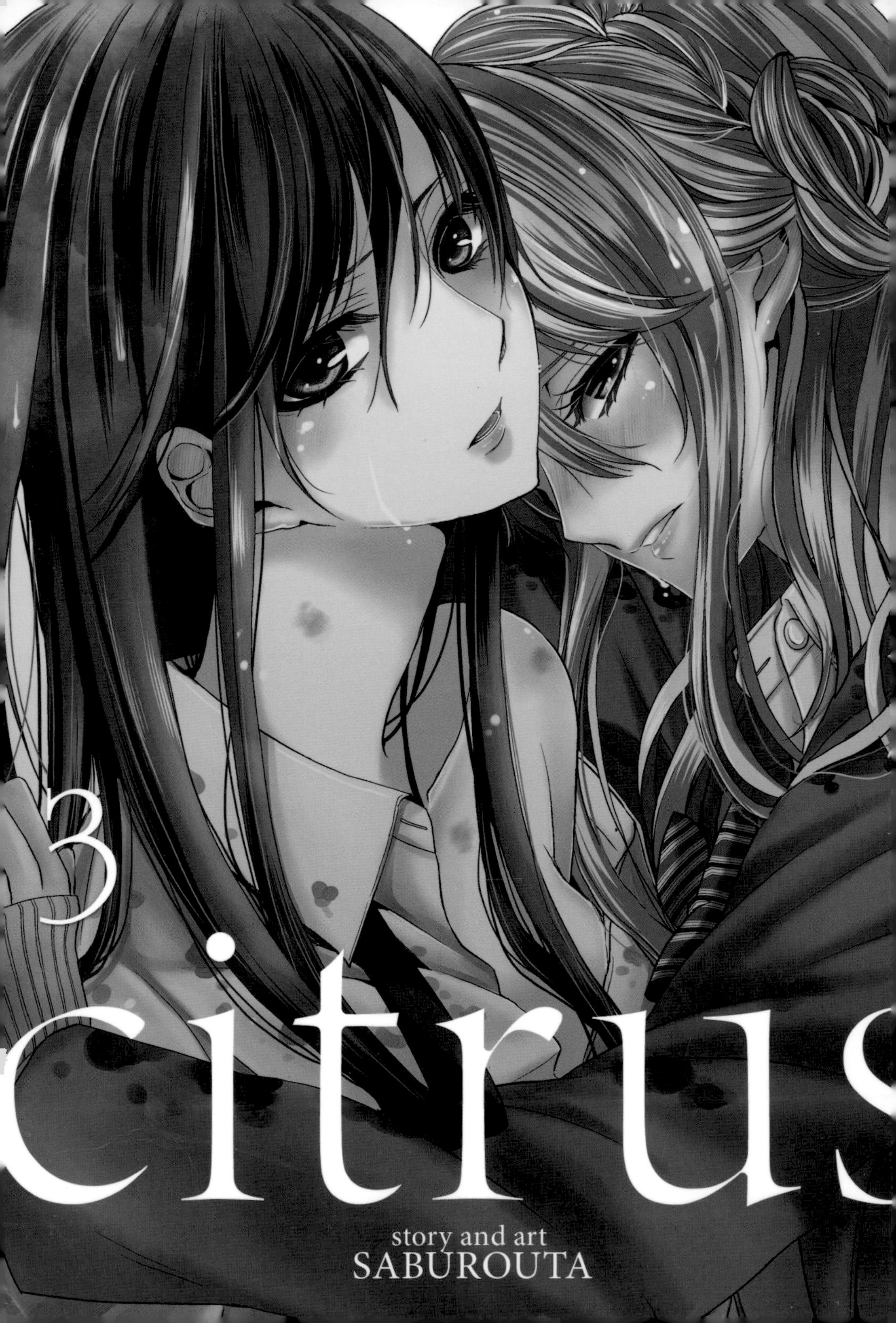
3
citrus
story and art
SABUROUTA

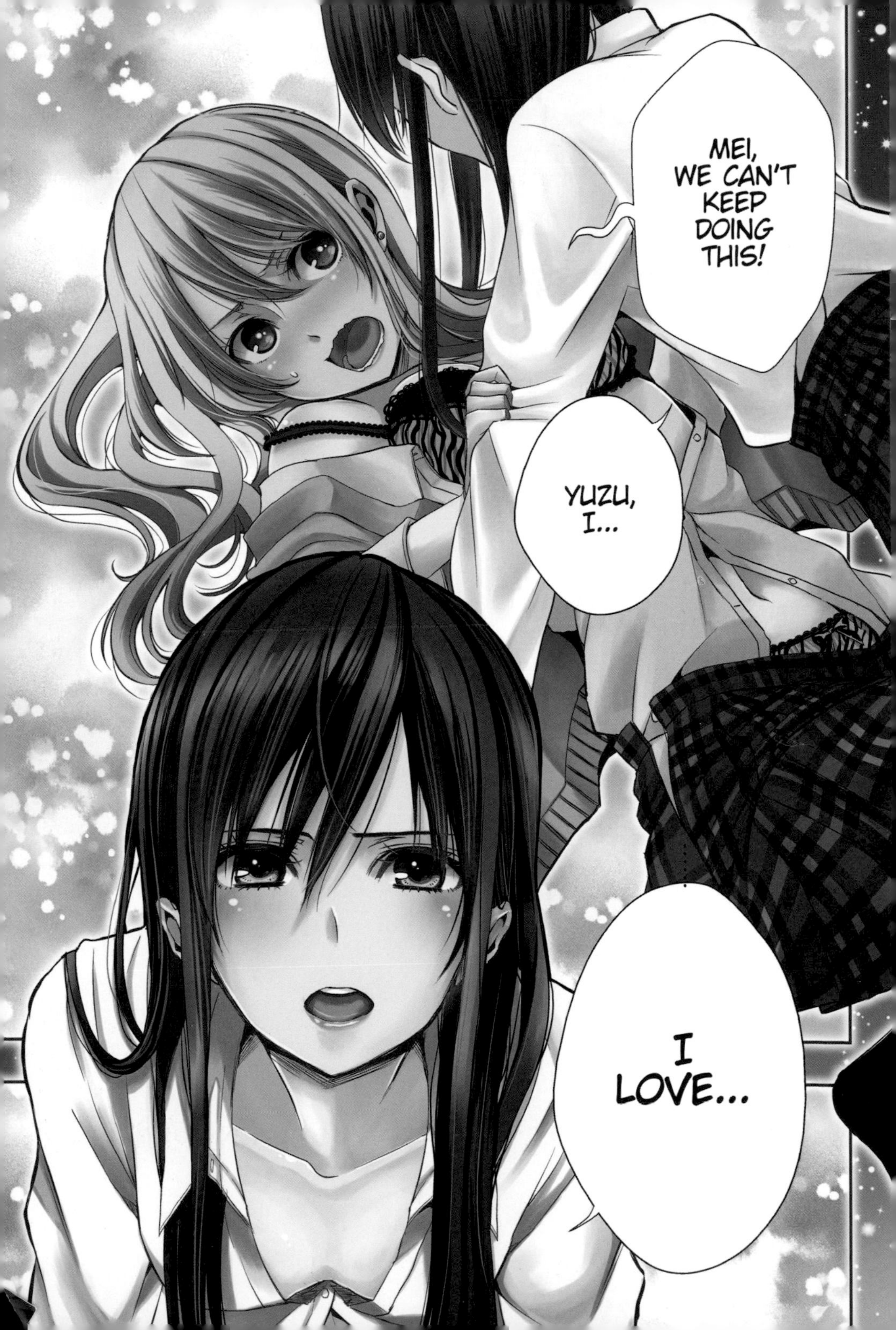
MEI, WE CAN'T KEEP DOING THIS!
YUZU, I...
I LOVE...

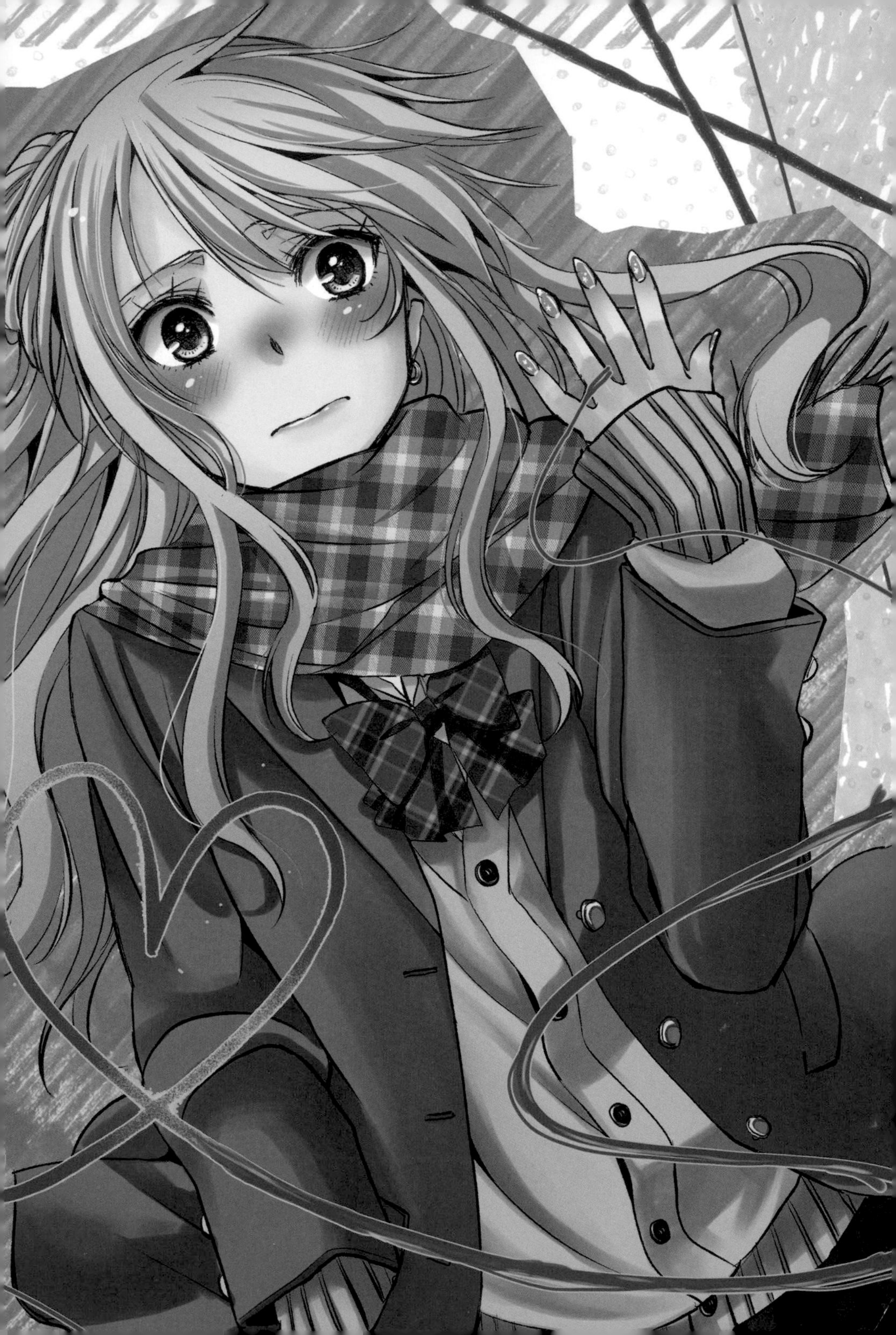

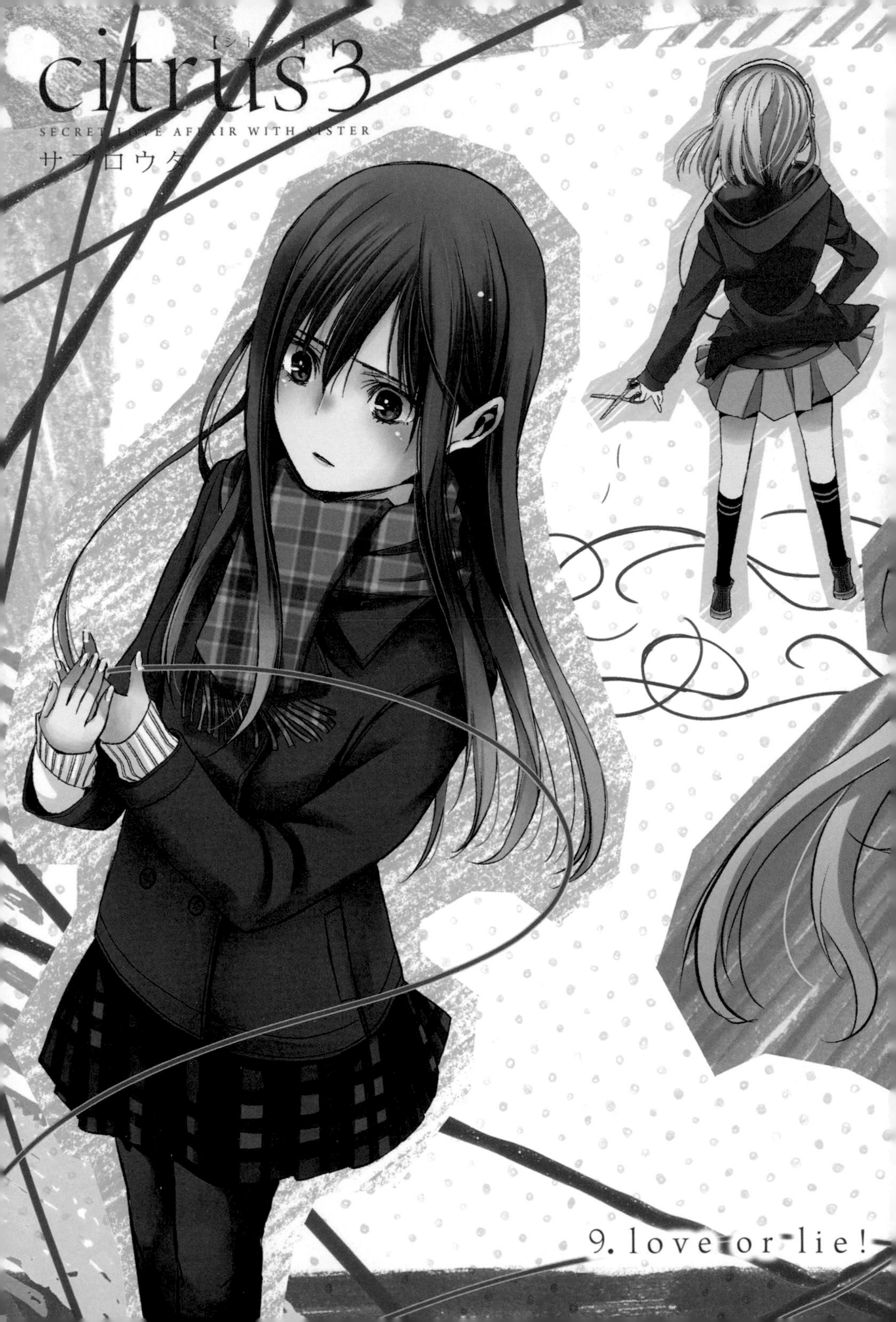
citrus 3
【シトラス】
SECRET LOVE AFFAIR WITH SISTER
サブロウタ
9. love or lie!

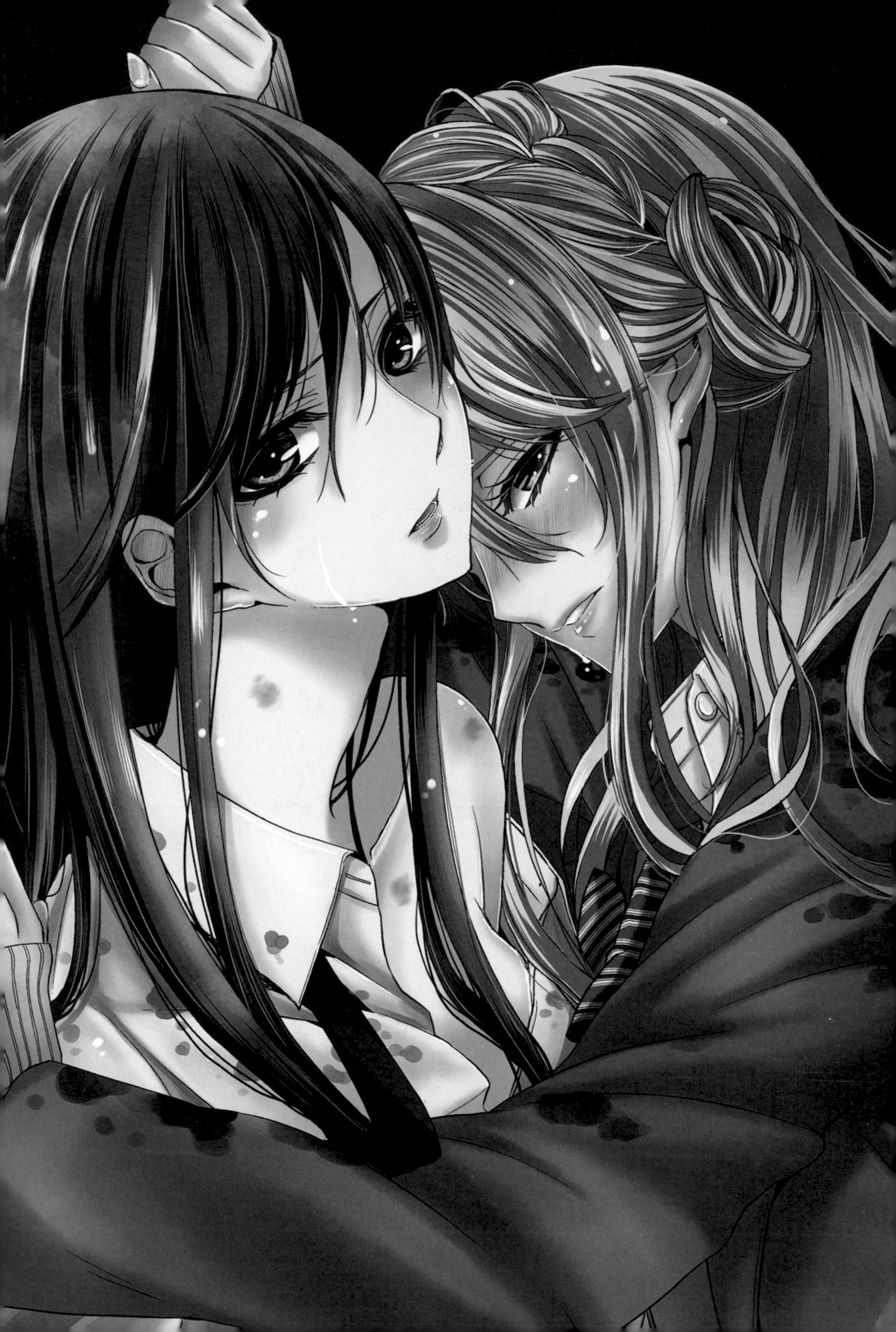

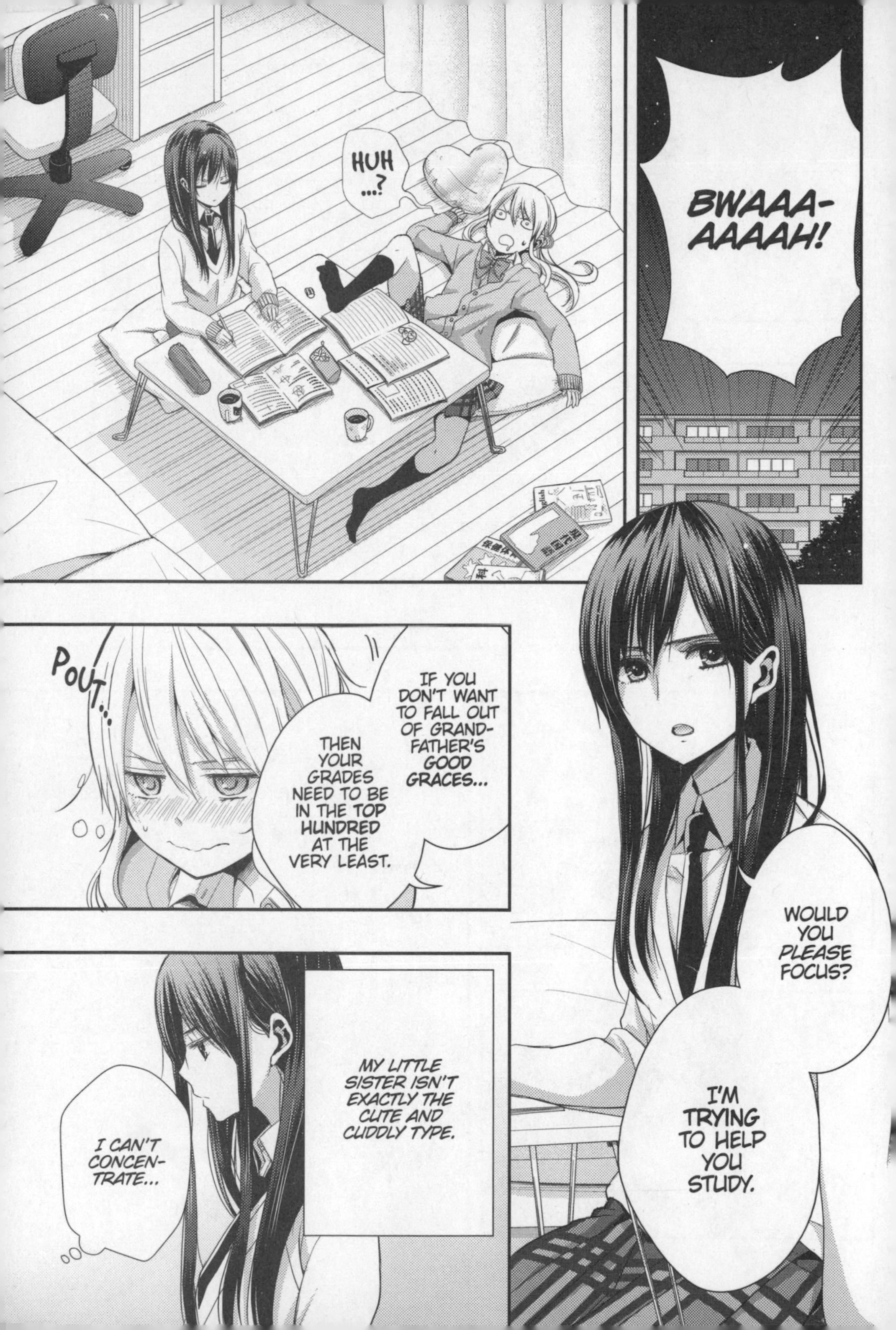
BWAAA-AAAAH!
HUH ...?
WOULD YOU PLEASE FOCUS?
I'M TRYING TO HELP YOU STUDY.
IF YOU DON'T WANT TO FALL OUT OF GRAND-FATHER'S GOOD GRACES...
THEN YOUR GRADES NEED TO BE IN THE TOP HUNDRED AT THE VERY LEAST.
POUT...
MY LITTLE SISTER ISN'T EXACTLY THE CUTE AND CUDDLY TYPE.
I CAN'T CONCEN-TRATE...

BUT, SHE KISSED ME LIKE THAT.

FLINCH

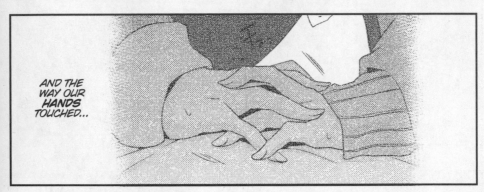

AND THE WAY OUR HANDS TOUCHED...

STARE

I THOUGHT IT WAS MEI'S WAY...

OF SAYING SHE LIKED ME TOO.

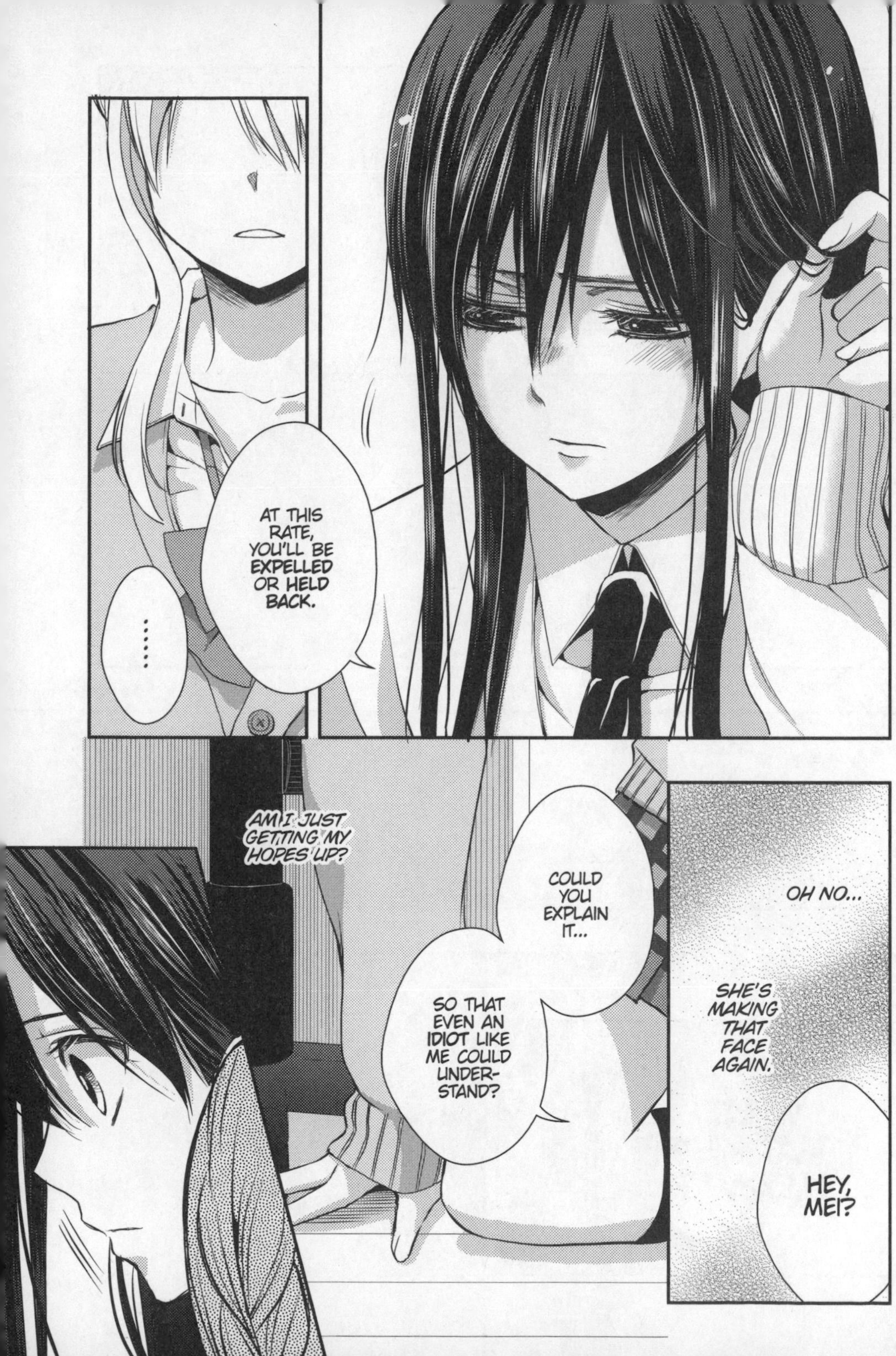
AT THIS RATE, YOU'LL BE EXPELLED OR HELD BACK.
......
OH NO...
SHE'S MAKING THAT FACE AGAIN.
HEY, MEI?
COULD YOU EXPLAIN IT...
SO THAT EVEN AN IDIOT LIKE ME COULD UNDER-STAND?
AM I JUST GETTING MY HOPES UP?

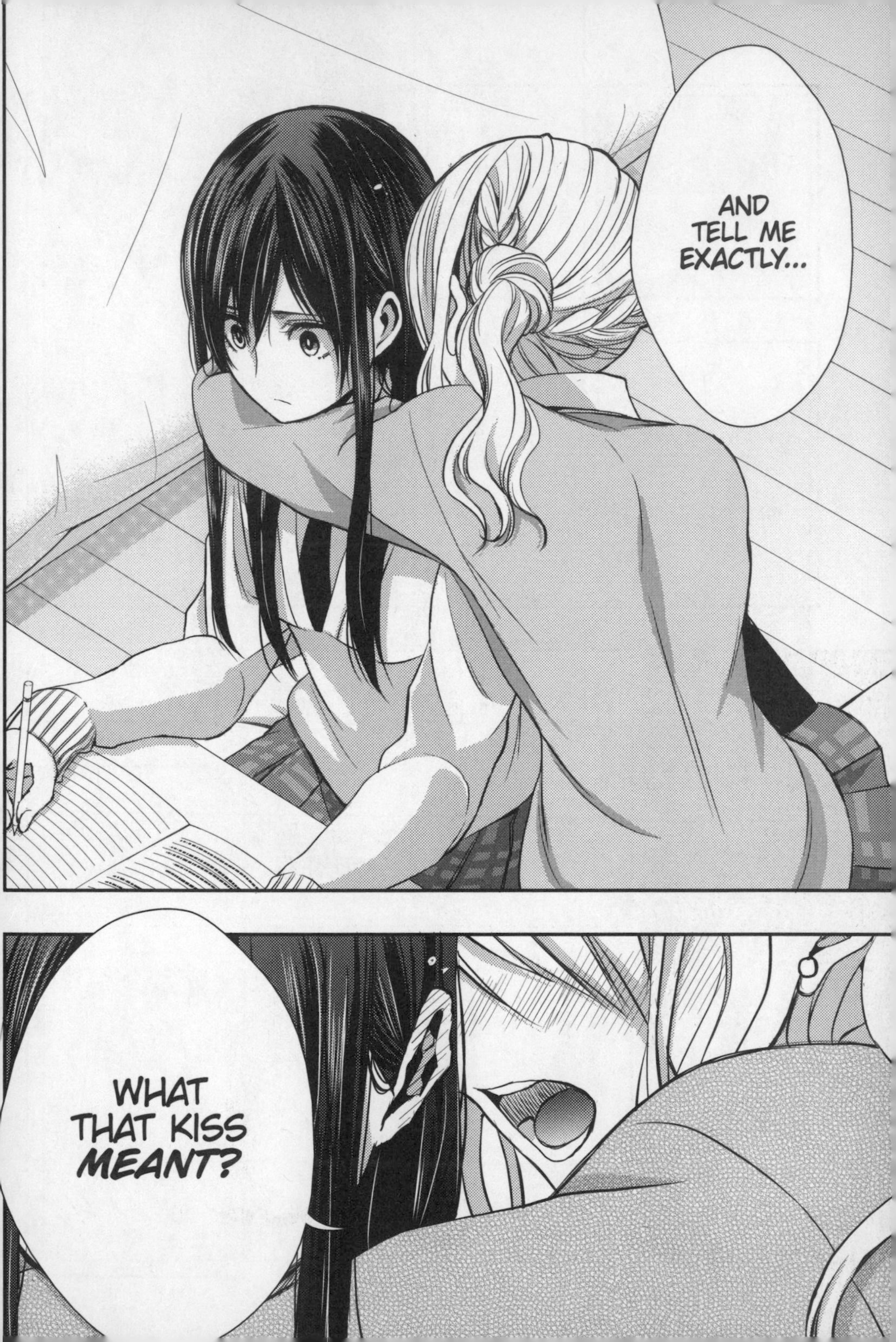
AND TELL ME EXACTLY...
WHAT THAT KISS *MEANT?*

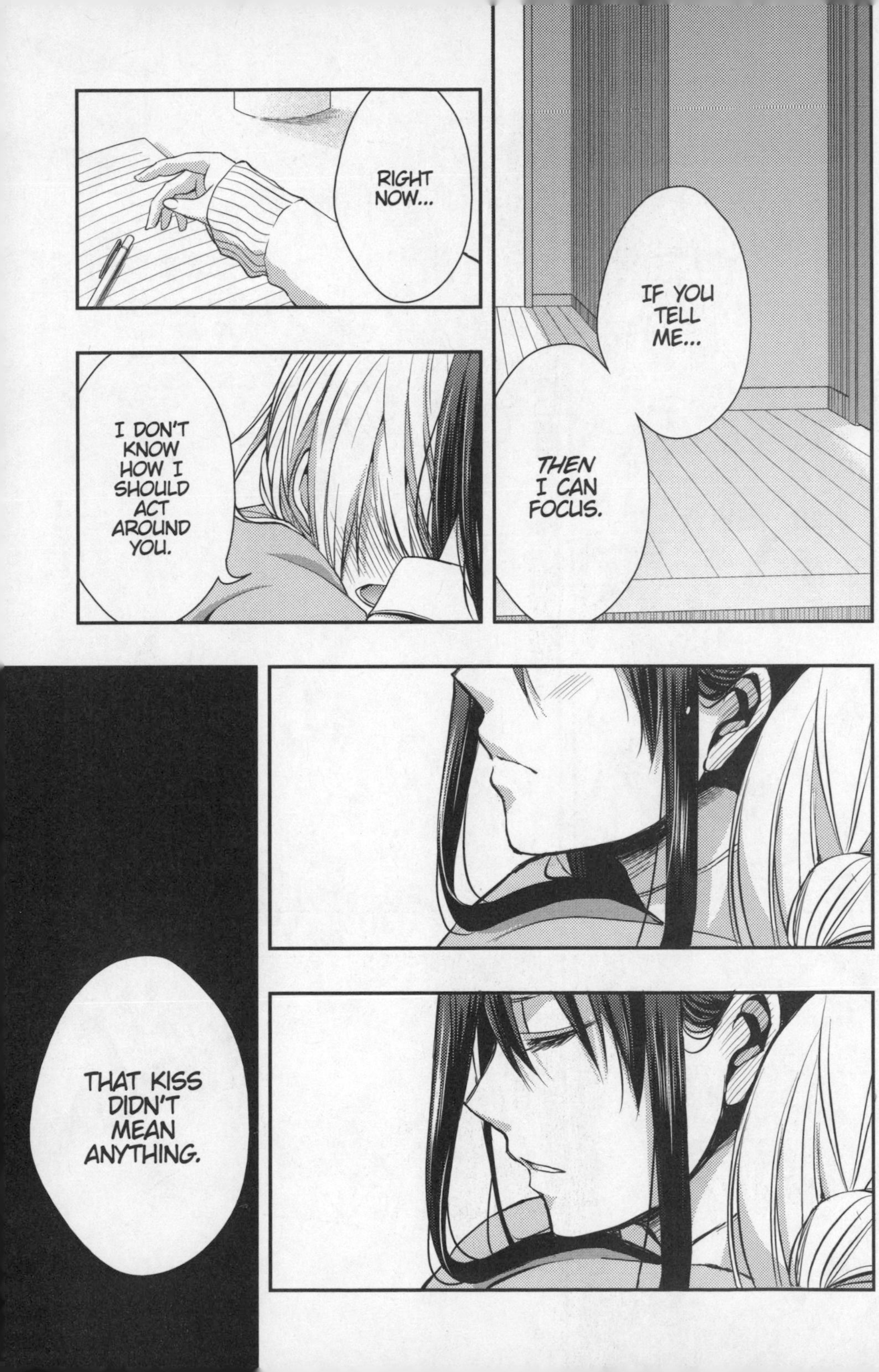
IF YOU TELL ME...
THEN I CAN FOCUS.
RIGHT NOW...
I DON'T KNOW HOW I SHOULD ACT AROUND YOU.
THAT KISS DIDN'T MEAN ANYTHING.

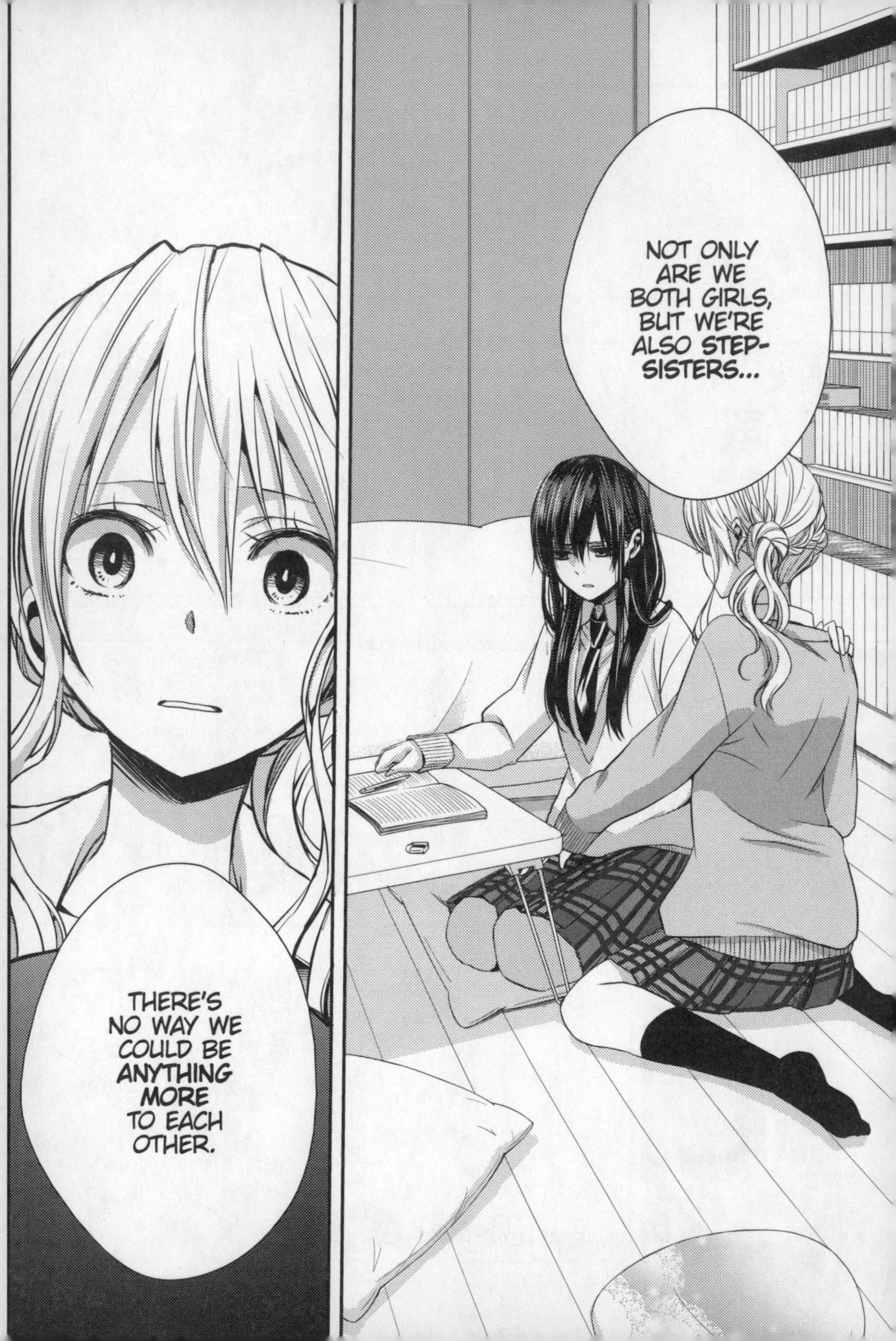
NOT ONLY ARE WE BOTH GIRLS, BUT WE'RE ALSO STEP-SISTERS...
THERE'S NO WAY WE COULD BE ANYTHING MORE TO EACH OTHER.

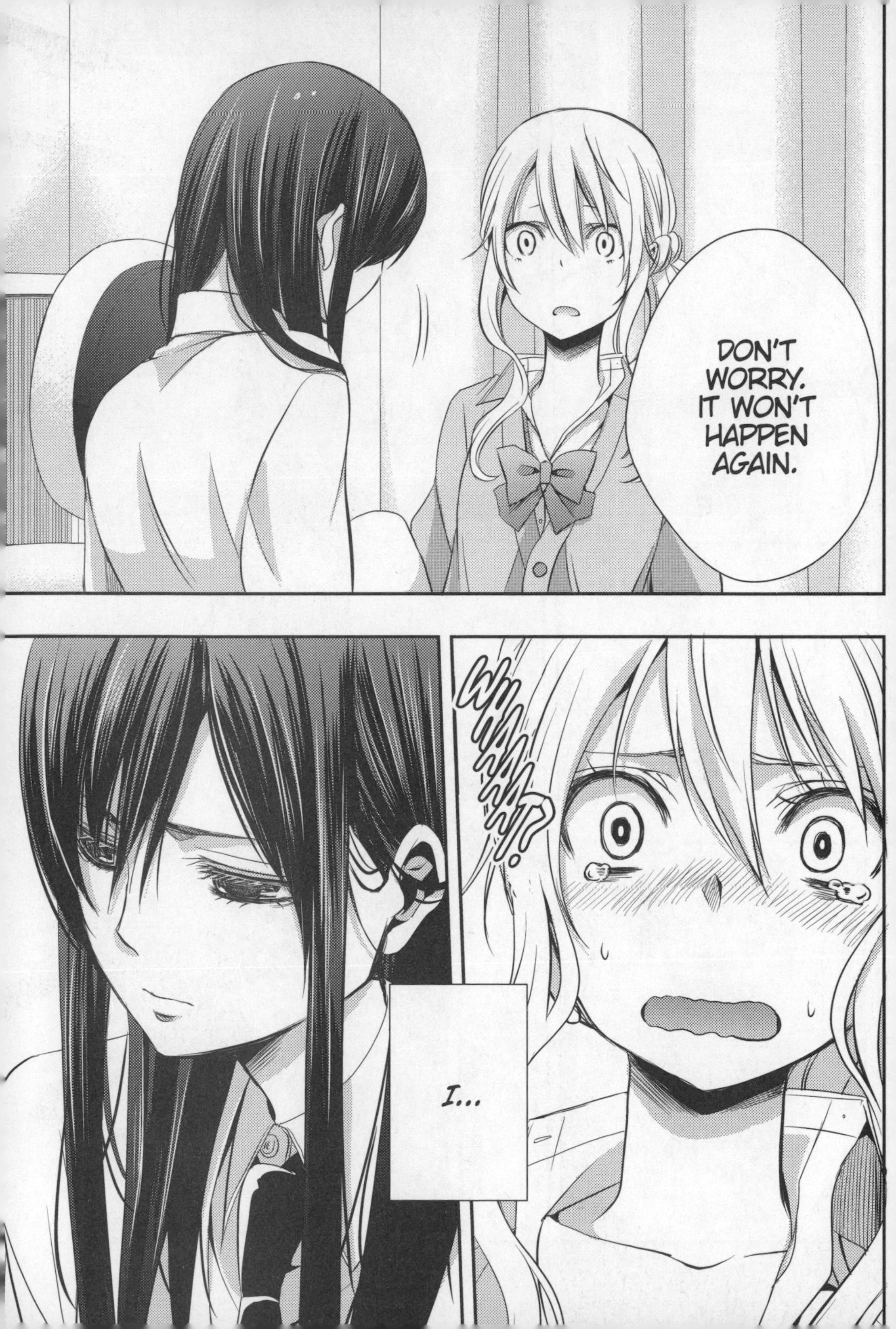
DON'T WORRY. IT WON'T HAPPEN AGAIN.
WHAAAT!?
I...

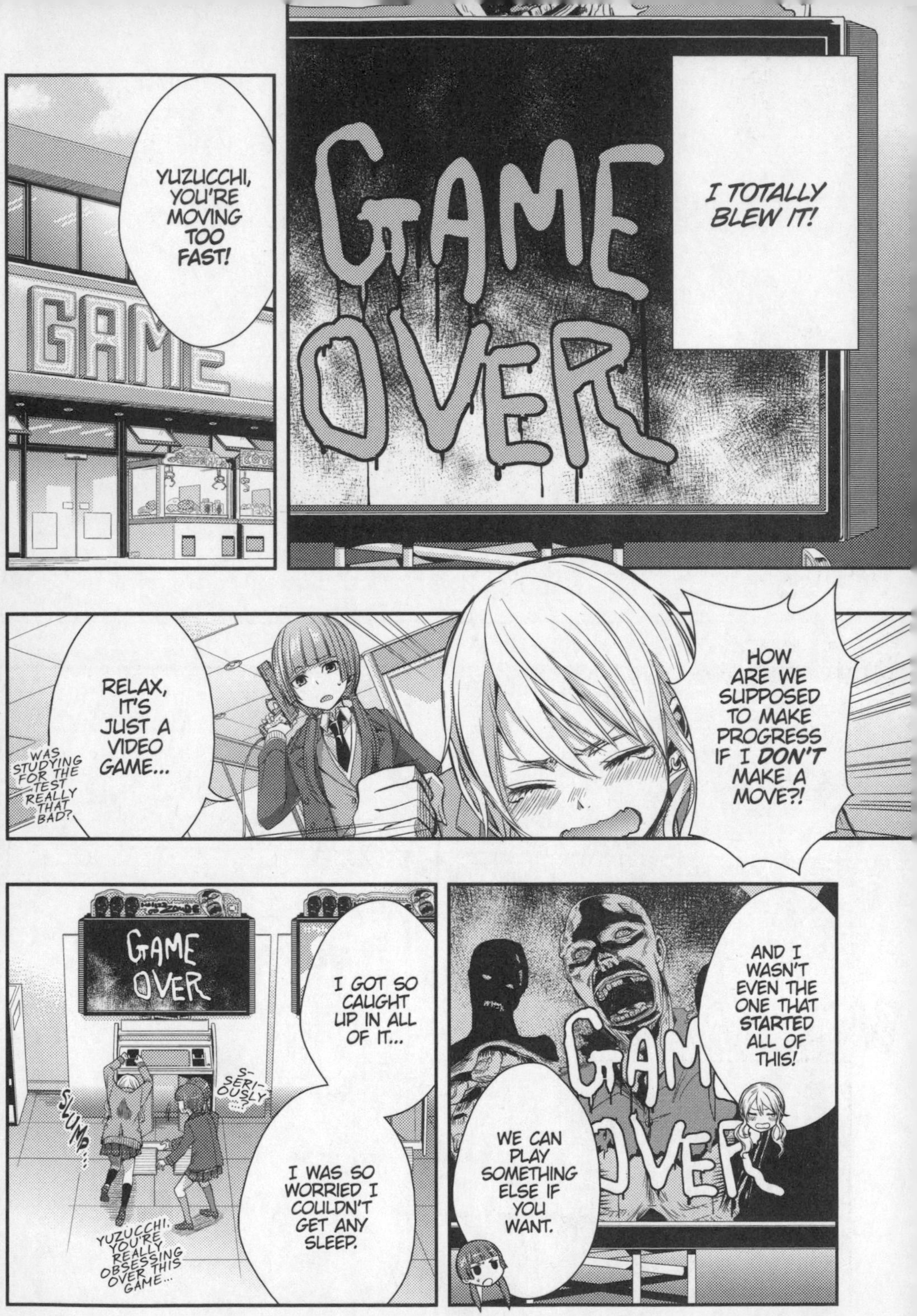
GAME OVER
I TOTALLY BLEW IT!
YUZUCCHI, YOU'RE MOVING TOO FAST!
GAME
HOW ARE WE SUPPOSED TO MAKE PROGRESS IF I *DON'T* MAKE A MOVE?!
RELAX, IT'S JUST A VIDEO GAME...
WAS STUDYING FOR THE TEST REALLY THAT BAD?
AND I WASN'T EVEN THE ONE THAT STARTED ALL OF THIS!
GAME OVER
WE CAN PLAY SOMETHING ELSE IF YOU WANT.
I GOT SO CAUGHT UP IN ALL OF IT...
I WAS SO WORRIED I COULDN'T GET ANY SLEEP.
GAME OVER
S-SERIOUSLY...?
SLUMP...
YUZUCCHI, YOU'RE REALLY OBSESSING OVER THIS GAME...

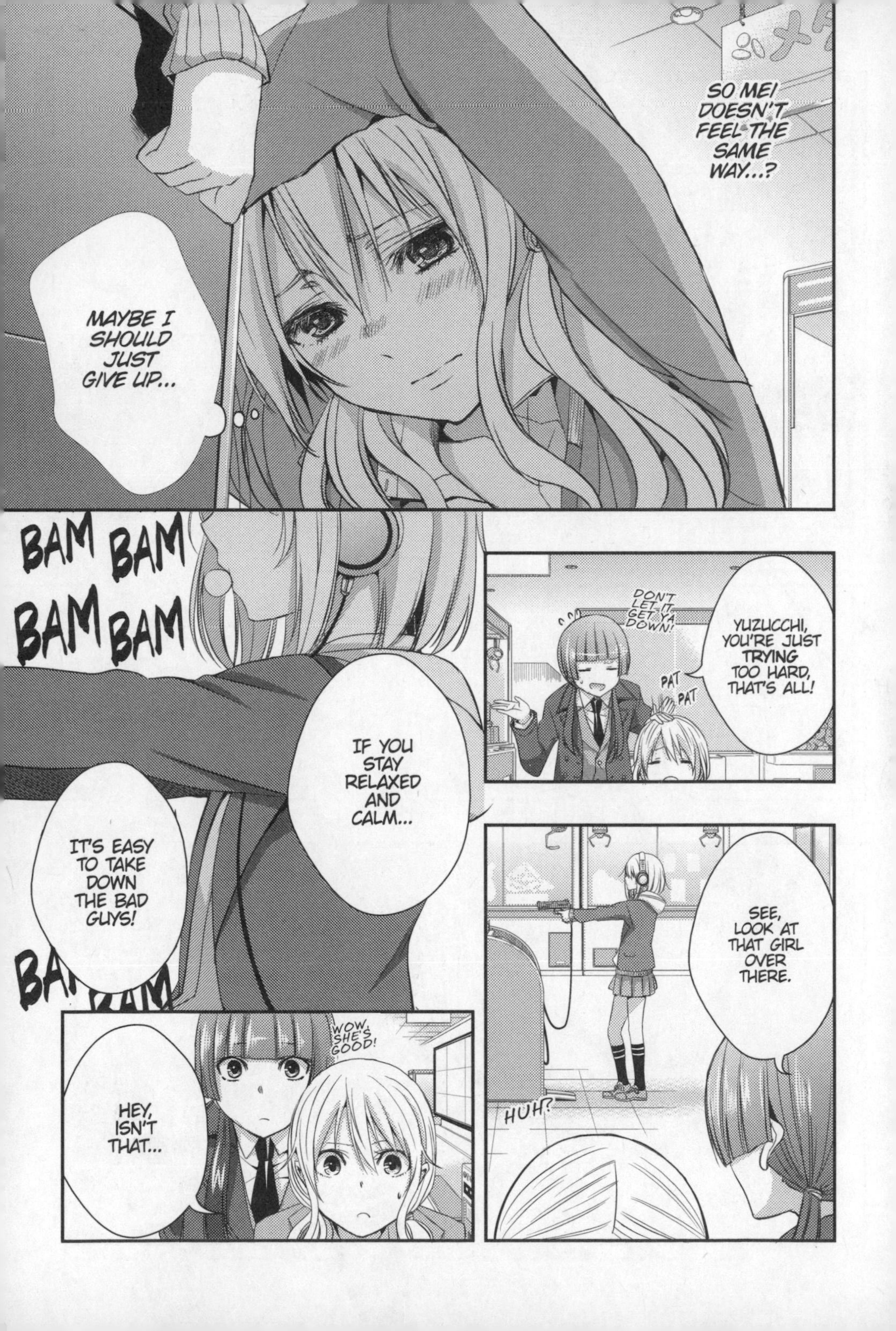
SO MEI DOESN'T FEEL THE SAME WAY...?
MAYBE I SHOULD JUST GIVE UP...
YUZUCCHI, YOU'RE JUST TRYING TOO HARD, THAT'S ALL!
PAT PAT
DON'T LET IT GET YA DOWN!
SEE, LOOK AT THAT GIRL OVER THERE.
HUH?
BAM BAM BAM BAM
IF YOU STAY RELAXED AND CALM...
IT'S EASY TO TAKE DOWN THE BAD GUYS!
BAM BAM
WOW, SHE'S GOOD!
HEY, ISN'T THAT...

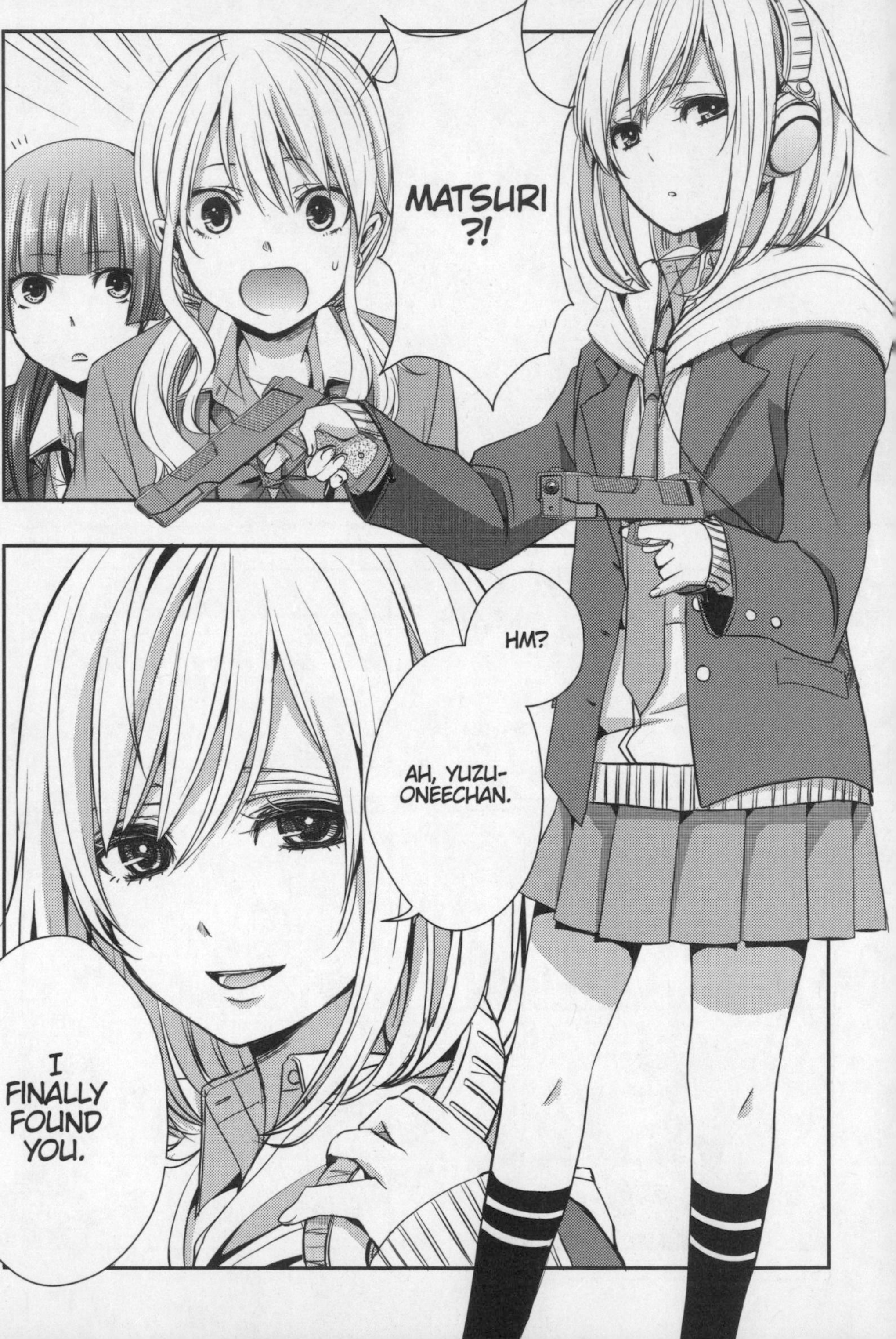
MATSURI ?!
HM?
AH, YUZU-ONEECHAN.
I FINALLY FOUND YOU.

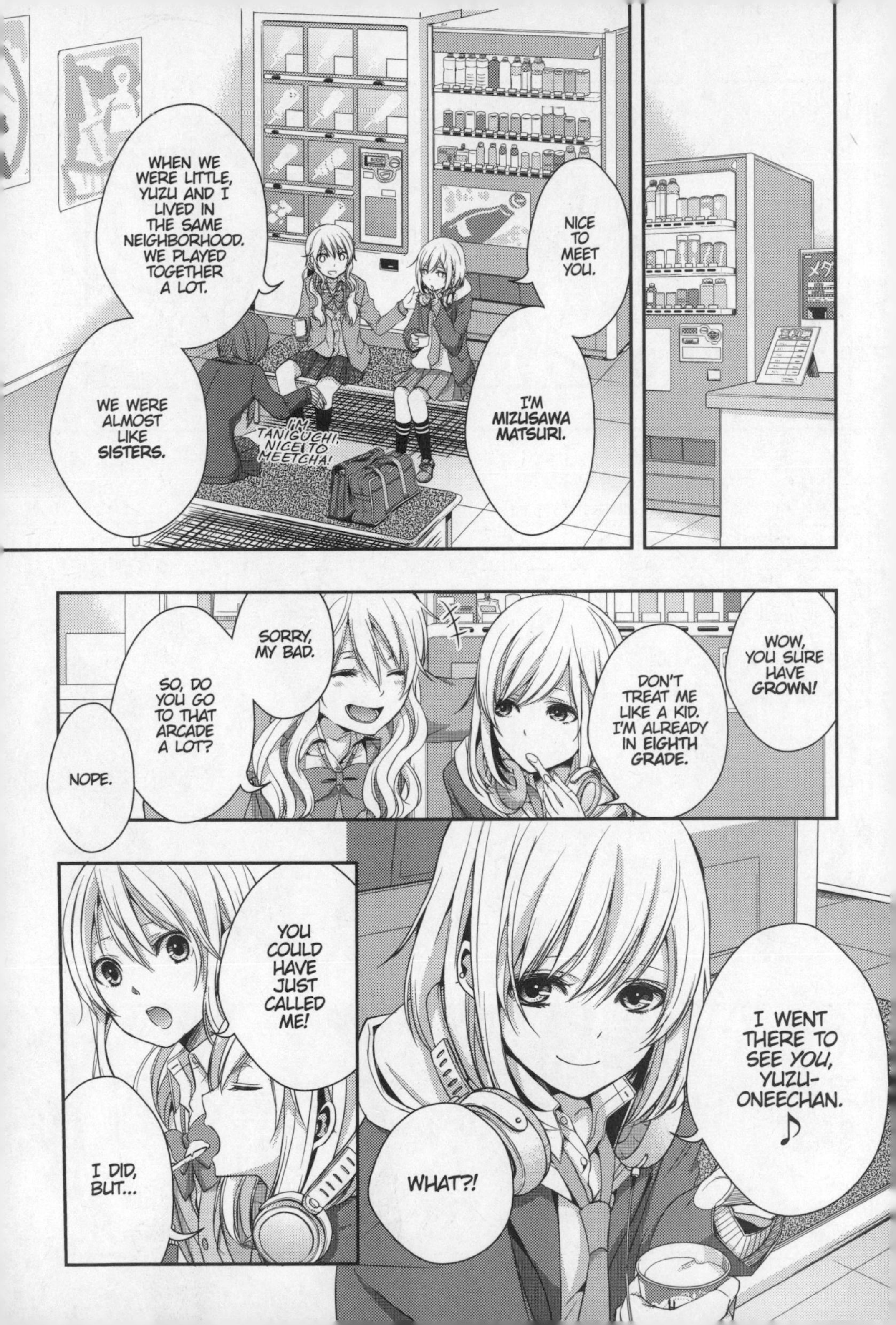
NICE TO MEET YOU.
I'M MIZUSAWA MATSURI.
I'M TANIGUCHI. NICE TO MEETCHA!
WHEN WE WERE LITTLE, YUZU AND I LIVED IN THE SAME NEIGHBORHOOD. WE PLAYED TOGETHER A LOT.
WE WERE ALMOST LIKE SISTERS.
WOW, YOU SURE HAVE GROWN!
DON'T TREAT ME LIKE A KID. I'M ALREADY IN EIGHTH GRADE.
SORRY, MY BAD.
SO, DO YOU GO TO THAT ARCADE A LOT?
NOPE.
I WENT THERE TO SEE YOU, YUZU-ONEECHAN. ♪
WHAT?!
YOU COULD HAVE JUST CALLED ME!
I DID, BUT...

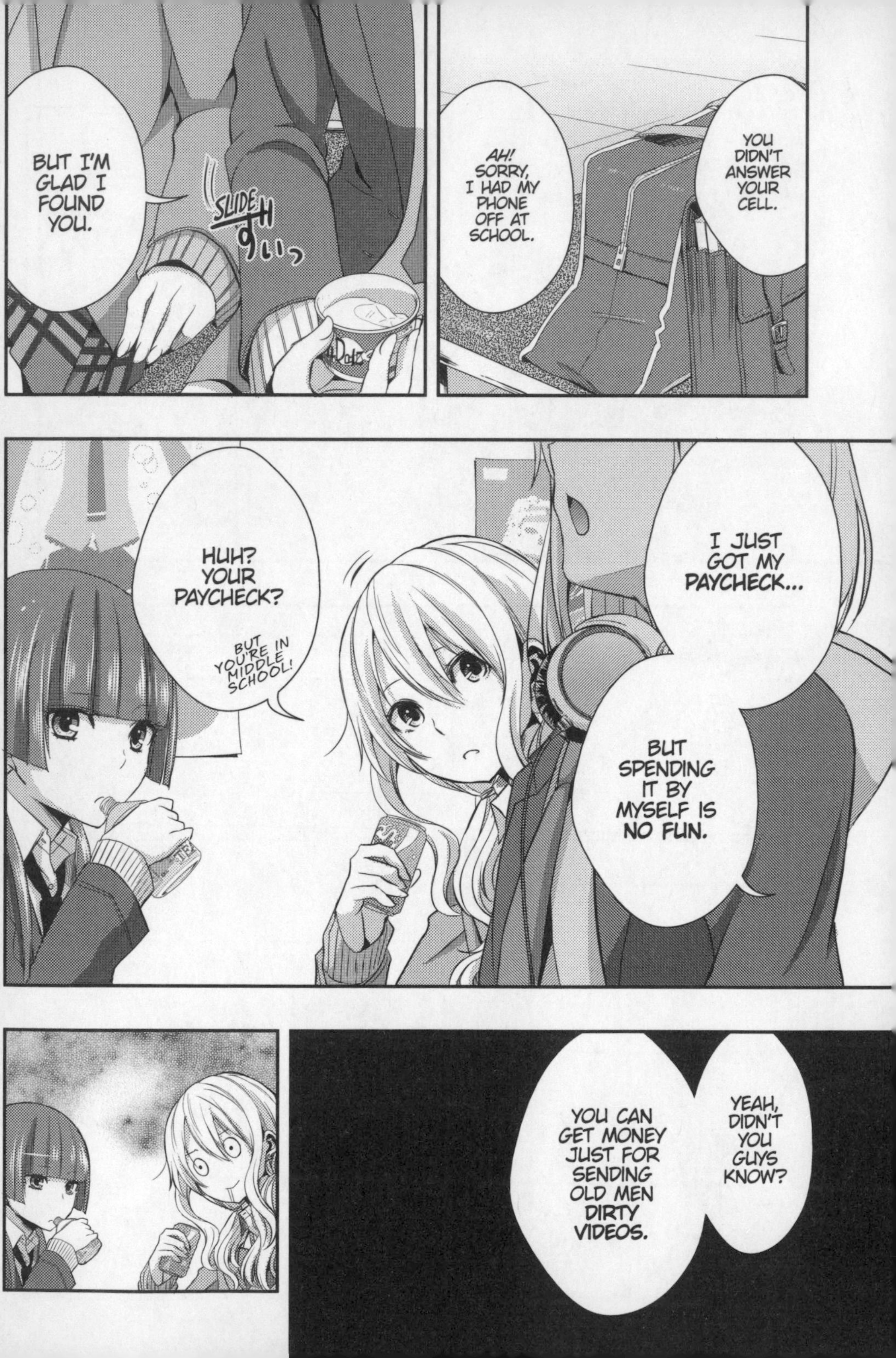
YOU DIDN'T ANSWER YOUR CELL.
AH! SORRY, I HAD MY PHONE OFF AT SCHOOL.
BUT I'M GLAD I FOUND YOU.
SLIDE すいっ
I JUST GOT MY PAYCHECK...
BUT SPENDING IT BY MYSELF IS NO FUN.
HUH? YOUR PAYCHECK?
BUT YOU'RE IN MIDDLE SCHOOL!
YEAH, DIDN'T YOU GUYS KNOW?
YOU CAN GET MONEY JUST FOR SENDING OLD MEN DIRTY VIDEOS.

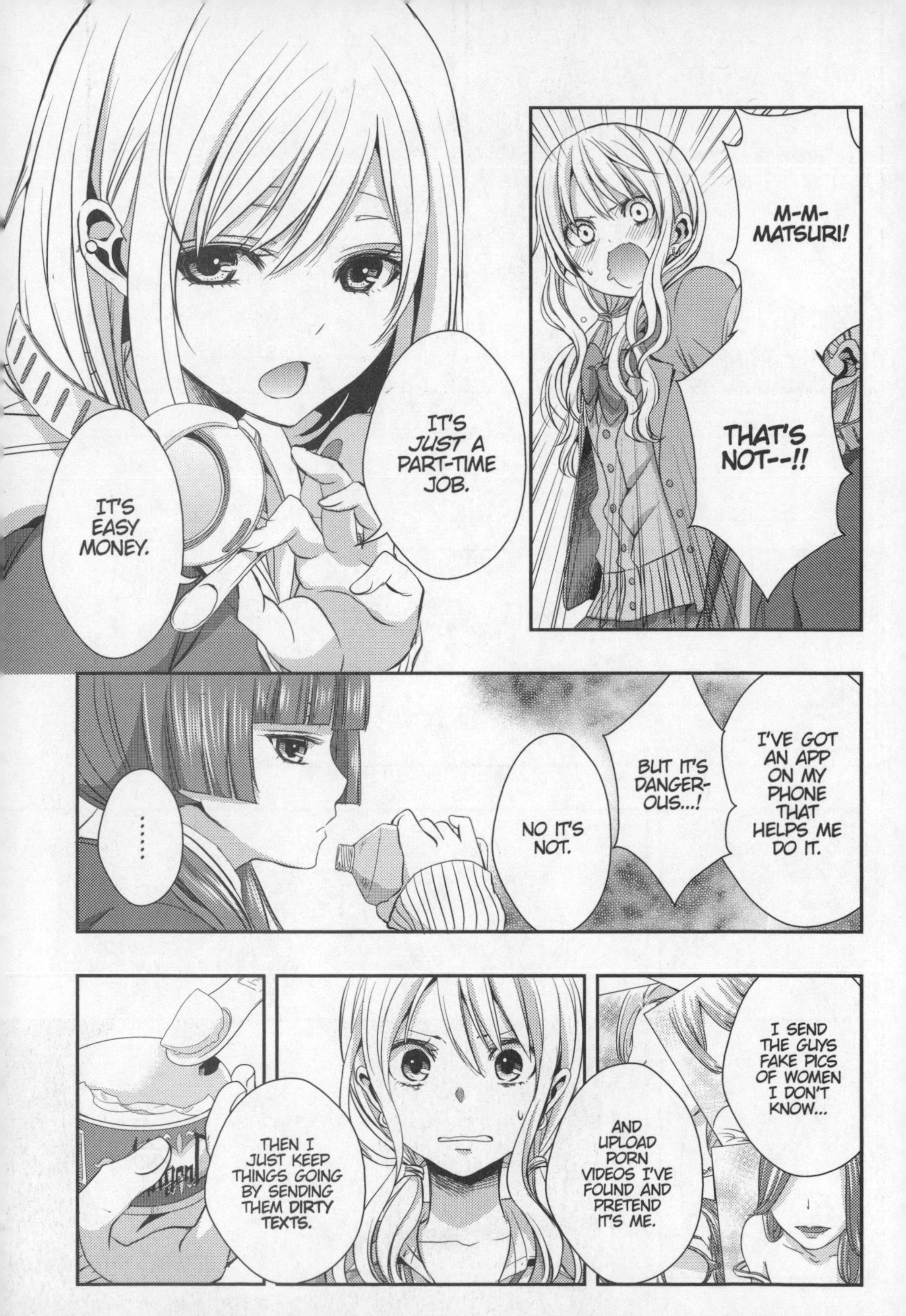
M-M-MATSURI!
THAT'S NOT--!!
IT'S JUST A PART-TIME JOB.
IT'S EASY MONEY.
I'VE GOT AN APP ON MY PHONE THAT HELPS ME DO IT.
BUT IT'S DANGER-OUS...!
NO IT'S NOT.
......
I SEND THE GUYS FAKE PICS OF WOMEN I DON'T KNOW...
AND UPLOAD PORN VIDEOS I'VE FOUND AND PRETEND IT'S ME.
THEN I JUST KEEP THINGS GOING BY SENDING THEM DIRTY TEXTS.

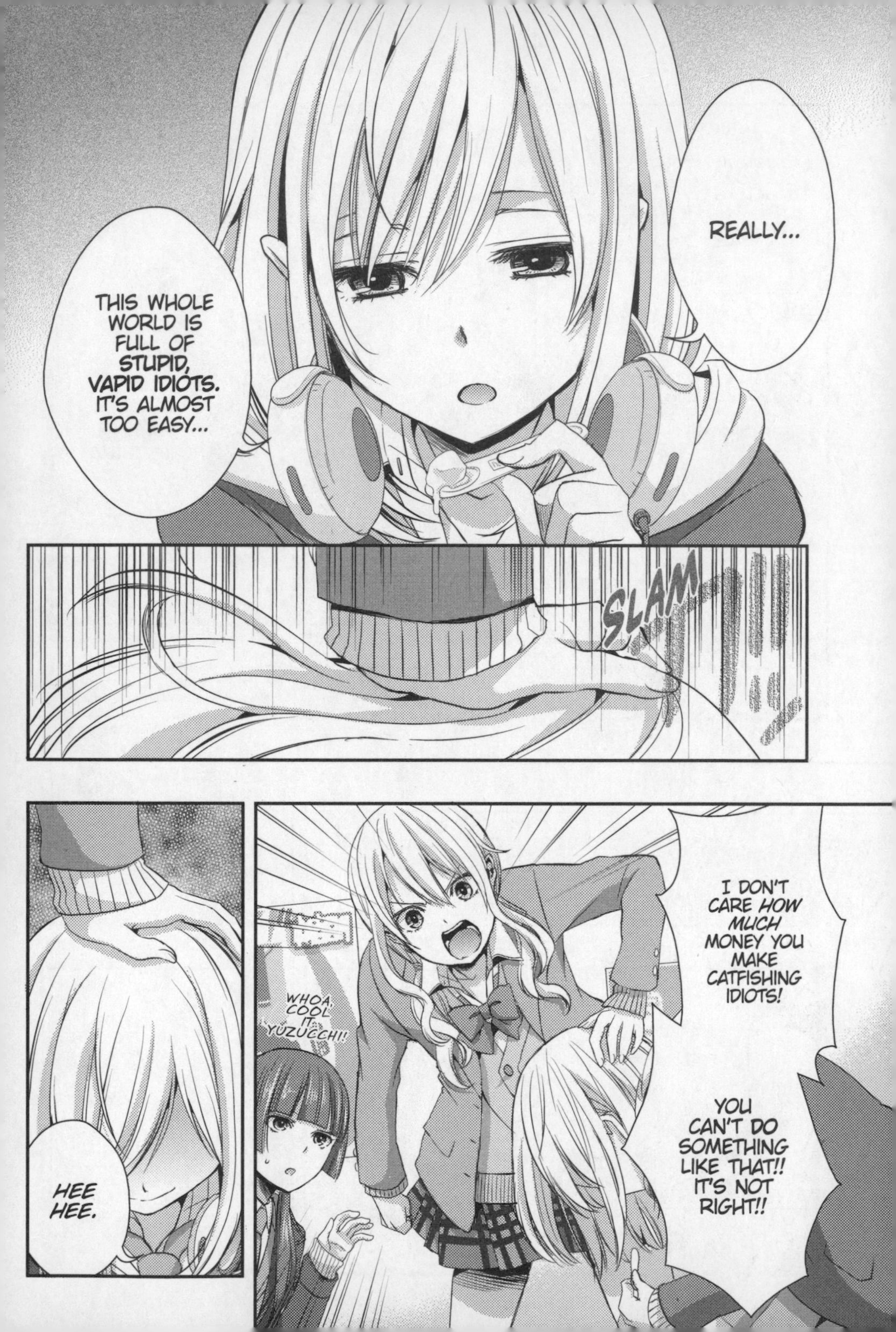
REALLY...
THIS WHOLE WORLD IS FULL OF STUPID, VAPID IDIOTS. IT'S ALMOST TOO EASY...
SLAM
I DON'T CARE *HOW MUCH* MONEY YOU MAKE CATFISHING IDIOTS!
YOU CAN'T DO SOMETHING LIKE THAT!! IT'S NOT RIGHT!!
WHOA, COOL IT, YUZUCCHI!
HEE HEE.

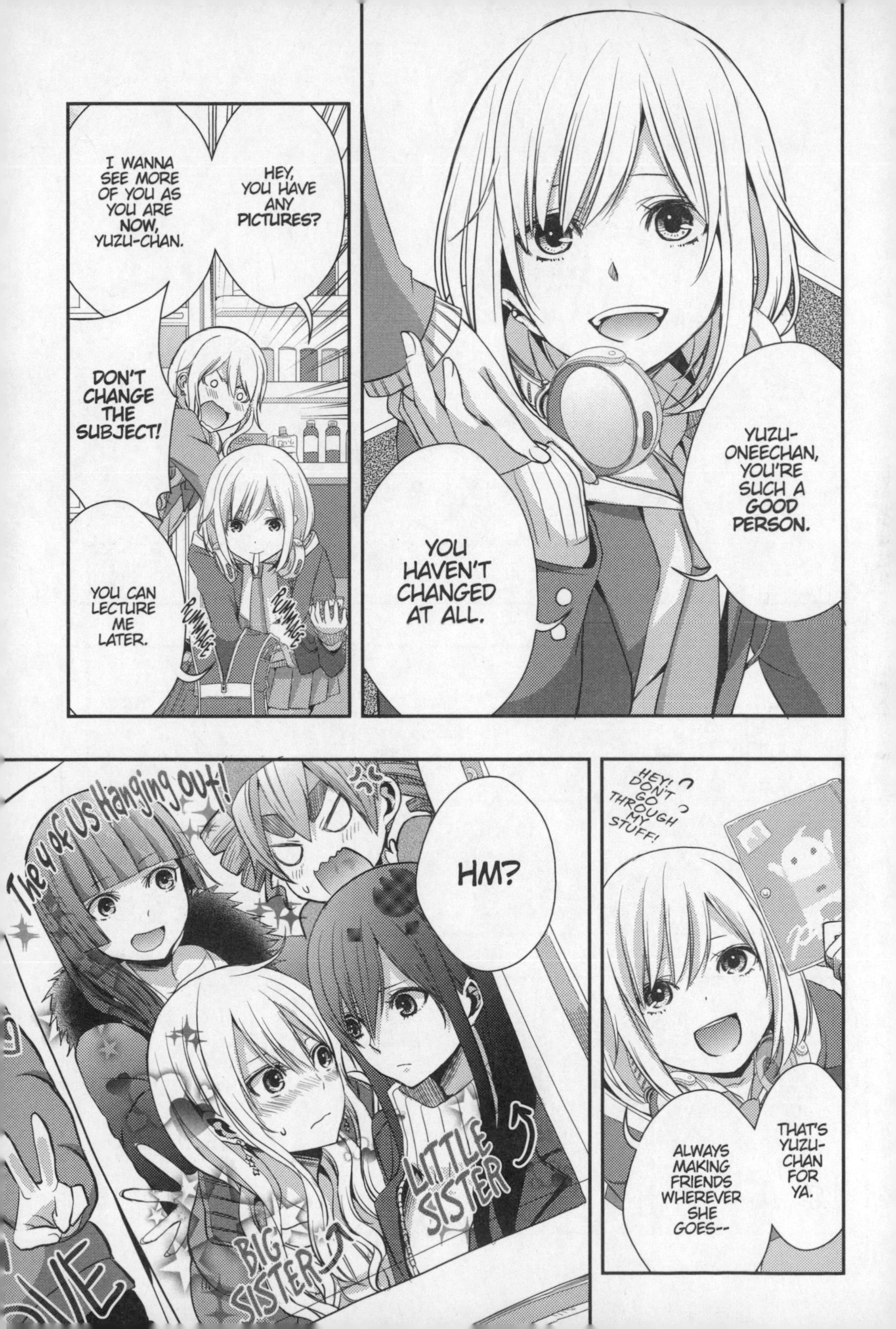
YUZU-ONEECHAN, YOU'RE SUCH A GOOD PERSON.
YOU HAVEN'T CHANGED AT ALL.
HEY, YOU HAVE ANY PICTURES?
I WANNA SEE MORE OF YOU AS YOU ARE NOW, YUZU-CHAN.
DON'T CHANGE THE SUBJECT!
YOU CAN LECTURE ME LATER.
RUMMAGE
RUMMAGE
HEY! DON'T GO THROUGH MY STUFF!
THAT'S YUZU-CHAN FOR YA.
ALWAYS MAKING FRIENDS WHEREVER SHE GOES--
HM?
The 4 of Us Hanging out!
LITTLE SISTER
BIG SISTER

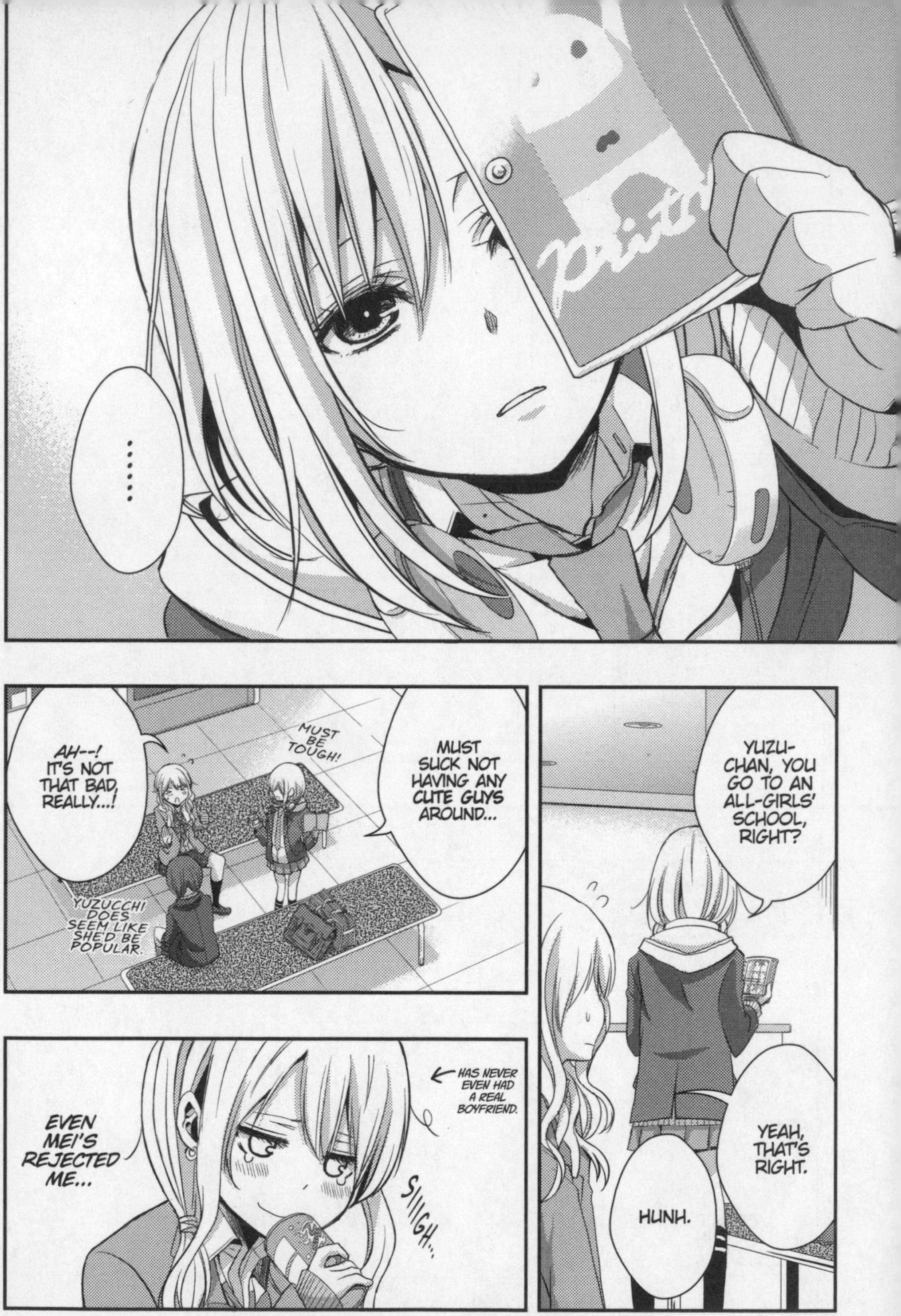
......
YUZU-CHAN, YOU GO TO AN ALL-GIRLS' SCHOOL, RIGHT?
YEAH, THAT'S RIGHT.
HUNH.
MUST SUCK NOT HAVING ANY CUTE GUYS AROUND...
MUST BE TOUGH!
AH--! IT'S NOT THAT BAD, REALLY...!
YUZUCCHI DOES SEEM LIKE SHE'D BE POPULAR.
HAS NEVER EVEN HAD A REAL BOYFRIEND.
SIIIGH...
EVEN MEI'S REJECTED ME...

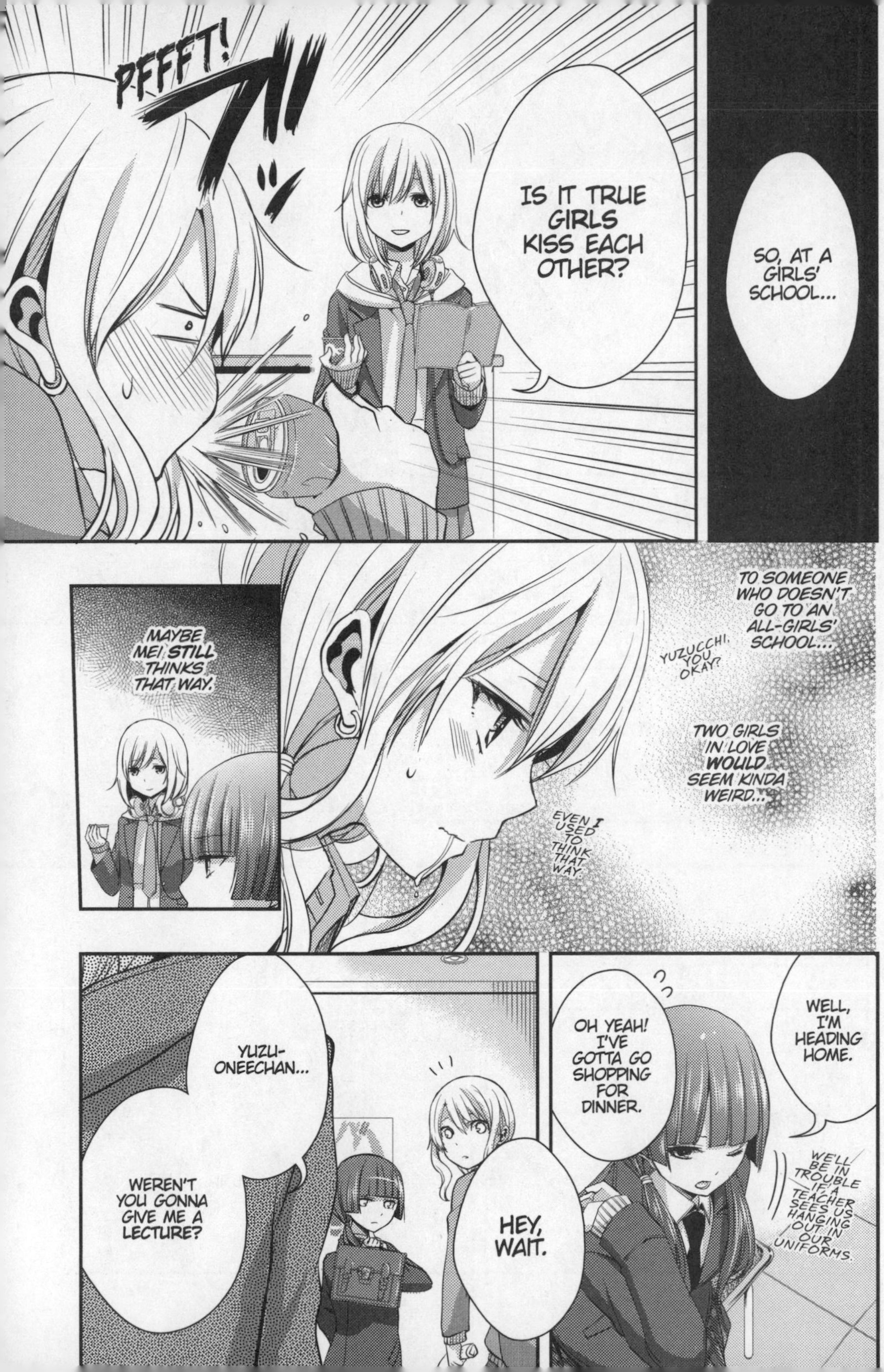
SO, AT A GIRLS' SCHOOL...
IS IT TRUE GIRLS KISS EACH OTHER?
PFFFT!
TO SOMEONE WHO DOESN'T GO TO AN ALL-GIRLS' SCHOOL...
YUZUCCHI, YOU OKAY?
TWO GIRLS IN LOVE WOULD SEEM KINDA WEIRD...
EVEN I USED TO THINK THAT WAY.
MAYBE MEI STILL THINKS THAT WAY.
WELL, I'M HEADING HOME.
WE'LL BE IN TROUBLE IF A TEACHER SEES US HANGING OUT IN OUR UNIFORMS.
OH YEAH! I'VE GOTTA GO SHOPPING FOR DINNER.
HEY, WAIT.
YUZU-ONEECHAN...
WEREN'T YOU GONNA GIVE ME A LECTURE?

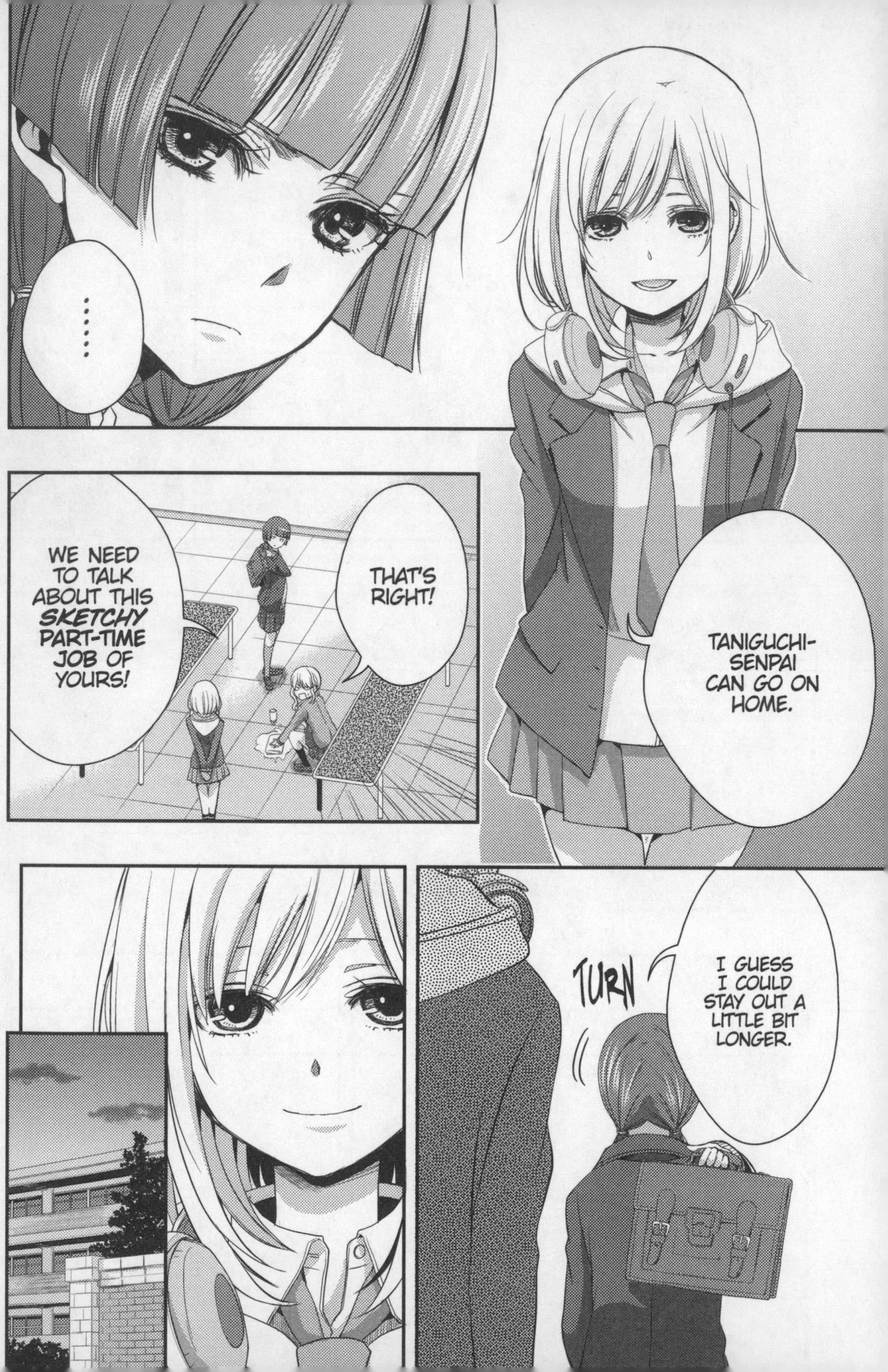
TANIGUCHI-SENPAI CAN GO ON HOME.
......
THAT'S RIGHT!
WE NEED TO TALK ABOUT THIS *SKETCHY* PART-TIME JOB OF YOURS!
I GUESS I COULD STAY OUT A LITTLE BIT LONGER.
TURN

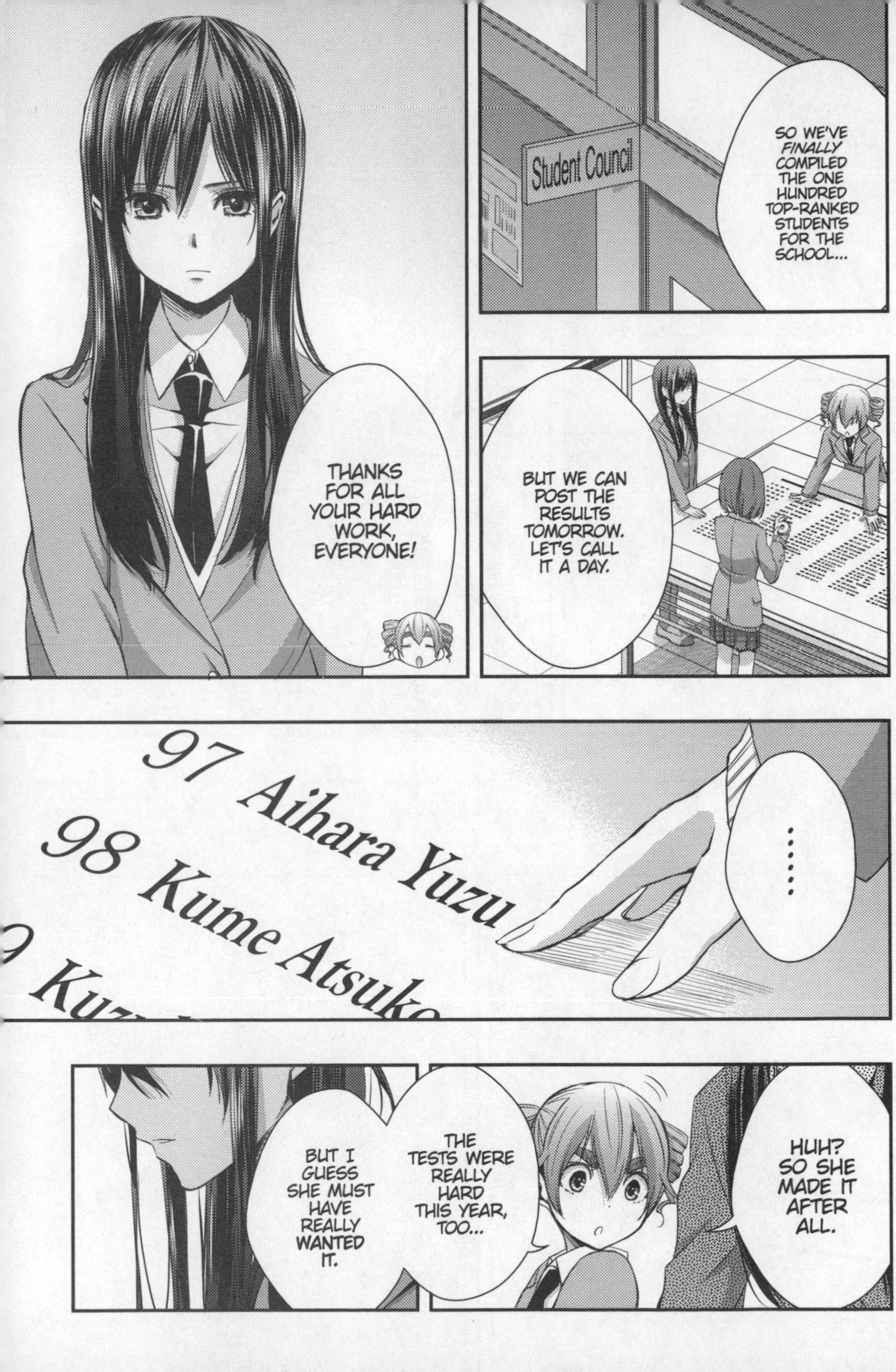
Student Council
SO WE'VE *FINALLY* COMPILED THE ONE HUNDRED TOP-RANKED STUDENTS FOR THE SCHOOL...
BUT WE CAN POST THE RESULTS TOMORROW. LET'S CALL IT A DAY.
THANKS FOR ALL YOUR HARD WORK, EVERYONE!
......
97 Aihara Yuzu
98 Kume Atsuko
HUH? SO SHE MADE IT AFTER ALL.
THE TESTS WERE REALLY HARD THIS YEAR, TOO...
BUT I GUESS SHE MUST HAVE REALLY WANTED IT.

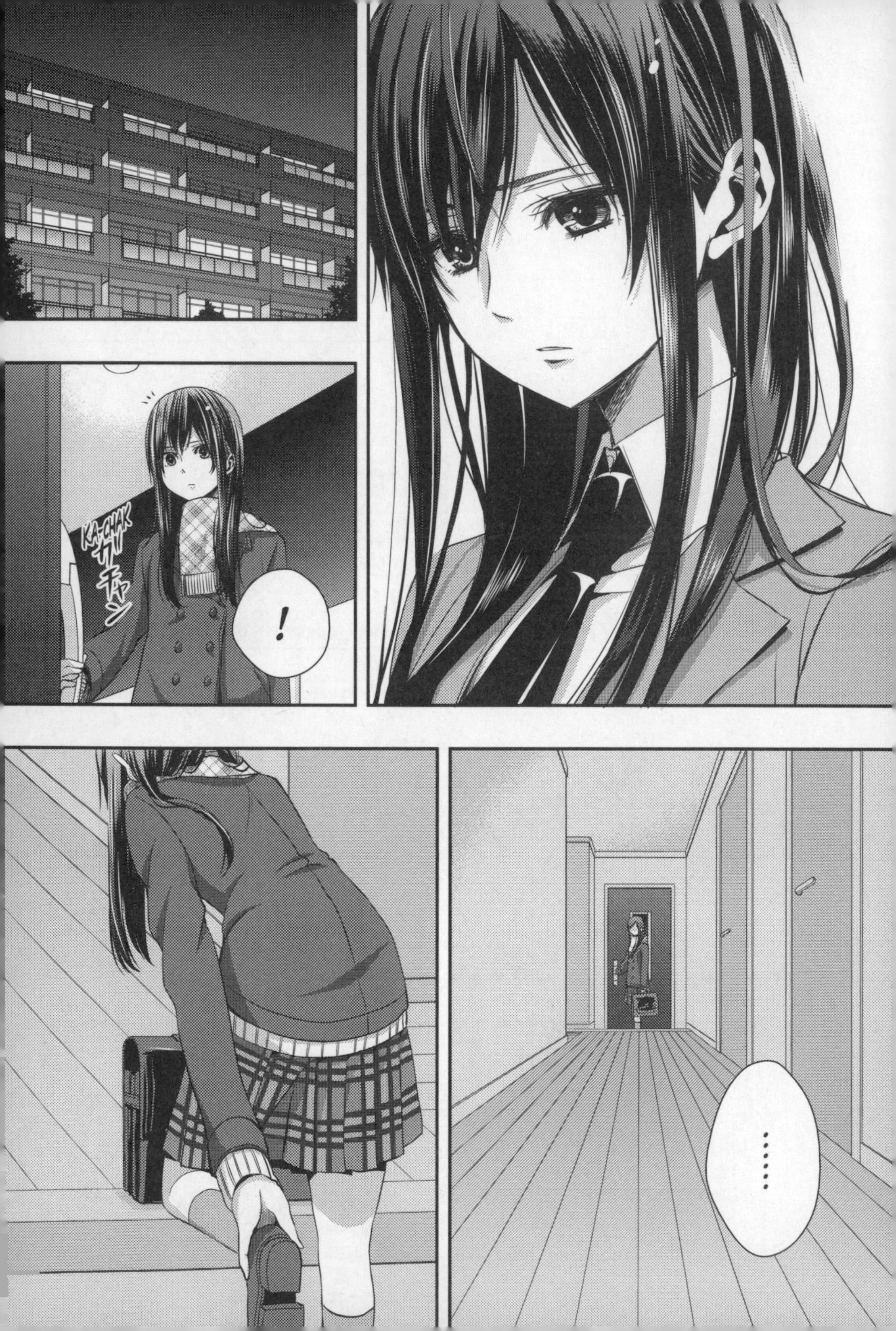
KA-CHAK
ガチャン
!
……

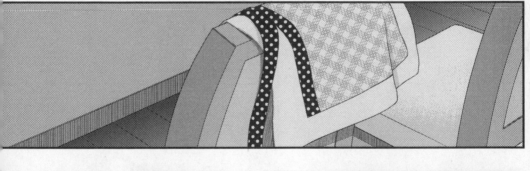

KA-
CHAK

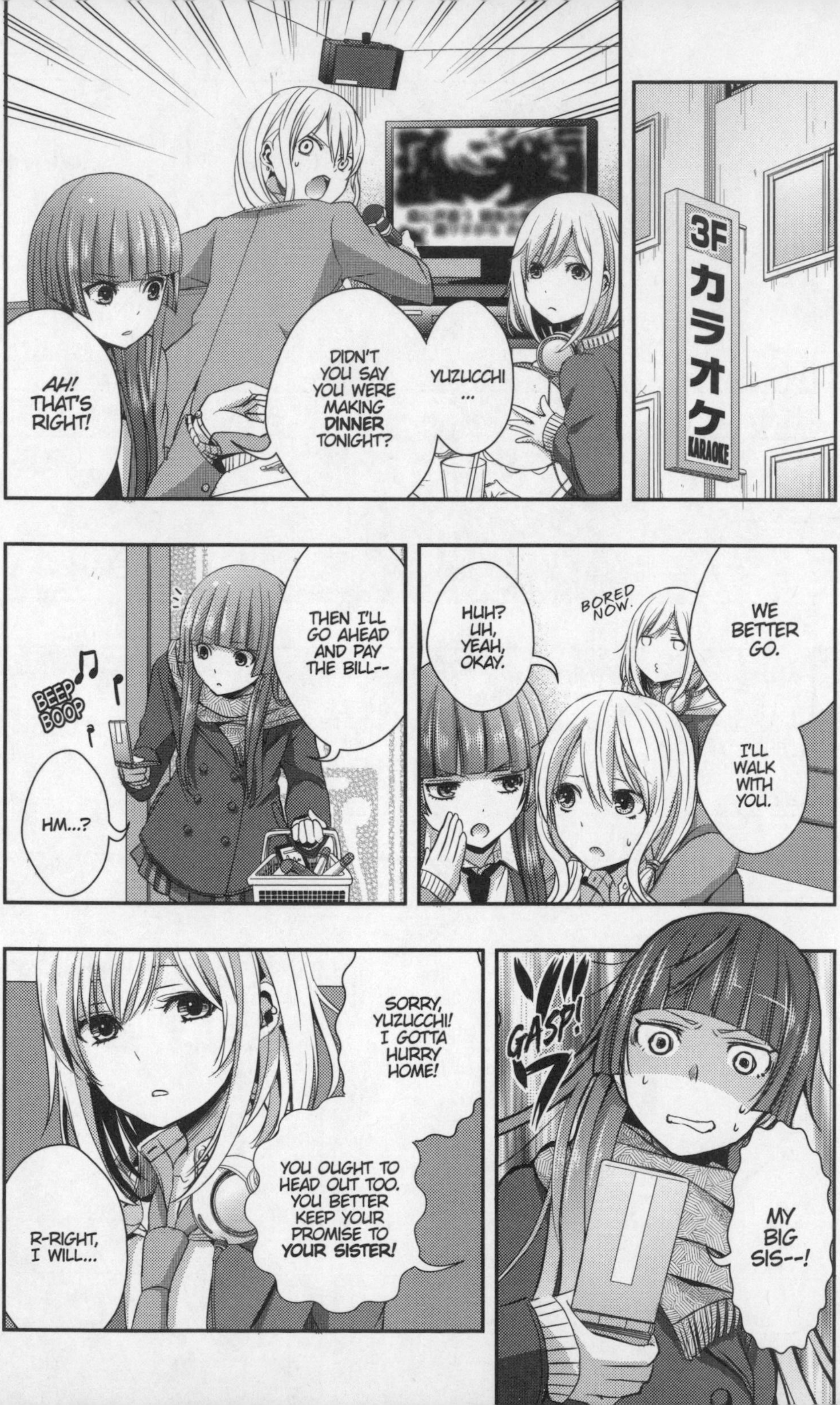
3F
カラオケ
KARAOKE
YUZUCCHI ...
DIDN'T YOU SAY YOU WERE MAKING DINNER TONIGHT?
AH! THAT'S RIGHT!
WE BETTER GO.
BORED NOW.
HUH? UH, YEAH, OKAY.
I'LL WALK WITH YOU.
THEN I'LL GO AHEAD AND PAY THE BILL--
BEEP BOOP
HM...?
GASP!
MY BIG SIS--!
SORRY, YUZUCCHI! I GOTTA HURRY HOME!
YOU OUGHT TO HEAD OUT TOO. YOU BETTER KEEP YOUR PROMISE TO YOUR SISTER!
R-RIGHT, I WILL...

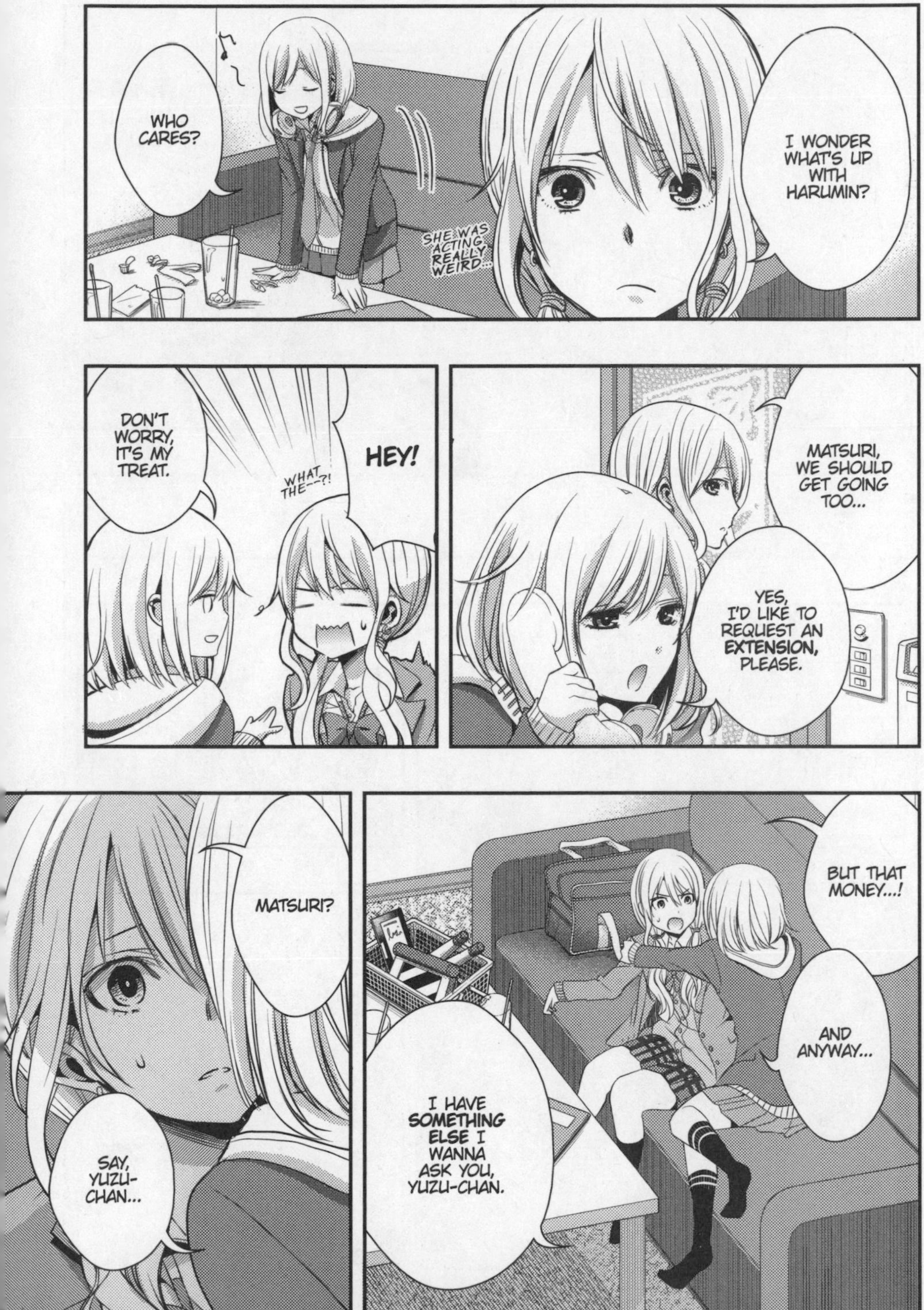
I WONDER WHAT'S UP WITH HARUMIN?
SHE WAS ACTING REALLY WEIRD...
WHO CARES?
MATSURI, WE SHOULD GET GOING TOO...
YES, I'D LIKE TO REQUEST AN EXTENSION, PLEASE.
HEY!
WHAT THE--?!
DON'T WORRY, IT'S MY TREAT.
BUT THAT MONEY...!
AND ANYWAY...
I HAVE SOMETHING ELSE I WANNA ASK YOU, YUZU-CHAN.
MATSURI?
SAY, YUZU-CHAN...

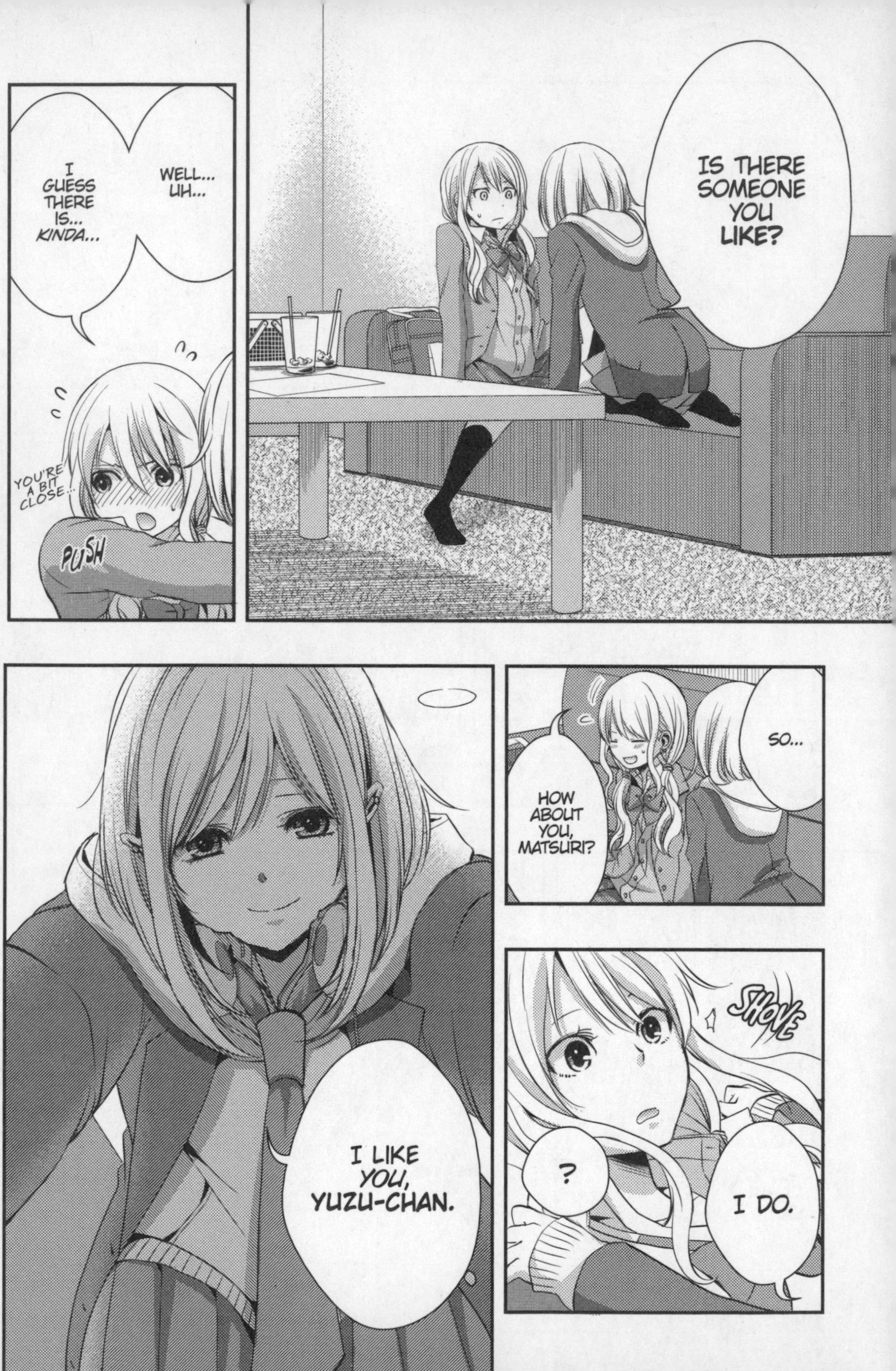
IS THERE SOMEONE YOU LIKE?
WELL... UH...
I GUESS THERE IS... *KINDA*...
YOU'RE A BIT CLOSE...
PUSH
SO...
HOW ABOUT YOU, MATSURI?
SHOVE
I DO.
?
I LIKE *YOU*, YUZU-CHAN.

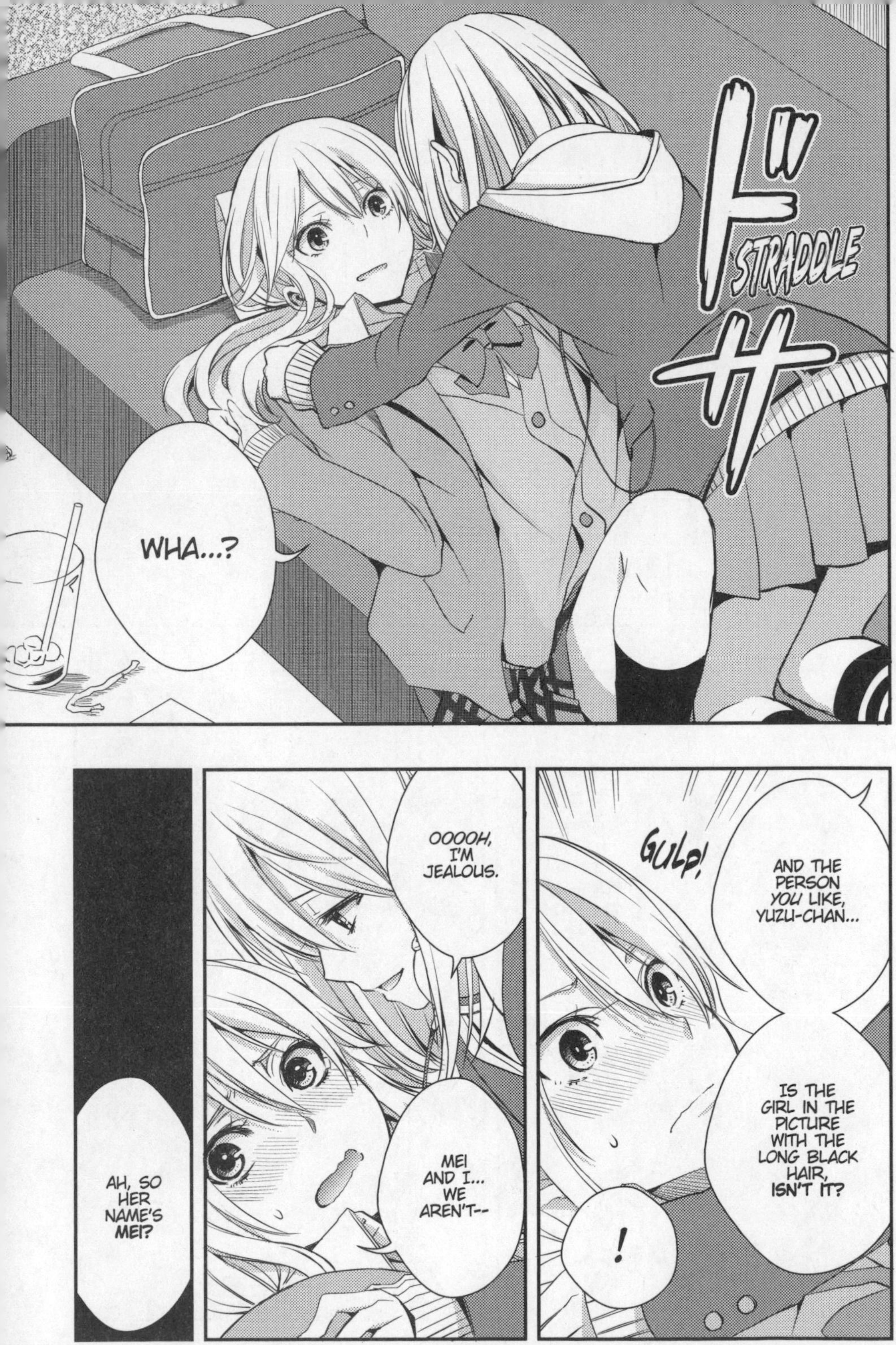
STRADDLE
WHA...?
GULP!
AND THE PERSON YOU LIKE, YUZU-CHAN...
IS THE GIRL IN THE PICTURE WITH THE LONG BLACK HAIR, ISN'T IT?
!
OOOOH, I'M JEALOUS.
MEI AND I... WE AREN'T--
AH, SO HER NAME'S MEI?

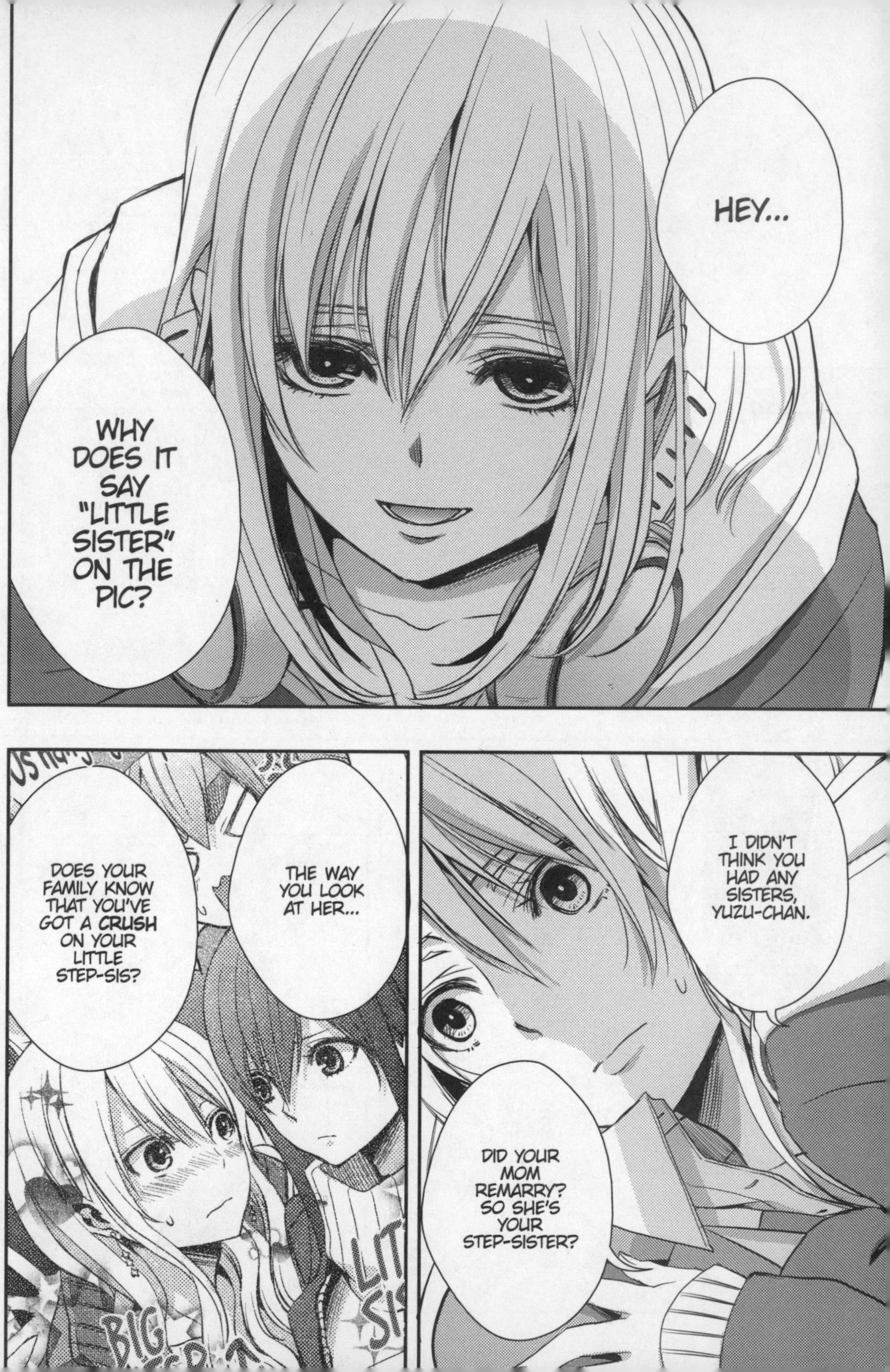
HEY...
WHY DOES IT SAY "LITTLE SISTER" ON THE PIC?
I DIDN'T THINK YOU HAD ANY SISTERS, YUZU-CHAN.
DID YOUR MOM REMARRY? SO SHE'S YOUR STEP-SISTER?
THE WAY YOU LOOK AT HER...
DOES YOUR FAMILY KNOW THAT YOU'VE GOT A CRUSH ON YOUR LITTLE STEP-SIS?

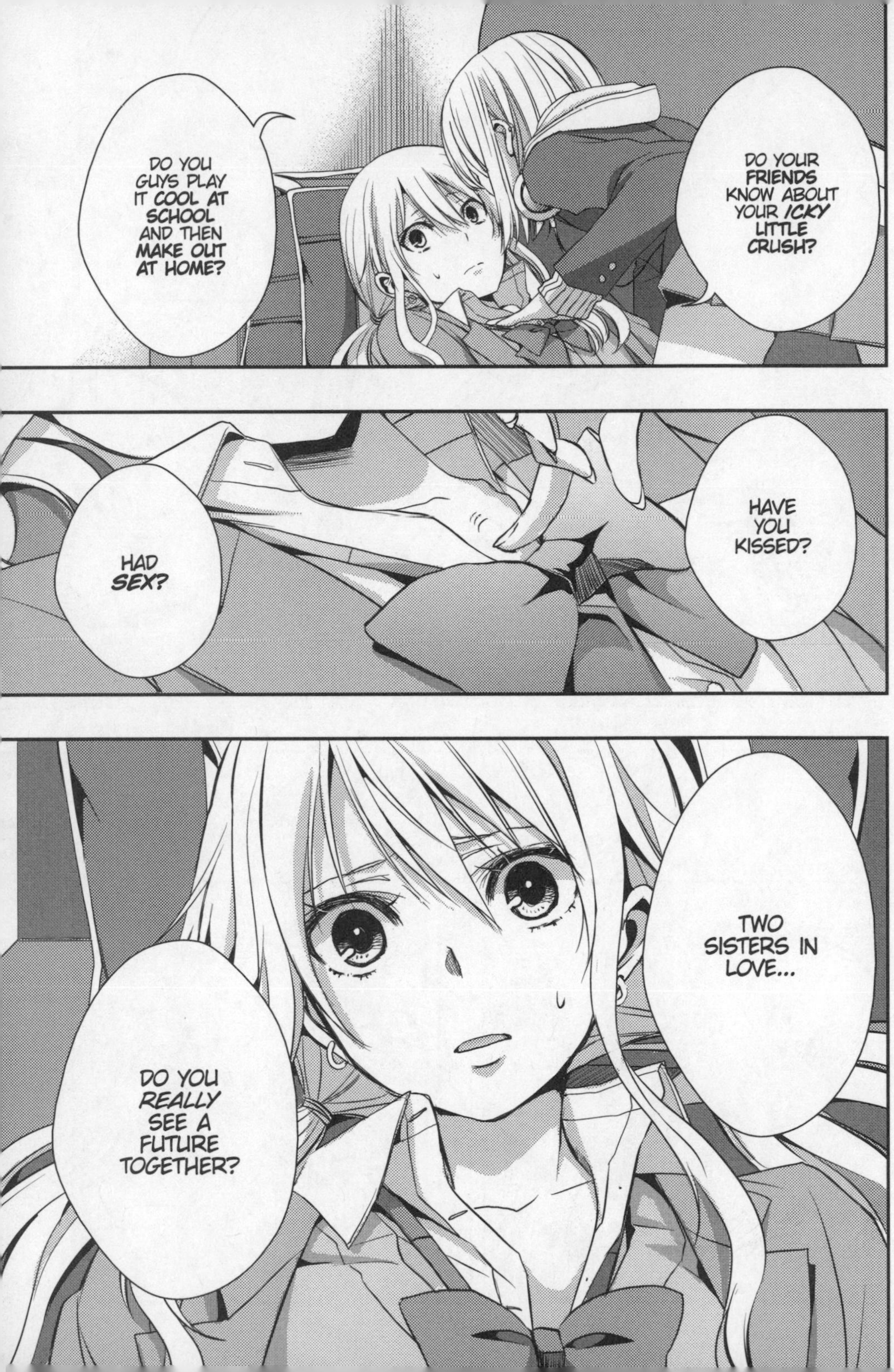
DO YOUR FRIENDS KNOW ABOUT YOUR *ICKY* LITTLE CRUSH?
DO YOU GUYS PLAY IT COOL AT SCHOOL AND THEN MAKE OUT AT HOME?
HAVE YOU KISSED?
HAD *SEX?*
TWO SISTERS IN LOVE...
DO YOU *REALLY* SEE A FUTURE TOGETHER?

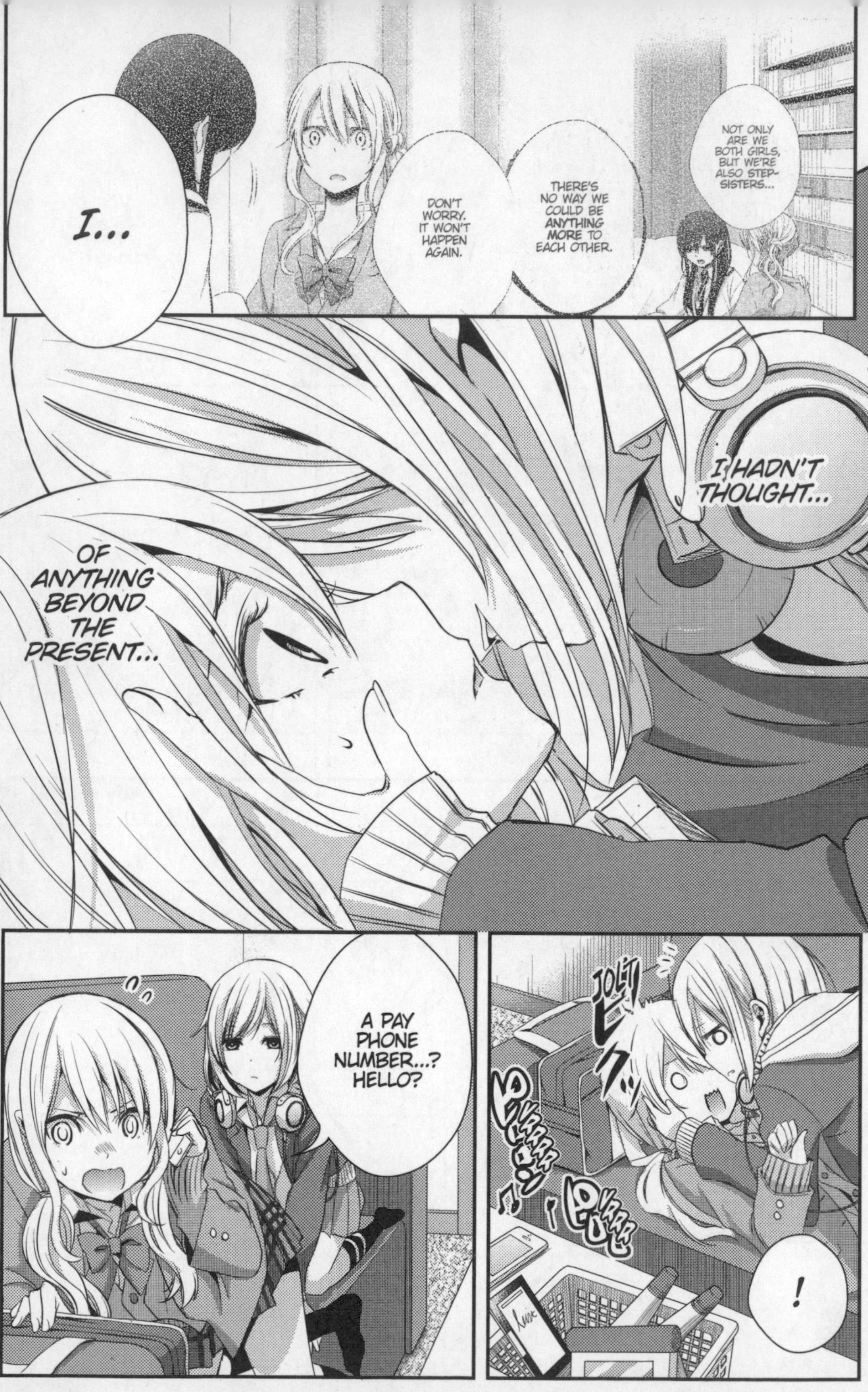
NOT ONLY ARE WE BOTH GIRLS, BUT WE'RE ALSO STEP-SISTERS...
THERE'S NO WAY WE COULD BE ANYTHING MORE TO EACH OTHER.
DON'T WORRY. IT WON'T HAPPEN AGAIN.
I...
I HADN'T THOUGHT...
OF ANYTHING BEYOND THE PRESENT...
JOLT!
!
A PAY PHONE NUMBER...? HELLO?

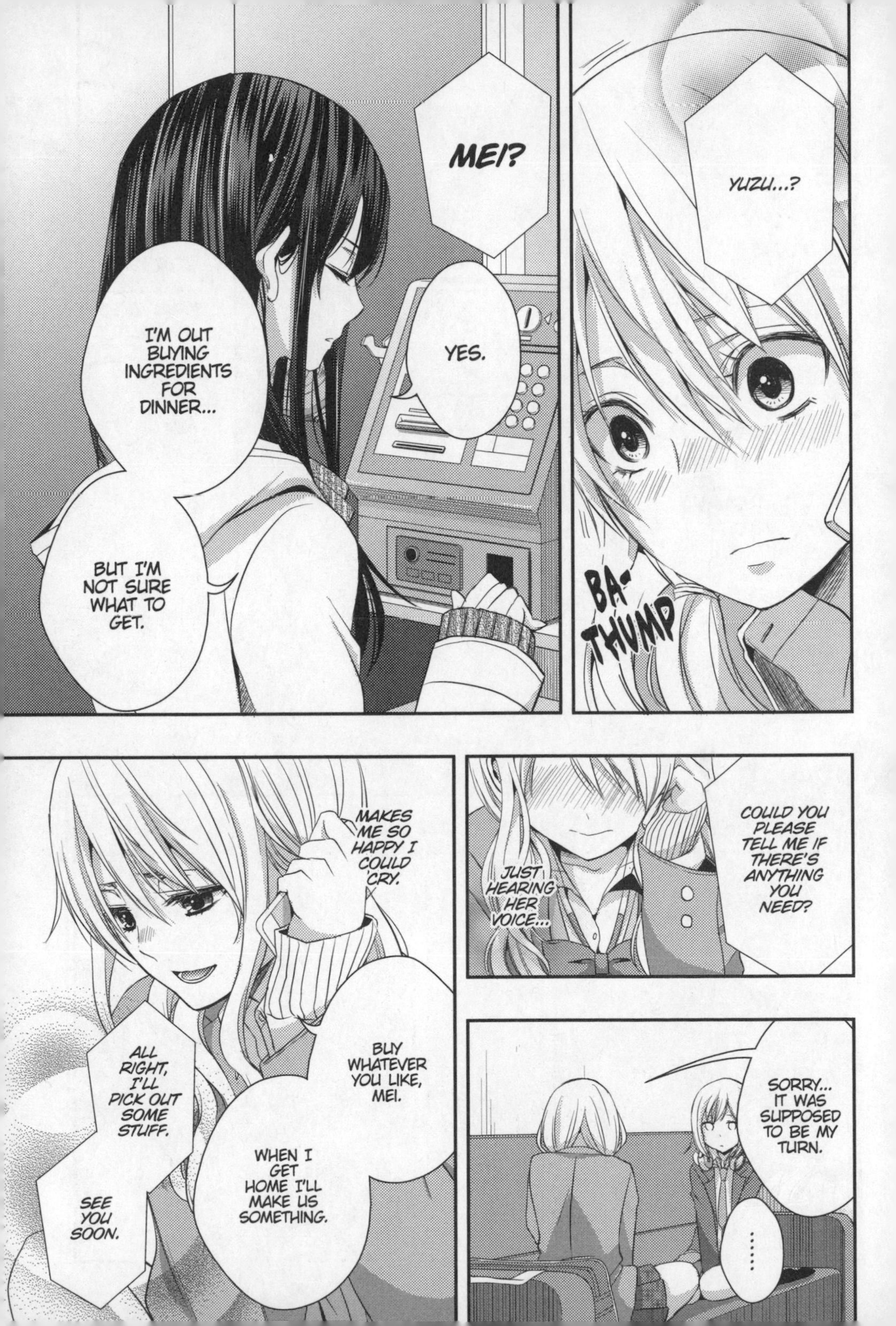
YUZU...?
BA-THUMP
MEI?
YES.
I'M OUT BUYING INGREDIENTS FOR DINNER...
BUT I'M NOT SURE WHAT TO GET.
COULD YOU PLEASE TELL ME IF THERE'S ANYTHING YOU NEED?
JUST HEARING HER VOICE...
SORRY... IT WAS SUPPOSED TO BE MY TURN.
......
MAKES ME SO HAPPY I COULD CRY.
BUY WHATEVER YOU LIKE, MEI.
WHEN I GET HOME I'LL MAKE US SOMETHING.
ALL RIGHT, I'LL PICK OUT SOME STUFF.
SEE YOU SOON.

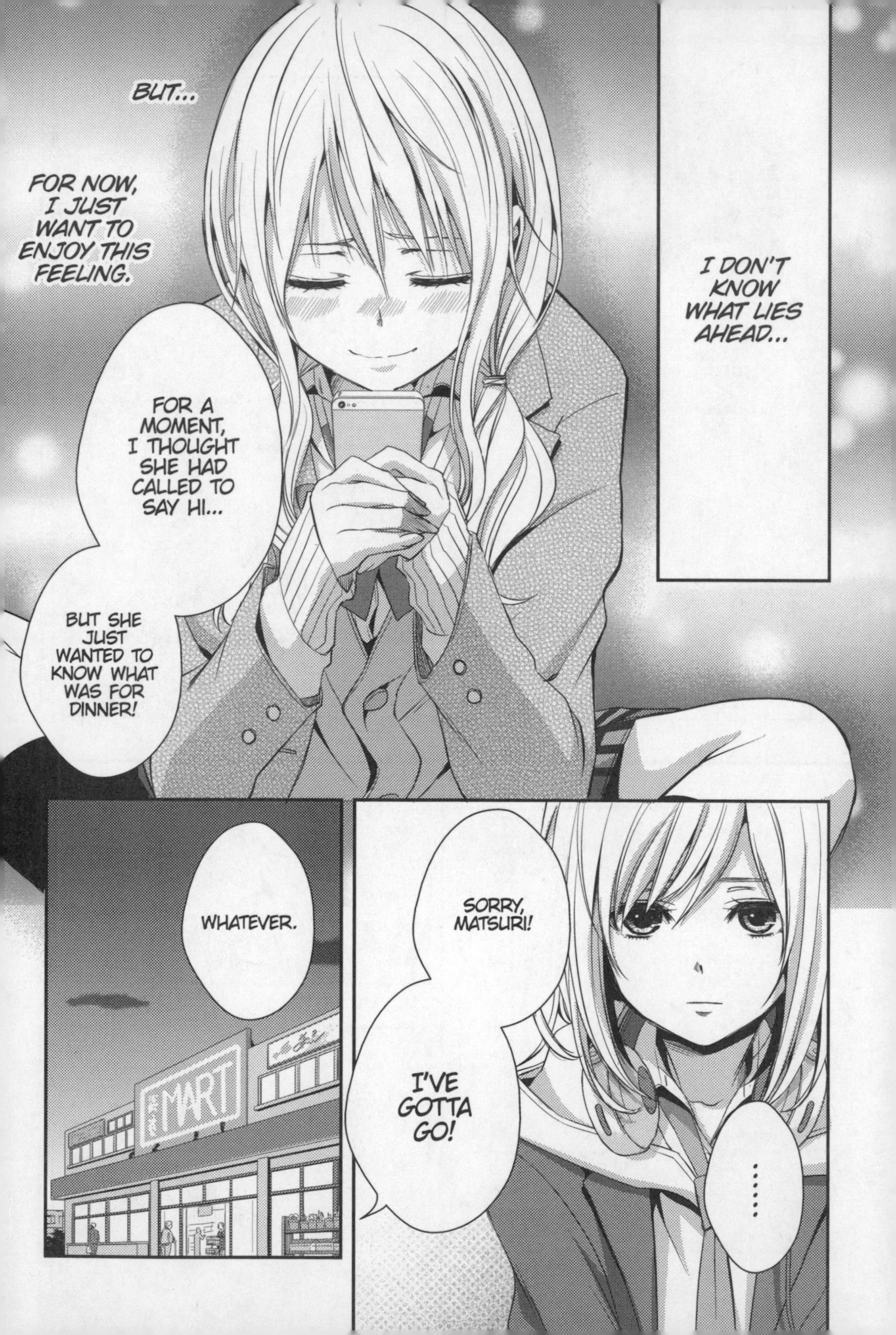
I DON'T KNOW WHAT LIES AHEAD...
BUT...
FOR NOW, I JUST WANT TO ENJOY THIS FEELING.
FOR A MOMENT, I THOUGHT SHE HAD CALLED TO SAY HI...
BUT SHE JUST WANTED TO KNOW WHAT WAS FOR DINNER!
SORRY, MATSURI!
I'VE GOTTA GO!
......
WHATEVER.
MART

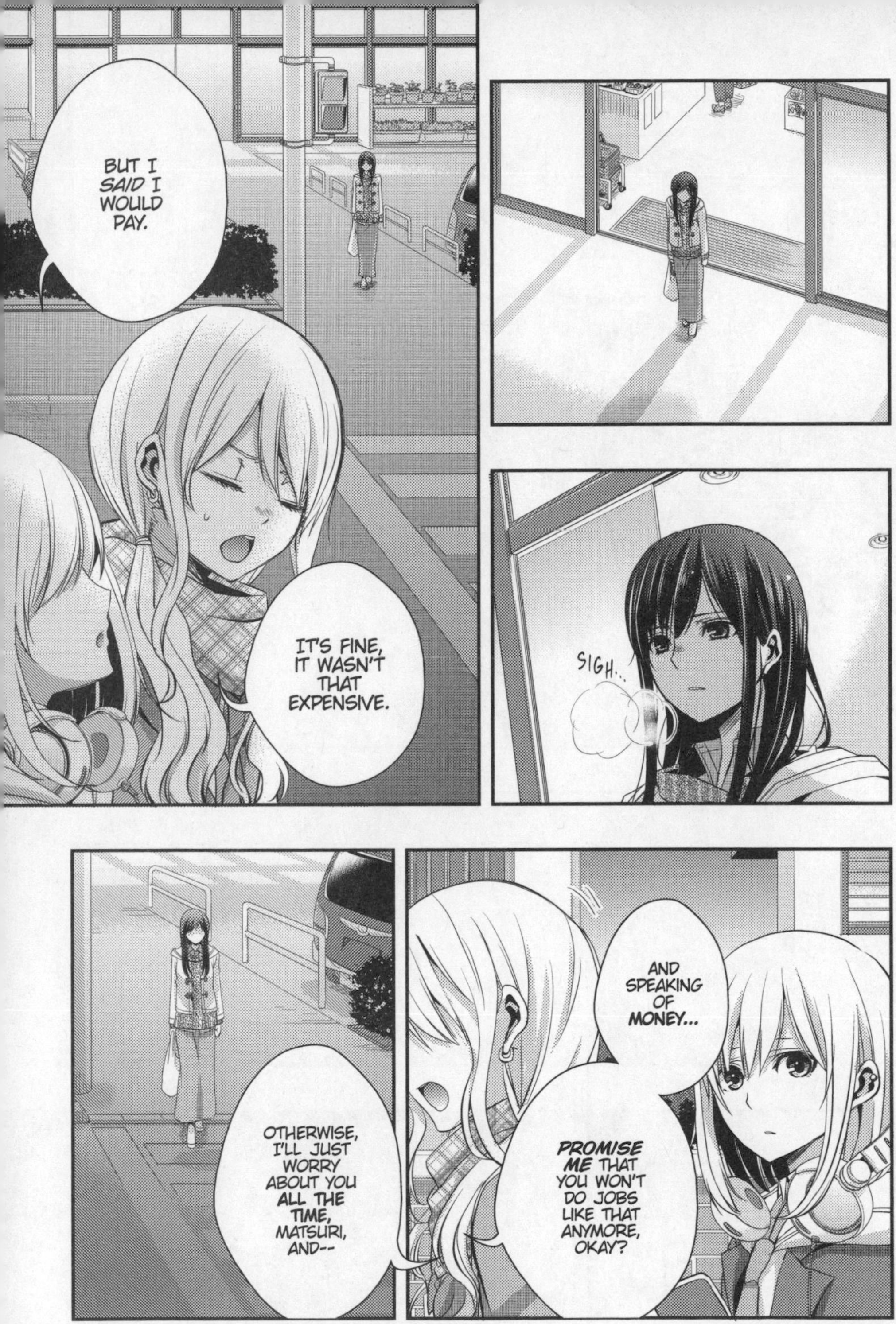
SIGH...
BUT I *SAID* I WOULD PAY.
IT'S FINE, IT WASN'T THAT EXPENSIVE.
AND SPEAKING OF **MONEY...**
PROMISE ME THAT YOU WON'T DO JOBS LIKE THAT ANYMORE, OKAY?
OTHERWISE, I'LL JUST WORRY ABOUT YOU **ALL THE TIME,** MATSURI, AND--

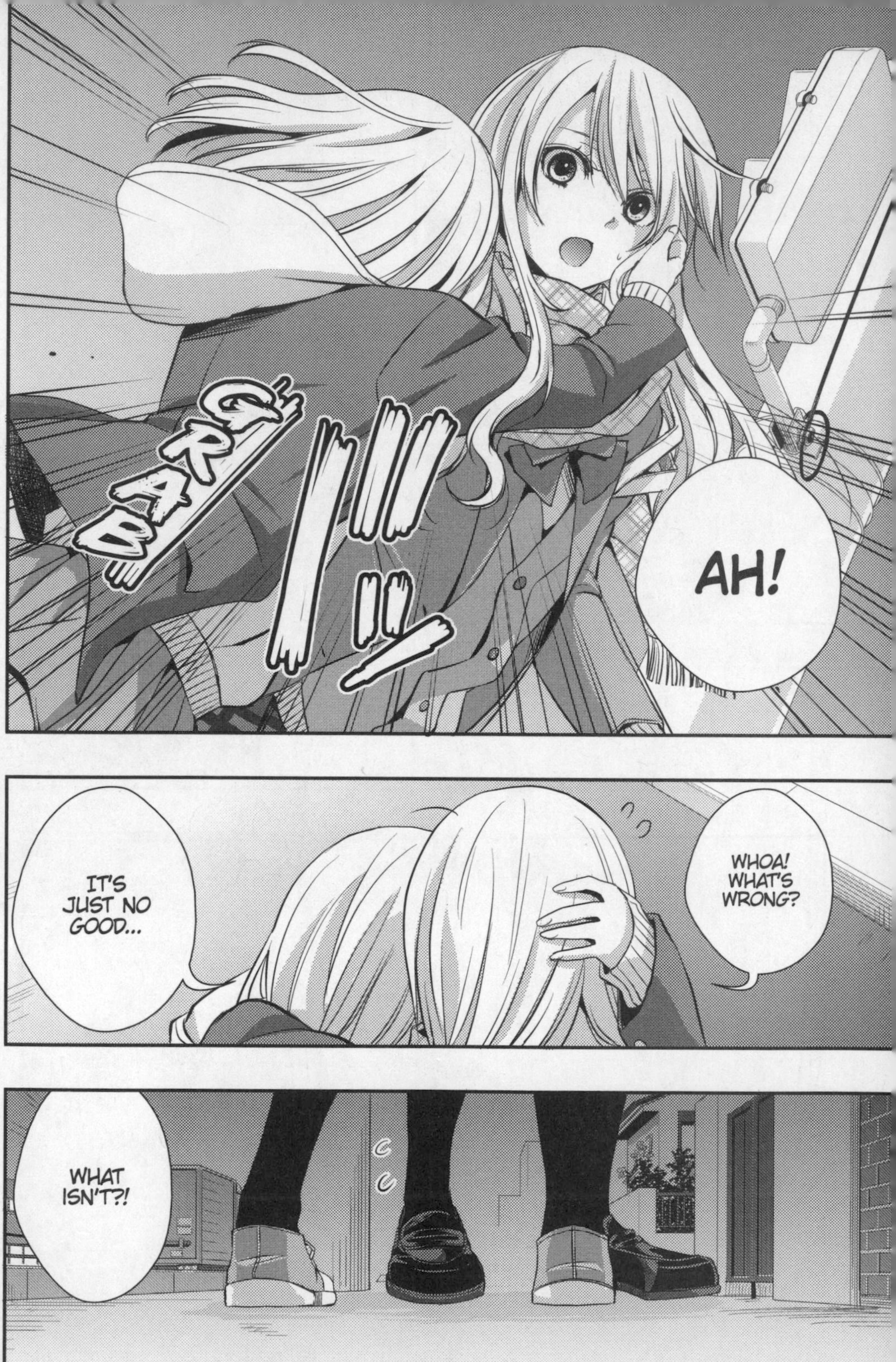
AH!
GRAB
WHOA! WHAT'S WRONG?
IT'S JUST NO GOOD...
WHAT ISN'T?!

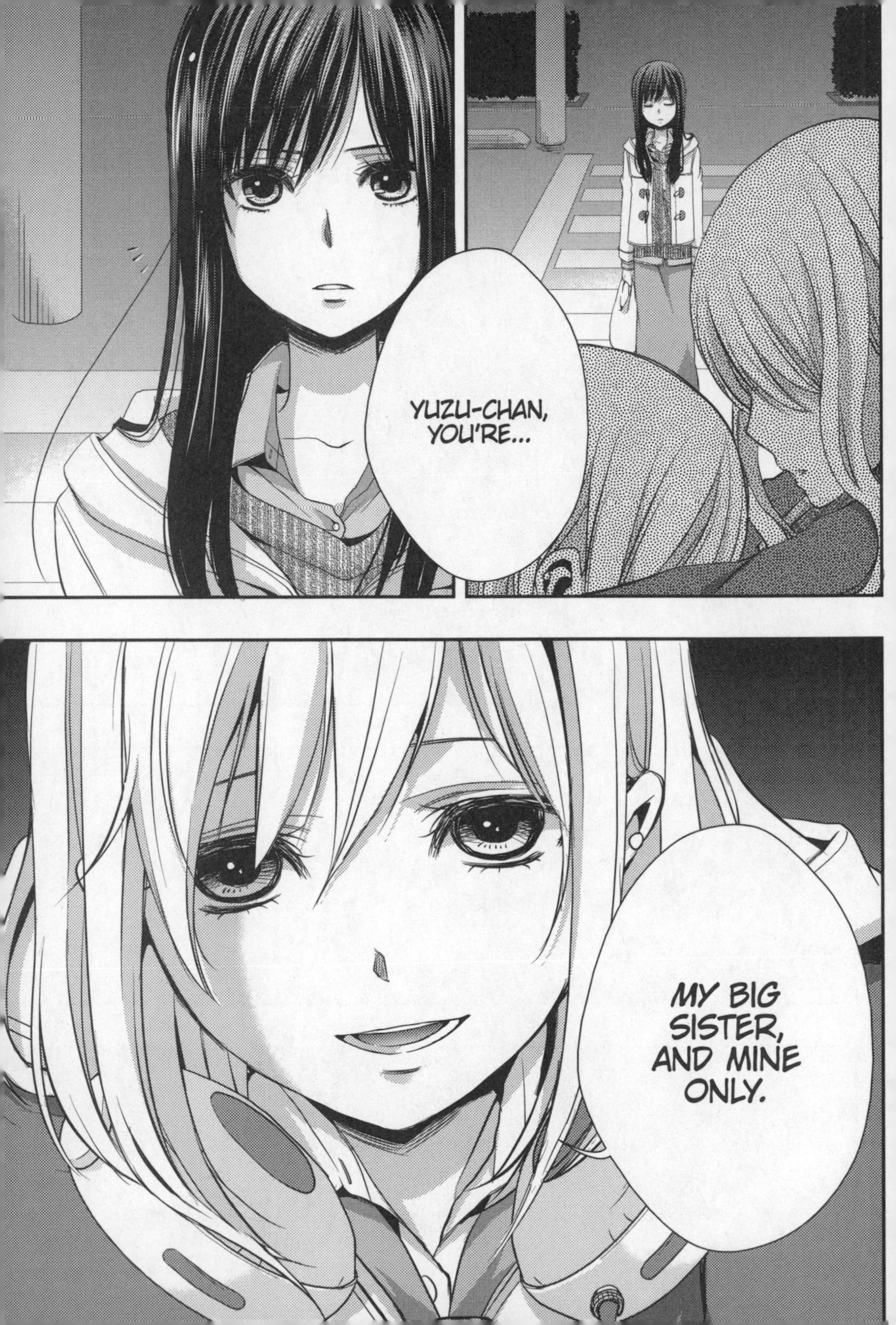
YUZU-CHAN, YOU'RE...
MY BIG SISTER, AND MINE ONLY.

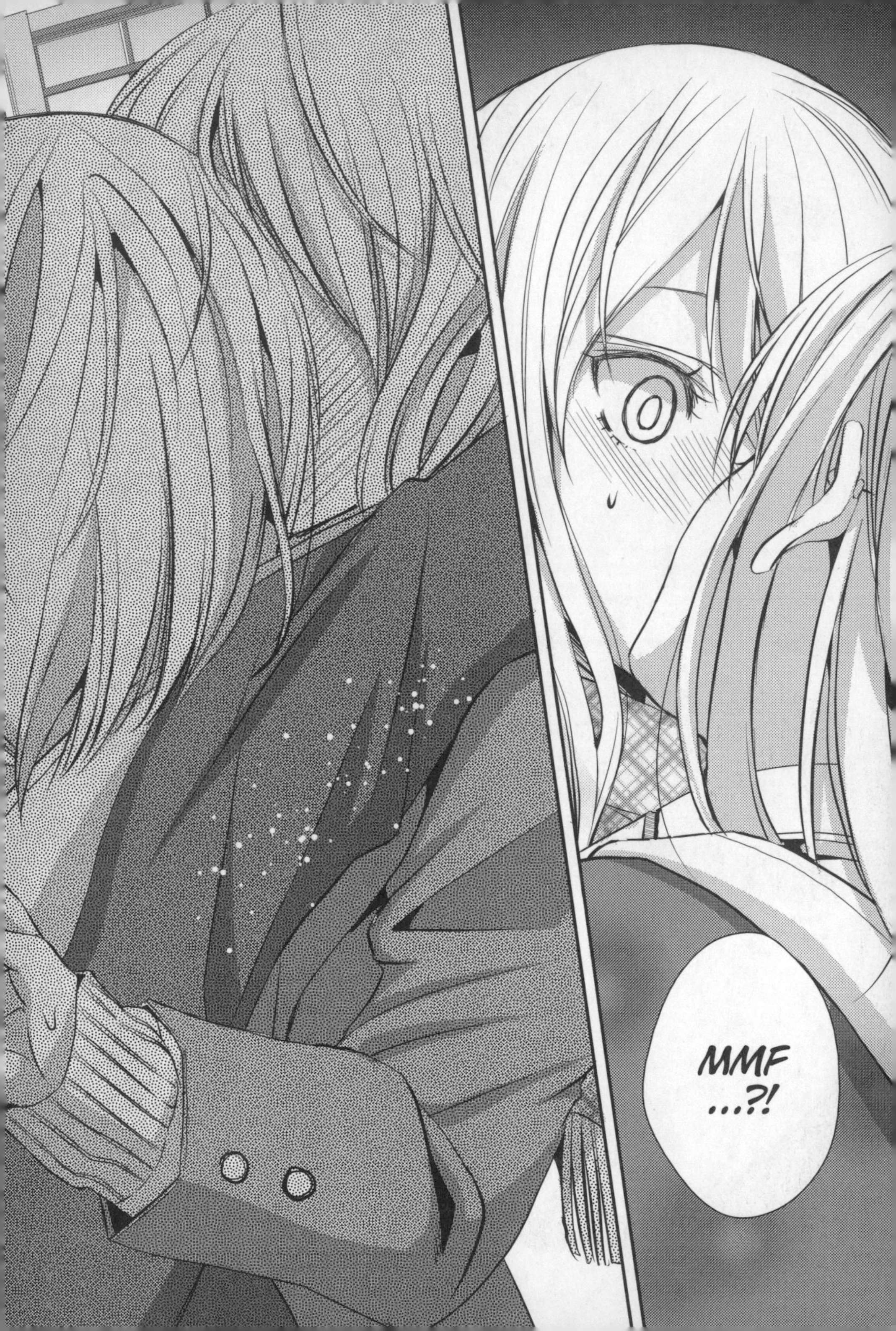
MMF ...?!

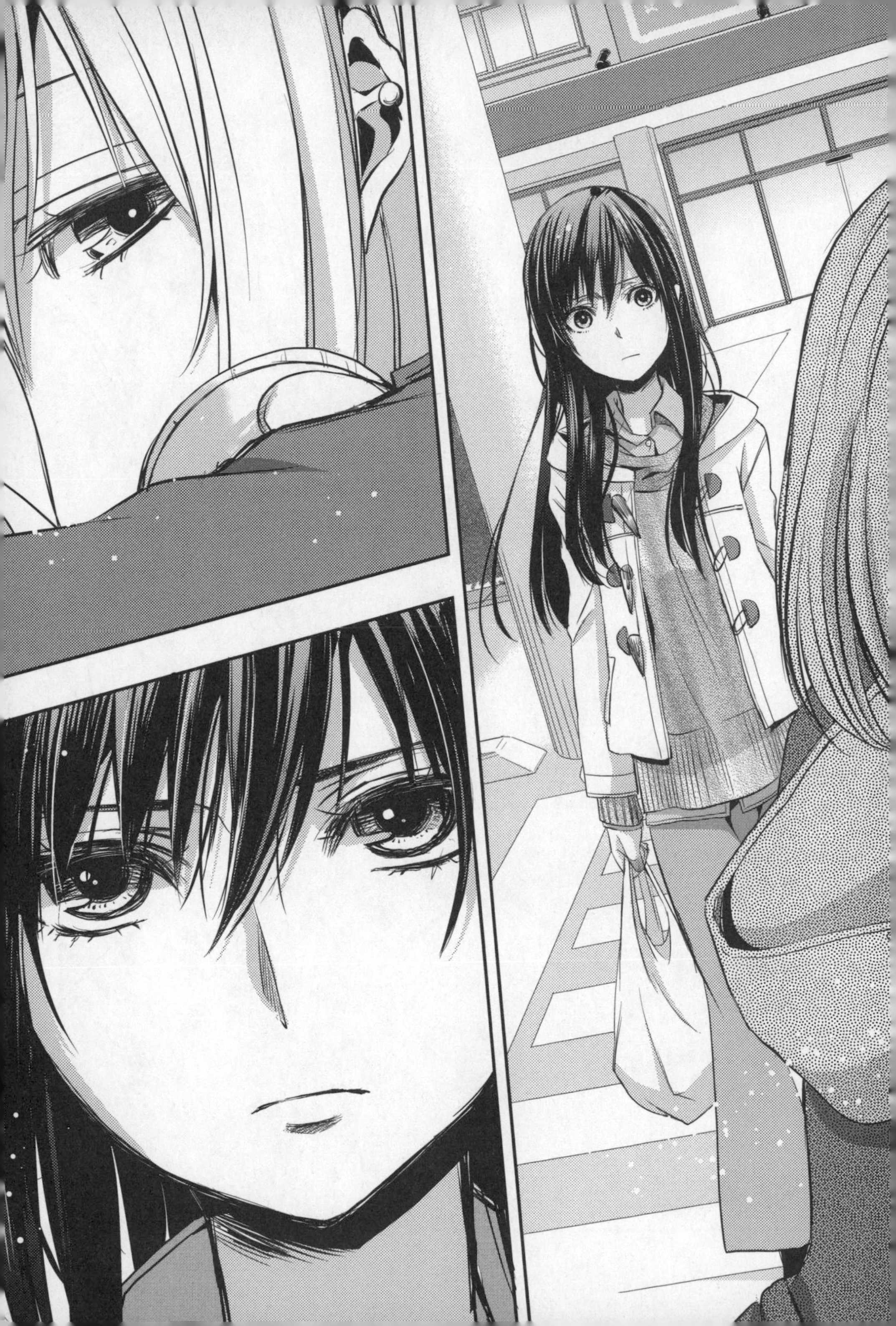

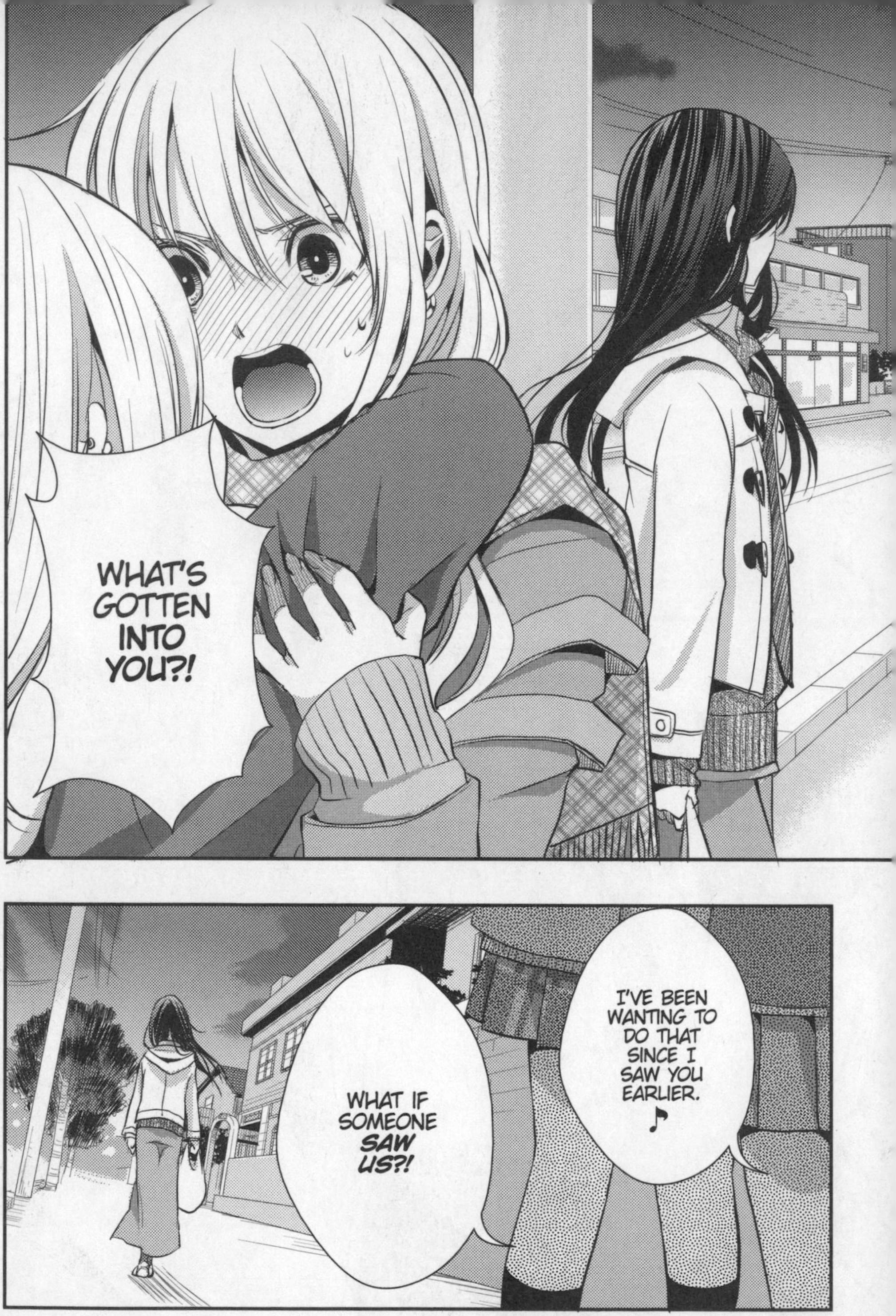
WHAT'S GOTTEN INTO YOU?!
I'VE BEEN WANTING TO DO THAT SINCE I SAW YOU EARLIER. ♪
WHAT IF SOMEONE *SAW* US?!

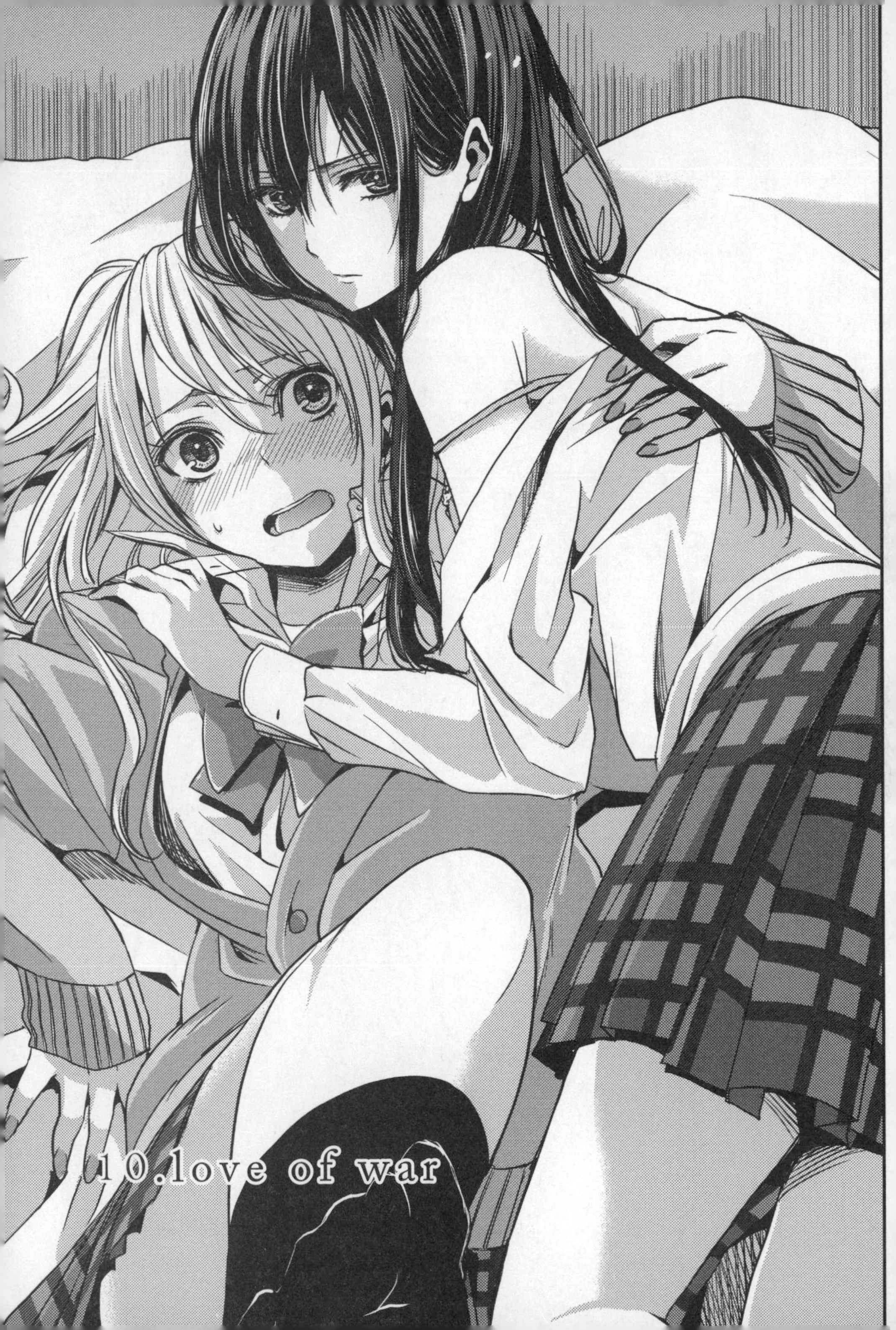
10.love of war

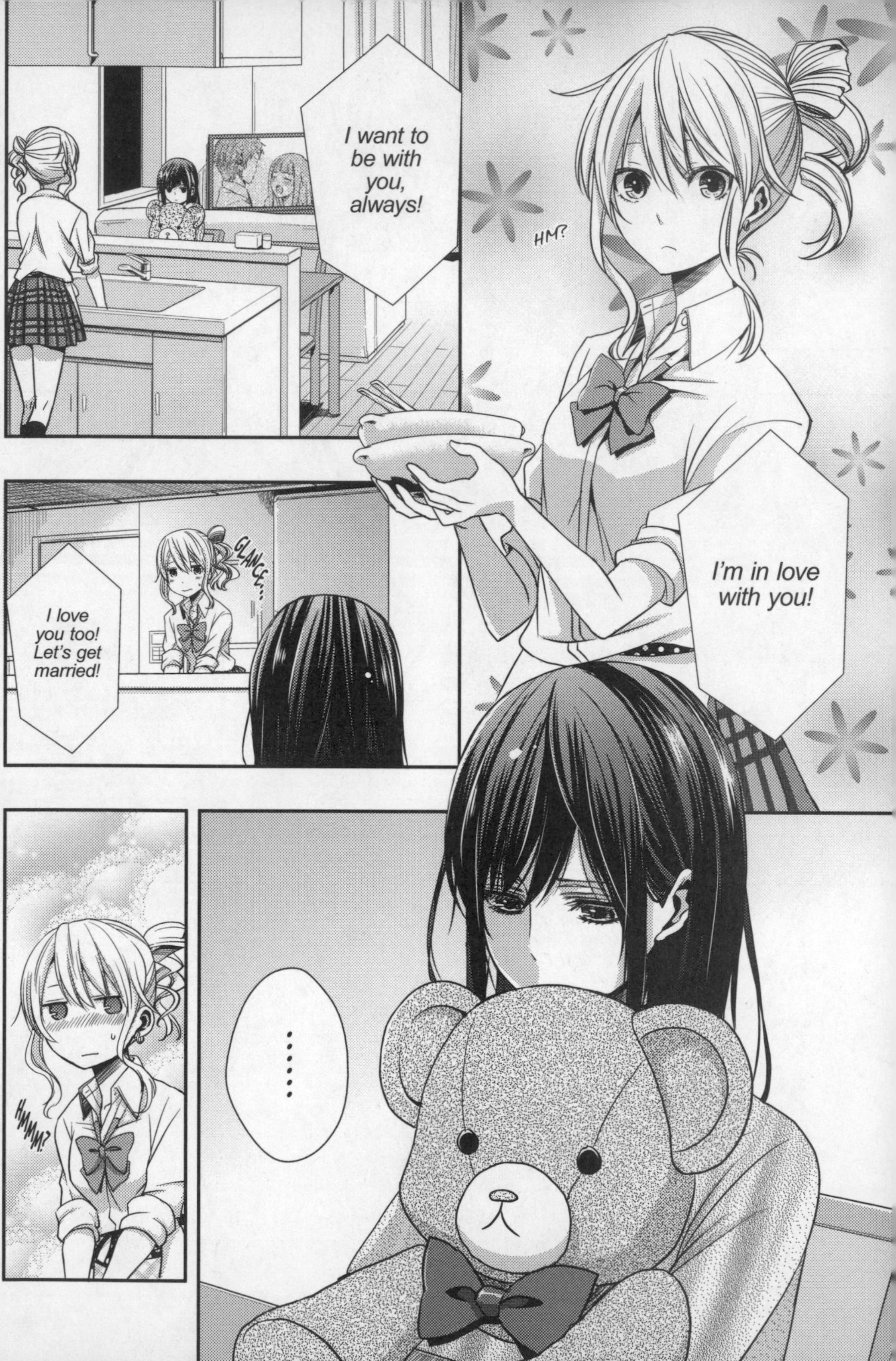
HM?
I'm in love with you!
I want to be with you, always!
GLANCE...
I love you too! Let's get married!
……
HMMM?

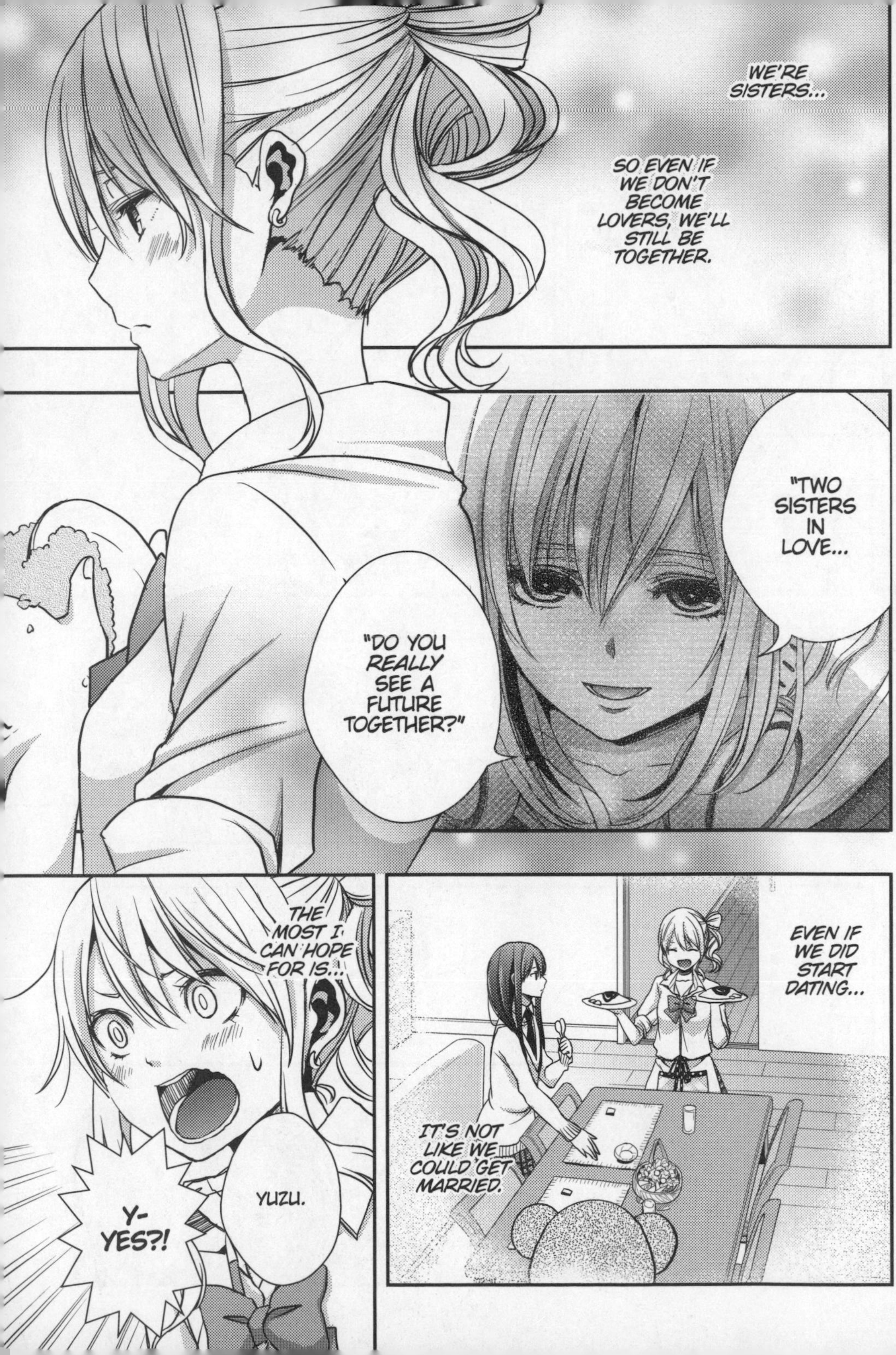
WE'RE SISTERS...
SO EVEN IF WE DON'T BECOME LOVERS, WE'LL STILL BE TOGETHER.
"TWO SISTERS IN LOVE...
"DO YOU REALLY SEE A FUTURE TOGETHER?"
EVEN IF WE DID START DATING...
IT'S NOT LIKE WE COULD GET MARRIED.
THE MOST I CAN HOPE FOR IS...
YUZU.
Y- YES?!

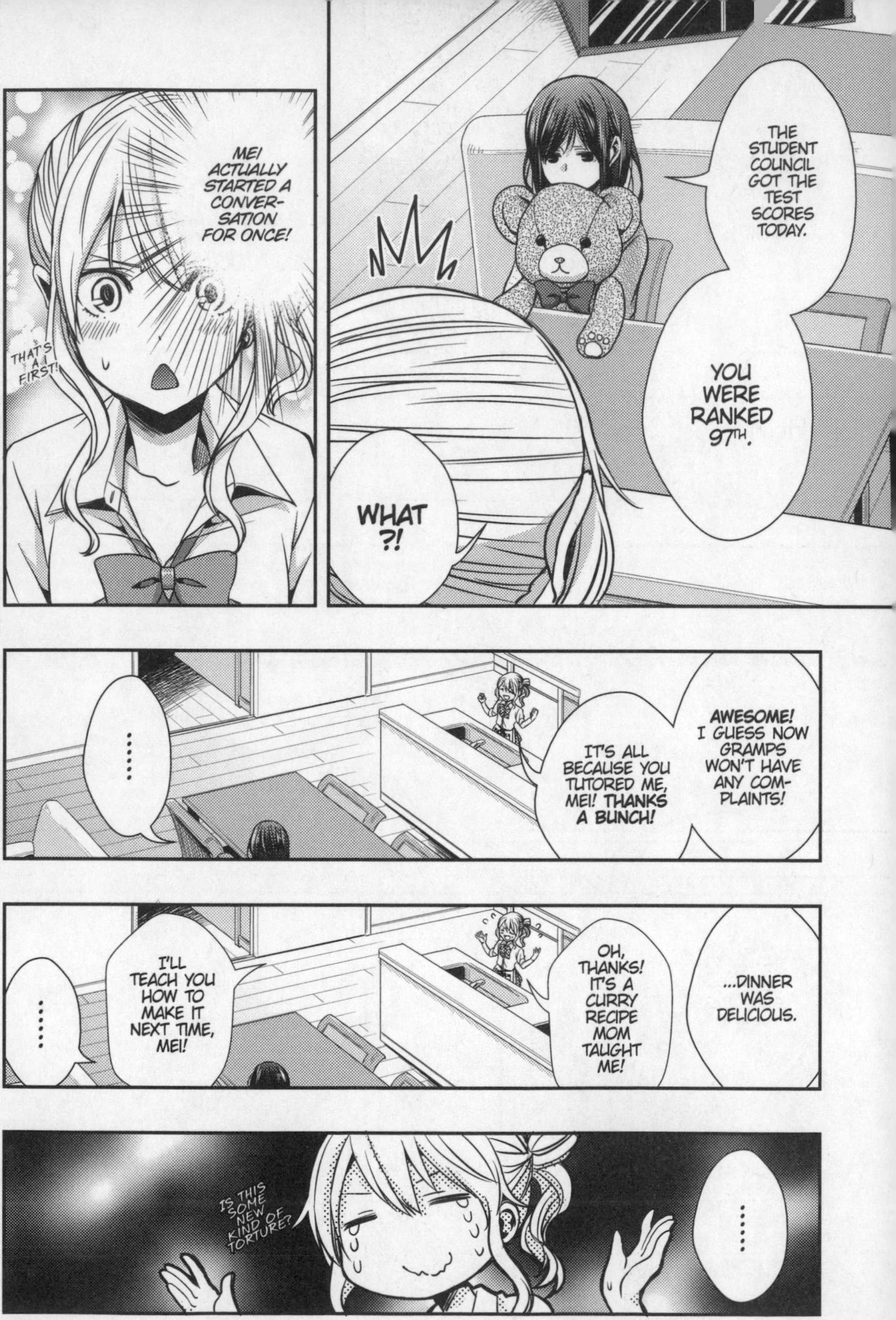
THE STUDENT COUNCIL GOT THE TEST SCORES TODAY.
YOU WERE RANKED 97TH.
WHAT?!
MEI ACTUALLY STARTED A CONVERSATION FOR ONCE!
THAT'S A FIRST!
AWESOME! I GUESS NOW GRAMPS WON'T HAVE ANY COMPLAINTS!
IT'S ALL BECAUSE YOU TUTORED ME, MEI! THANKS A BUNCH!
......
...DINNER WAS DELICIOUS.
OH, THANKS! IT'S A CURRY RECIPE MOM TAUGHT ME!
I'LL TEACH YOU HOW TO MAKE IT NEXT TIME, MEI!
......
......
IS THIS SOME NEW KIND OF TORTURE?

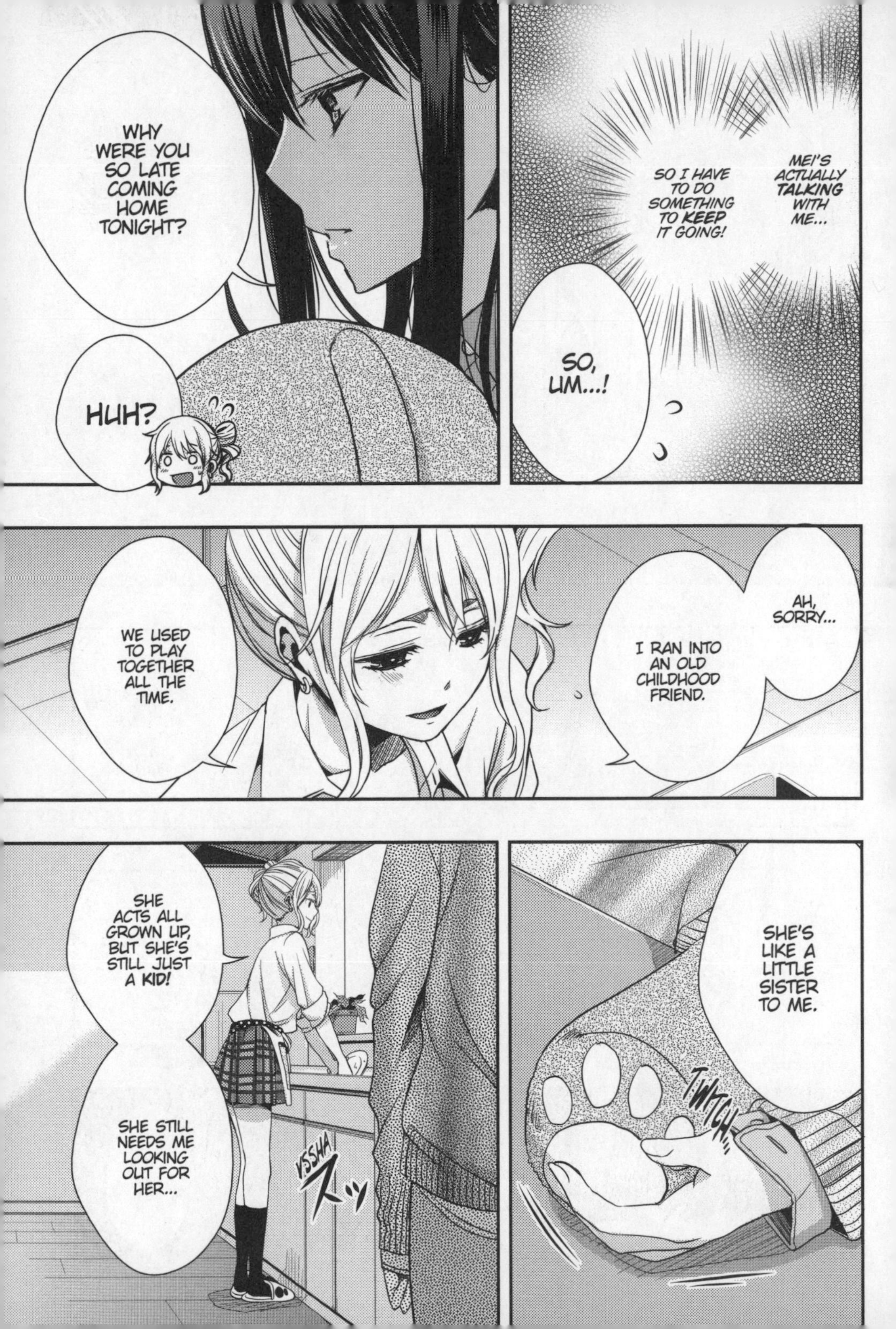
MEI'S ACTUALLY TALKING WITH ME...
SO I HAVE TO DO SOMETHING TO KEEP IT GOING!
SO, UM...!
WHY WERE YOU SO LATE COMING HOME TONIGHT?
HUH?
AH, SORRY...
I RAN INTO AN OLD CHILDHOOD FRIEND.
WE USED TO PLAY TOGETHER ALL THE TIME.
SHE'S LIKE A LITTLE SISTER TO ME.
TWITCH...
SHE ACTS ALL GROWN UP, BUT SHE'S STILL JUST A KID!
SHE STILL NEEDS ME LOOKING OUT FOR HER...
VSSHA
スッ

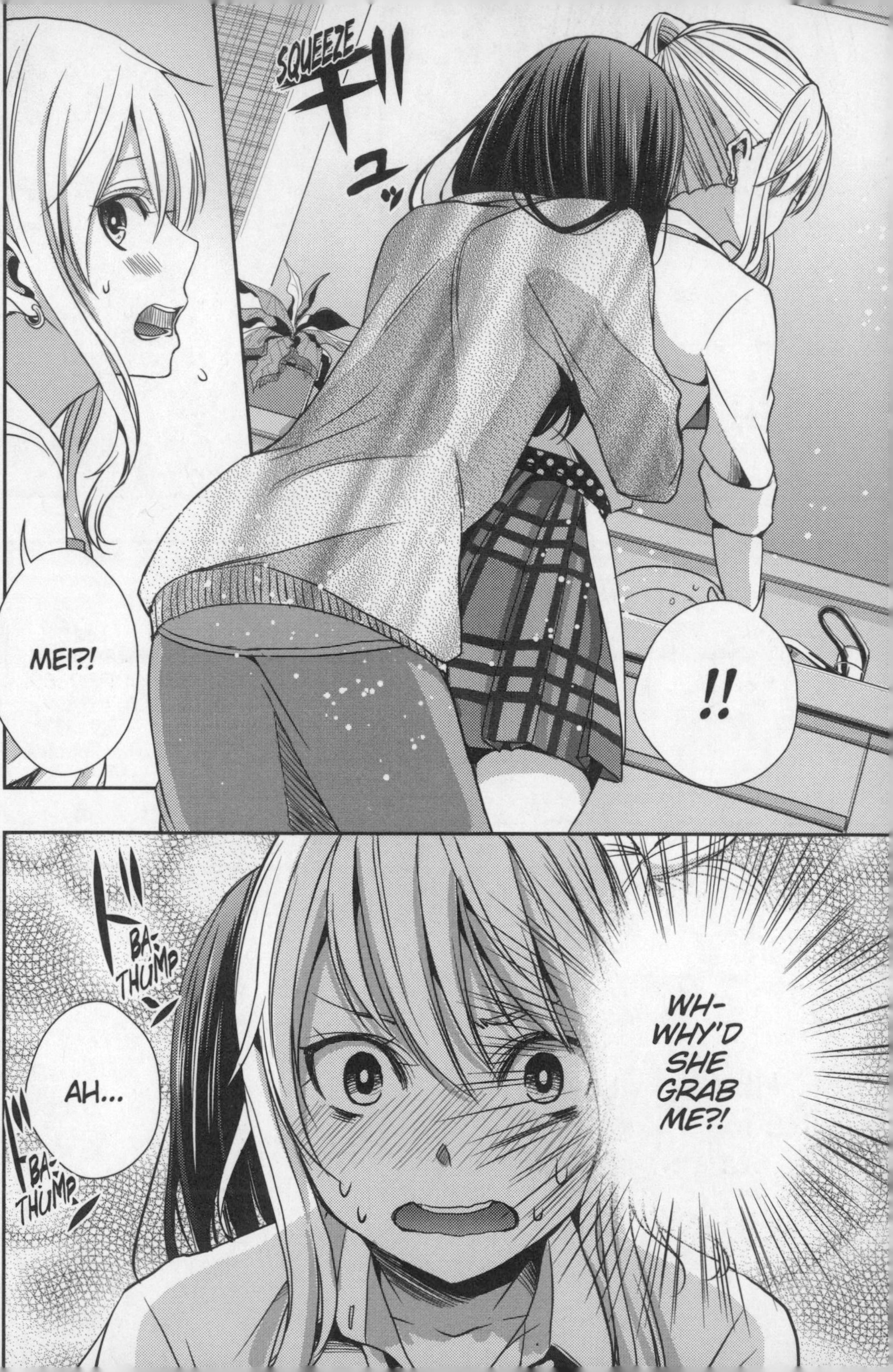
SQUEEZE
!!
MEI?!
WH- WHY'D SHE GRAB ME?!
BA-THUMP
AH...
BA-THUMP

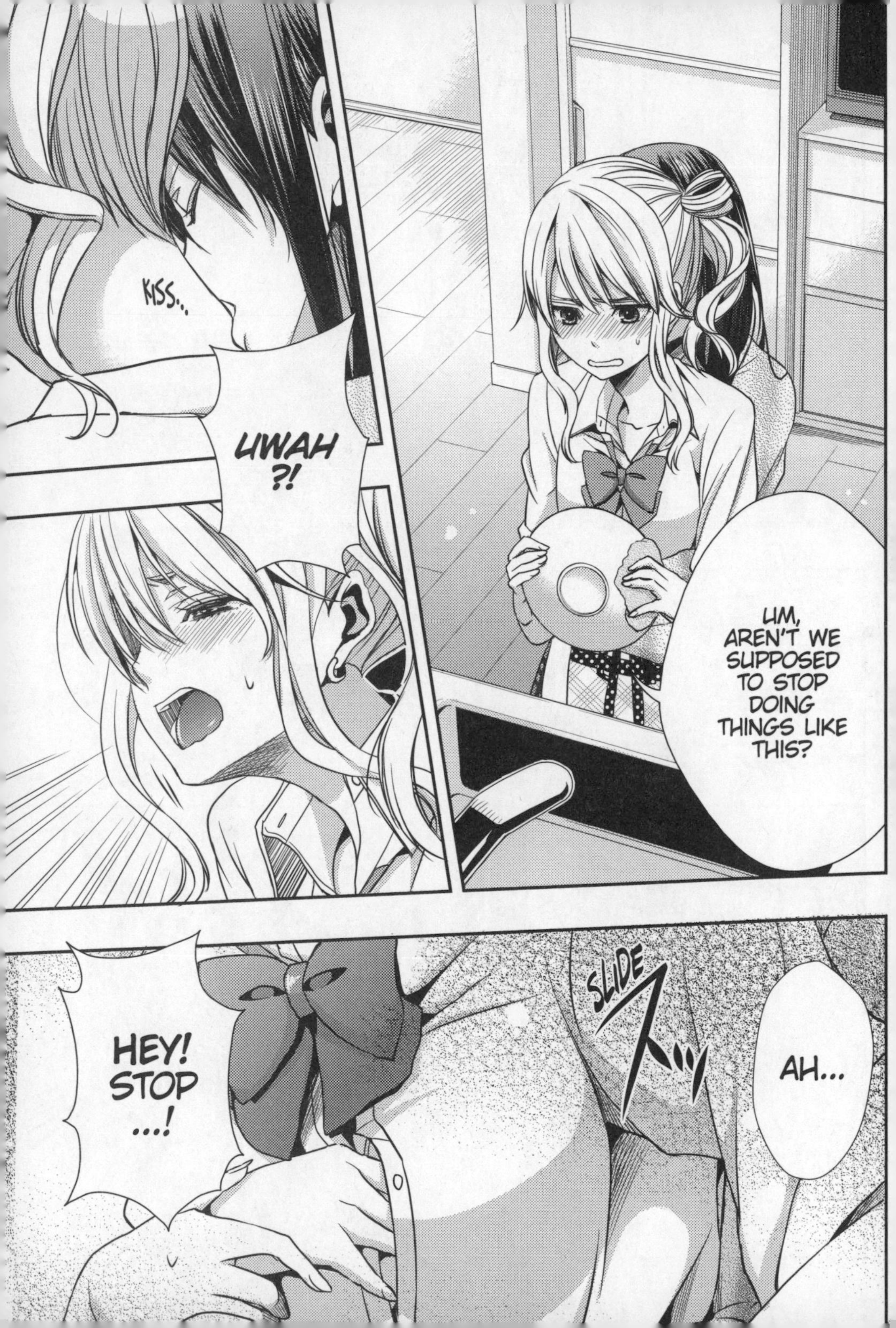
UM, AREN'T WE SUPPOSED TO STOP DOING THINGS LIKE THIS?
KISS...
UWAH ?!
AH...
SLIDE
HEY! STOP ...!

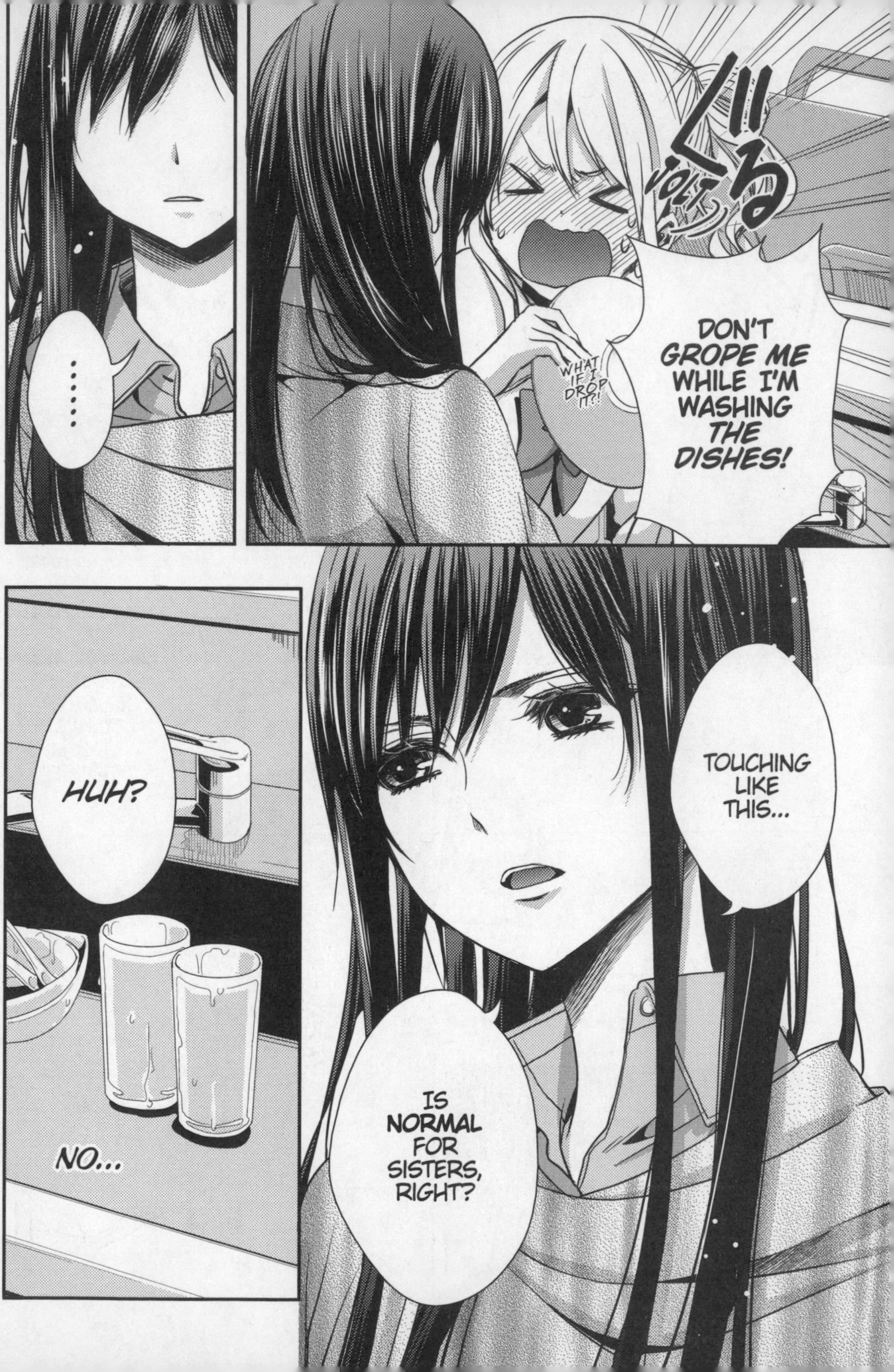
DON'T GROPE ME WHILE I'M WASHING THE DISHES!
WHAT IF I DROP IT?!
......
TOUCHING LIKE THIS...
IS NORMAL FOR SISTERS, RIGHT?
HUH?
NO...

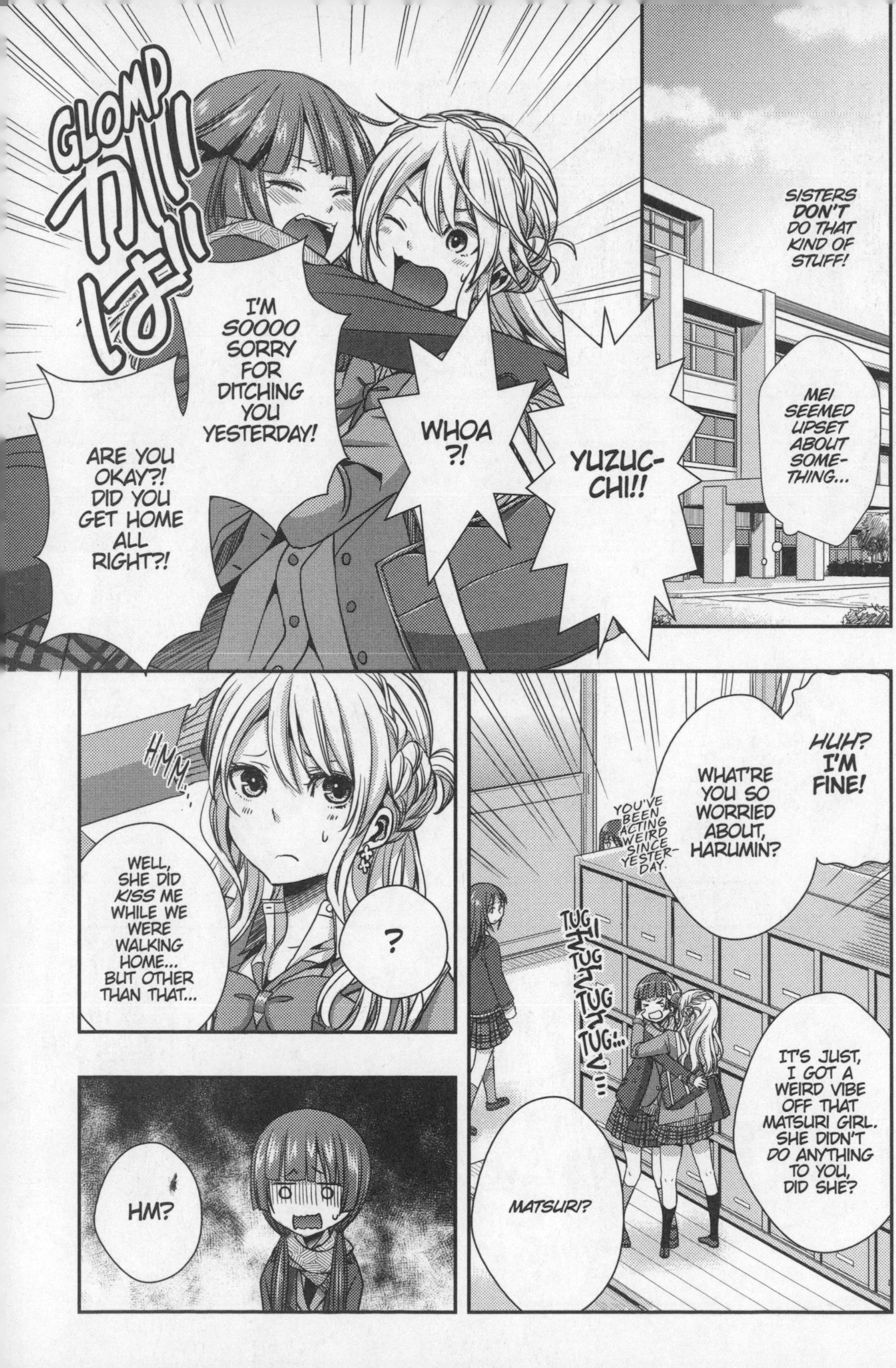
SISTERS DON'T DO THAT KIND OF STUFF!
MEI SEEMED UPSET ABOUT SOMETHING...
YUZUC-CHI!!
WHOA?!
GLOMP
I'M SOOOO SORRY FOR DITCHING YOU YESTERDAY!
ARE YOU OKAY?! DID YOU GET HOME ALL RIGHT?!
HUH? I'M FINE!
WHAT'RE YOU SO WORRIED ABOUT, HARUMIN?
YOU'VE BEEN ACTING WEIRD SINCE YESTER-DAY.
TUG TUG TUG TUG...
IT'S JUST, I GOT A WEIRD VIBE OFF THAT MATSURI GIRL. SHE DIDN'T DO ANYTHING TO YOU, DID SHE?
MATSURI?
HMM
?
WELL, SHE DID KISS ME WHILE WE WERE WALKING HOME... BUT OTHER THAN THAT...
HM?

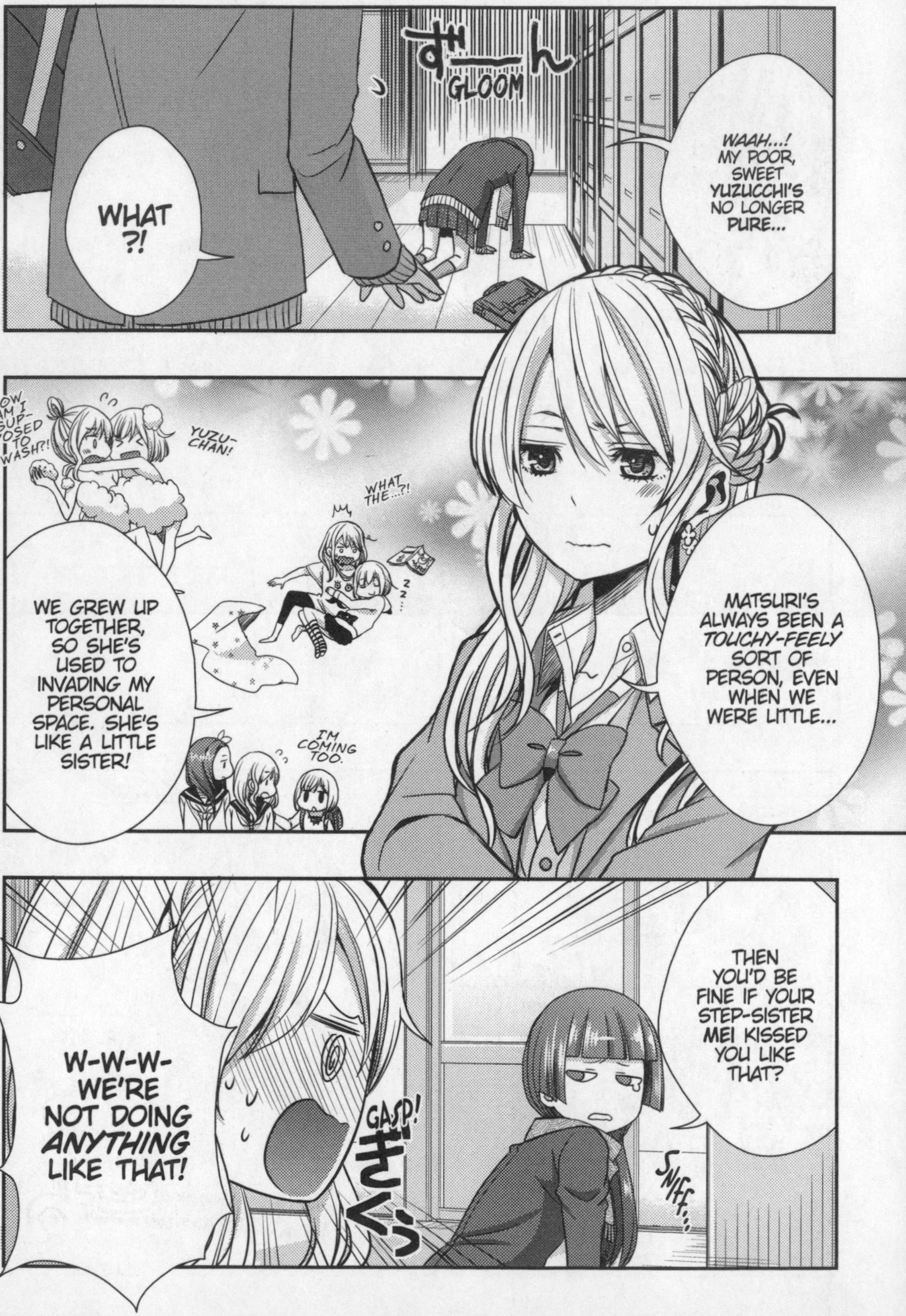
ずーん
GLOOM
WAAH...! MY POOR, SWEET YUZUCCHI'S NO LONGER PURE...
WHAT ?!
MATSURI'S ALWAYS BEEN A *TOUCHY-FEELY* SORT OF PERSON, EVEN WHEN WE WERE LITTLE...
YUZU-CHAN!
HOW AM I SUPPOSED TO WASH?!
WHAT THE...?!
WE GREW UP TOGETHER, SO SHE'S USED TO INVADING MY PERSONAL SPACE. SHE'S LIKE A LITTLE SISTER!
I'M COMING TOO.
THEN YOU'D BE FINE IF YOUR STEP-SISTER MEI KISSED YOU LIKE THAT?
SNIFF...
GASP!
ぎくぅ
W-W-W-WE'RE NOT DOING *ANYTHING* LIKE THAT!

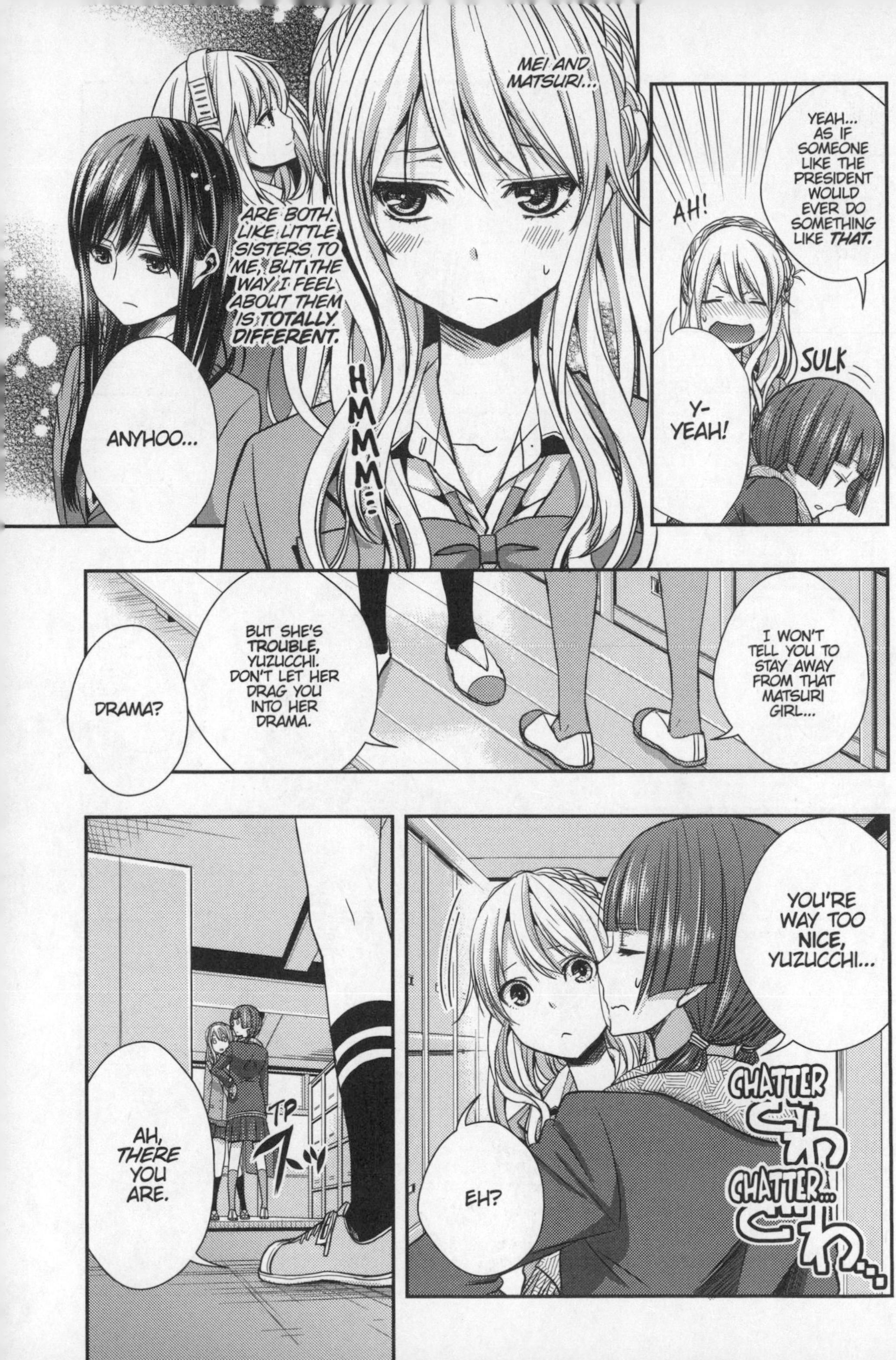
YEAH... AS IF SOMEONE LIKE THE PRESIDENT WOULD EVER DO SOMETHING LIKE *THAT.*
AH!
Y- YEAH!
SULK
MEI AND MATSURI...
ARE BOTH LIKE LITTLE SISTERS TO ME, BUT THE WAY I FEEL ABOUT THEM IS *TOTALLY DIFFERENT.*
HMMM...
ANYHOO...
I WON'T TELL YOU TO STAY AWAY FROM THAT MATSURI GIRL...
BUT SHE'S TROUBLE, YUZUCCHI. DON'T LET HER DRAG YOU INTO HER DRAMA.
DRAMA?
YOU'RE WAY TOO NICE, YUZUCCHI...
EH?
CHATTER ざわ
CHATTER... ざわ...
TAP
AH, THERE YOU ARE.

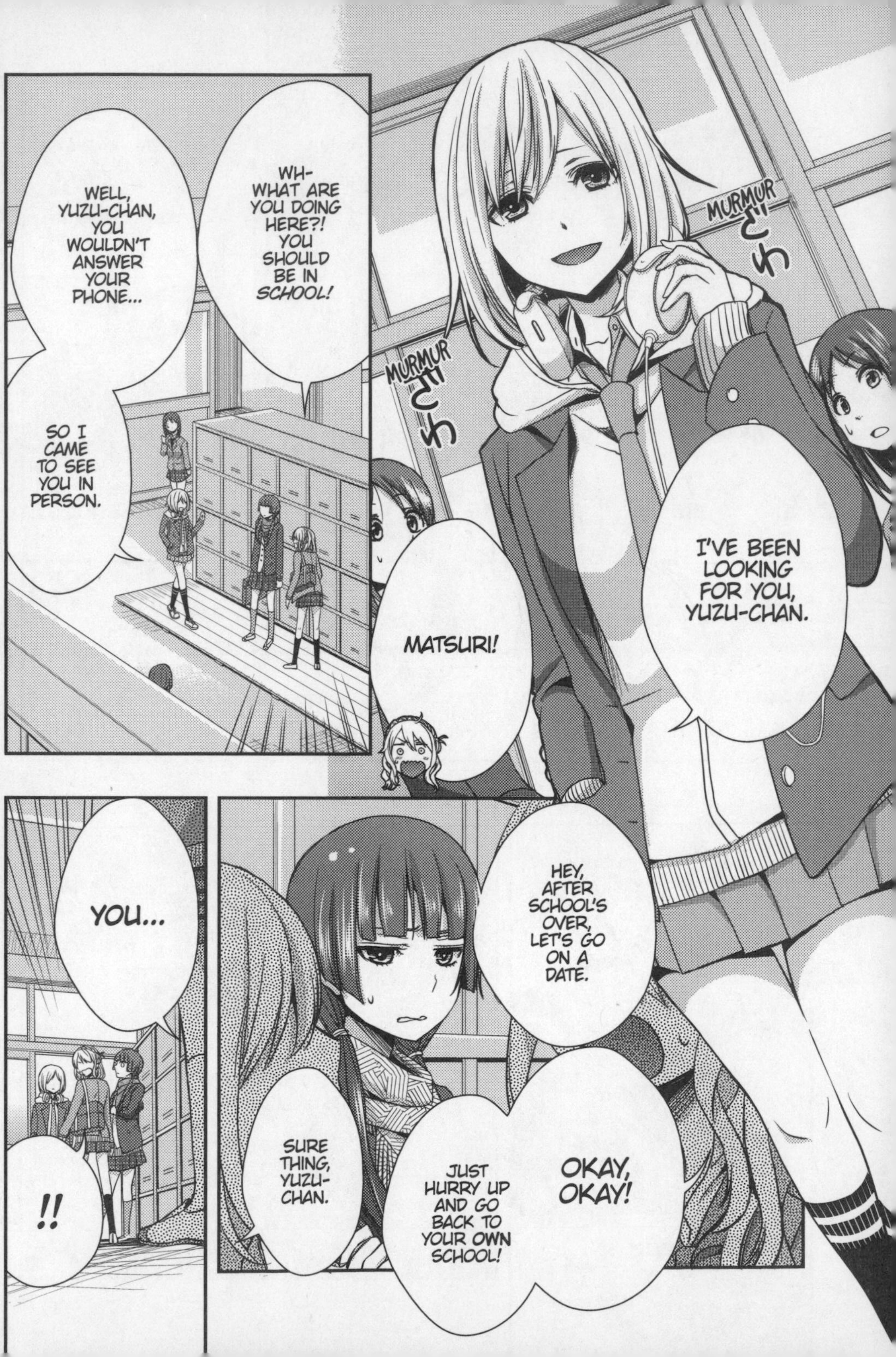
I'VE BEEN LOOKING FOR YOU, YUZU-CHAN.
MURMUR ざわ
MURMUR ざわ
MATSURI!
WH- WHAT ARE YOU DOING HERE?! YOU SHOULD BE IN SCHOOL!
WELL, YUZU-CHAN, YOU WOULDN'T ANSWER YOUR PHONE...
SO I CAME TO SEE YOU IN PERSON.
HEY, AFTER SCHOOL'S OVER, LET'S GO ON A DATE.
OKAY, OKAY!
JUST HURRY UP AND GO BACK TO YOUR OWN SCHOOL!
SURE THING, YUZU-CHAN.
YOU...
!!

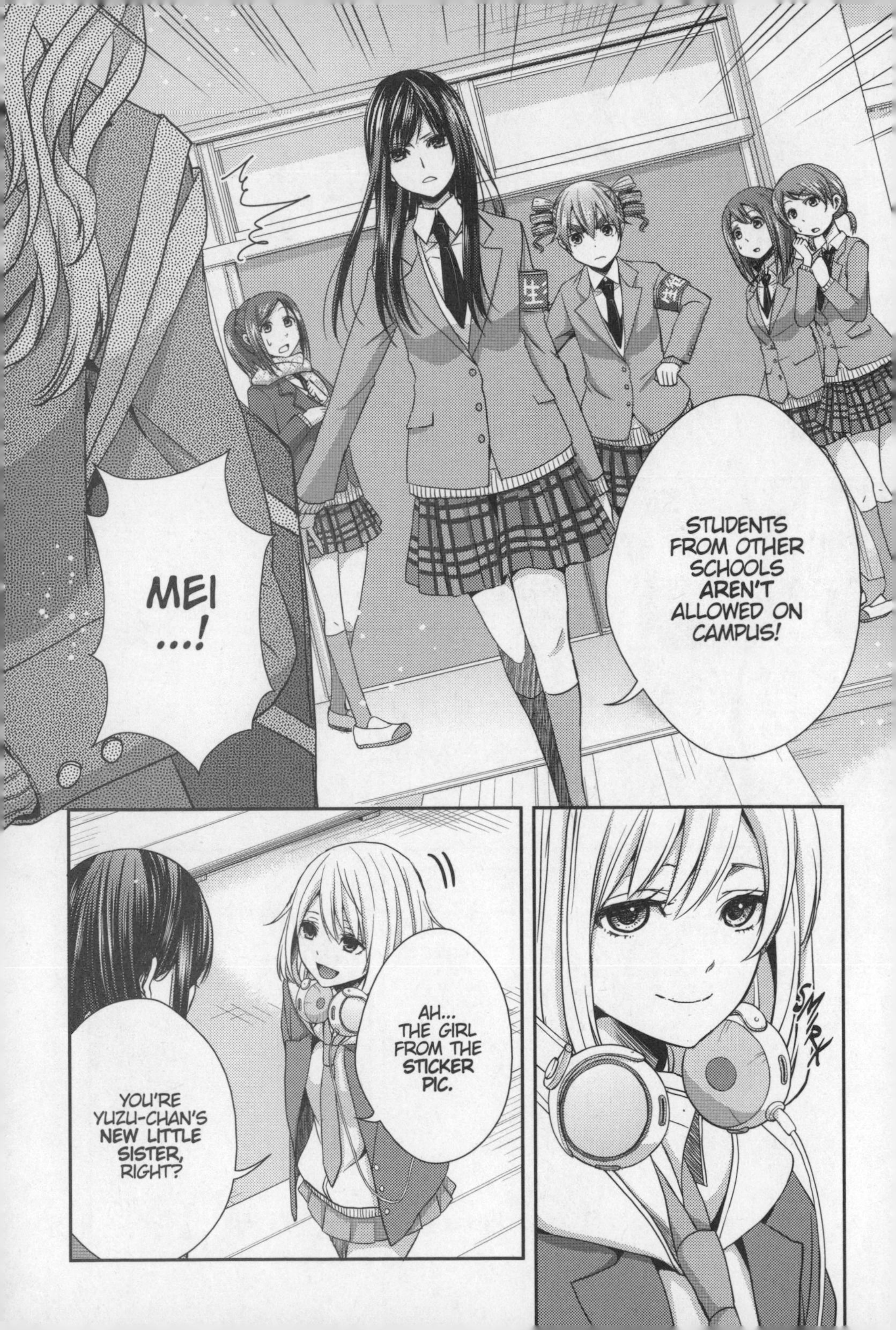
STUDENTS FROM OTHER SCHOOLS AREN'T ALLOWED ON CAMPUS!
MEI ...!
SMIRK
AH... THE GIRL FROM THE STICKER PIC.
YOU'RE YUZU-CHAN'S NEW LITTLE SISTER, RIGHT?

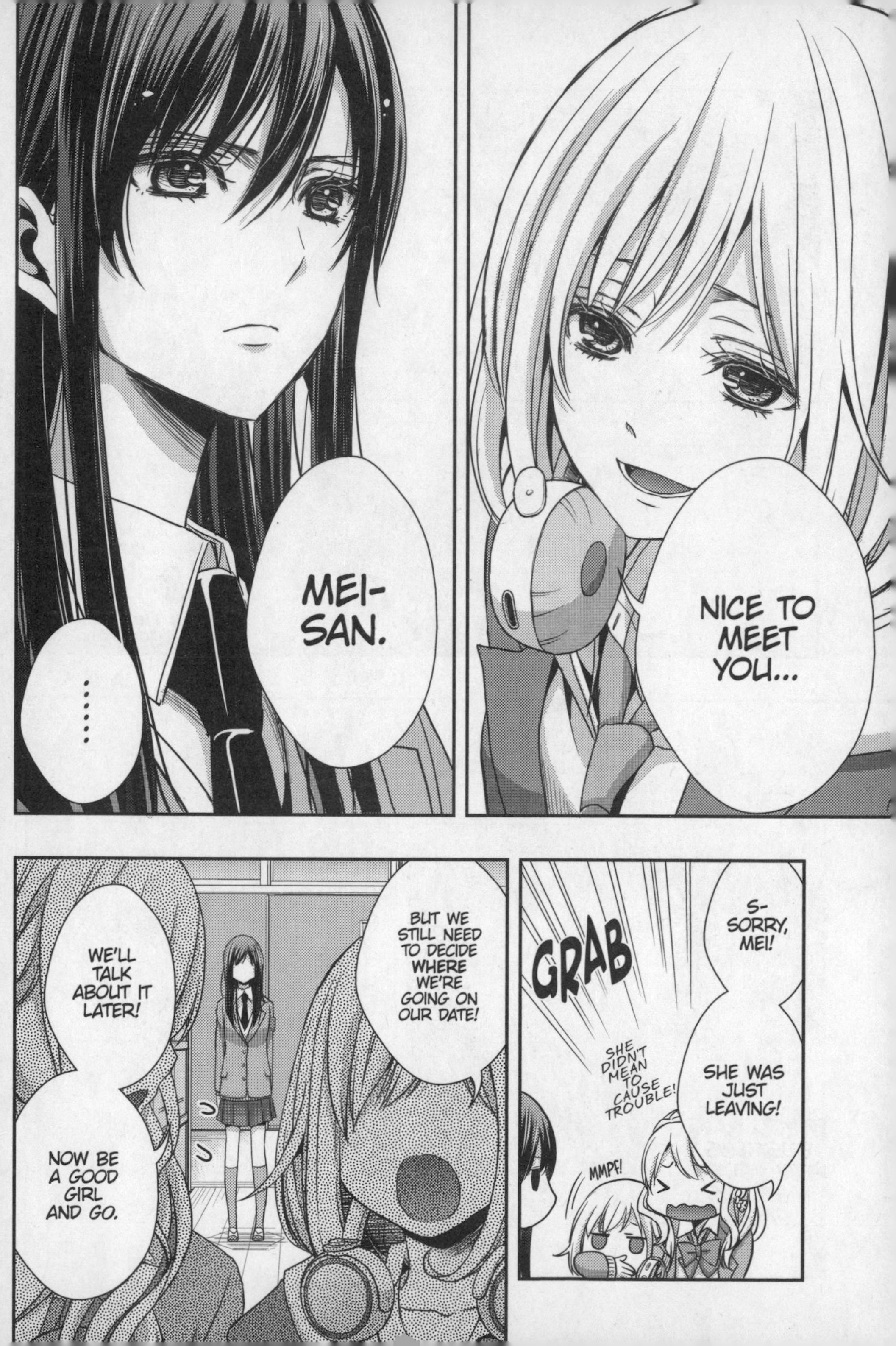
NICE TO MEET YOU...
MEI-SAN.
......
S- SORRY, MEI!
SHE WAS JUST LEAVING!
SHE DIDN'T MEAN TO CAUSE TROUBLE!
GRAB
MMPF!
BUT WE STILL NEED TO DECIDE WHERE WE'RE GOING ON OUR DATE!
WE'LL TALK ABOUT IT LATER!
NOW BE A GOOD GIRL AND GO.

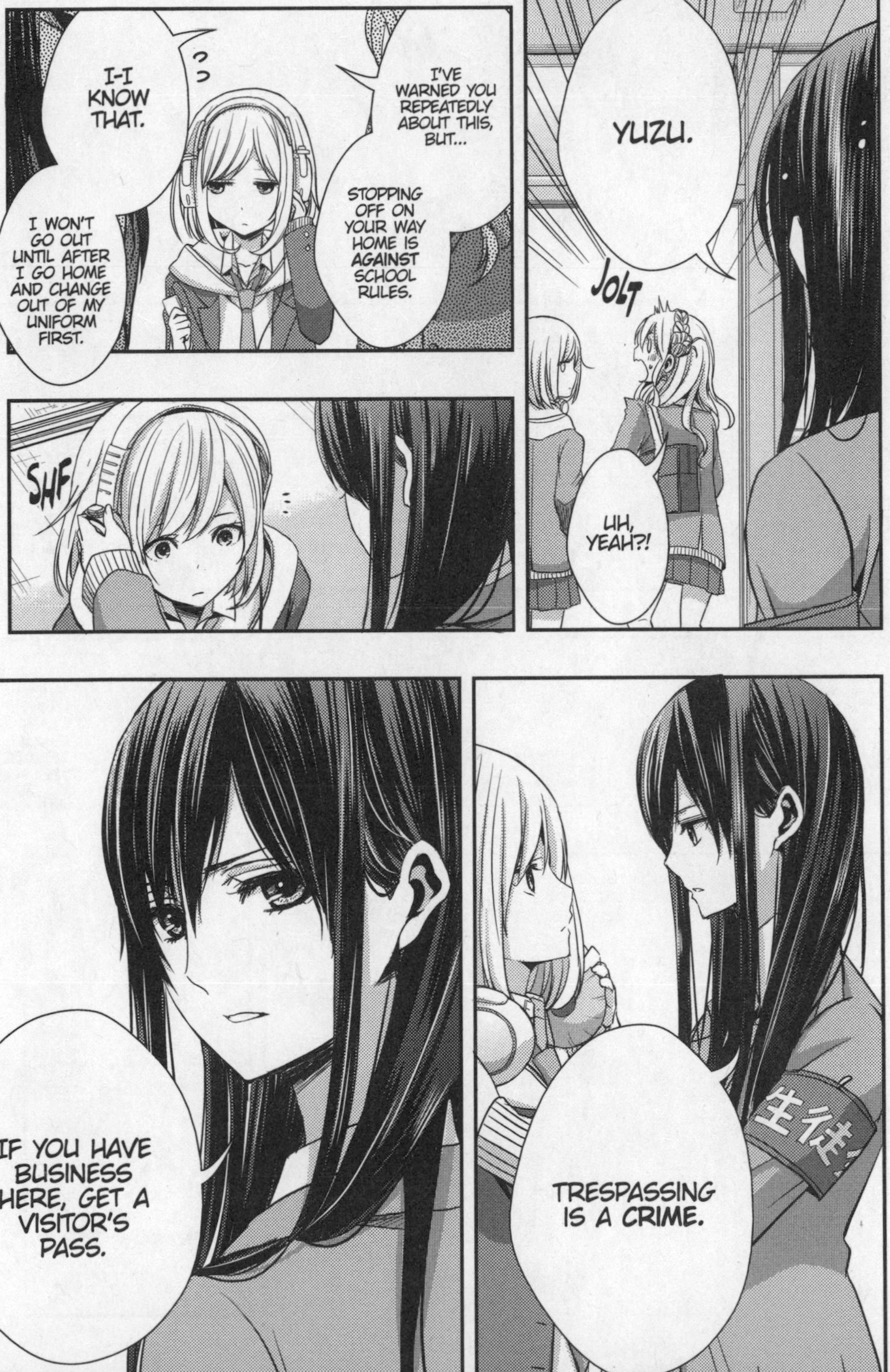
YUZU.
JOLT
UH, YEAH?!
I'VE WARNED YOU REPEATEDLY ABOUT THIS, BUT...
STOPPING OFF ON YOUR WAY HOME IS AGAINST SCHOOL RULES.
I-I KNOW THAT.
I WON'T GO OUT UNTIL AFTER I GO HOME AND CHANGE OUT OF MY UNIFORM FIRST.
SHF
TRESPASSING IS A CRIME.
生徒
IF YOU HAVE BUSINESS HERE, GET A VISITOR'S PASS.

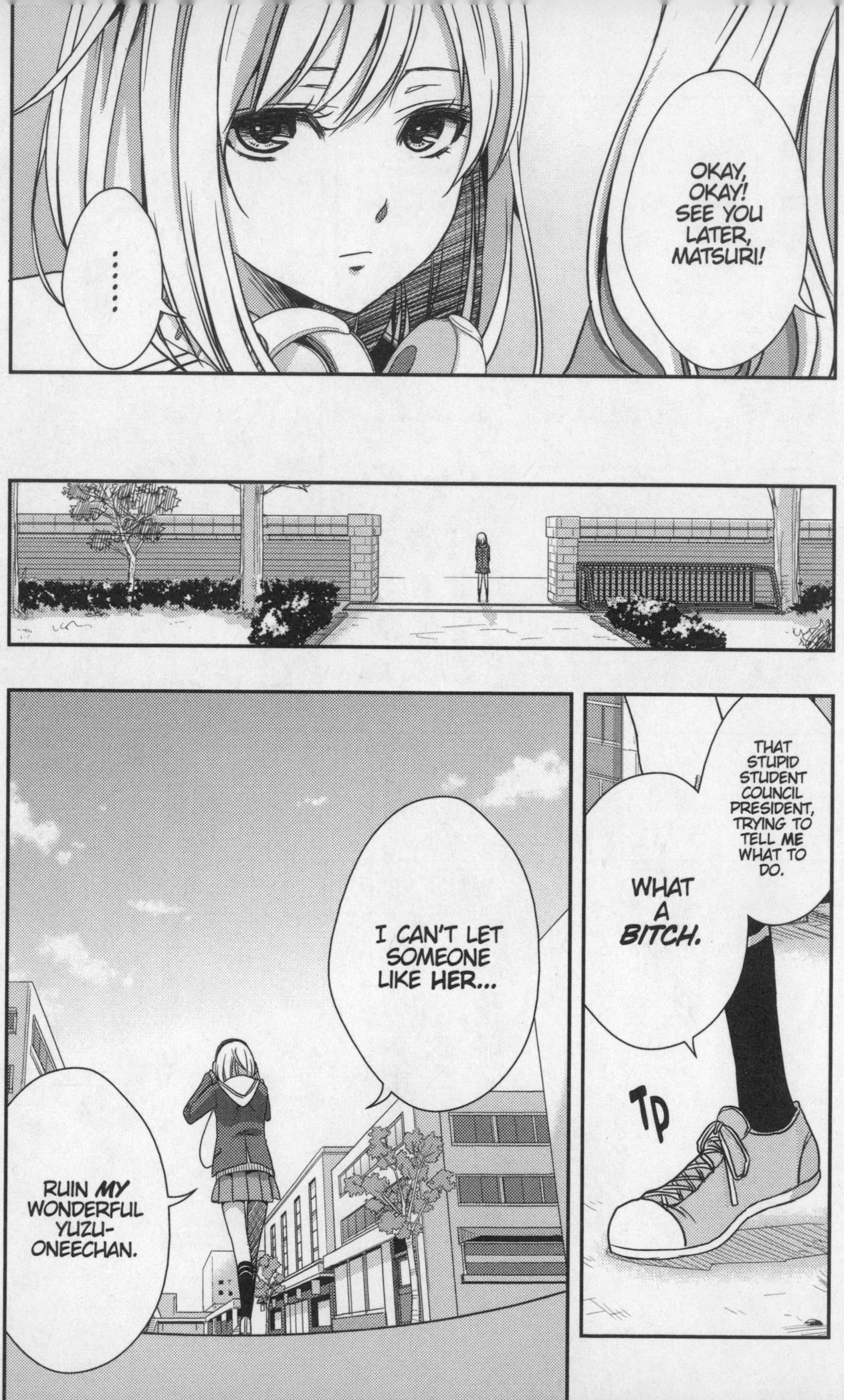
OKAY, OKAY! SEE YOU LATER, MATSURI!
......
THAT STUPID STUDENT COUNCIL PRESIDENT, TRYING TO TELL ME WHAT TO DO.
WHAT A *BITCH.*
TP
I CAN'T LET SOMEONE LIKE HER...
RUIN *MY* WONDERFUL YUZU-ONEECHAN.

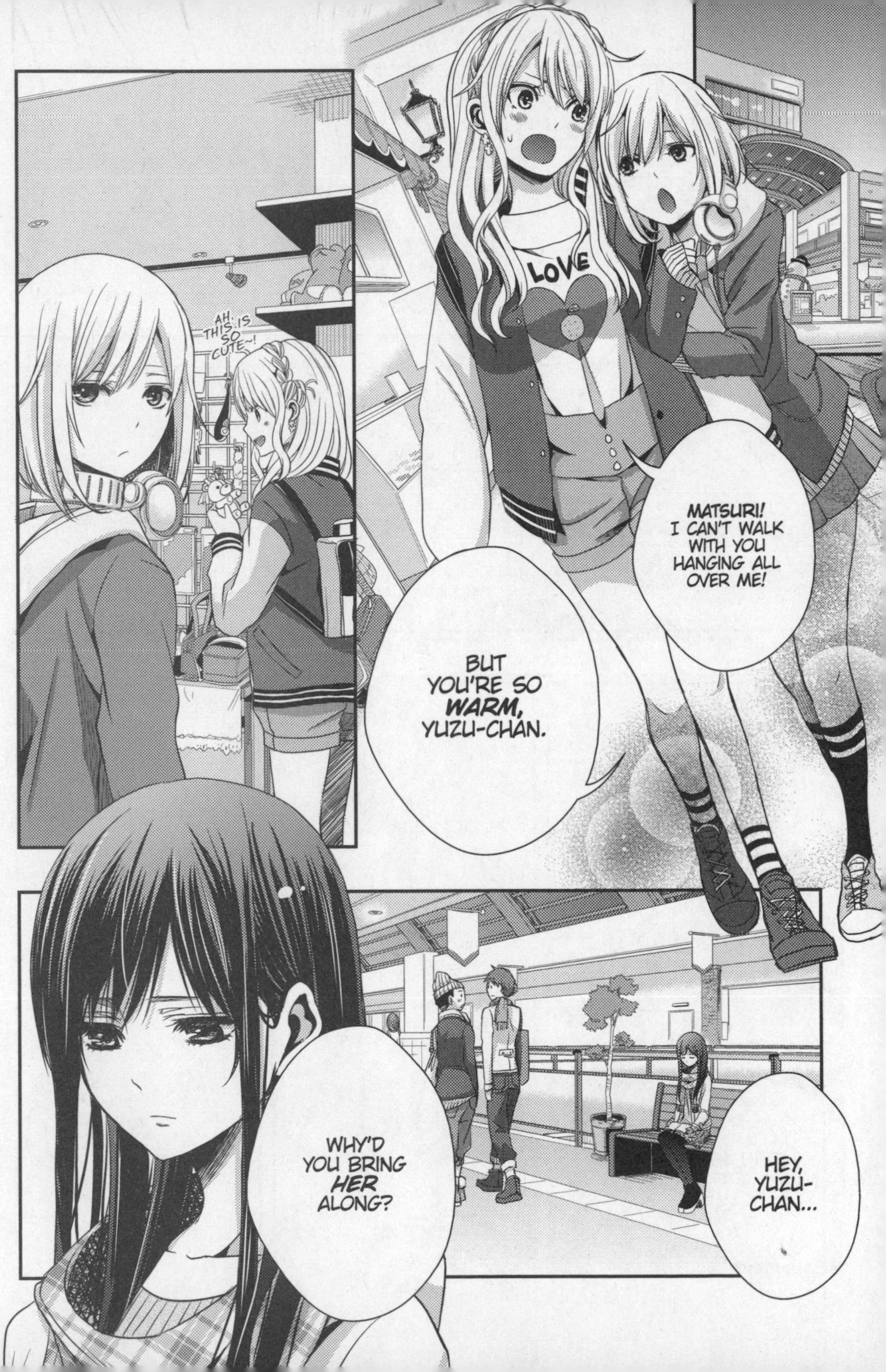
MATSURI! I CAN'T WALK WITH YOU HANGING ALL OVER ME!
BUT YOU'RE SO WARM, YUZU-CHAN.
AH, THIS IS SO CUTE~!
HEY, YUZU-CHAN...
WHY'D YOU BRING HER ALONG?

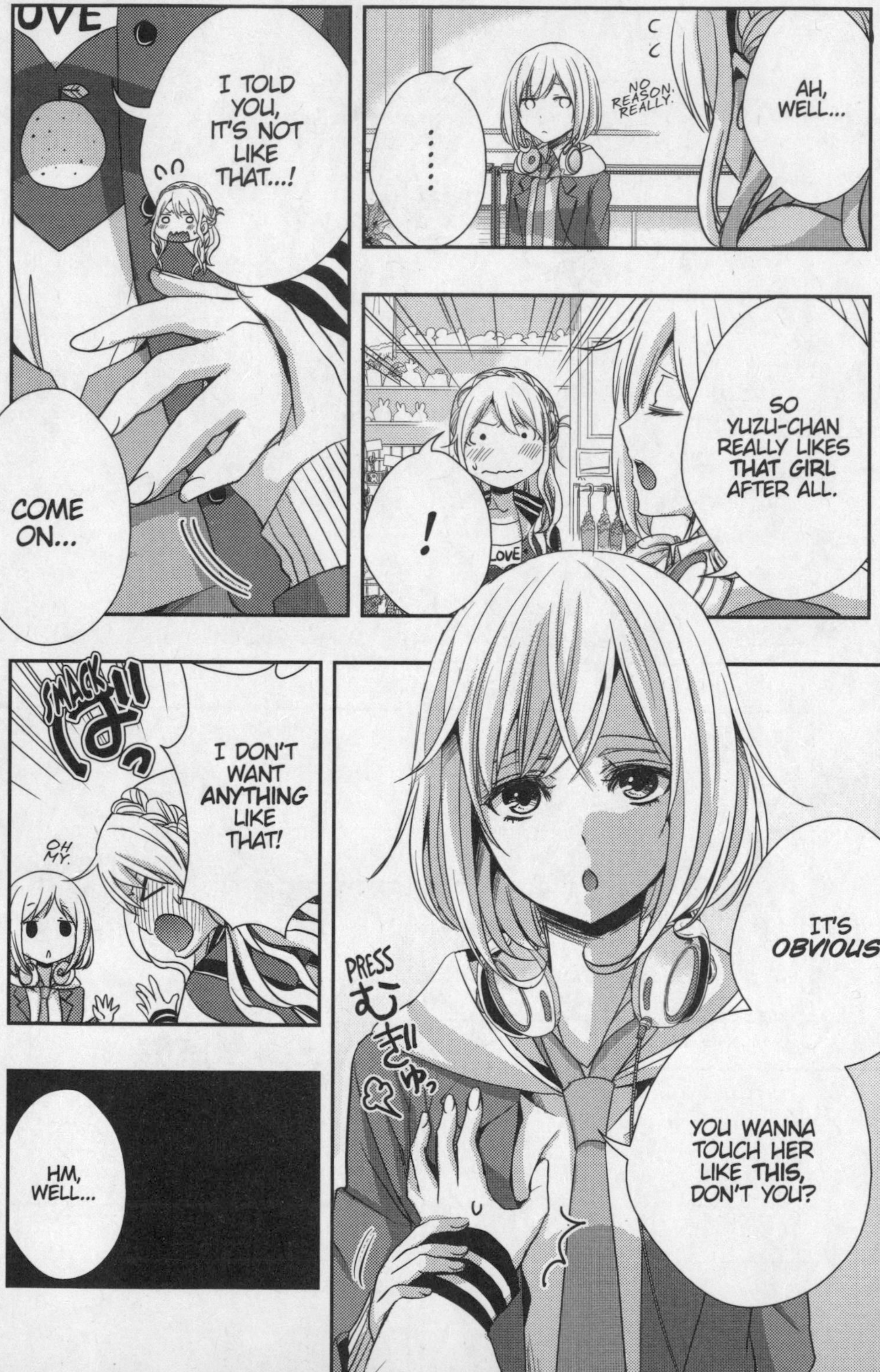
AH, WELL...
NO REASON. REALLY.
......
SO YUZU-CHAN REALLY LIKES THAT GIRL AFTER ALL.
!
LOVE
I TOLD YOU, IT'S NOT LIKE THAT...!
COME ON...
IT'S OBVIOUS.
YOU WANNA TOUCH HER LIKE THIS, DON'T YOU?
PRESS
SMACK
I DON'T WANT ANYTHING LIKE THAT!
OH MY.
HM, WELL...

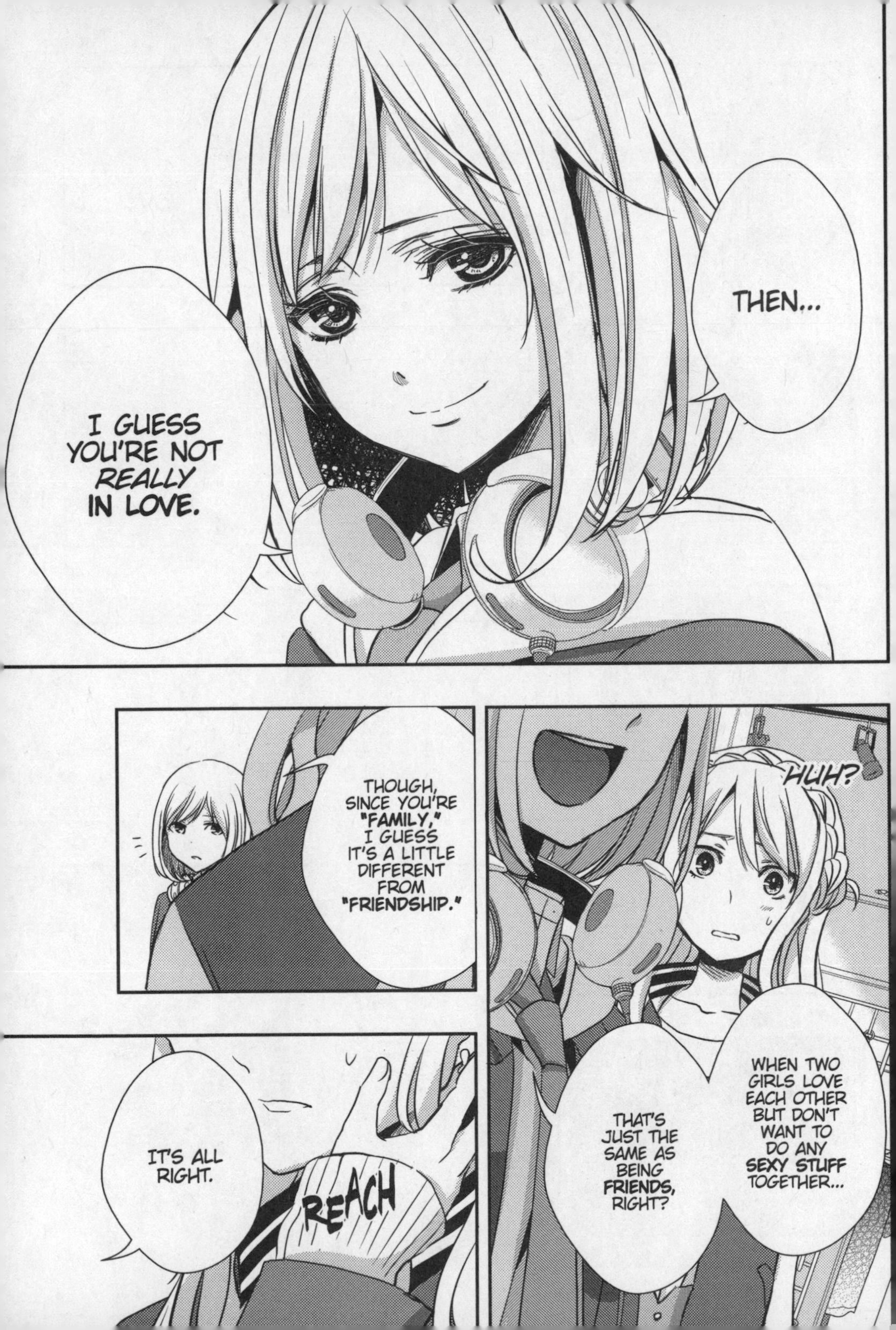
THEN...
I GUESS YOU'RE NOT *REALLY* IN LOVE.
HUH?
WHEN TWO GIRLS LOVE EACH OTHER BUT DON'T WANT TO DO ANY **SEXY STUFF** TOGETHER...
THAT'S JUST THE SAME AS BEING **FRIENDS,** RIGHT?
THOUGH, SINCE YOU'RE **"FAMILY,"** I GUESS IT'S A LITTLE DIFFERENT FROM **"FRIENDSHIP."**
IT'S ALL RIGHT.
REACH

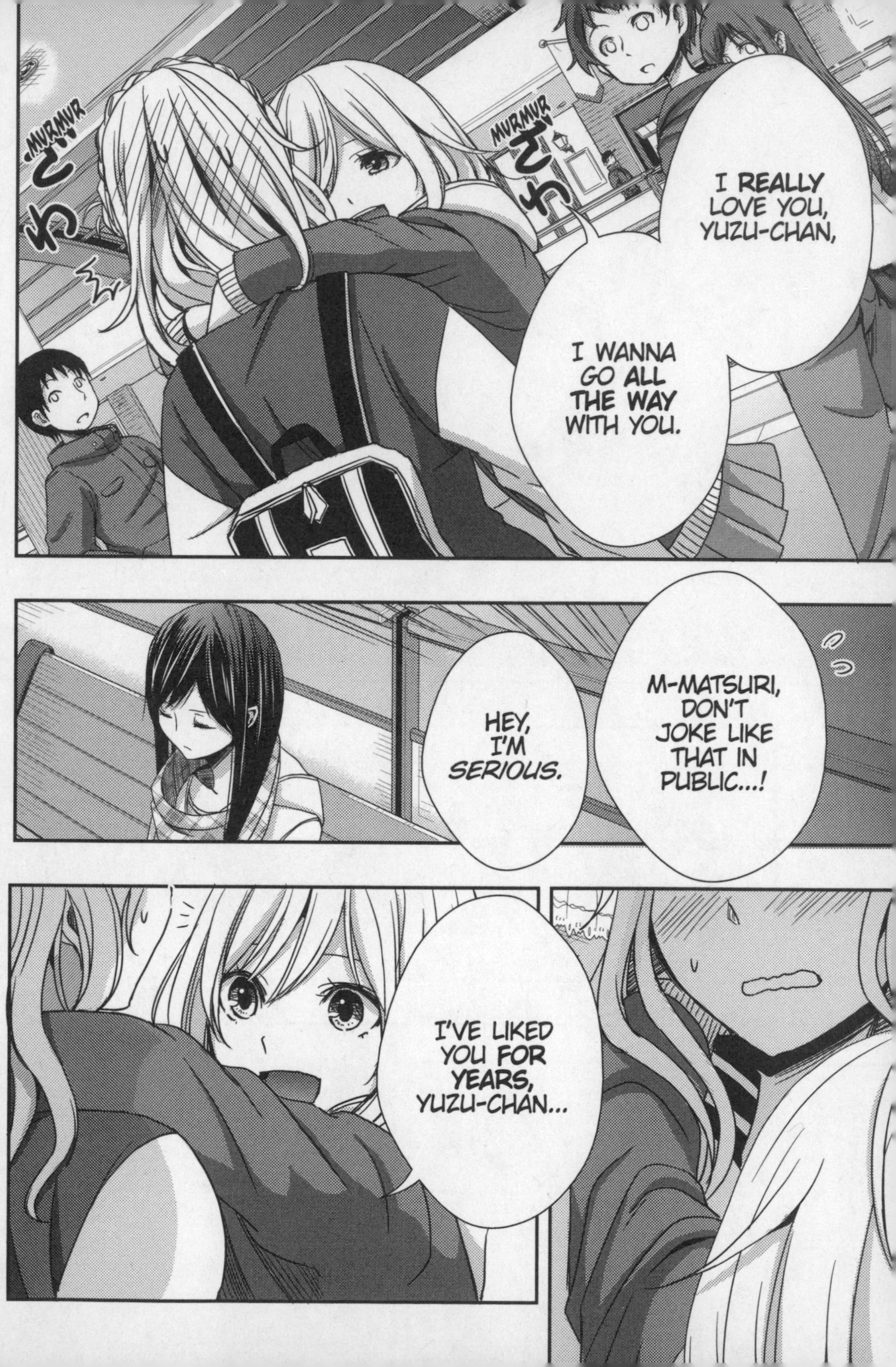
MURMUR
MURMUR
I REALLY LOVE YOU, YUZU-CHAN,
I WANNA GO ALL THE WAY WITH YOU.
M-MATSURI, DON'T JOKE LIKE THAT IN PUBLIC...!
HEY, I'M SERIOUS.
I'VE LIKED YOU FOR YEARS, YUZU-CHAN...

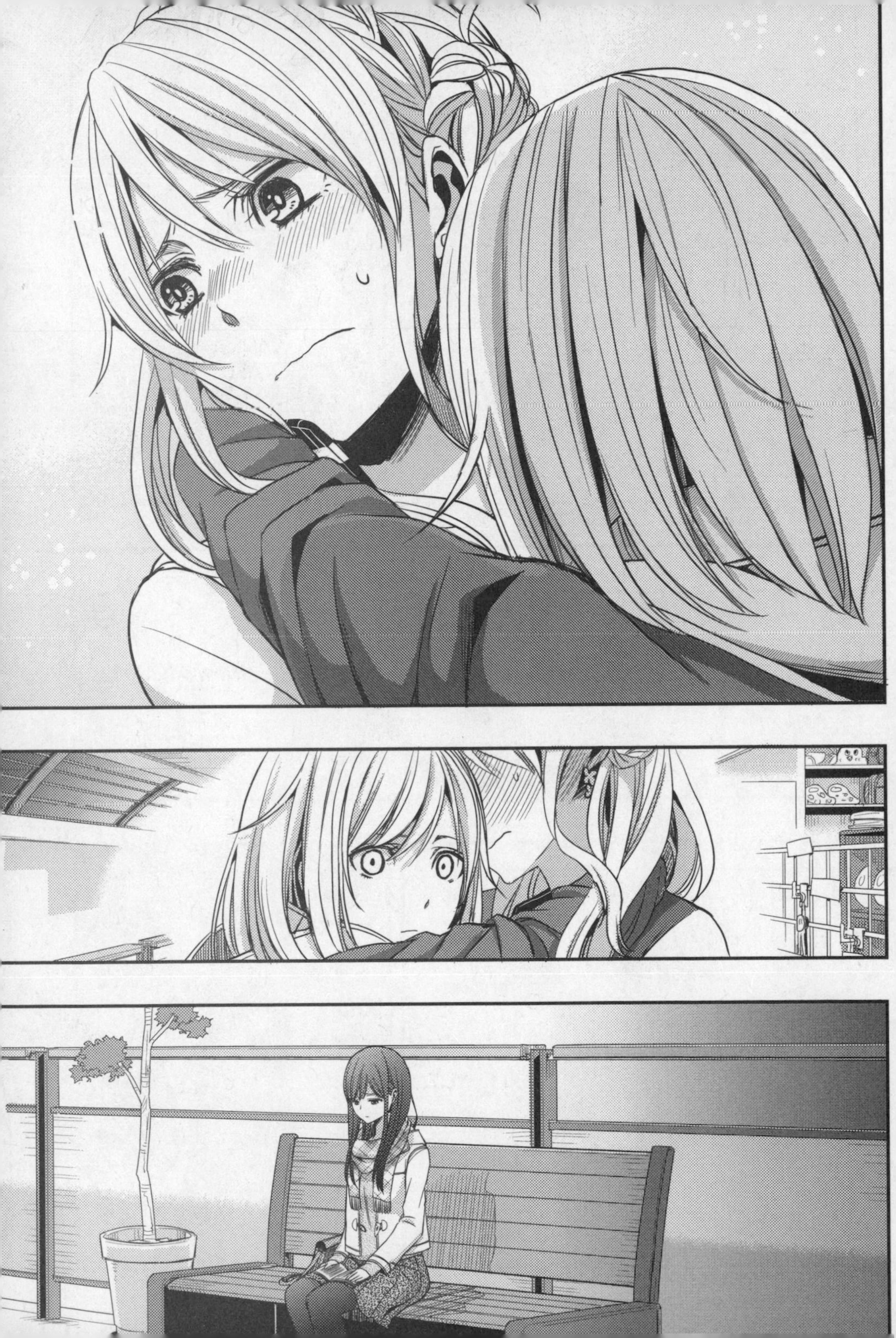

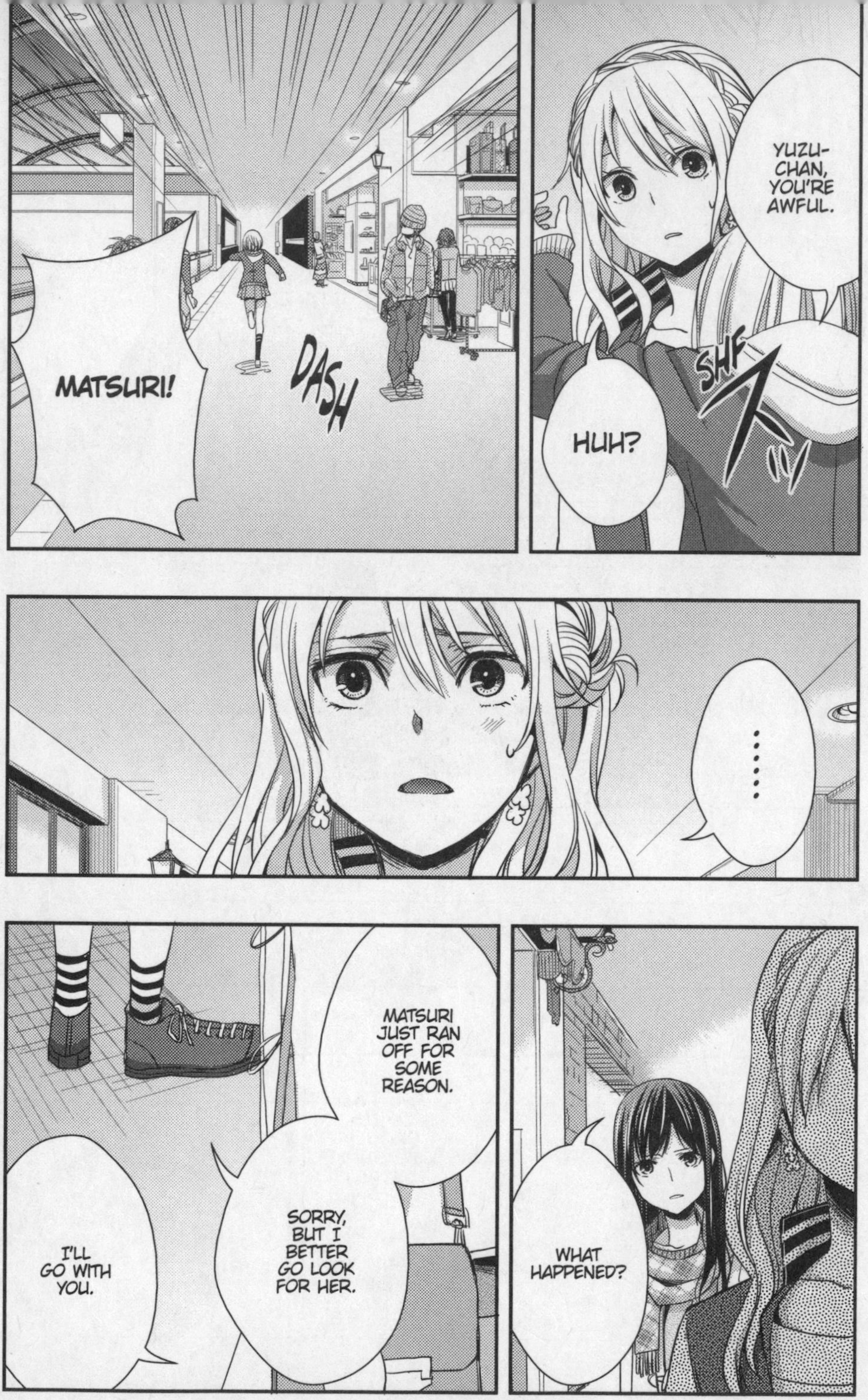
YUZU-CHAN, YOU'RE AWFUL.
SHF
HUH?
MATSURI!
DASH
......
WHAT HAPPENED?
MATSURI JUST RAN OFF FOR SOME REASON.
SORRY, BUT I BETTER GO LOOK FOR HER.
I'LL GO WITH YOU.

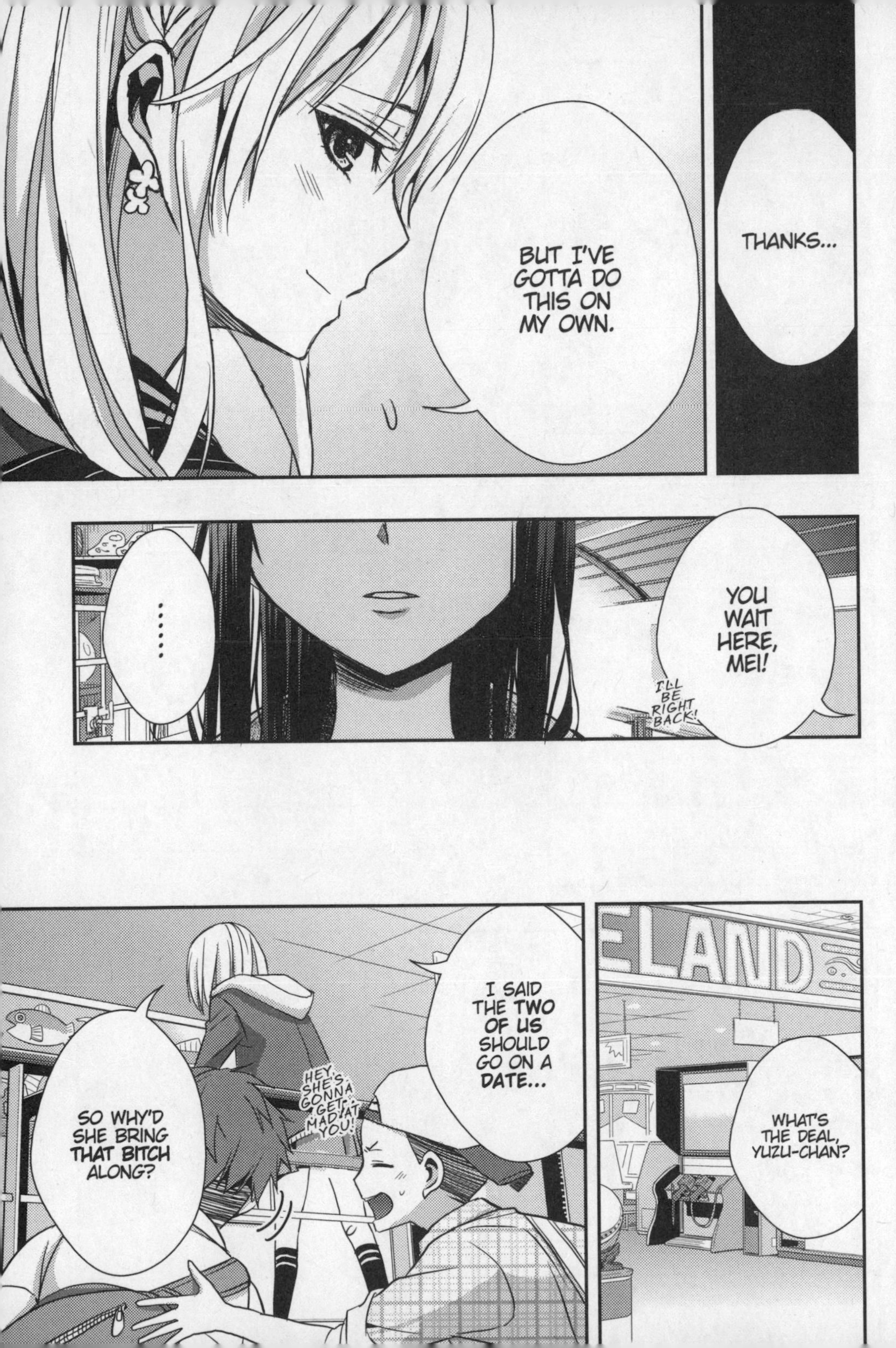
THANKS...
BUT I'VE GOTTA DO THIS ON MY OWN.
YOU WAIT HERE, MEI!
I'LL BE RIGHT BACK!
......
WHAT'S THE DEAL, YUZU-CHAN?
I SAID THE TWO OF US SHOULD GO ON A DATE...
HEY, SHE'S GONNA GET MAD AT YOU!
SO WHY'D SHE BRING THAT BITCH ALONG?

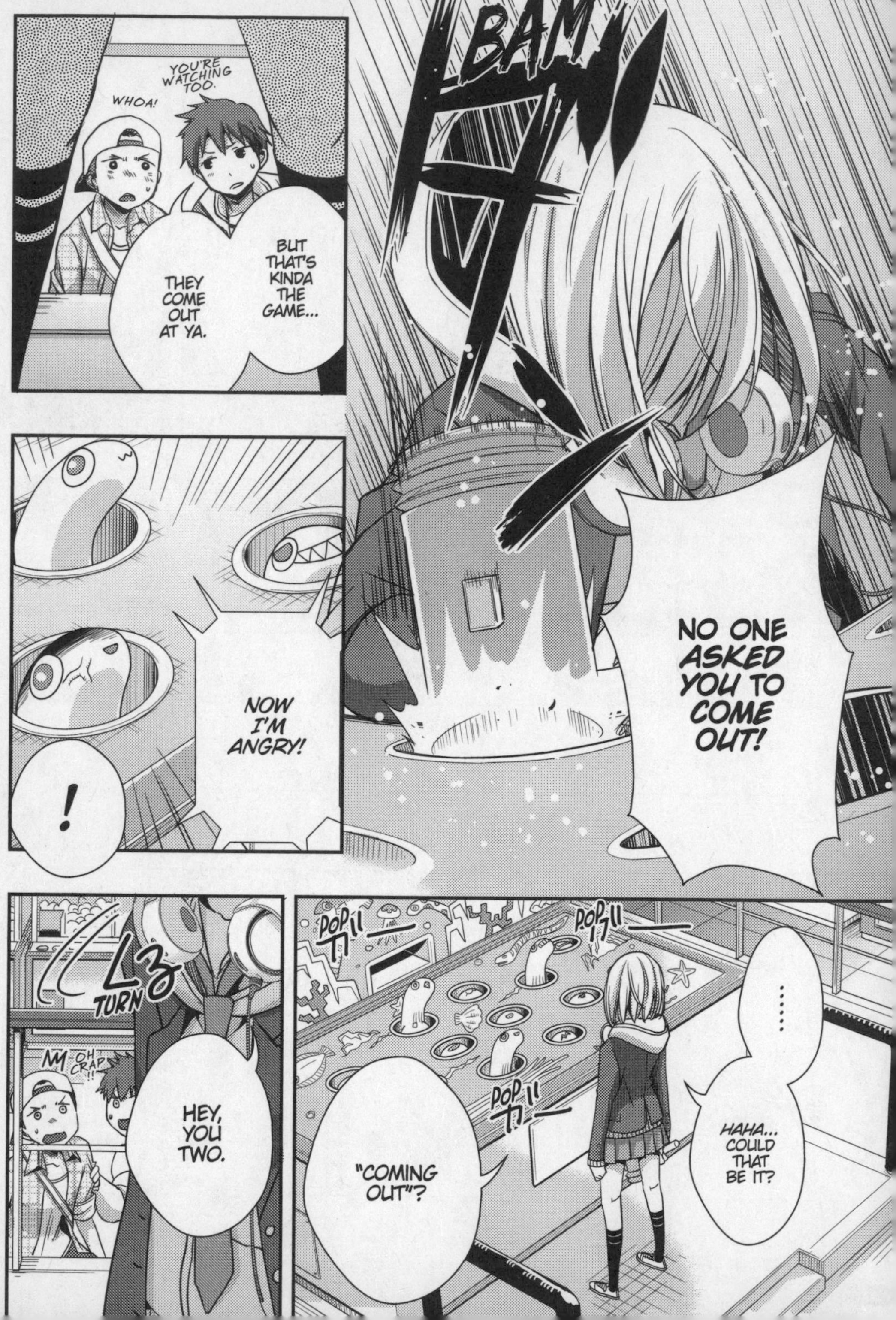
BAM
NO ONE ASKED YOU TO COME OUT!
YOU'RE WATCHING TOO.
WHOA!
BUT THAT'S KINDA THE GAME...
THEY COME OUT AT YA.
NOW I'M ANGRY!
!
POP
POP
......
HAHA... COULD THAT BE IT?
POP
"COMING OUT"?
TURN
OH CRAP!!
HEY, YOU TWO.

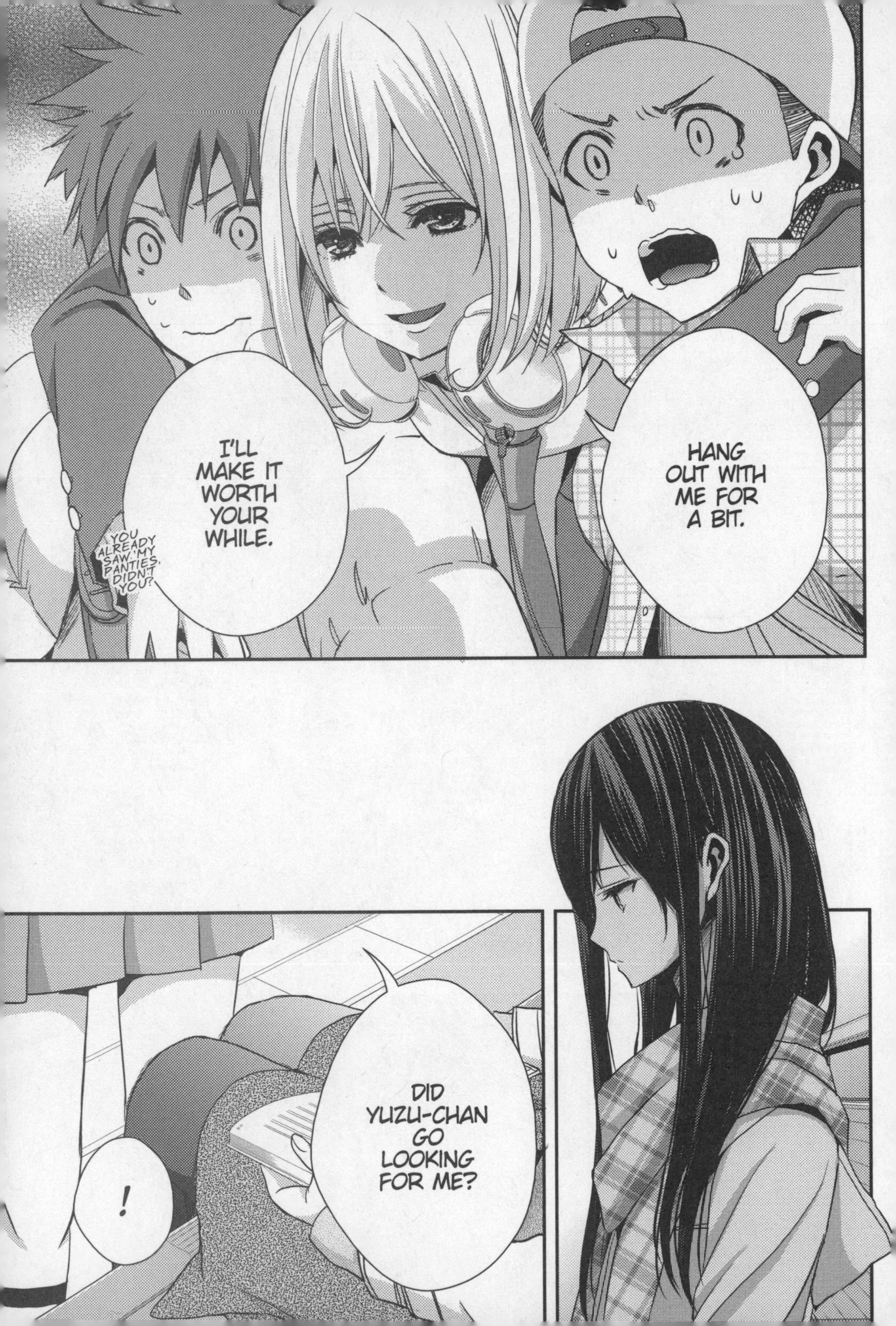
HANG OUT WITH ME FOR A BIT.
I'LL MAKE IT WORTH YOUR WHILE.
YOU ALREADY SAW MY PANTIES, DIDN'T YOU?
DID YUZU-CHAN GO LOOKING FOR ME?
!

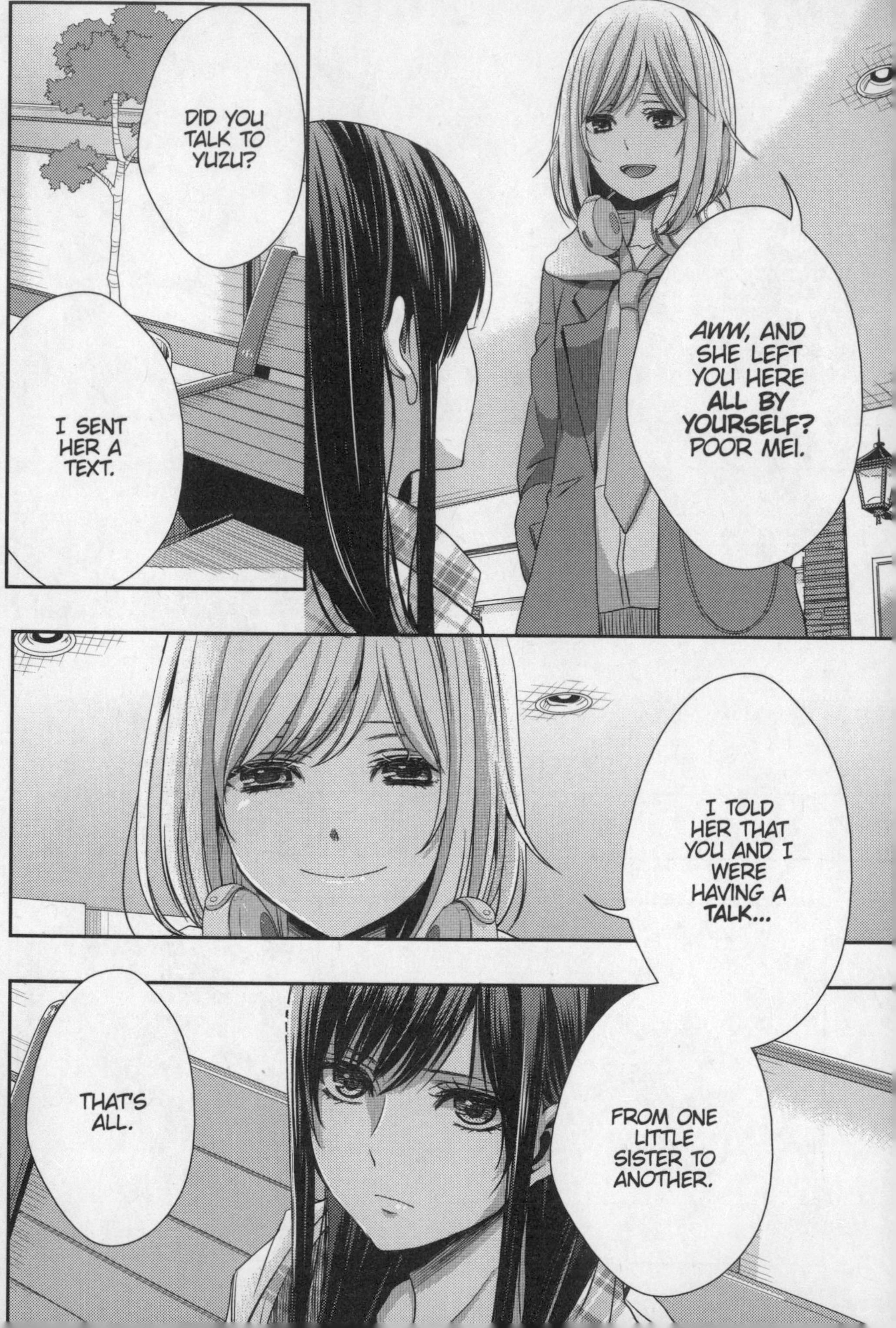
DID YOU TALK TO YUZU?
I SENT HER A TEXT.
AWW, AND SHE LEFT YOU HERE ALL BY YOURSELF? POOR MEI.
I TOLD HER THAT YOU AND I WERE HAVING A TALK...
FROM ONE LITTLE SISTER TO ANOTHER.
THAT'S ALL.

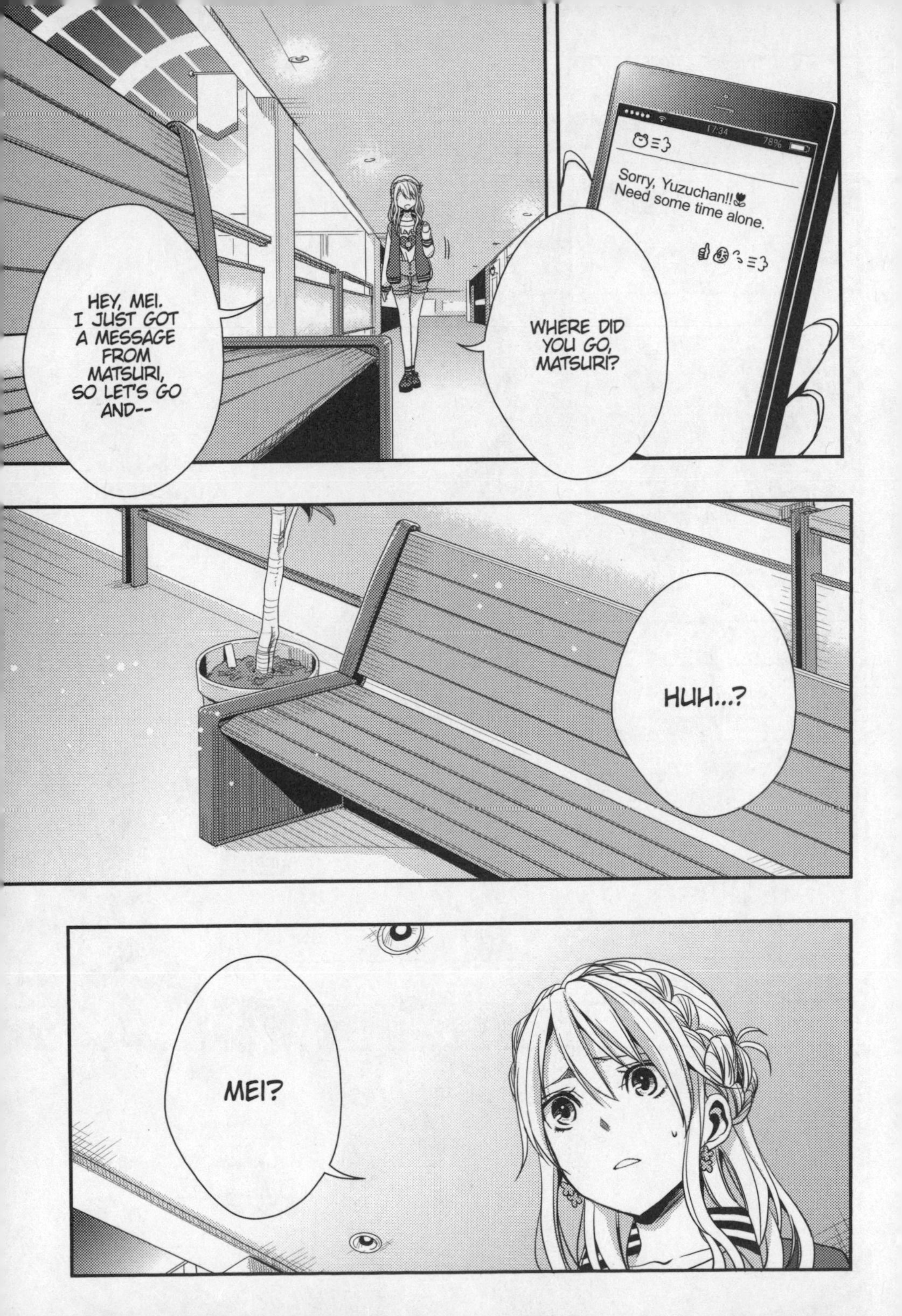
17:34
78%
Sorry, Yuzuchan!!
Need some time alone.
WHERE DID YOU GO, MATSURI?
HEY, MEI. I JUST GOT A MESSAGE FROM MATSURI, SO LET'S GO AND--
HUH...?
MEI?

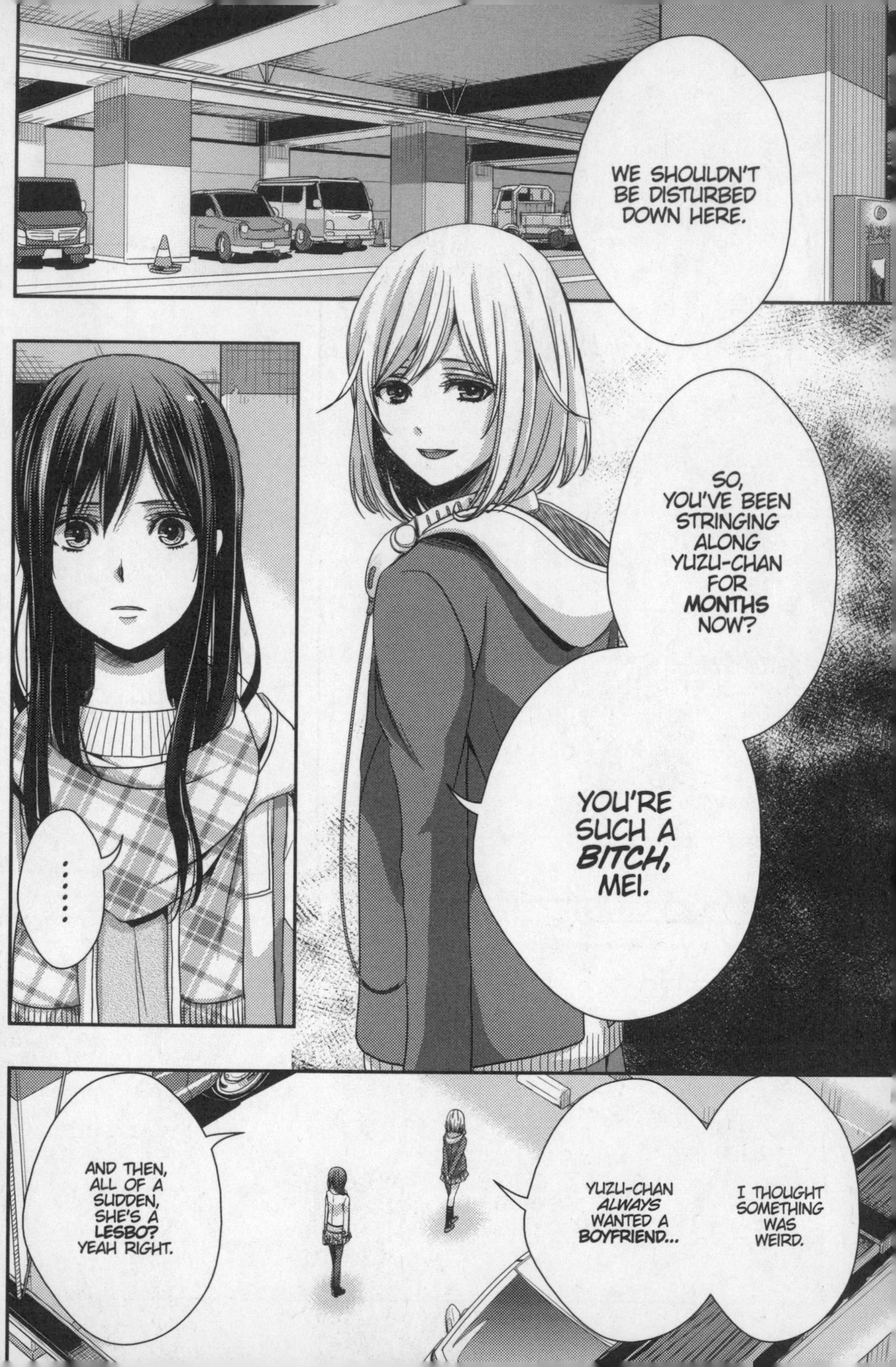
WE SHOULDN'T BE DISTURBED DOWN HERE.
SO, YOU'VE BEEN STRINGING ALONG YUZU-CHAN FOR MONTHS NOW?
YOU'RE SUCH A *BITCH*, MEI.
......
I THOUGHT SOMETHING WAS WEIRD.
YUZU-CHAN *ALWAYS* WANTED A BOYFRIEND...
AND THEN, ALL OF A SUDDEN, SHE'S A LESBO? YEAH RIGHT.

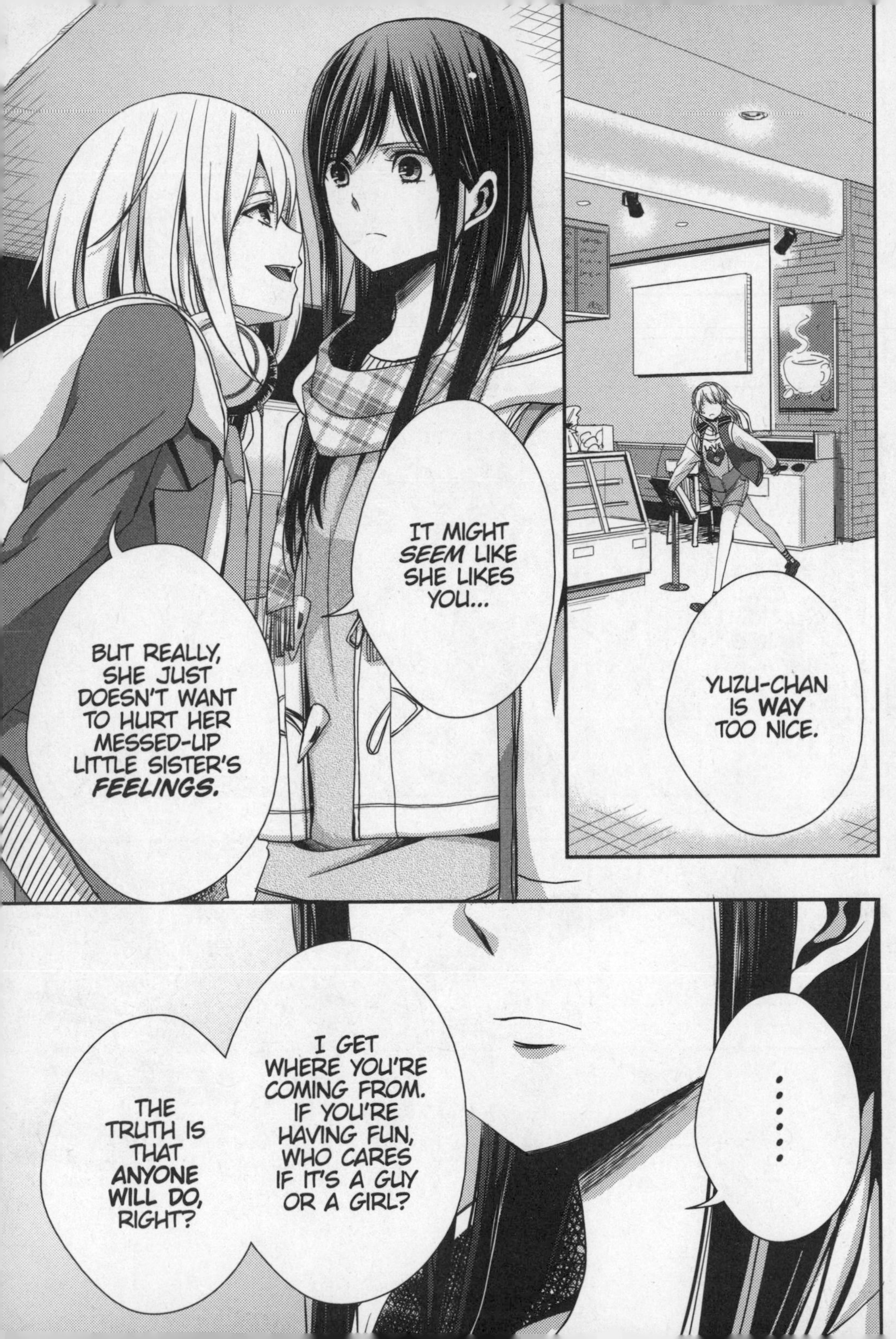
YUZU-CHAN IS WAY TOO NICE.
IT MIGHT *SEEM* LIKE SHE LIKES YOU...
BUT REALLY, SHE JUST DOESN'T WANT TO HURT HER MESSED-UP LITTLE SISTER'S *FEELINGS.*
......
I GET WHERE YOU'RE COMING FROM. IF YOU'RE HAVING FUN, WHO CARES IF IT'S A GUY OR A GIRL?
THE TRUTH IS THAT ANYONE WILL DO, RIGHT?

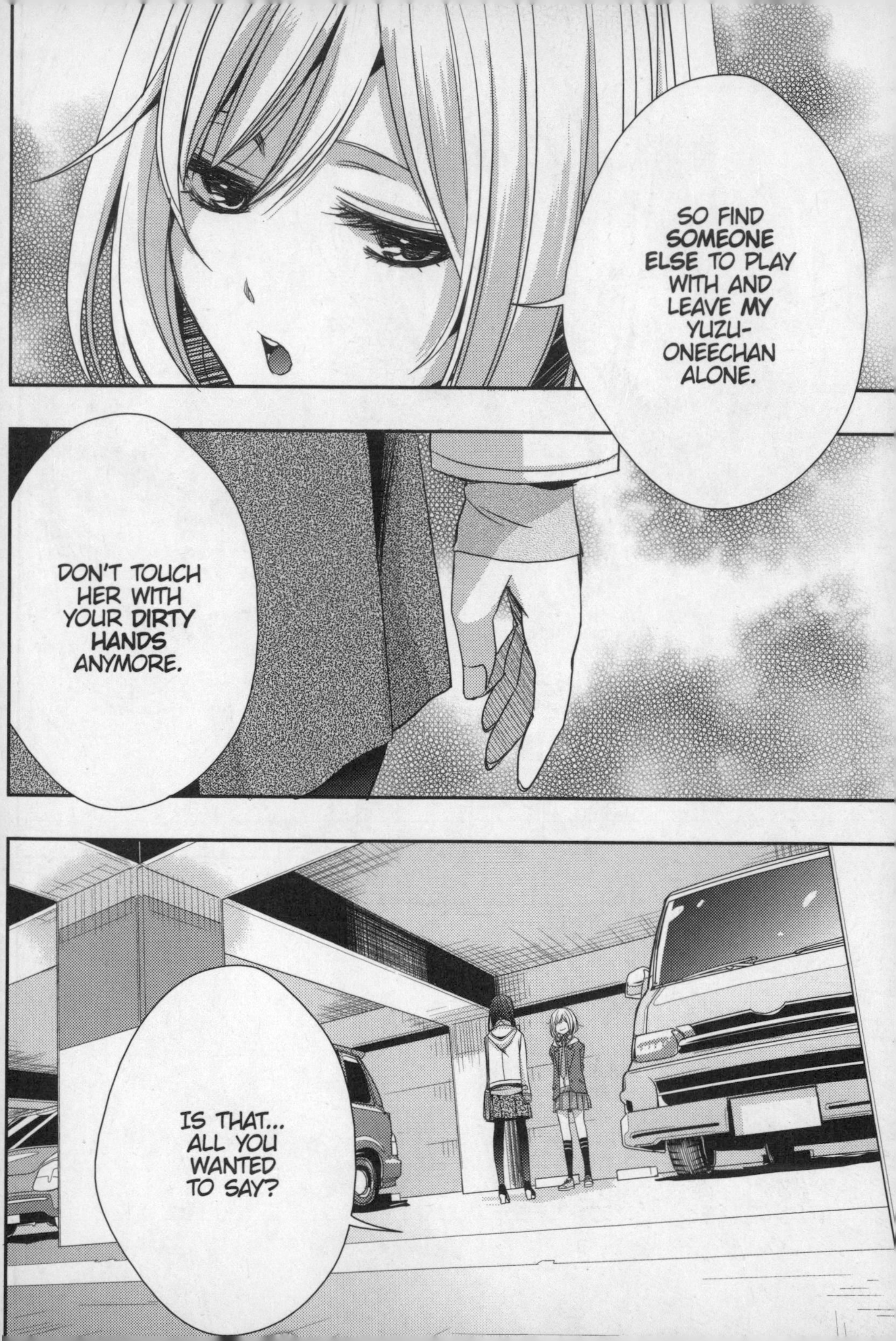
SO FIND SOMEONE ELSE TO PLAY WITH AND LEAVE MY YUZU-ONEECHAN ALONE.
DON'T TOUCH HER WITH YOUR DIRTY HANDS ANYMORE.
IS THAT... ALL YOU WANTED TO SAY?

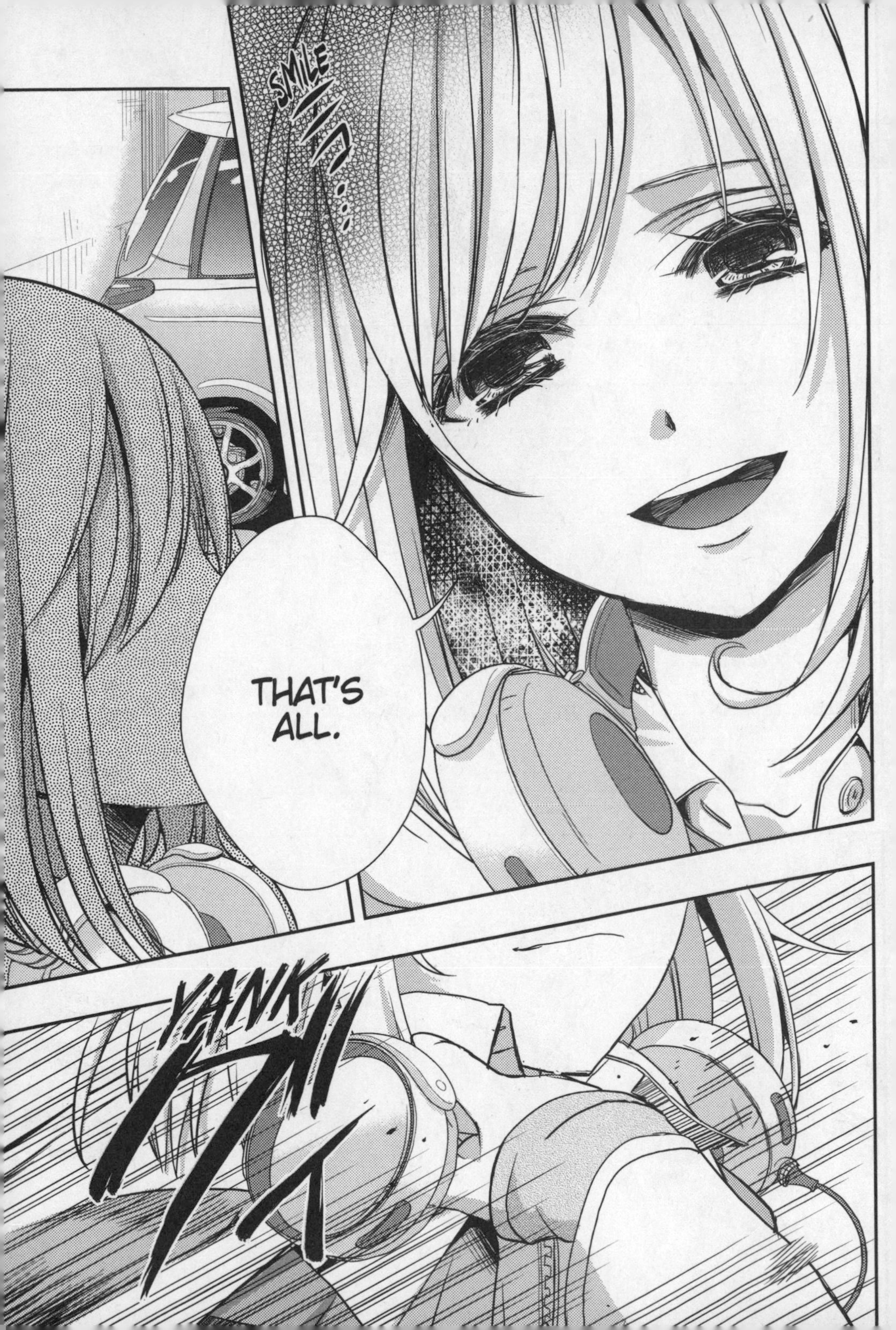
SMILE
THAT'S ALL.
YANK!

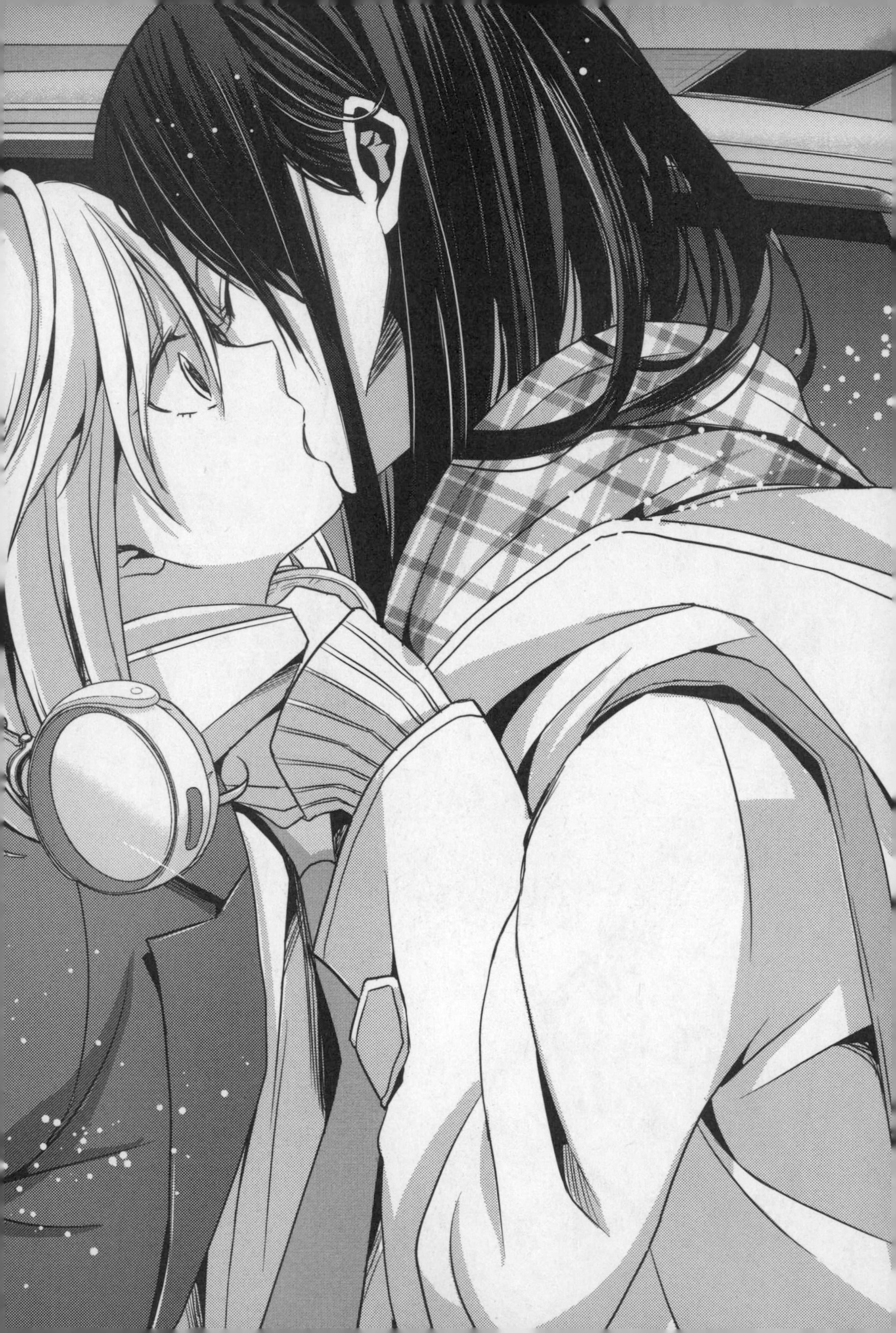

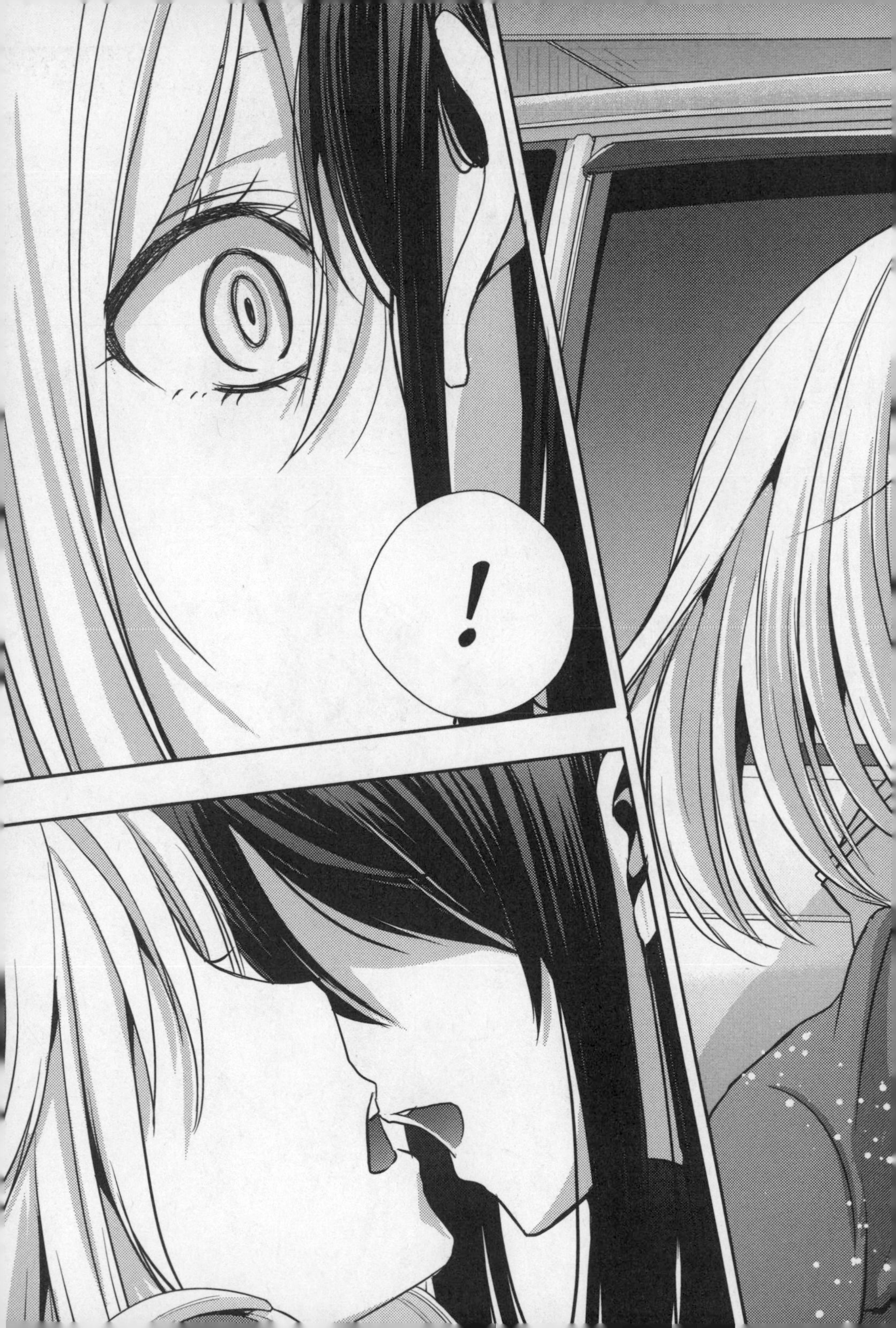
!

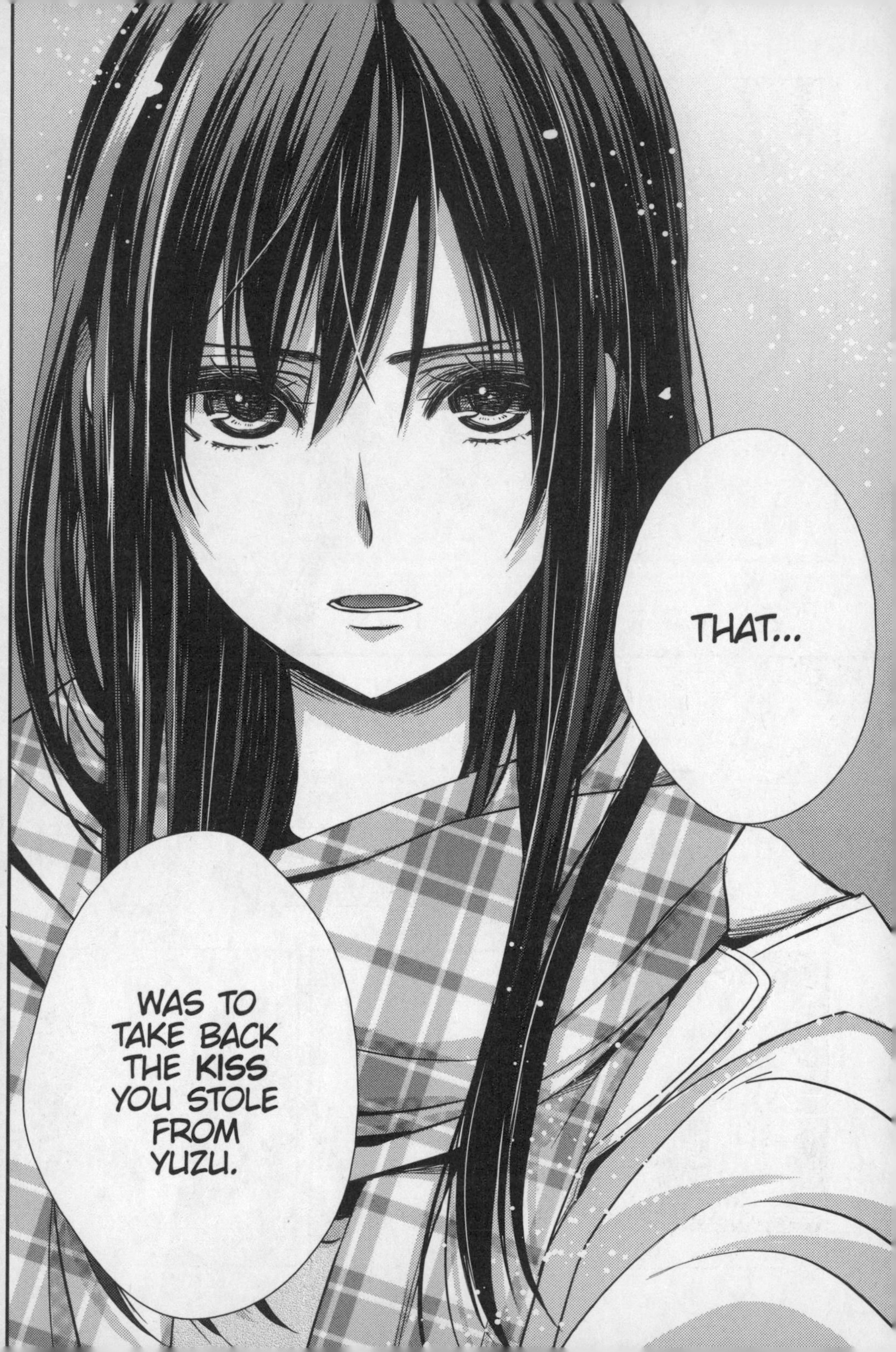
THAT...
WAS TO TAKE BACK THE KISS YOU STOLE FROM YUZU.

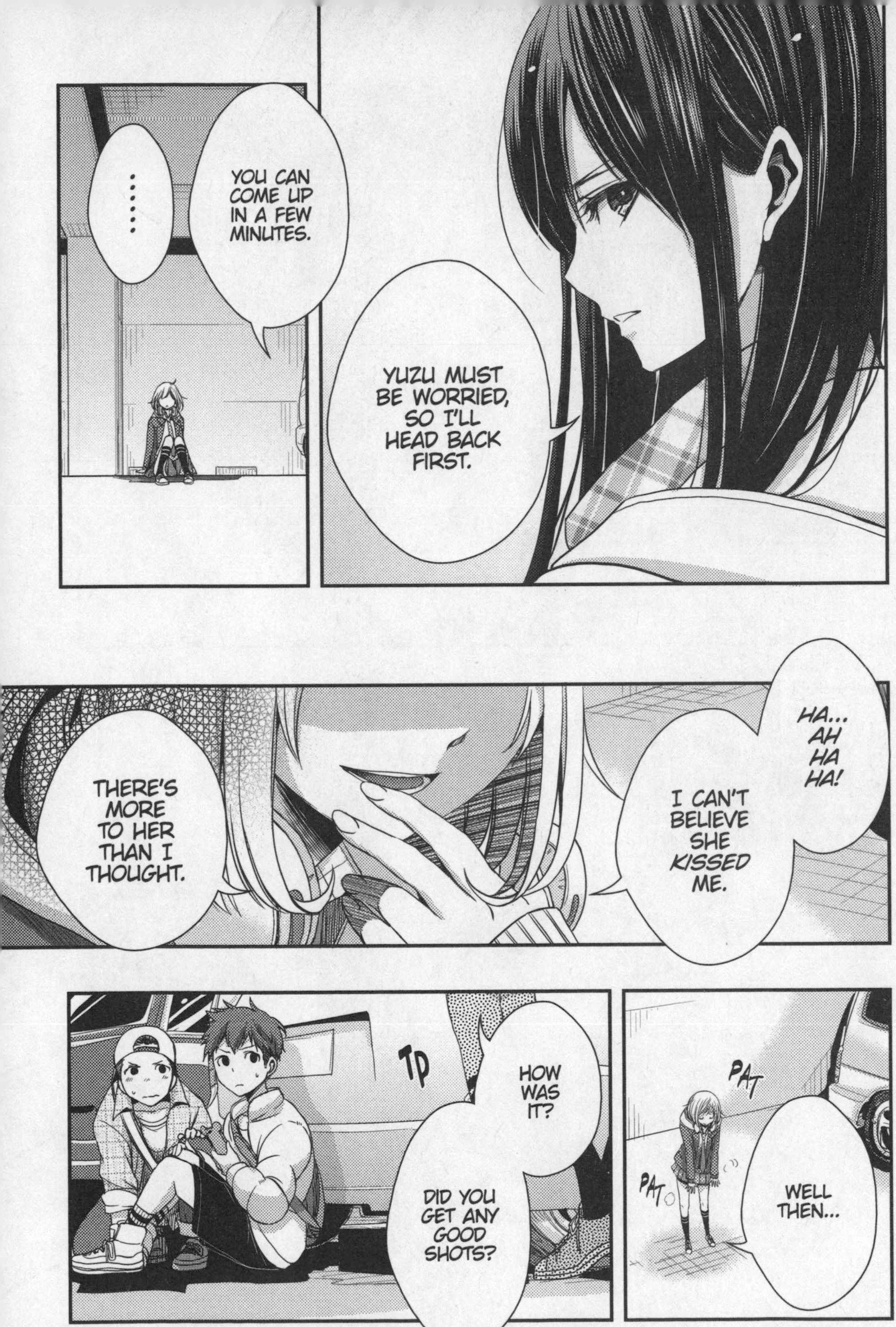
YUZU MUST BE WORRIED, SO I'LL HEAD BACK FIRST.
YOU CAN COME UP IN A FEW MINUTES.
......
HA... AH HA HA!
I CAN'T BELIEVE SHE KISSED ME.
THERE'S MORE TO HER THAN I THOUGHT.
PAT
WELL THEN...
PAT
TP
HOW WAS IT?
DID YOU GET ANY GOOD SHOTS?

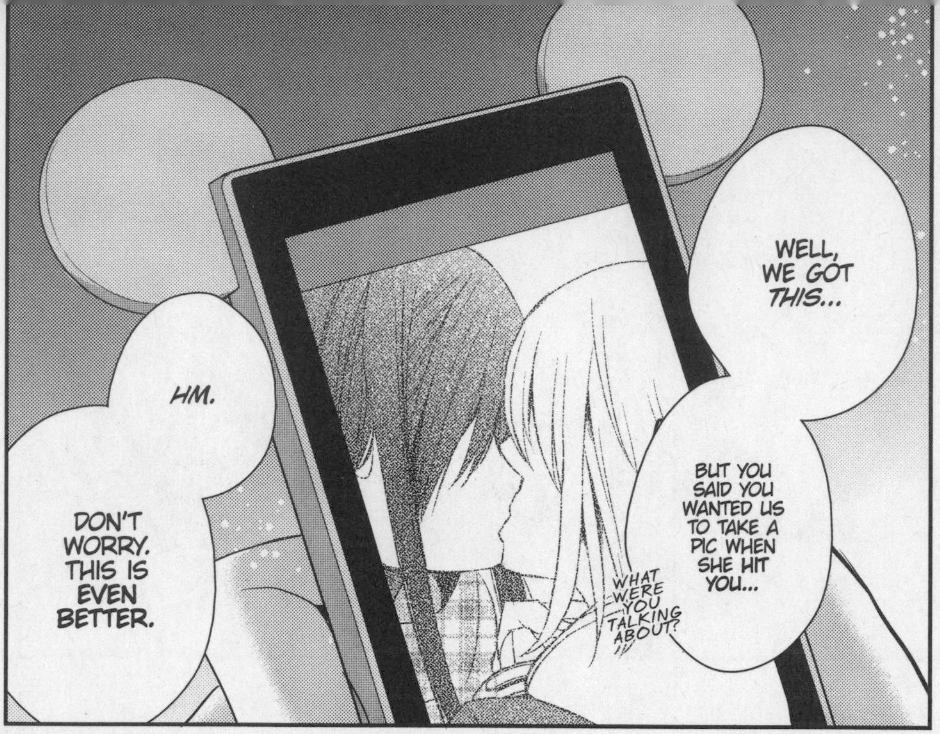
WELL, WE GOT *THIS*...
BUT YOU SAID YOU WANTED US TO TAKE A PIC WHEN SHE HIT YOU...
WHAT WERE YOU TALKING ABOUT?
HM.
DON'T WORRY. THIS IS EVEN BETTER.

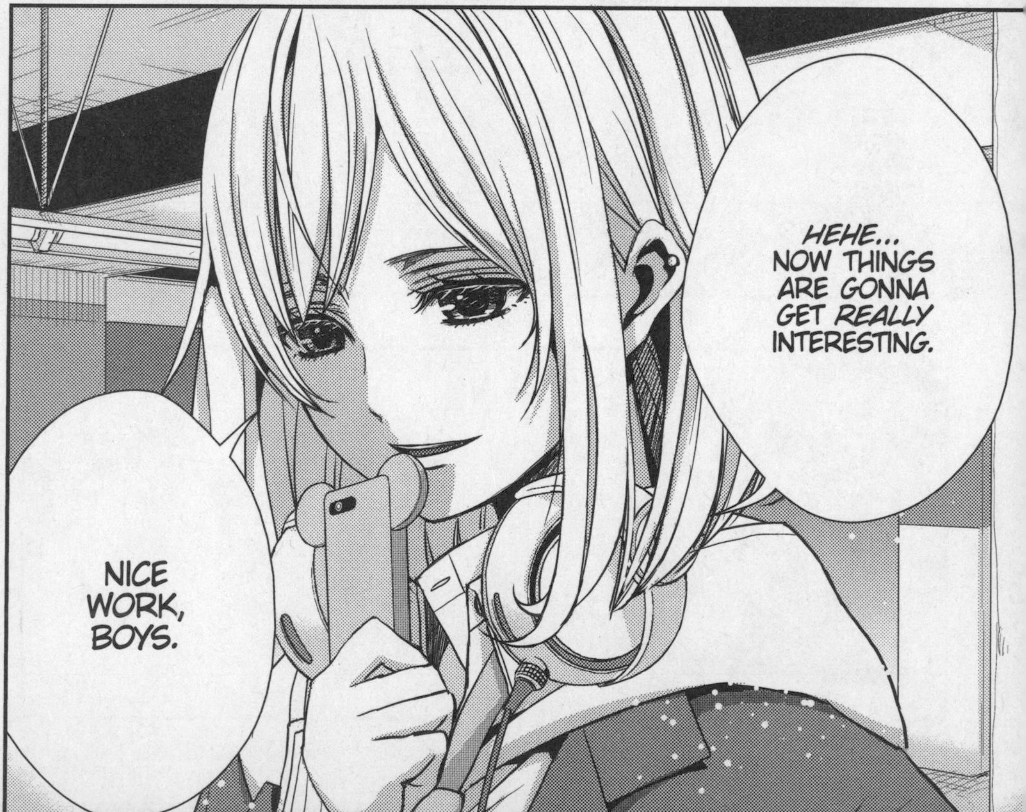
HEHE... NOW THINGS ARE GONNA GET *REALLY* INTERESTING.
NICE WORK, BOYS.

citrus

【シトラス】

SECRET LOVE AFFAIR WITH SISTER

citrus

SABUROUTA PRESENTS SECRET LOVE AFFAIR WITH SISTER

3

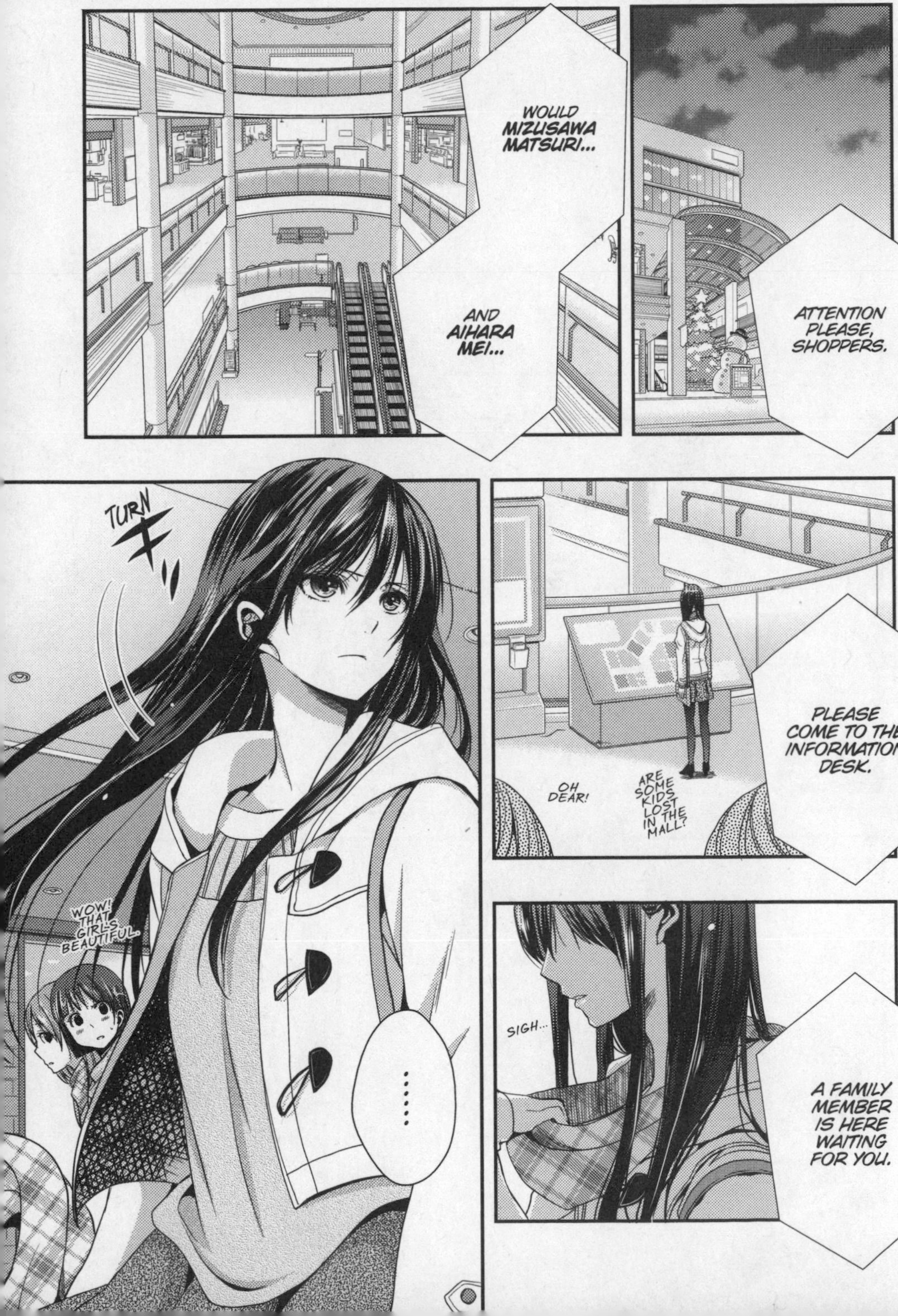
ATTENTION PLEASE, SHOPPERS.
WOULD MIZUSAWA MATSURI...
AND AIHARA MEI...
PLEASE COME TO THE INFORMATION DESK.
ARE SOME KIDS LOST IN THE MALL?
OH DEAR!
A FAMILY MEMBER IS HERE WAITING FOR YOU.
SIGH...
TURN
......
WOW! THAT GIRL'S BEAUTIFUL.

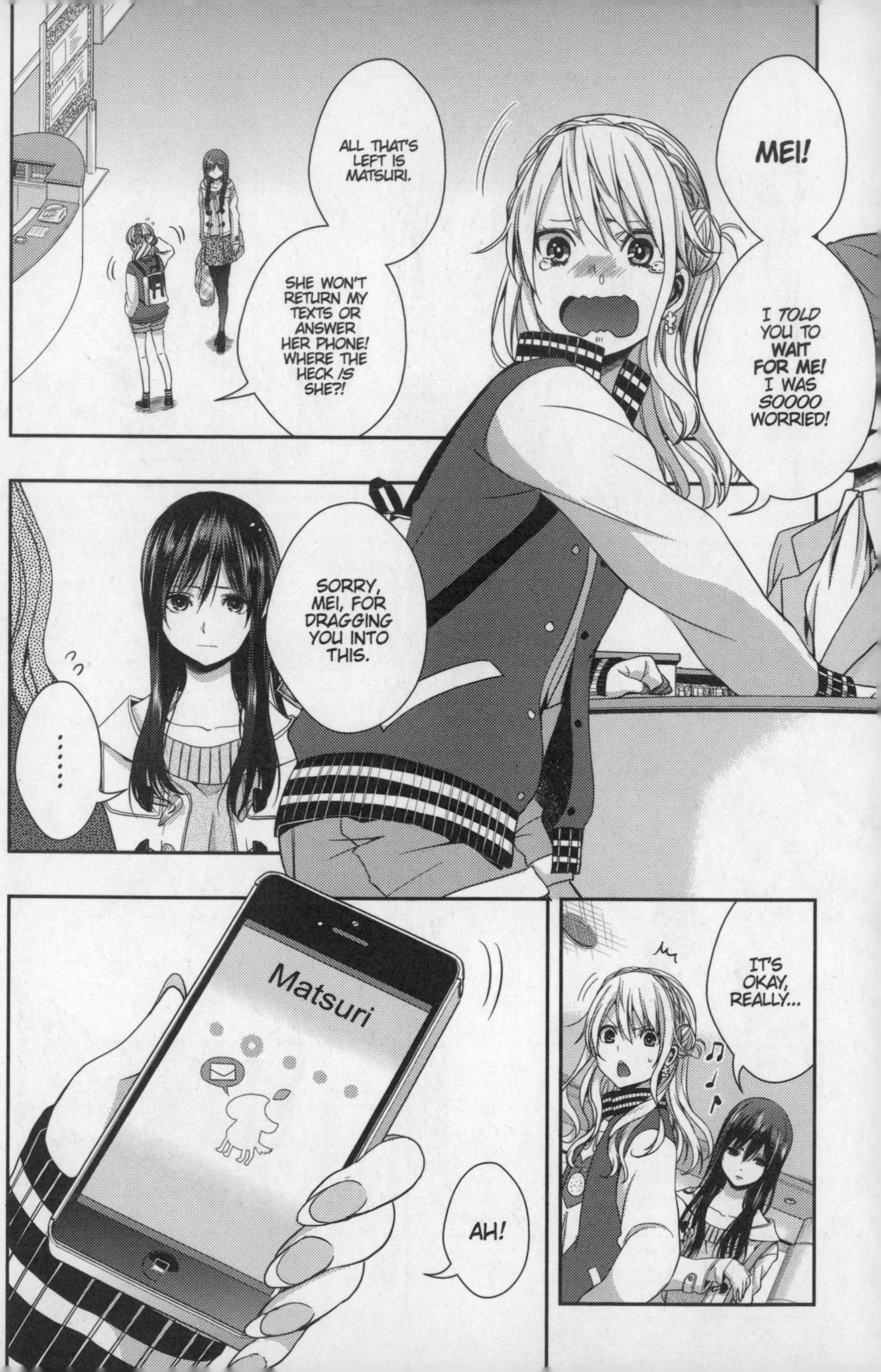
ALL THAT'S LEFT IS MATSURI.
SHE WON'T RETURN MY TEXTS OR ANSWER HER PHONE! WHERE THE HECK *IS* SHE?!
MEI!
I *TOLD* YOU TO WAIT FOR ME! I WAS *SOOOO* WORRIED!
SORRY, MEI, FOR DRAGGING YOU INTO THIS.
......
IT'S OKAY, REALLY...
Matsuri
AH!

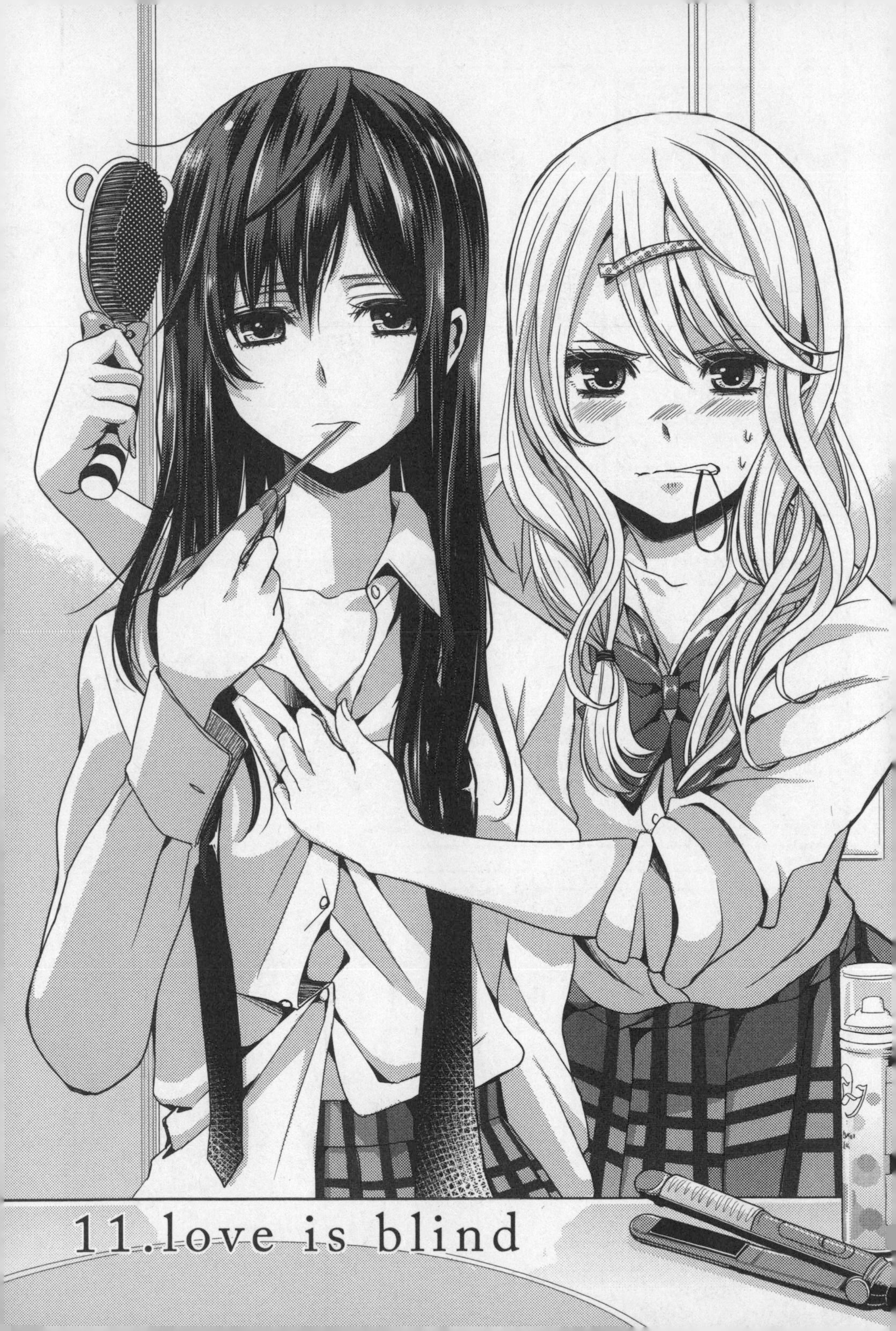

11. love is blind

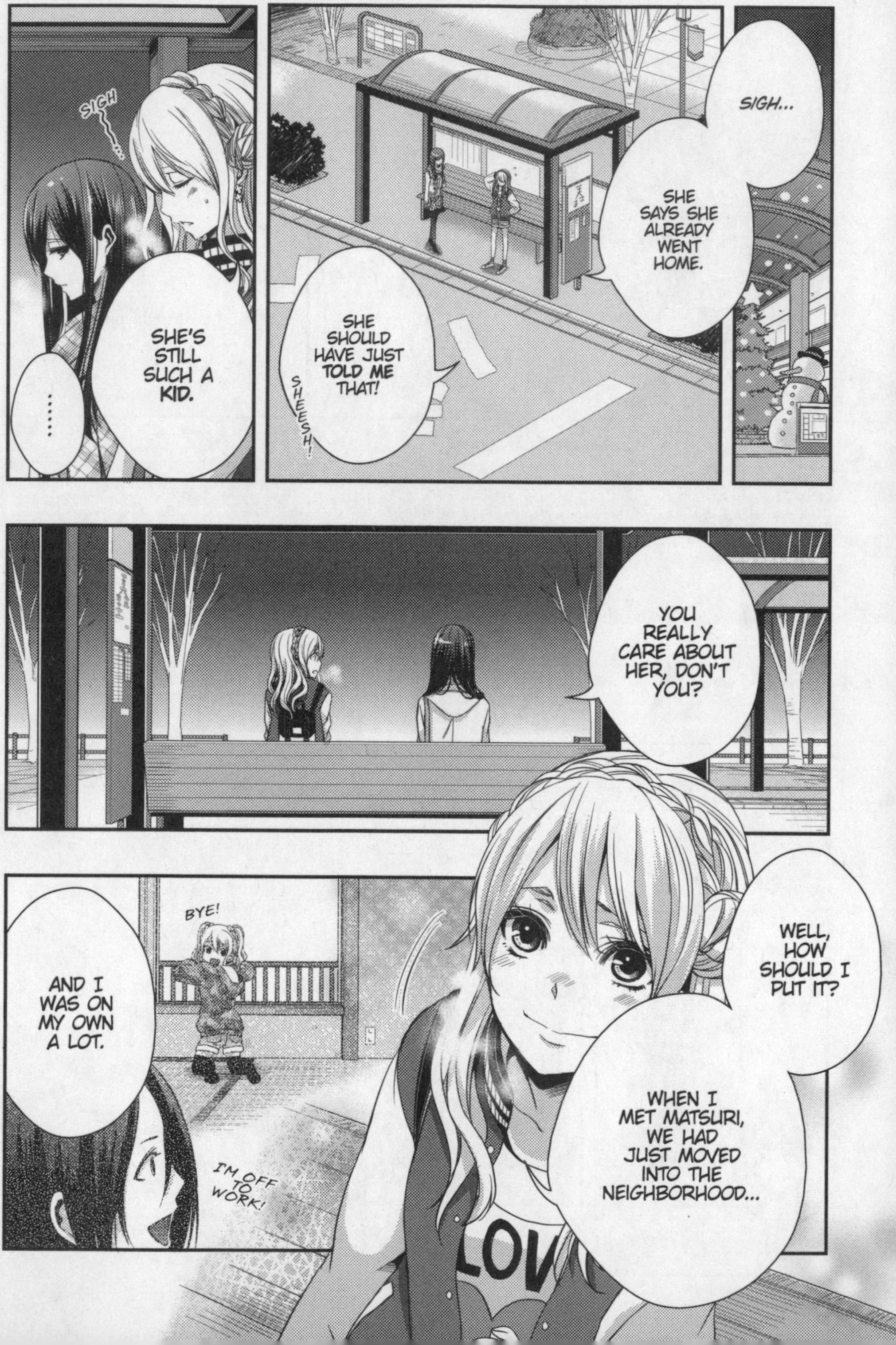
SIGH...
SHE SAYS SHE ALREADY WENT HOME.
SHE SHOULD HAVE JUST TOLD ME THAT!
SHEESH!
SIGH
SHE'S STILL SUCH A KID.
......
YOU REALLY CARE ABOUT HER, DON'T YOU?
WELL, HOW SHOULD I PUT IT?
WHEN I MET MATSURI, WE HAD JUST MOVED INTO THE NEIGHBORHOOD...
LOV
BYE!
AND I WAS ON MY OWN A LOT.
I'M OFF TO WORK!

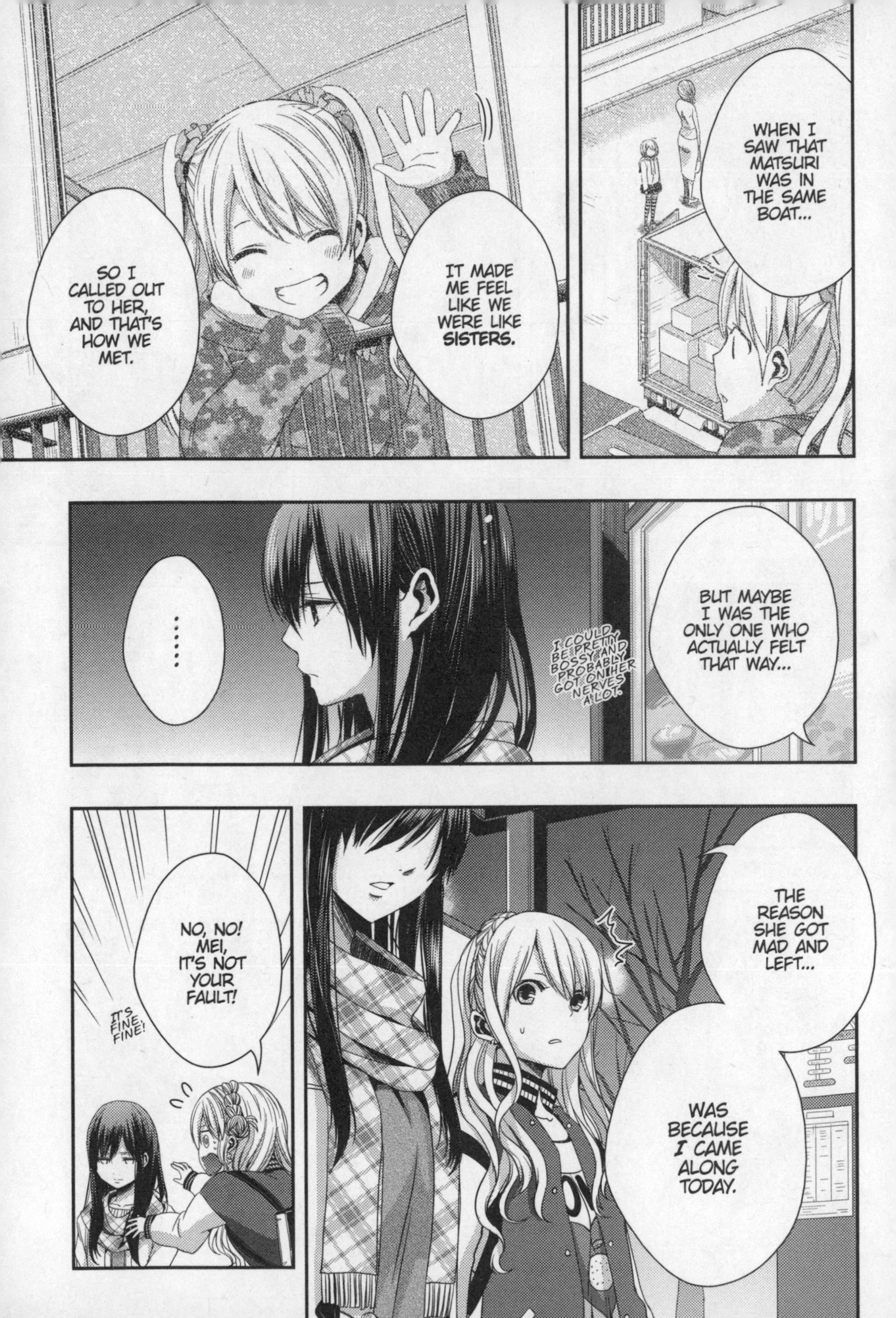
WHEN I SAW THAT MATSURI WAS IN THE SAME BOAT...
IT MADE ME FEEL LIKE WE WERE LIKE SISTERS.
SO I CALLED OUT TO HER, AND THAT'S HOW WE MET.
BUT MAYBE I WAS THE ONLY ONE WHO ACTUALLY FELT THAT WAY...
I COULD BE PRETTY BOSSY AND PROBABLY GOT ON HER NERVES A LOT.
......
THE REASON SHE GOT MAD AND LEFT...
WAS BECAUSE I CAME ALONG TODAY.
NO, NO! MEI, IT'S NOT YOUR FAULT!
IT'S FINE, FINE!

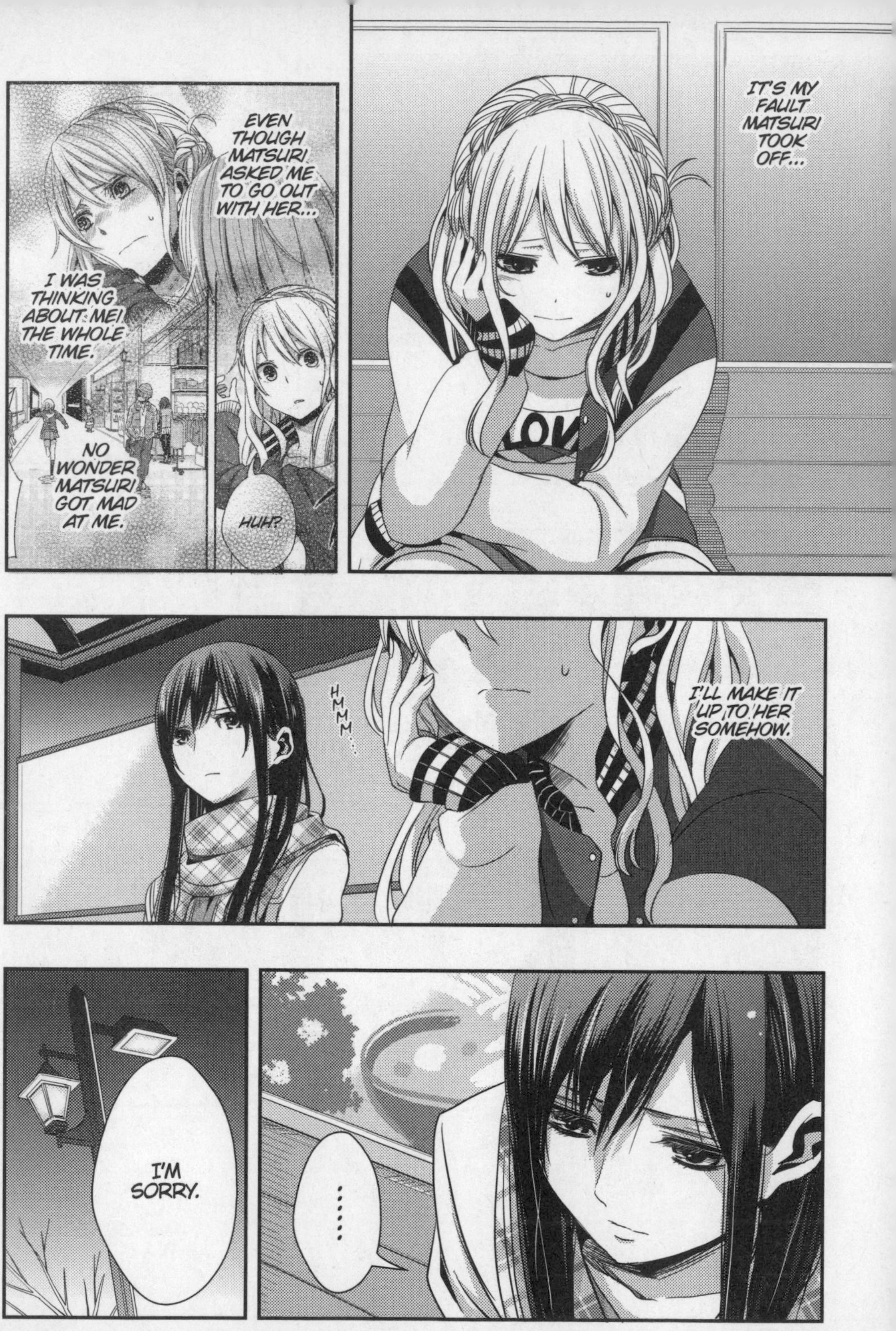
IT'S MY FAULT MATSURI TOOK OFF...
EVEN THOUGH MATSURI ASKED ME TO GO OUT WITH HER...
I WAS THINKING ABOUT MEI THE WHOLE TIME.
HUH?
NO WONDER MATSURI GOT MAD AT ME.
I'LL MAKE IT UP TO HER SOMEHOW.
HMMM...
......
I'M SORRY.

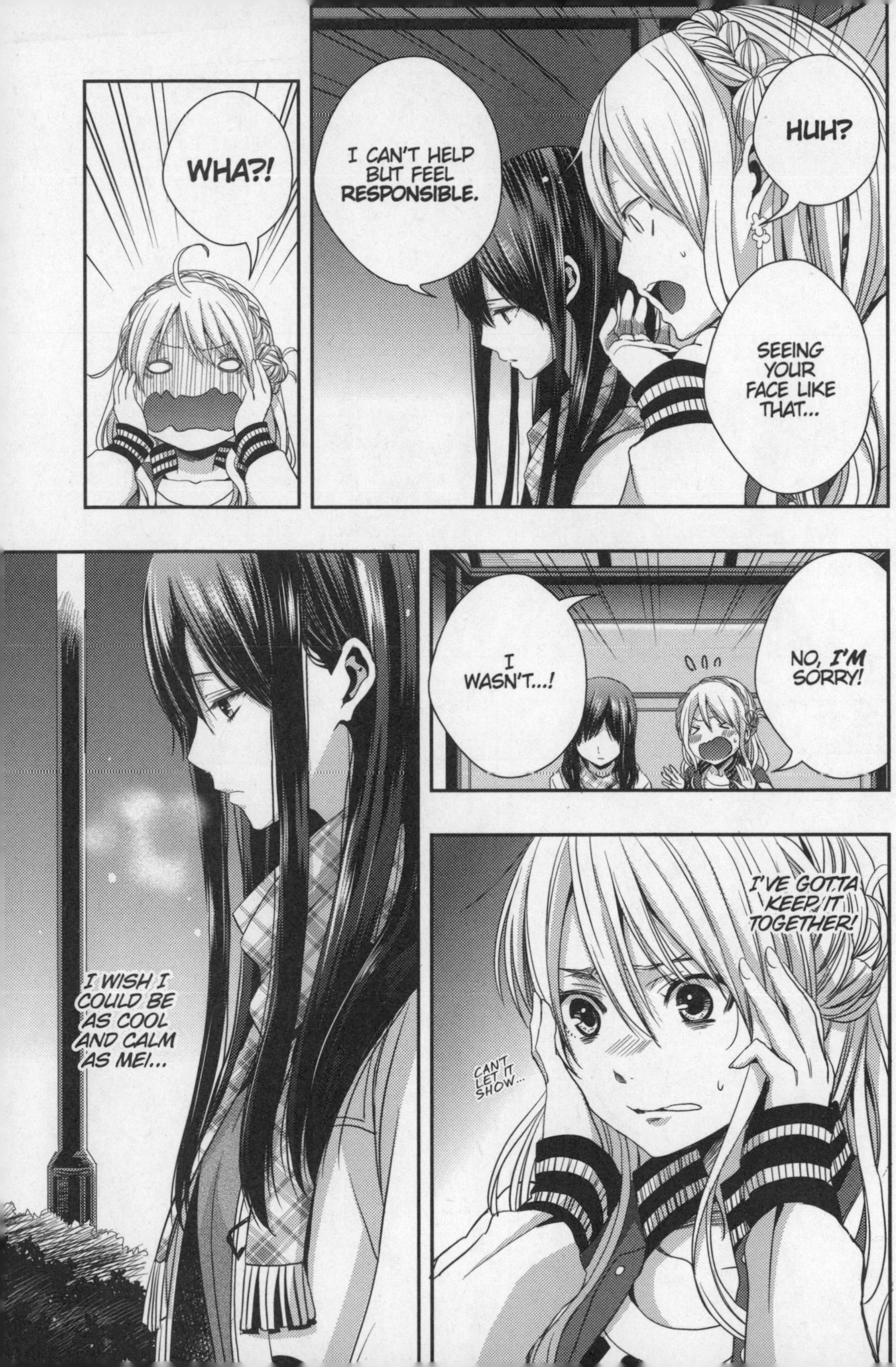
HUH?
I CAN'T HELP BUT FEEL RESPONSIBLE.
SEEING YOUR FACE LIKE THAT...
WHA?!
NO, *I'M* SORRY!
I WASN'T...!
I'VE GOTTA KEEP IT TOGETHER!
CAN'T LET IT SHOW...
I WISH I COULD BE AS COOL AND CALM AS MEI...

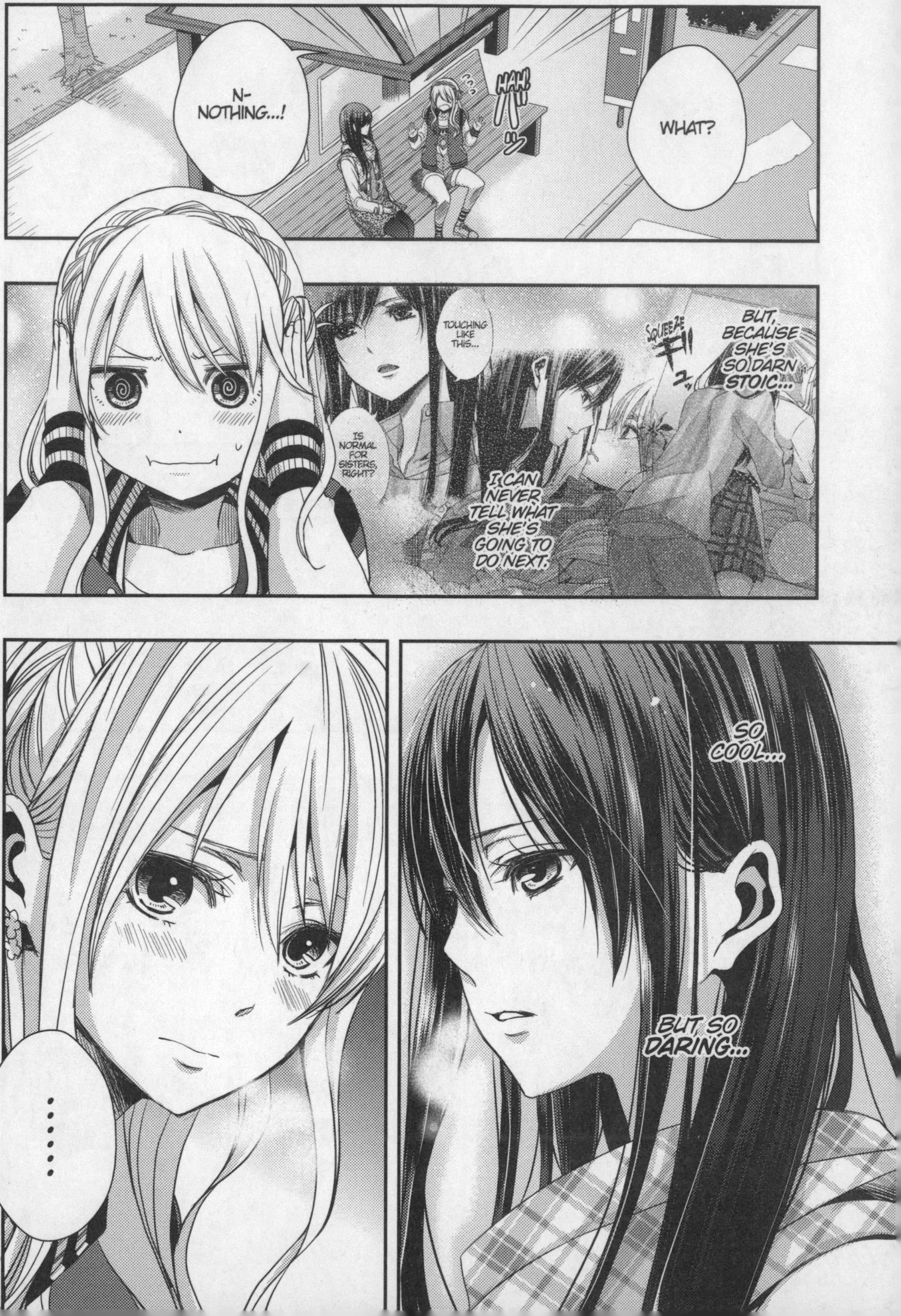

WHAT?
HAH!
N-NOTHING...!
BUT, BECAUSE SHE'S SO DARN STOIC...
SQUEEZE
TOUCHING LIKE THIS...
IS NORMAL FOR SISTERS, RIGHT?
I CAN NEVER TELL WHAT SHE'S GOING TO DO NEXT.
SO COOL...
BUT SO DARING...
......

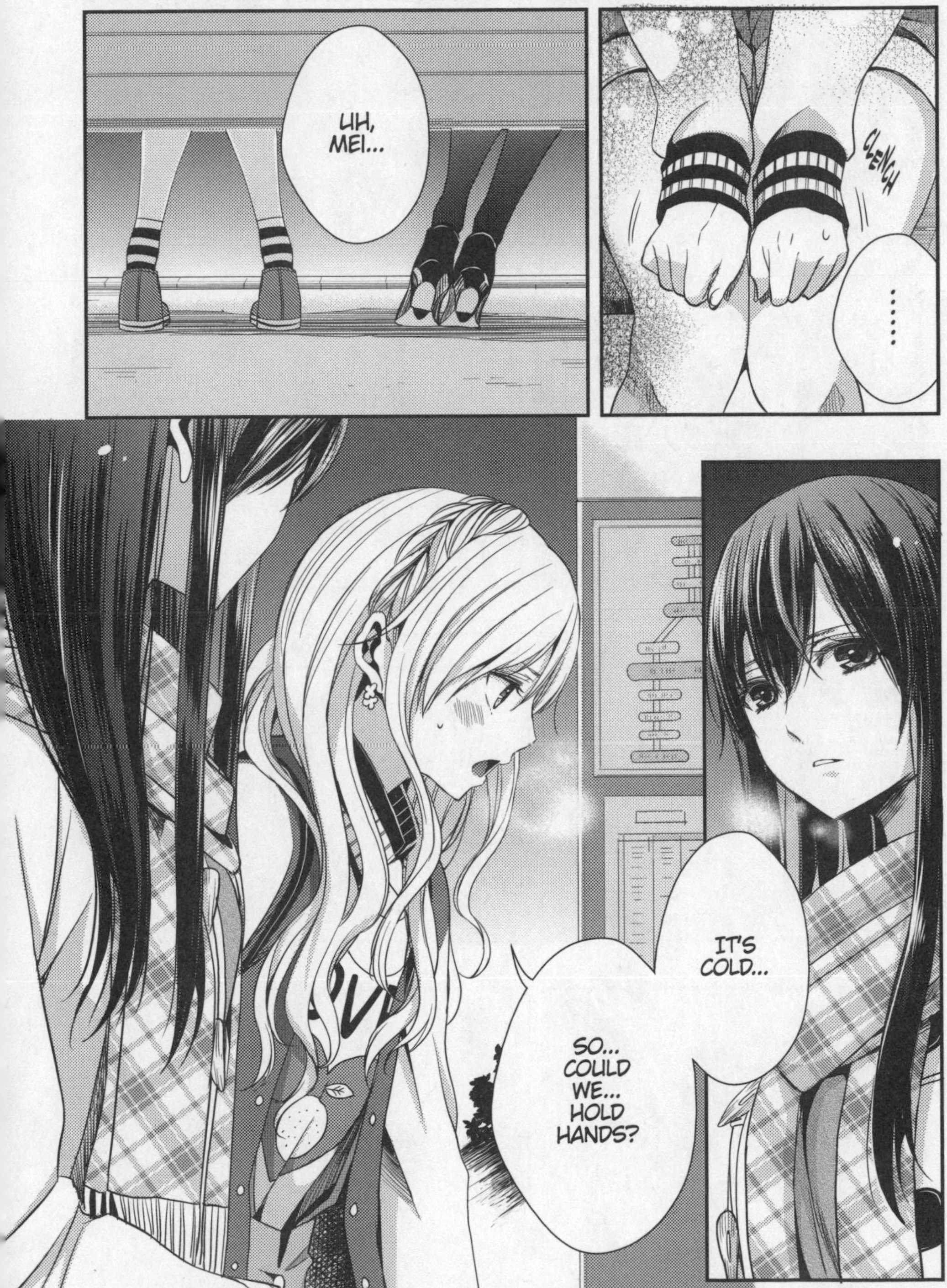
CLENCH
......
UH, MEI...
IT'S COLD...
SO... COULD WE... HOLD HANDS?

......

ALL RIGHT.

SLIDE ズッ

FOR SISTERS, IT'S NO BIG DEAL, RIGHT?

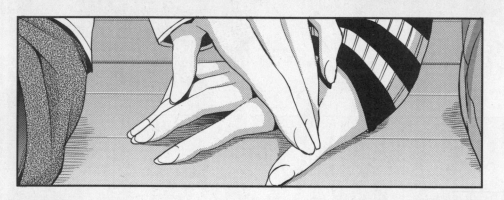

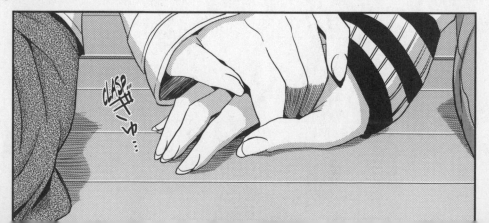

CLASP ギュ...

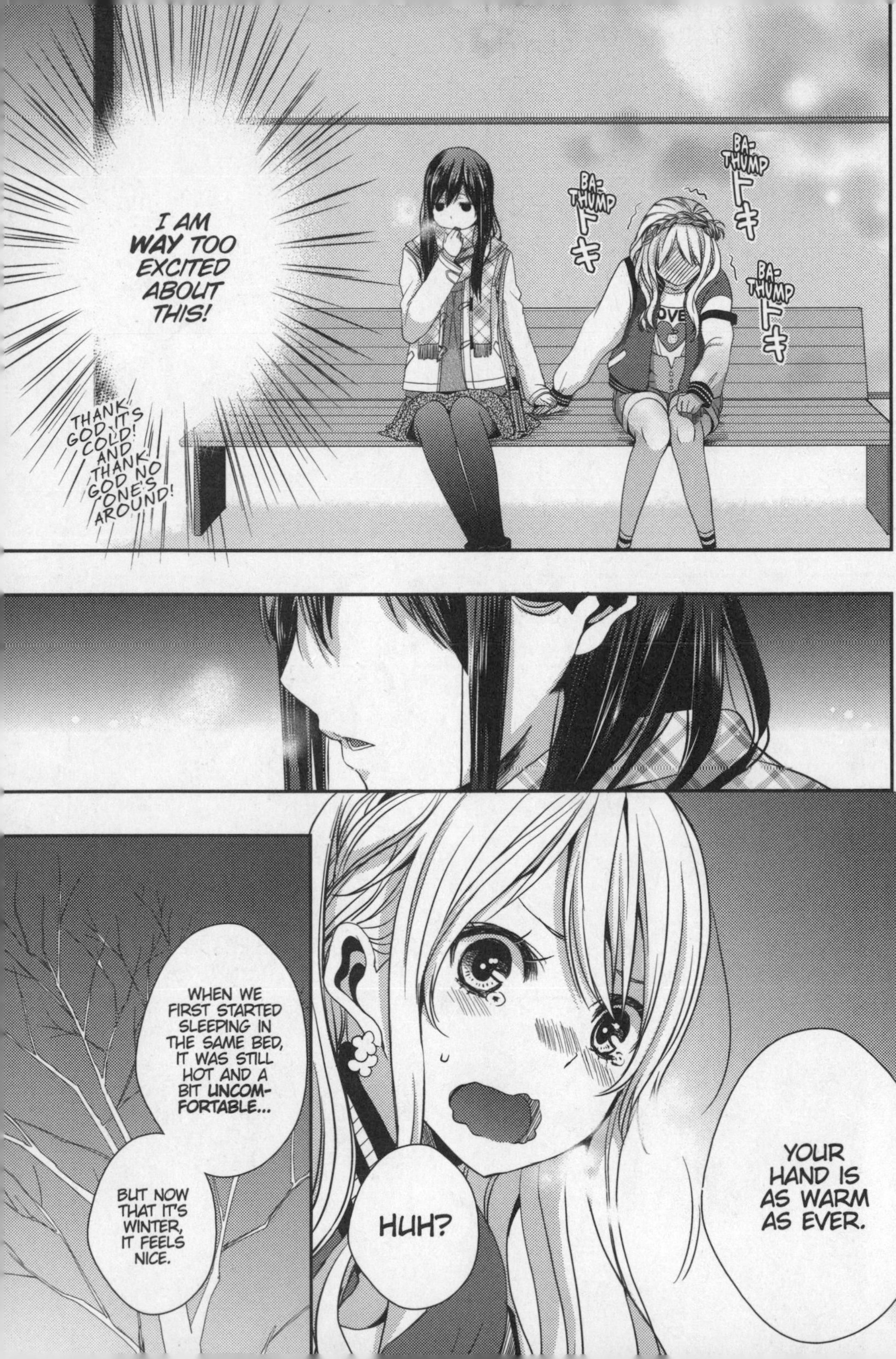
BA-THUMP トキ
BA-THUMP トキ
BA-THUMP トキ
I AM WAY TOO EXCITED ABOUT THIS!
THANK GOD IT'S COLD! AND THANK GOD NO ONE'S AROUND!
YOUR HAND IS AS WARM AS EVER.
HUH?
WHEN WE FIRST STARTED SLEEPING IN THE SAME BED, IT WAS STILL HOT AND A BIT UNCOM-FORTABLE...
BUT NOW THAT IT'S WINTER, IT FEELS NICE.

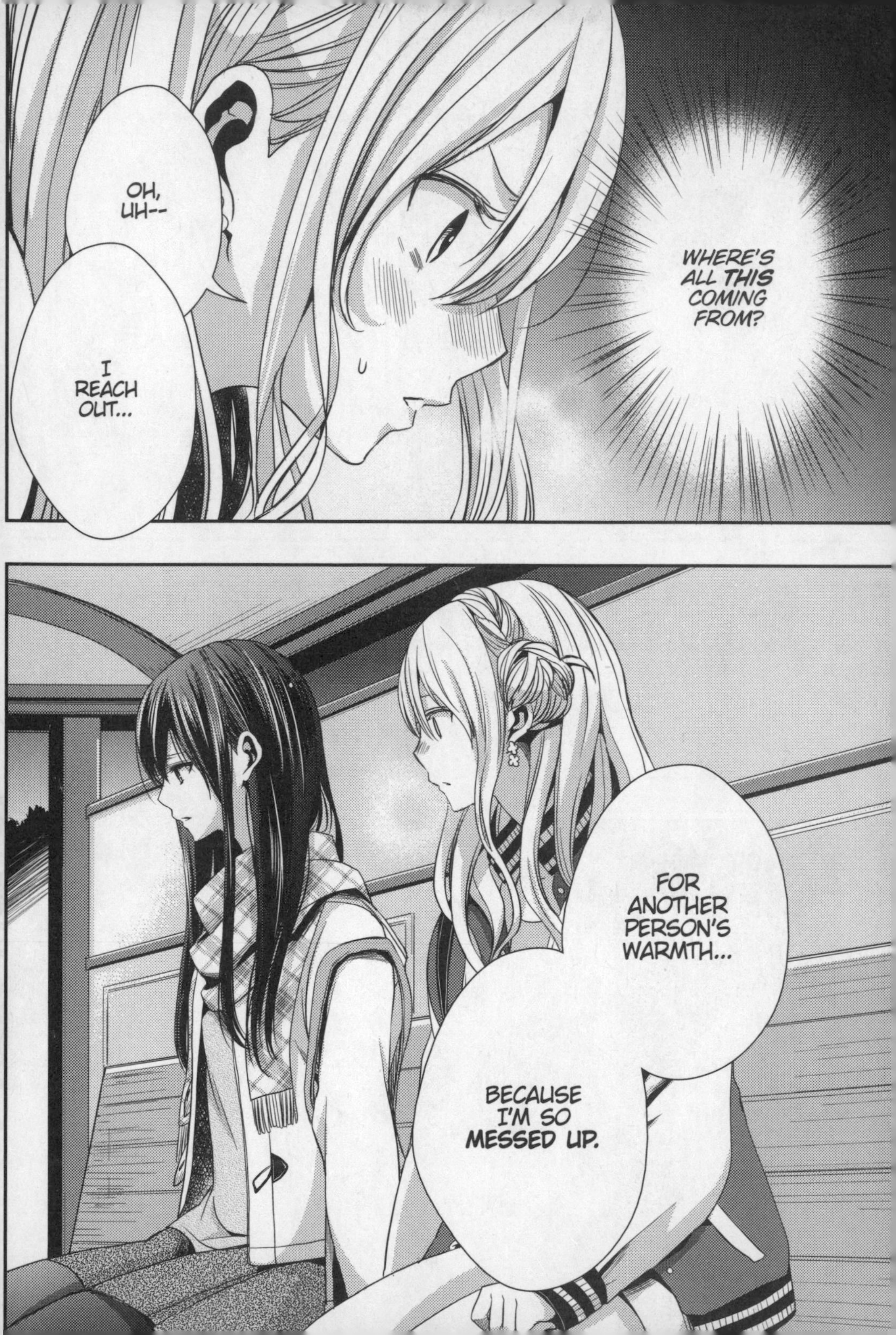
WHERE'S ALL THIS COMING FROM?
OH, UH--
I REACH OUT...
FOR ANOTHER PERSON'S WARMTH...
BECAUSE I'M SO MESSED UP.

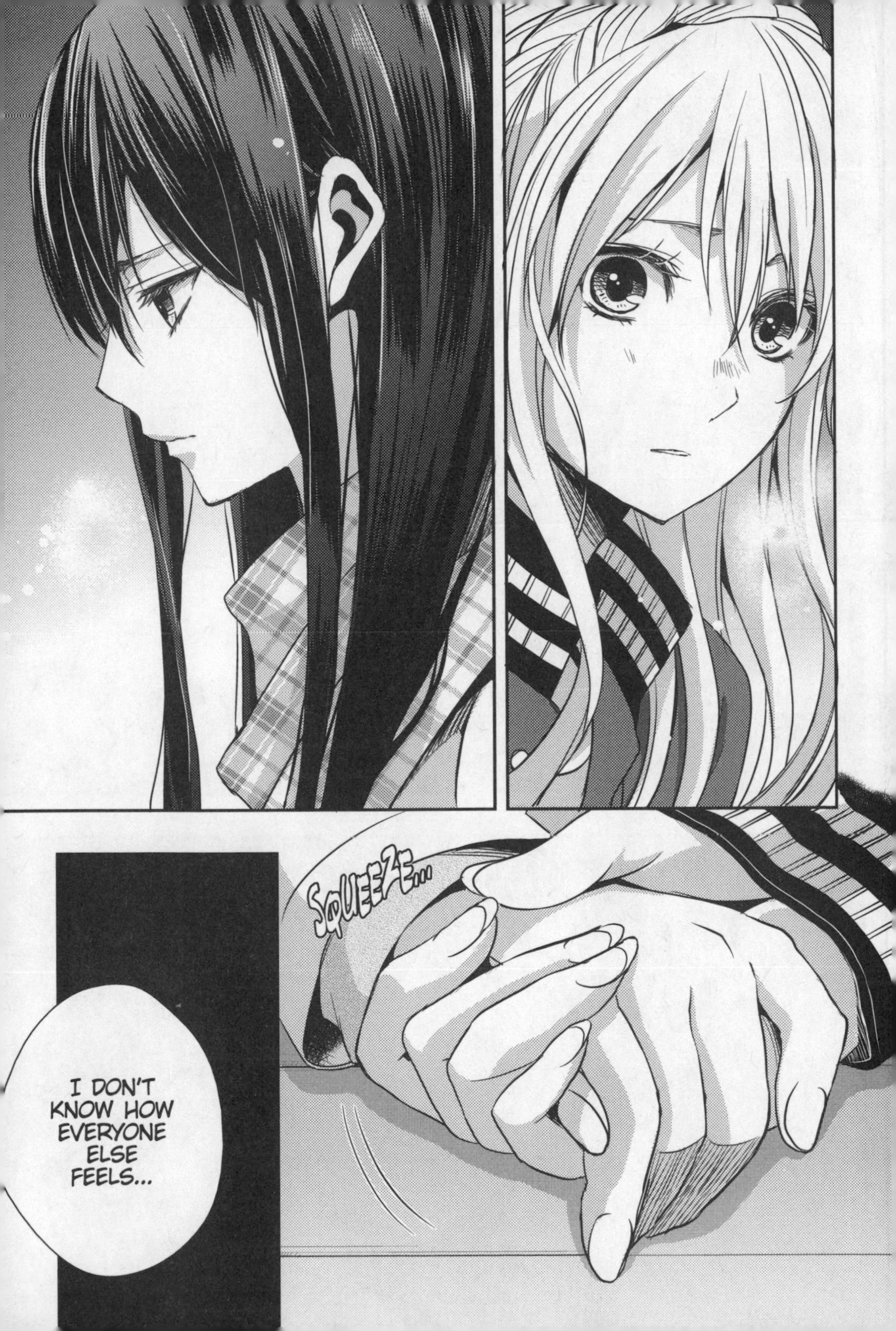
SQUEEZE...
I DON'T KNOW HOW EVERYONE ELSE FEELS...

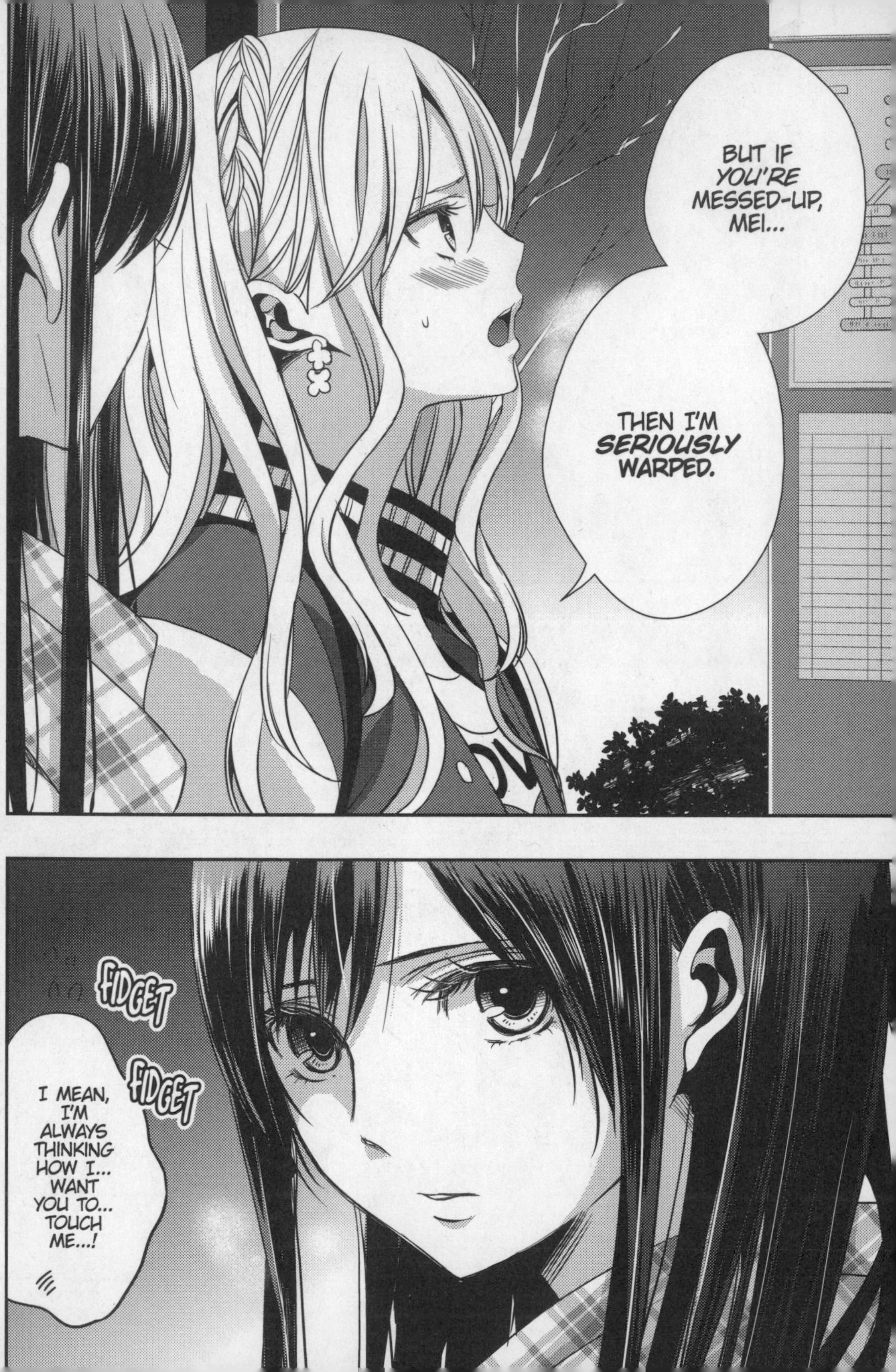
BUT IF *YOU'RE* MESSED-UP, MEI...
THEN I'M ***SERIOUSLY*** WARPED.
FIDGET
FIDGET
I MEAN, I'M ALWAYS THINKING HOW I... WANT YOU TO... TOUCH ME...!

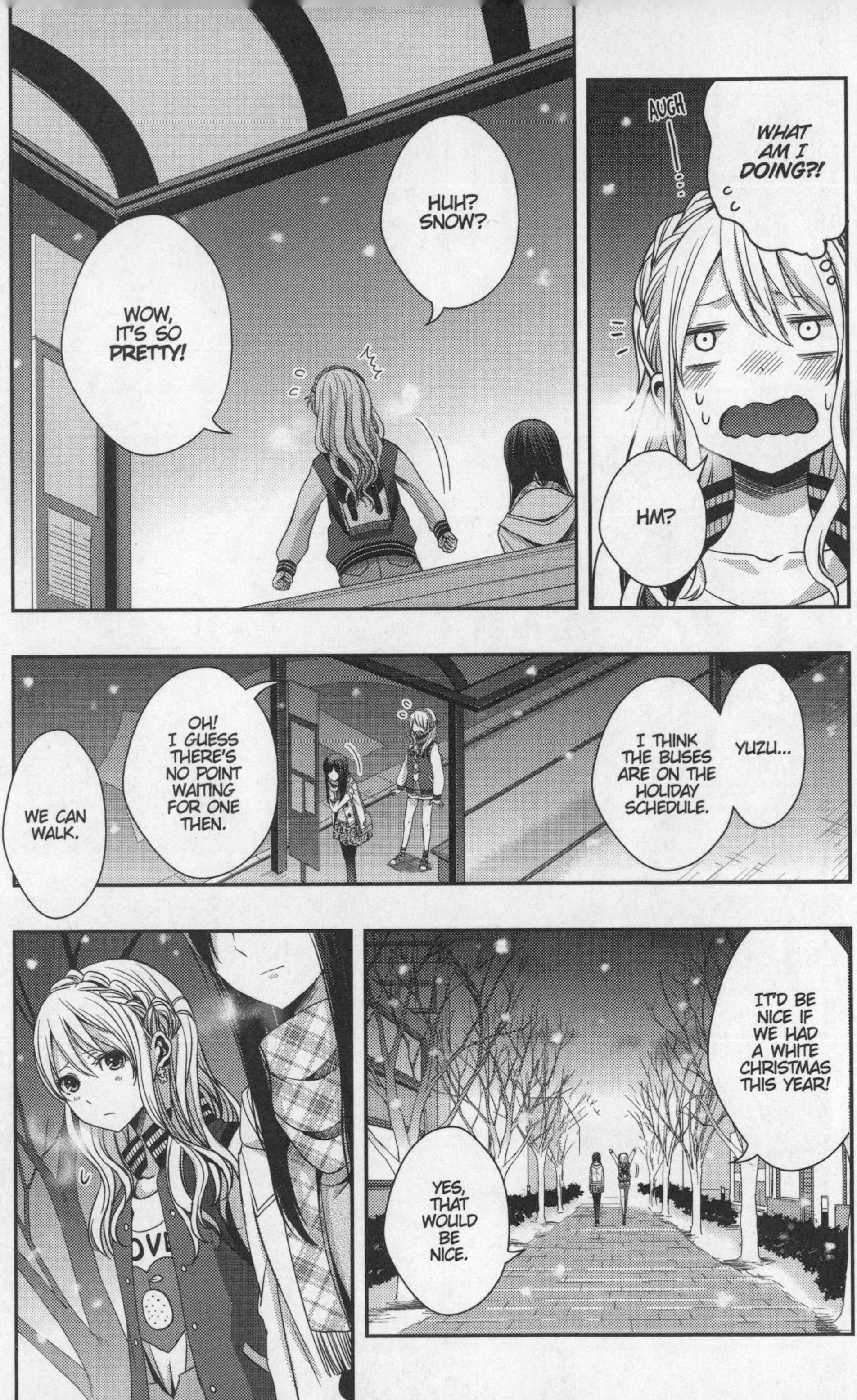
WHAT AM I DOING?!
AUGH
HM?
HUH? SNOW?
WOW, IT'S SO PRETTY!
YUZU...
I THINK THE BUSES ARE ON THE HOLIDAY SCHEDULE.
OH! I GUESS THERE'S NO POINT WAITING FOR ONE THEN.
WE CAN WALK.
IT'D BE NICE IF WE HAD A WHITE CHRISTMAS THIS YEAR!
YES, THAT WOULD BE NICE.

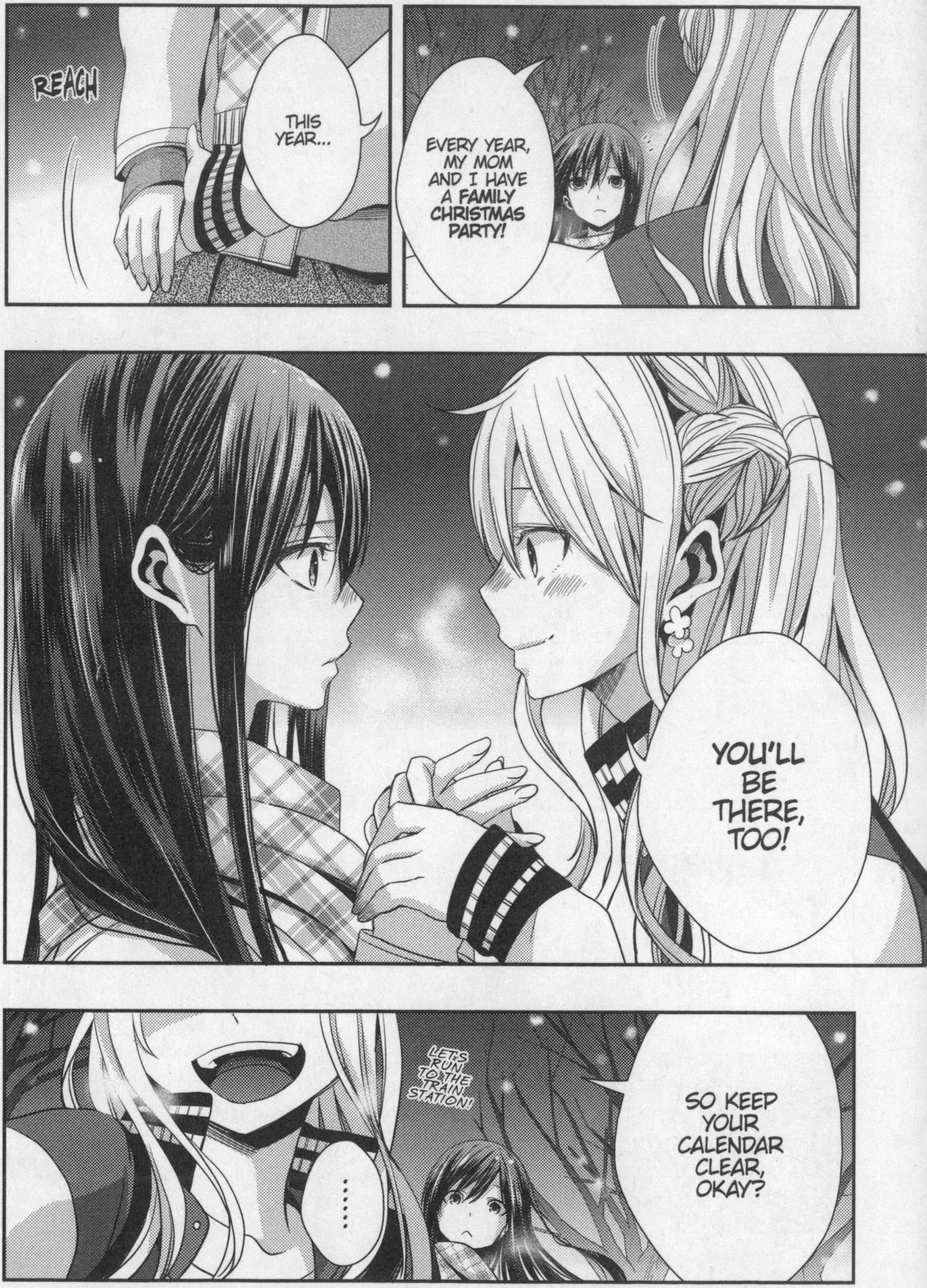
EVERY YEAR, MY MOM AND I HAVE A FAMILY CHRISTMAS PARTY!
THIS YEAR...
REACH
YOU'LL BE THERE, TOO!
SO KEEP YOUR CALENDAR CLEAR, OKAY?
LET'S RUN TO THE TRAIN STATION!
......

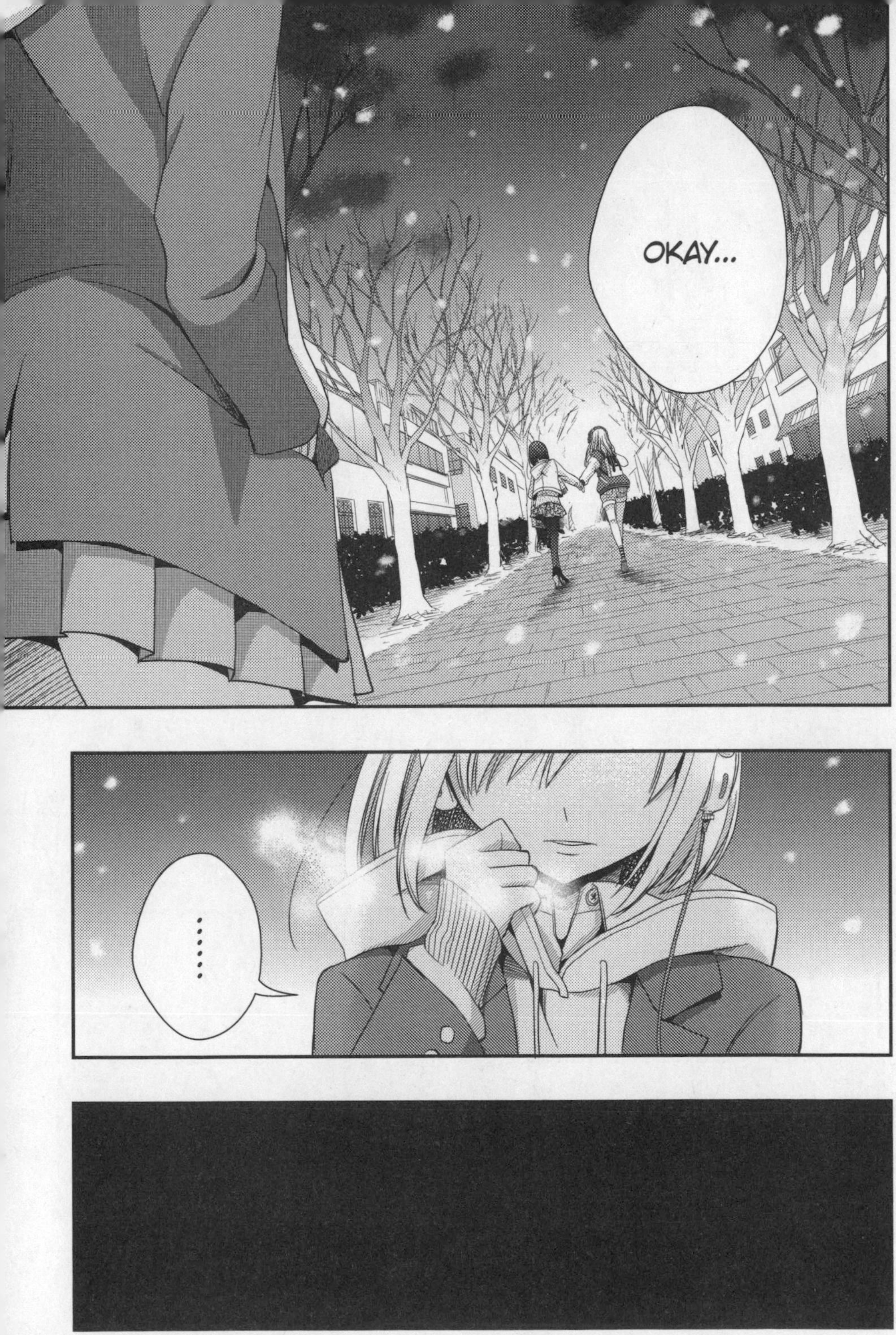
OKAY...
......

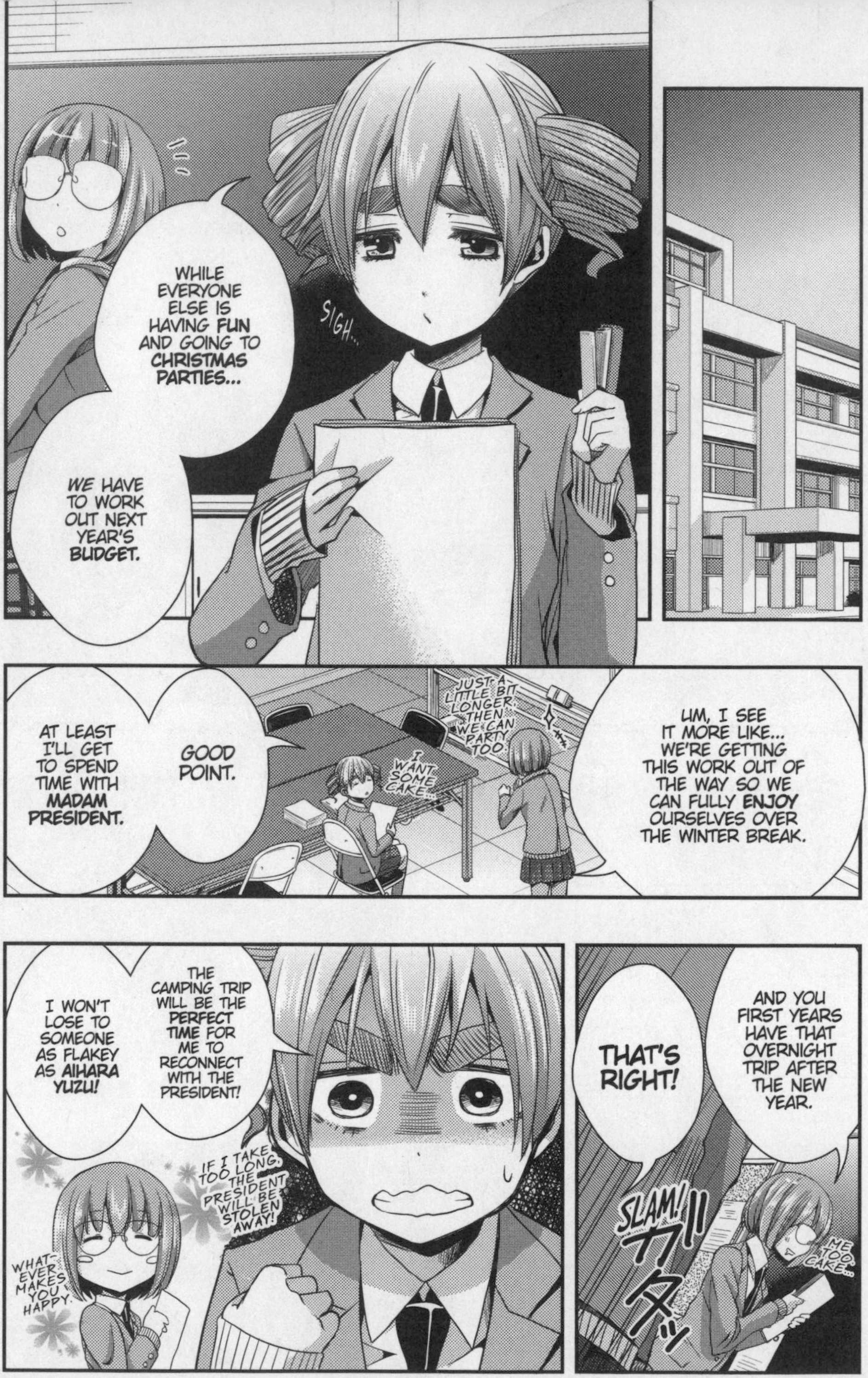
WHILE EVERYONE ELSE IS HAVING FUN AND GOING TO CHRISTMAS PARTIES...
SIGH...
WE HAVE TO WORK OUT NEXT YEAR'S BUDGET.
UM, I SEE IT MORE LIKE... WE'RE GETTING THIS WORK OUT OF THE WAY SO WE CAN FULLY ENJOY OURSELVES OVER THE WINTER BREAK.
JUST A LITTLE BIT LONGER. THEN WE CAN PARTY TOO.
I WANT SOME CAKE...
GOOD POINT.
AT LEAST I'LL GET TO SPEND TIME WITH MADAM PRESIDENT.
AND YOU FIRST YEARS HAVE THAT OVERNIGHT TRIP AFTER THE NEW YEAR.
THAT'S RIGHT!
ME TOO. CAKE...
SLAM!
ガタッ
THE CAMPING TRIP WILL BE THE PERFECT TIME FOR ME TO RECONNECT WITH THE PRESIDENT!
I WON'T LOSE TO SOMEONE AS FLAKEY AS AIHARA YUZU!
IF I TAKE TOO LONG, THE PRESIDENT WILL BE STOLEN AWAY!
WHATEVER MAKES YOU HAPPY.

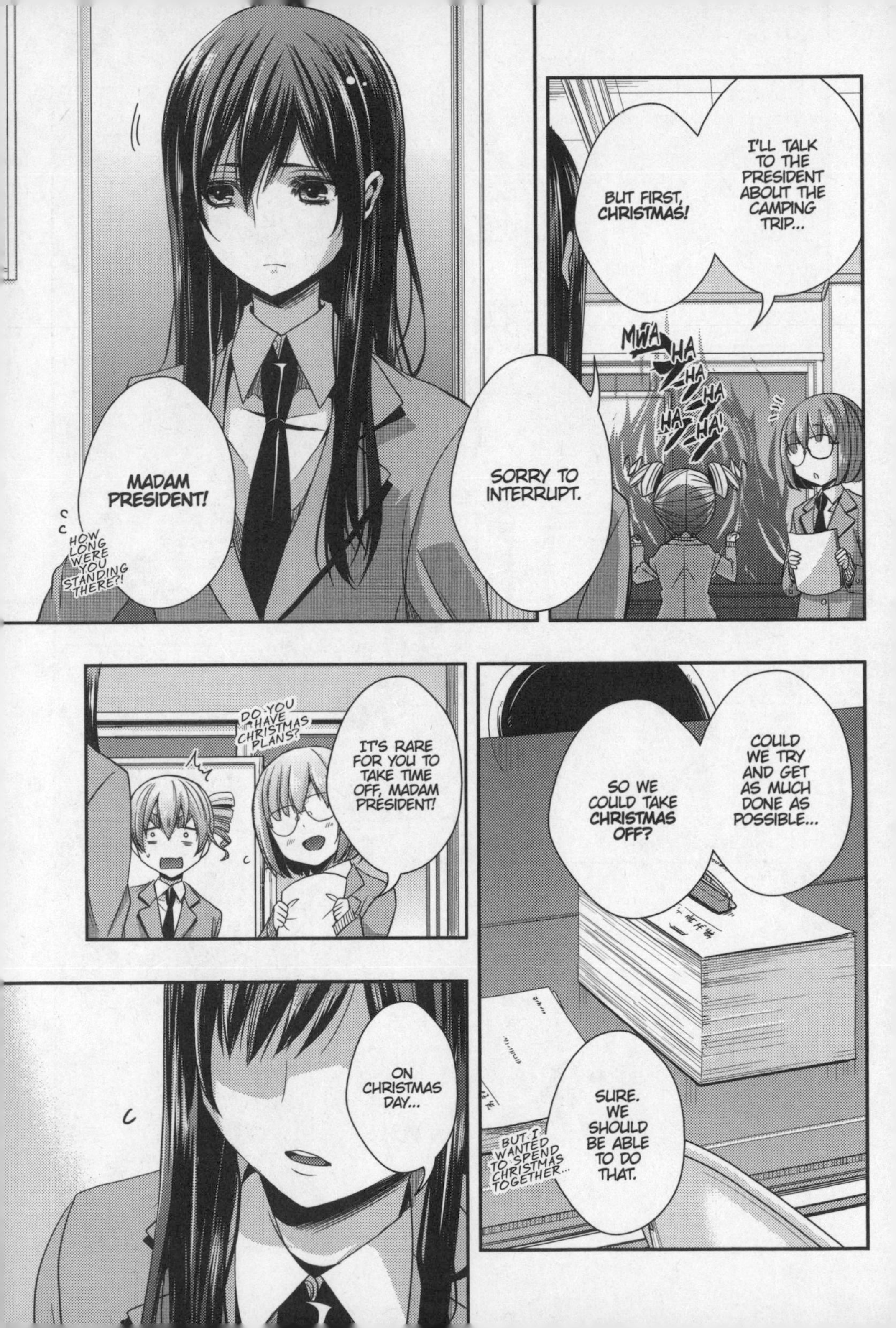
I'LL TALK TO THE PRESIDENT ABOUT THE CAMPING TRIP...
BUT FIRST, CHRISTMAS!
MWA HA HA HA HA HA!
SORRY TO INTERRUPT.
MADAM PRESIDENT!
HOW LONG WERE YOU STANDING THERE?!
COULD WE TRY AND GET AS MUCH DONE AS POSSIBLE...
SO WE COULD TAKE CHRISTMAS OFF?
SURE. WE SHOULD BE ABLE TO DO THAT.
BUT I WANTED TO SPEND CHRISTMAS TOGETHER...
IT'S RARE FOR YOU TO TAKE TIME OFF, MADAM PRESIDENT!
DO YOU HAVE CHRISTMAS PLANS?
ON CHRISTMAS DAY...

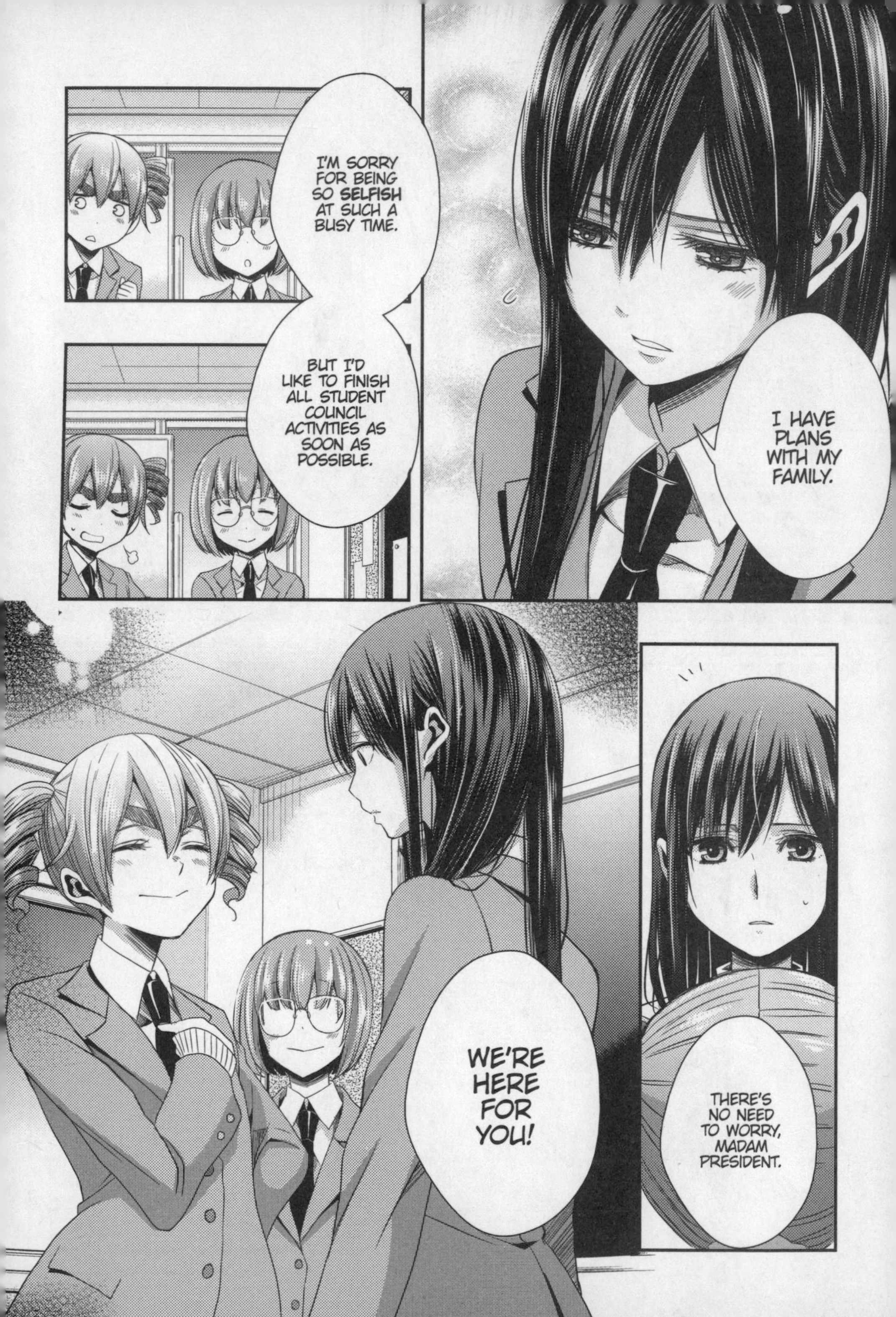
I HAVE PLANS WITH MY FAMILY.
I'M SORRY FOR BEING SO SELFISH AT SUCH A BUSY TIME.
BUT I'D LIKE TO FINISH ALL STUDENT COUNCIL ACTIVITIES AS SOON AS POSSIBLE.
THERE'S NO NEED TO WORRY, MADAM PRESIDENT.
WE'RE HERE FOR YOU!

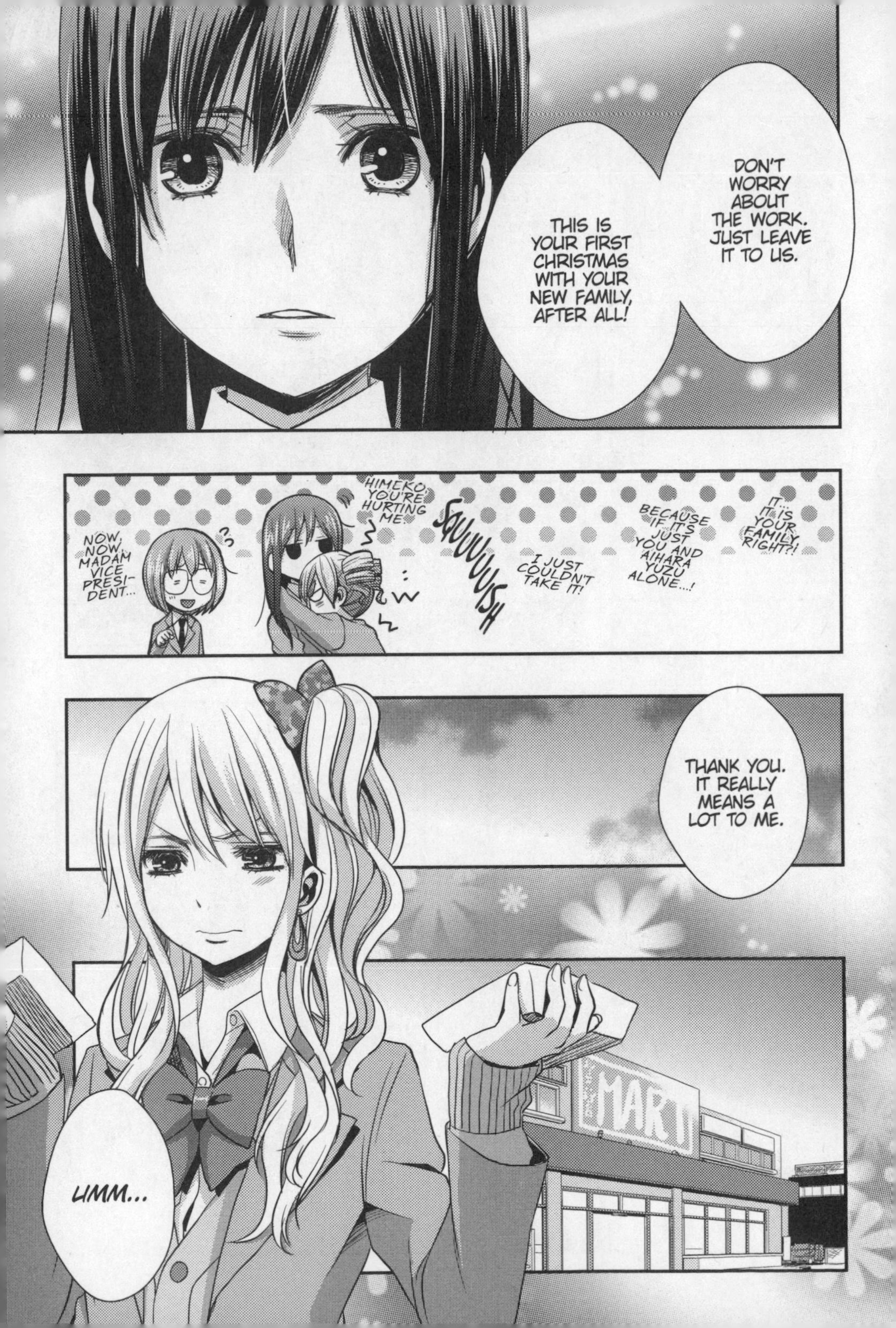
DON'T WORRY ABOUT THE WORK. JUST LEAVE IT TO US.
THIS IS YOUR FIRST CHRISTMAS WITH YOUR NEW FAMILY, AFTER ALL!
IT... IT IS YOUR FAMILY, RIGHT?!
BECAUSE IF IT'S JUST YOU AND AIHARA YUZU ALONE...!
I JUST COULDN'T TAKE IT!
SQUUUUUISH
HIMEKO, YOU'RE HURTING ME.
NOW, NOW, MADAM VICE PRESIDENT...
THANK YOU. IT REALLY MEANS A LOT TO ME.
MART
UMM...

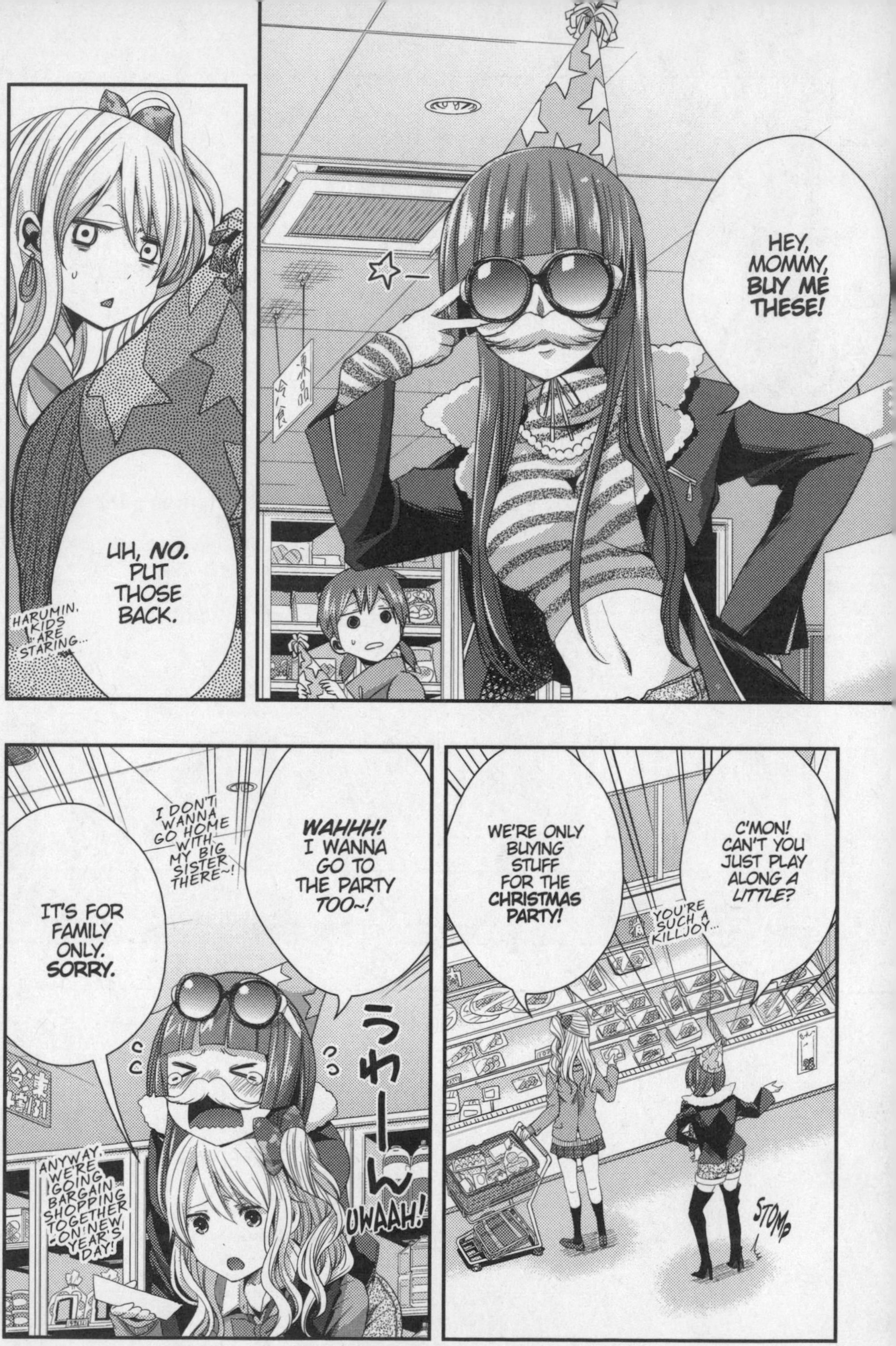
HEY, MOMMY, BUY ME THESE!
UH, NO. PUT THOSE BACK.
HARUMIN, KIDS ARE STARING...
C'MON! CAN'T YOU JUST PLAY ALONG A LITTLE?
YOU'RE SUCH A KILLJOY...
WE'RE ONLY BUYING STUFF FOR THE CHRISTMAS PARTY!
STOMP
WAHHH! I WANNA GO TO THE PARTY TOO~!
I DON'T WANNA GO HOME WITH MY BIG SISTER THERE~!
IT'S FOR FAMILY ONLY. SORRY.
うわーん
UWAAH!
ANYWAY, WE'RE GOING BARGAIN SHOPPING TOGETHER ON NEW YEAR'S DAY!

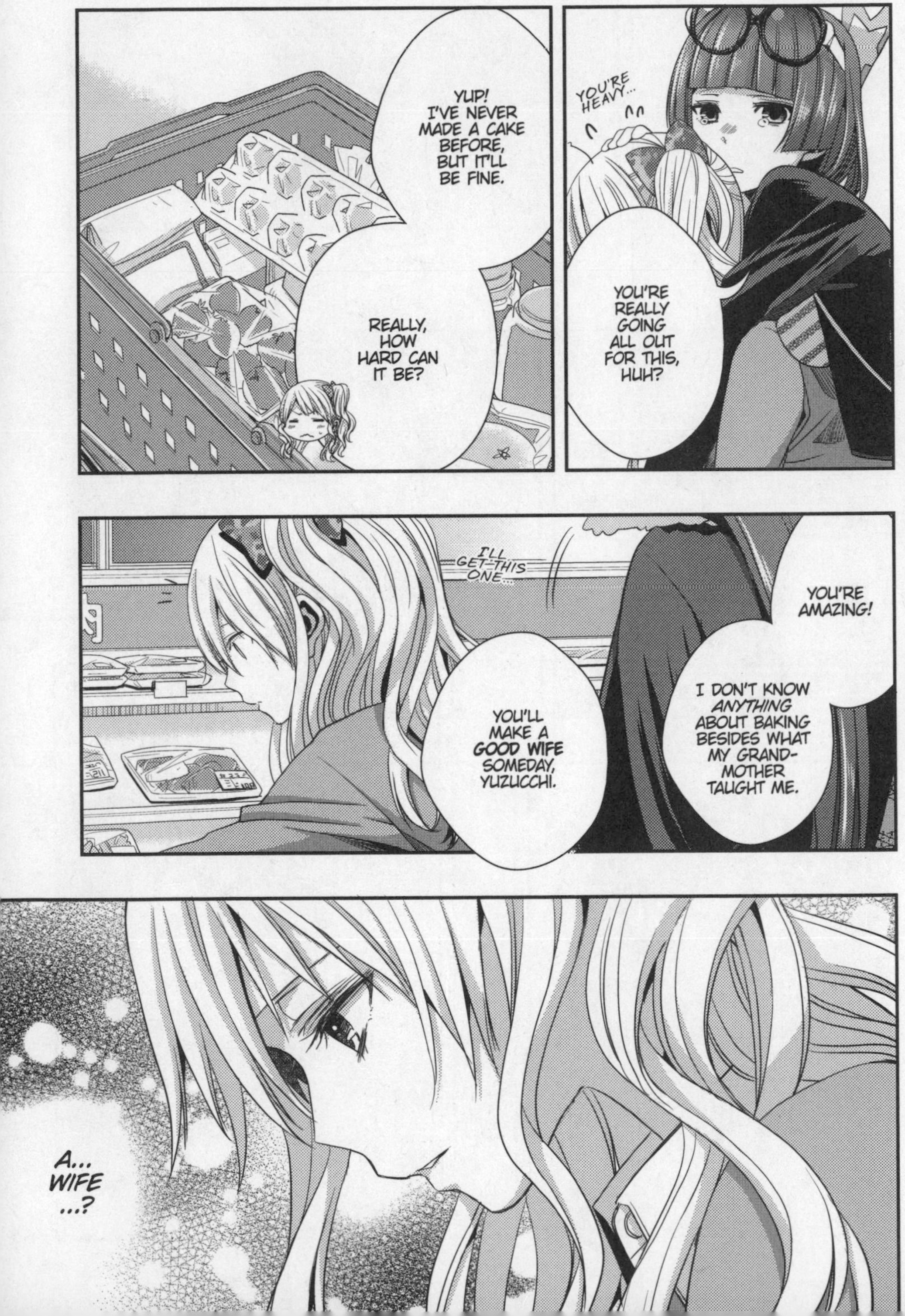
YOU'RE HEAVY...
YOU'RE REALLY GOING ALL OUT FOR THIS, HUH?
YUP! I'VE NEVER MADE A CAKE BEFORE, BUT IT'LL BE FINE.
REALLY, HOW HARD CAN IT BE?
YOU'RE AMAZING!
I DON'T KNOW *ANYTHING* ABOUT BAKING BESIDES WHAT MY GRAND-MOTHER TAUGHT ME.
I'LL GET THIS ONE...
YOU'LL MAKE A **GOOD WIFE** SOMEDAY, YUZUCCHI.
A... WIFE ...?

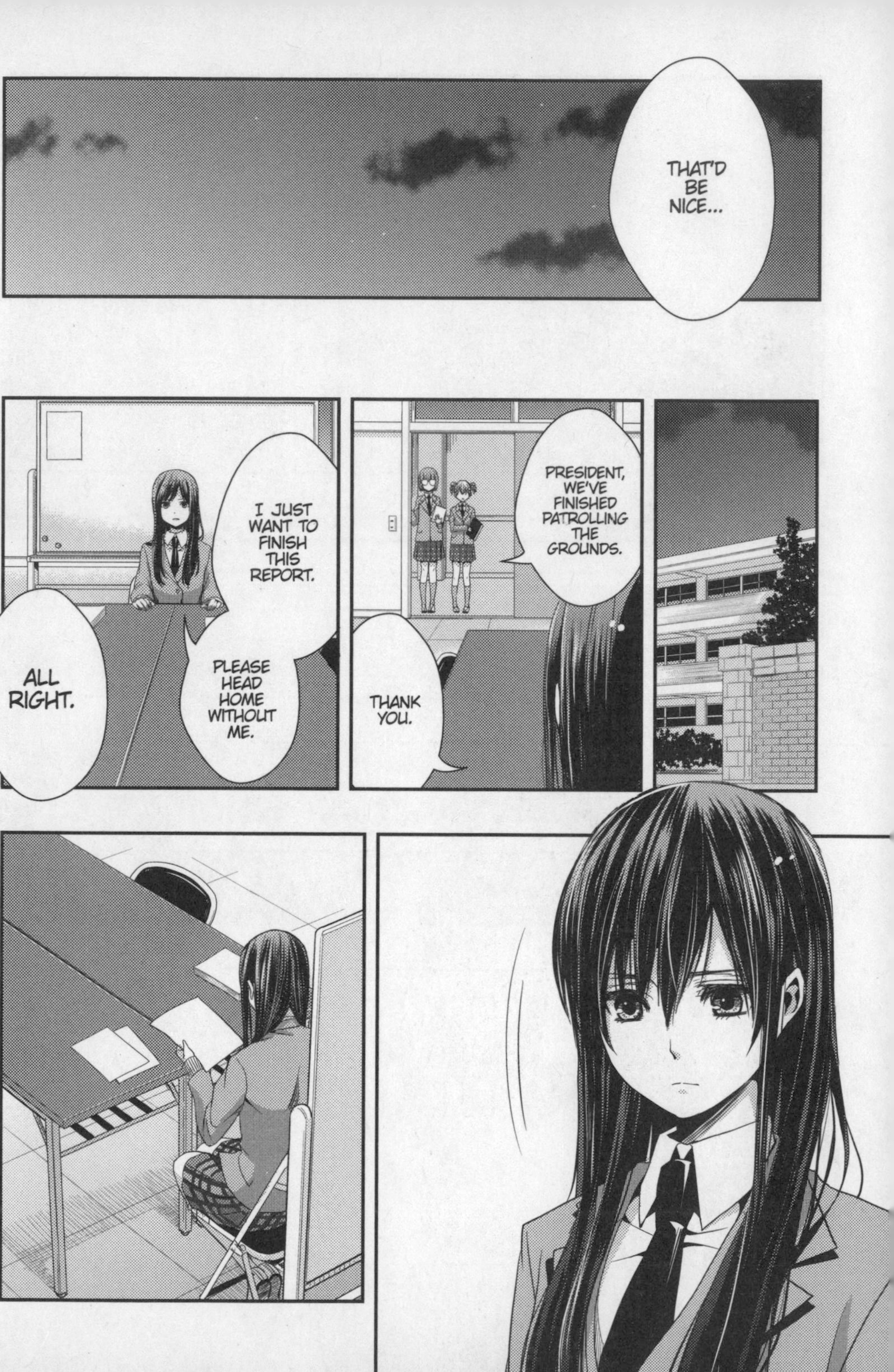
THAT'D BE NICE...
PRESIDENT, WE'VE FINISHED PATROLLING THE GROUNDS.
THANK YOU.
I JUST WANT TO FINISH THIS REPORT.
PLEASE HEAD HOME WITHOUT ME.
ALL RIGHT.

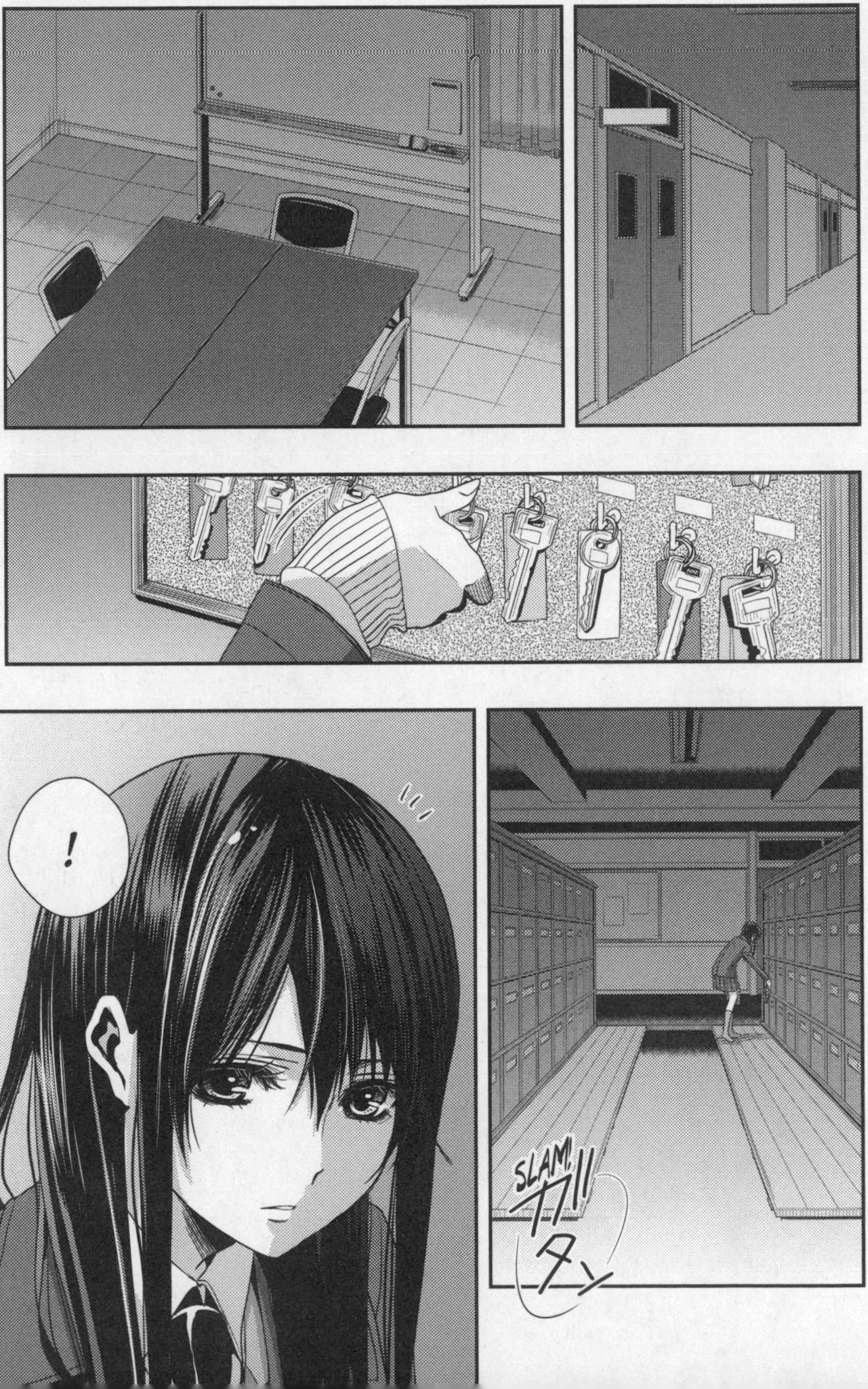
SLAM!
タン
!

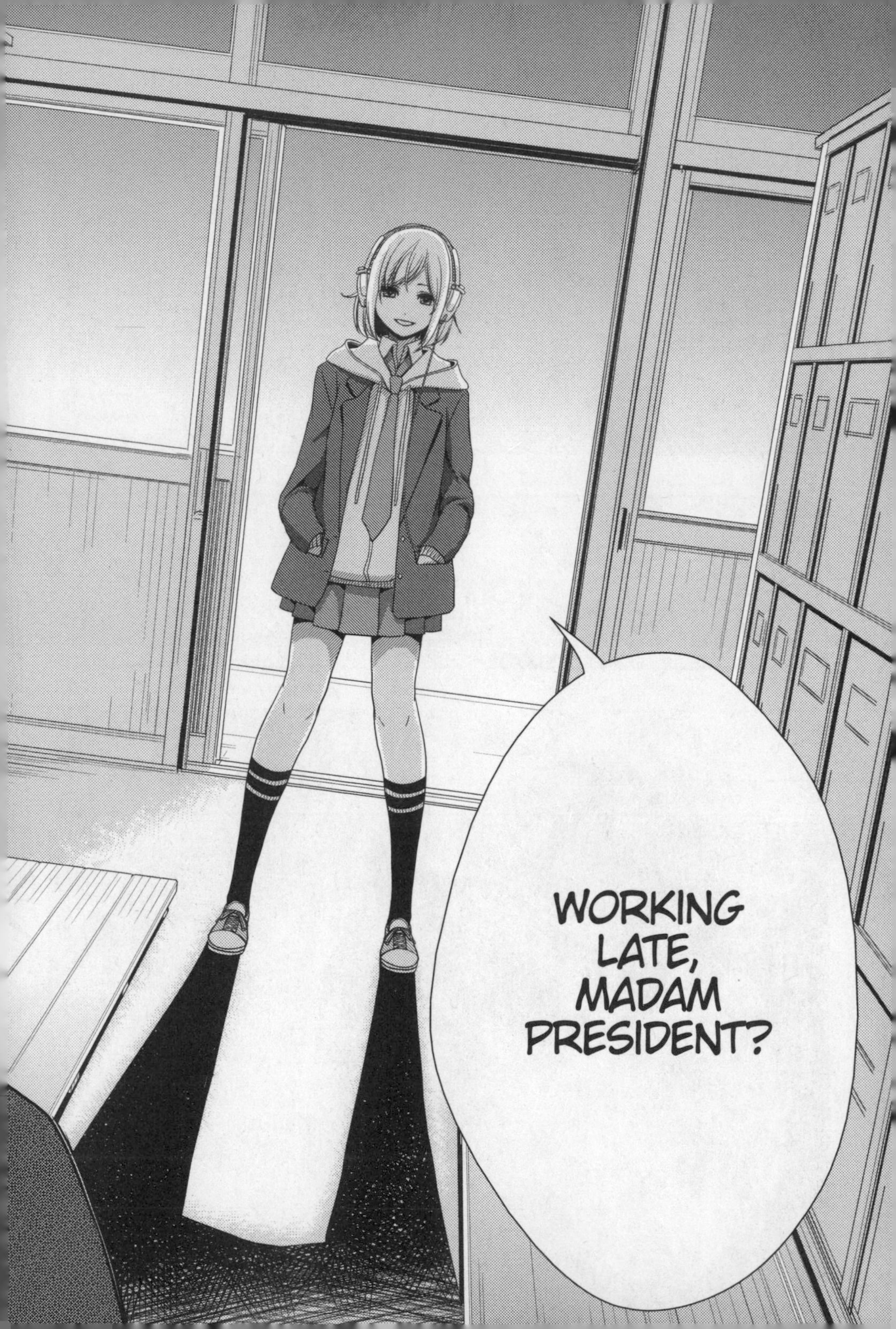
WORKING LATE, MADAM PRESIDENT?

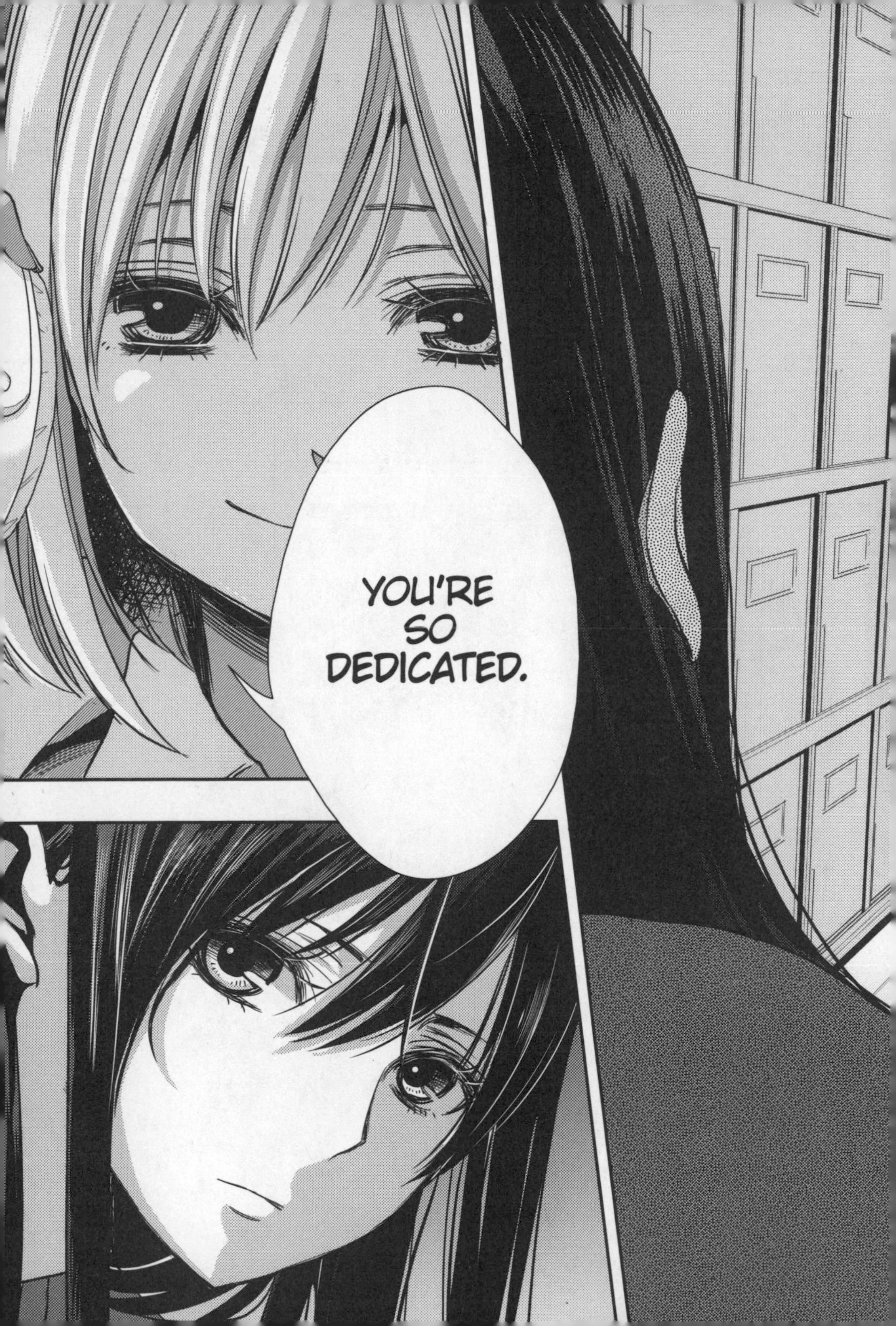
YOU'RE SO DEDICATED.

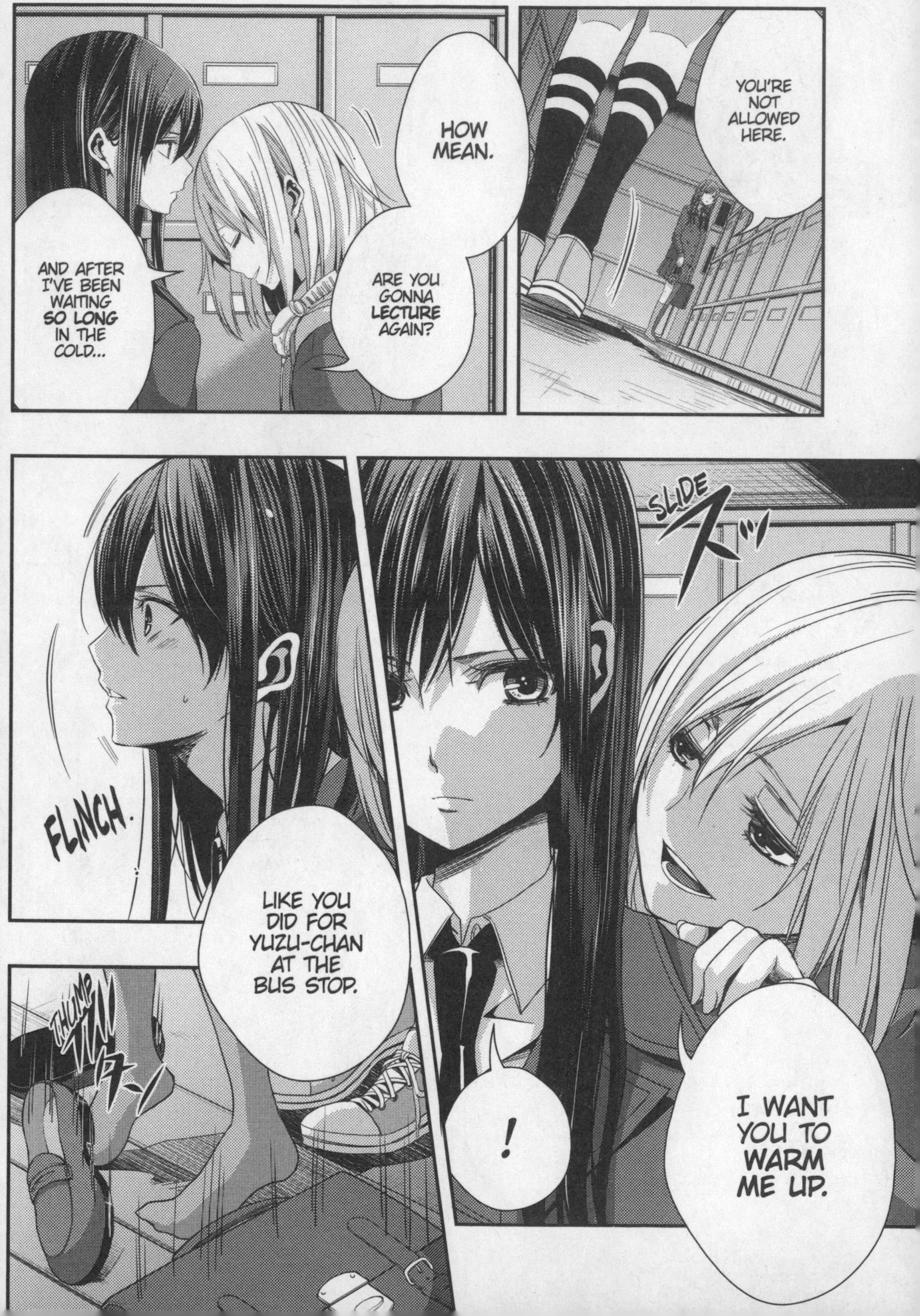
YOU'RE NOT ALLOWED HERE.
HOW MEAN.
ARE YOU GONNA LECTURE AGAIN?
AND AFTER I'VE BEEN WAITING SO LONG IN THE COLD...
SLIDE
I WANT YOU TO WARM ME UP.
LIKE YOU DID FOR YUZU-CHAN AT THE BUS STOP.
!
FLINCH.
THUMP

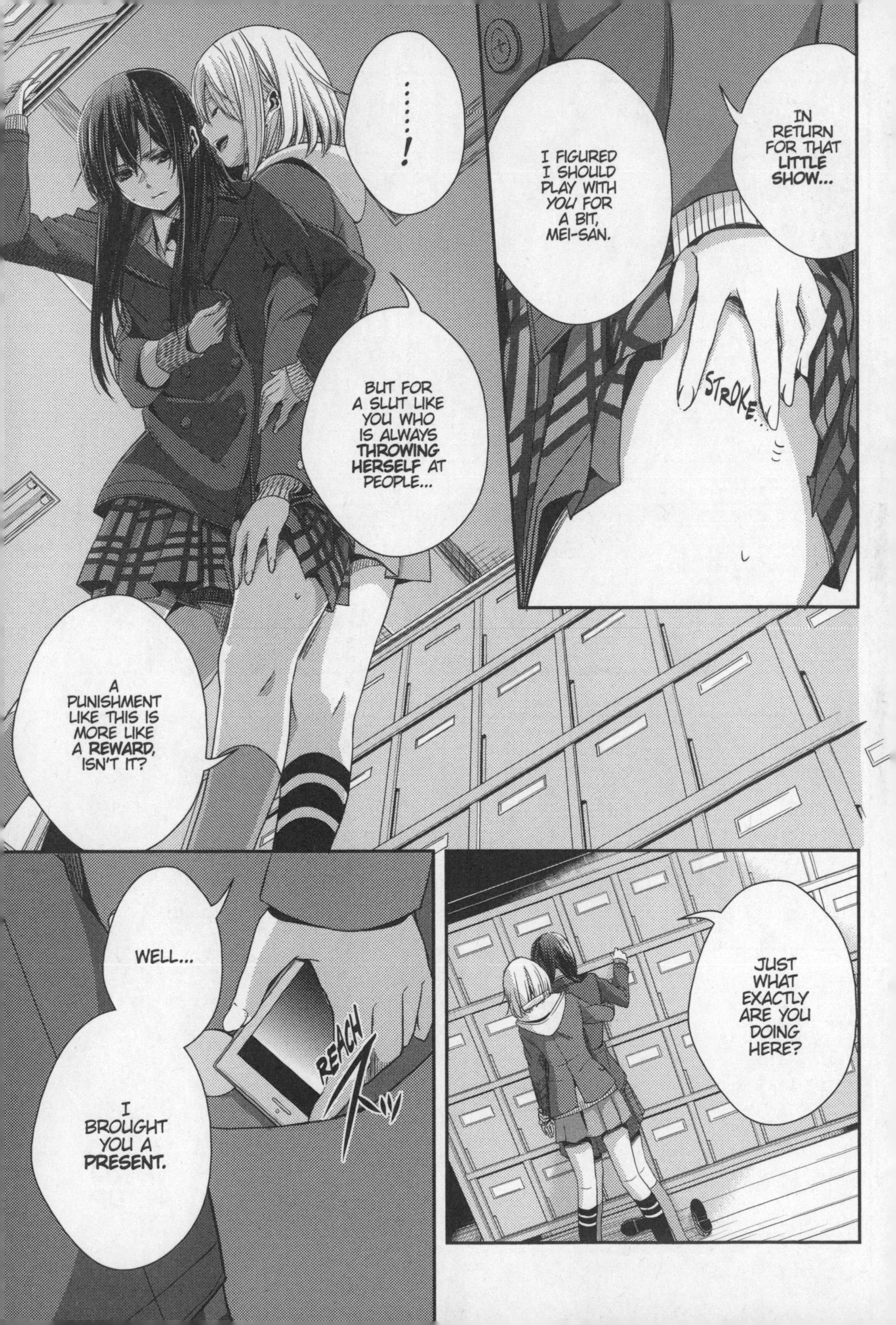
IN RETURN FOR THAT LITTLE SHOW...
I FIGURED I SHOULD PLAY WITH YOU FOR A BIT, MEI-SAN.
STROKE...
......!
BUT FOR A SLUT LIKE YOU WHO IS ALWAYS THROWING HERSELF AT PEOPLE...
A PUNISHMENT LIKE THIS IS MORE LIKE A REWARD, ISN'T IT?
JUST WHAT EXACTLY ARE YOU DOING HERE?
WELL...
REACH
I BROUGHT YOU A PRESENT.

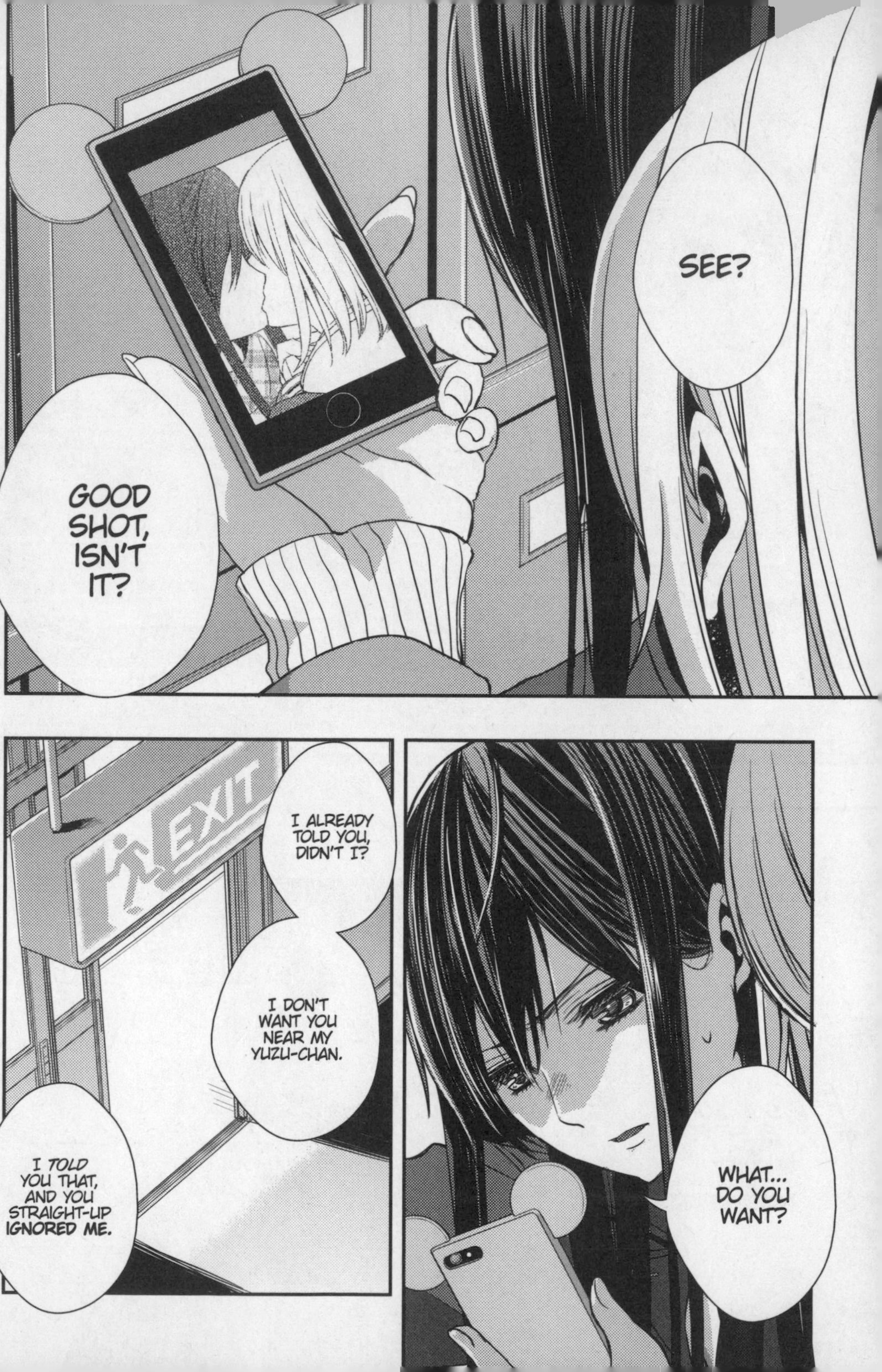
SEE?
GOOD SHOT, ISN'T IT?
WHAT... DO YOU WANT?
I ALREADY TOLD YOU, DIDN'T I?
I DON'T WANT YOU NEAR MY YUZU-CHAN.
I *TOLD* YOU THAT, AND YOU STRAIGHT-UP IGNORED ME.

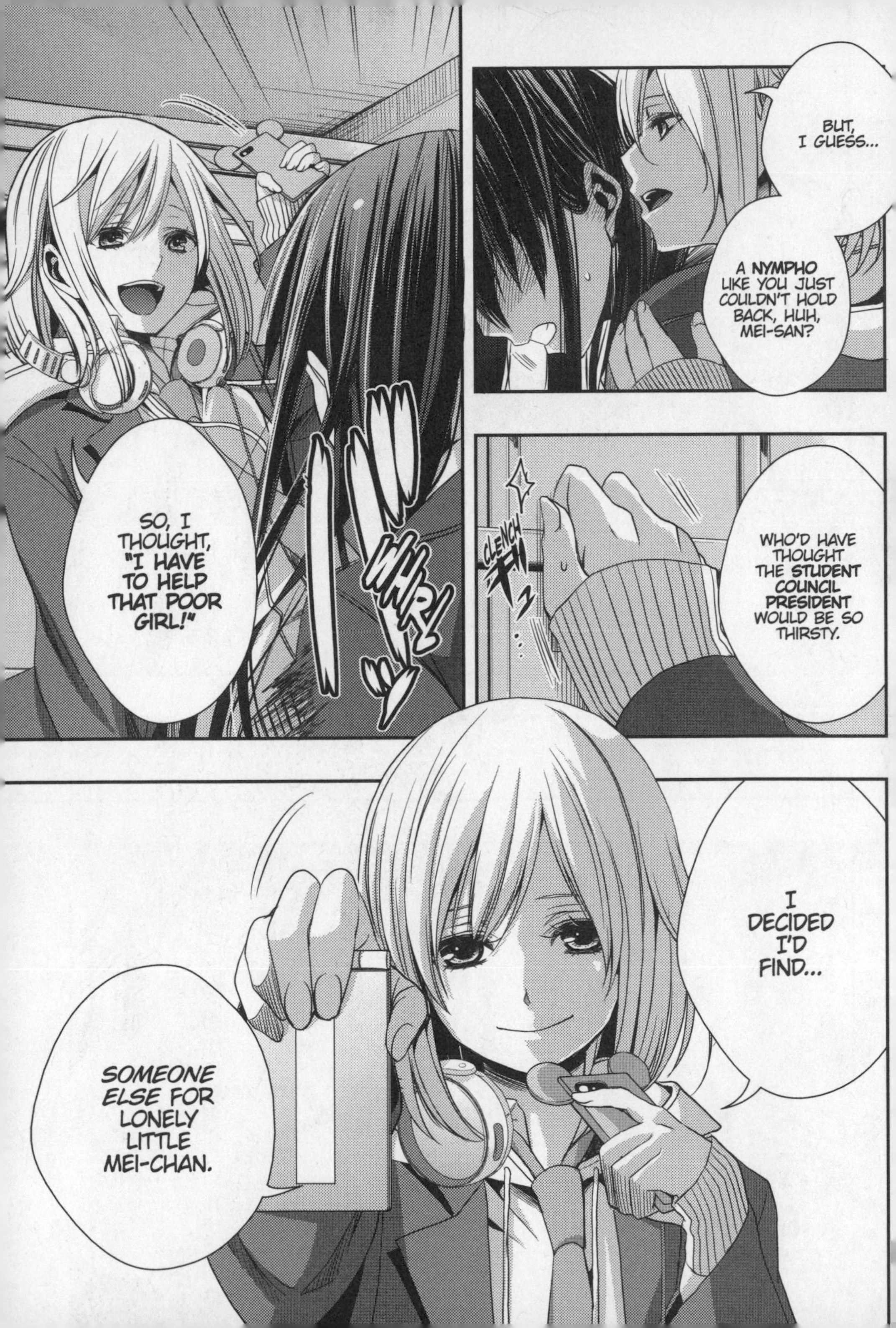
BUT, I GUESS...
A NYMPHO LIKE YOU JUST COULDN'T HOLD BACK, HUH, MEI-SAN?
CLENCH
WHO'D HAVE THOUGHT THE STUDENT COUNCIL PRESIDENT WOULD BE SO THIRSTY.
WHIRL
SO, I THOUGHT, "I HAVE TO HELP THAT POOR GIRL!"
I DECIDED I'D FIND...
SOMEONE ELSE FOR LONELY LITTLE MEI-CHAN.

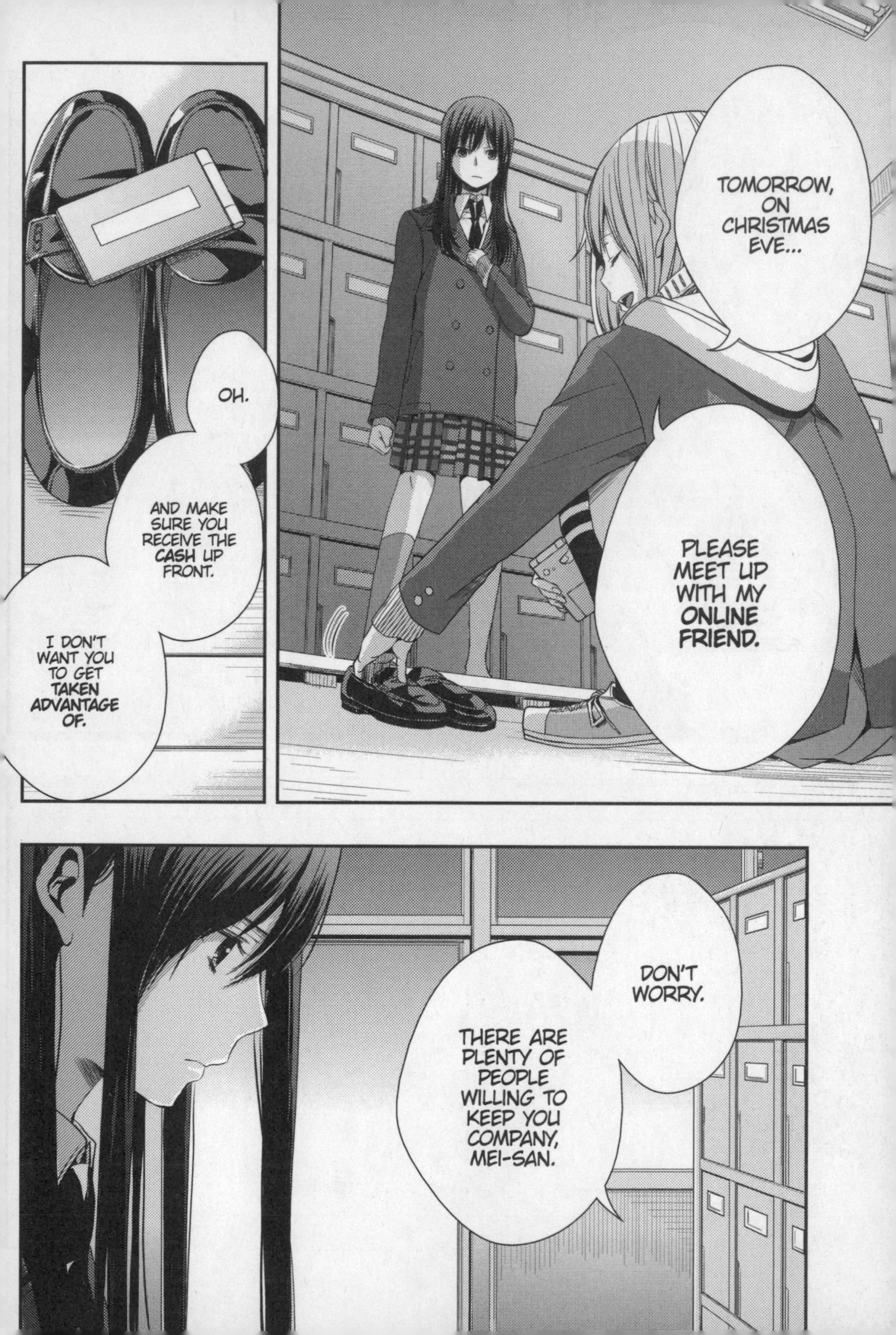
TOMORROW, ON CHRISTMAS EVE...
PLEASE MEET UP WITH MY ONLINE FRIEND.
OH.
AND MAKE SURE YOU RECEIVE THE CASH UP FRONT.
I DON'T WANT YOU TO GET TAKEN ADVANTAGE OF.
DON'T WORRY.
THERE ARE PLENTY OF PEOPLE WILLING TO KEEP YOU COMPANY, MEI-SAN.

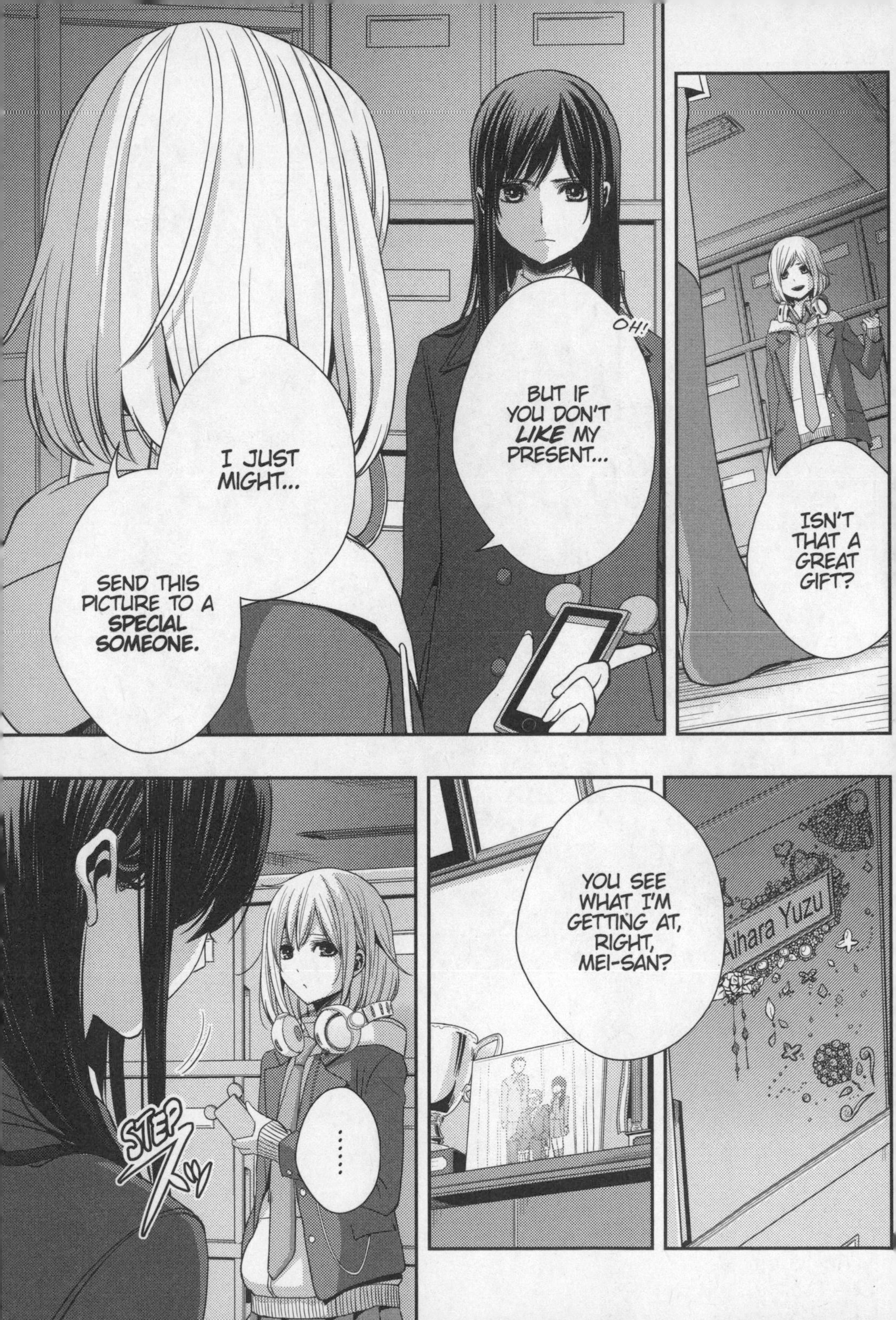
ISN'T THAT A GREAT GIFT?
OH!
BUT IF YOU DON'T *LIKE* MY PRESENT...
I JUST MIGHT...
SEND THIS PICTURE TO A SPECIAL SOMEONE.
Aihara Yuzu
YOU SEE WHAT I'M GETTING AT, RIGHT, MEI-SAN?
......
STEP

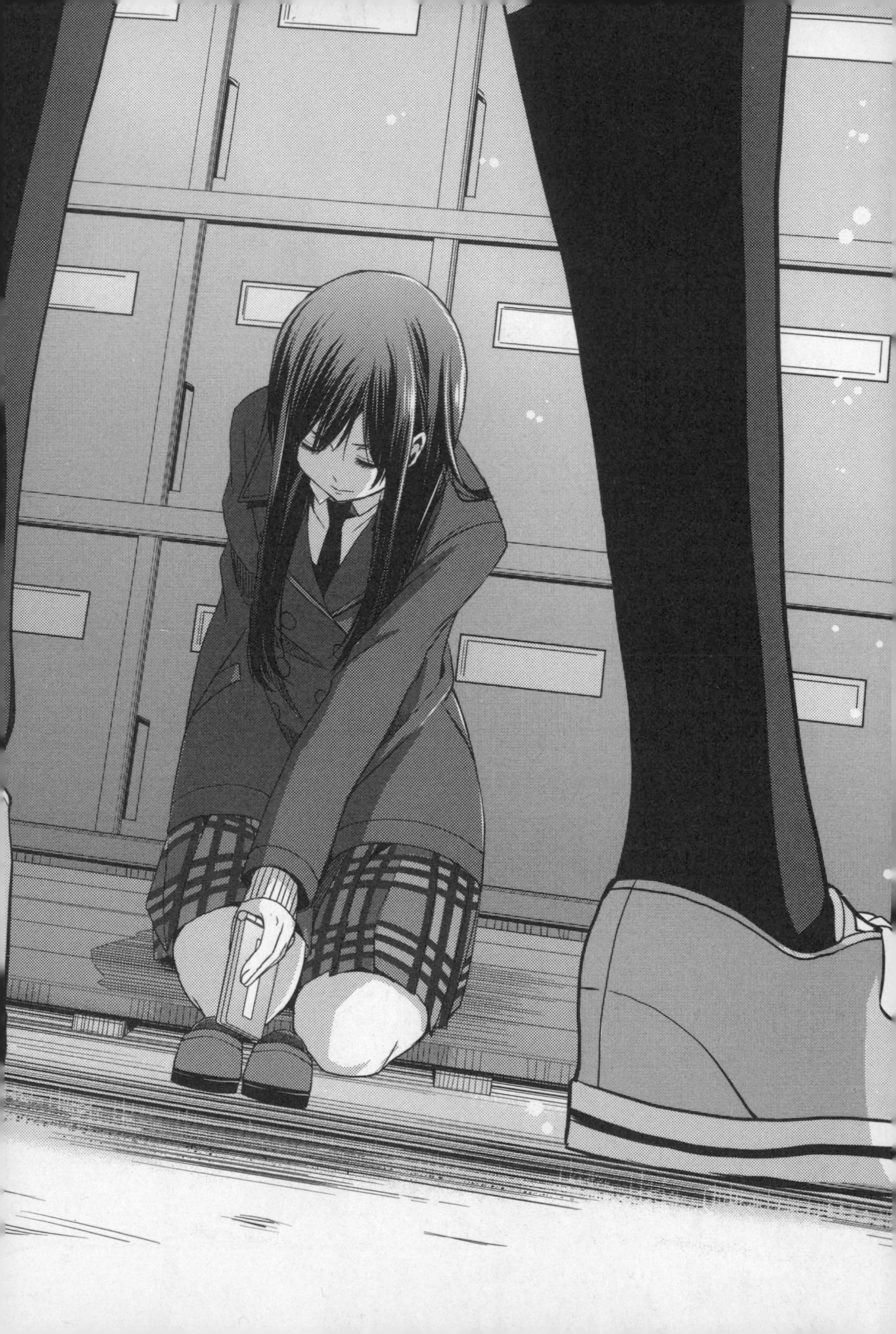

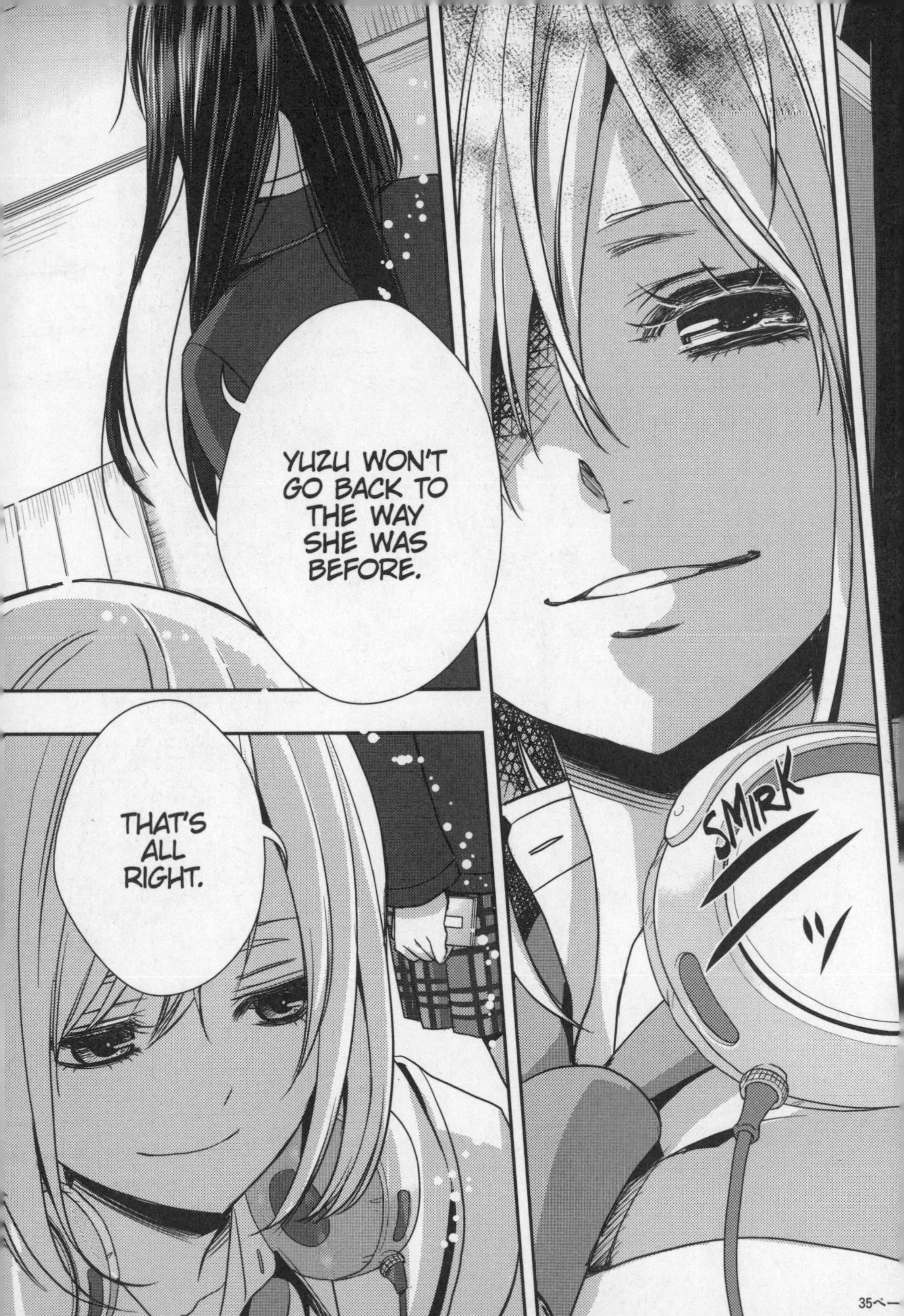
YUZU WON'T GO BACK TO THE WAY SHE WAS BEFORE.
SMIRK
THAT'S ALL RIGHT.

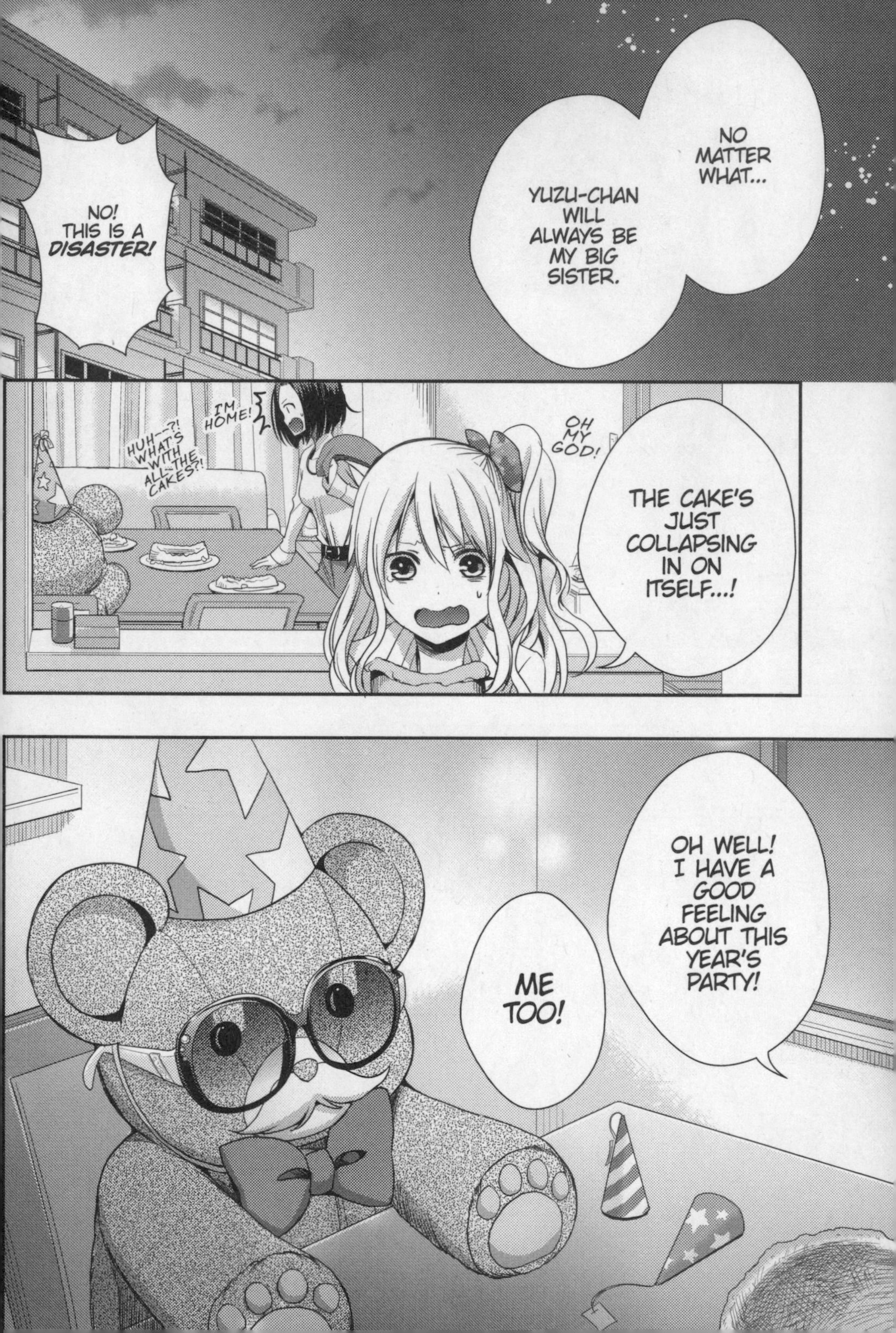
NO MATTER WHAT... YUZU-CHAN WILL ALWAYS BE MY BIG SISTER.
NO! THIS IS A DISASTER!
OH MY GOD!
THE CAKE'S JUST COLLAPSING IN ON ITSELF...!
I'M HOME!
HUH--?! WHAT'S WITH ALL THE CAKES?!
OH WELL! I HAVE A GOOD FEELING ABOUT THIS YEAR'S PARTY!
ME TOO!

citrus

【シトラス】

SECRET LOVE AFFAIR WITH SISTER

citrus

SABUROUTA PRESENTS SECRET LOVE AFFAIR WITH SISTER

3

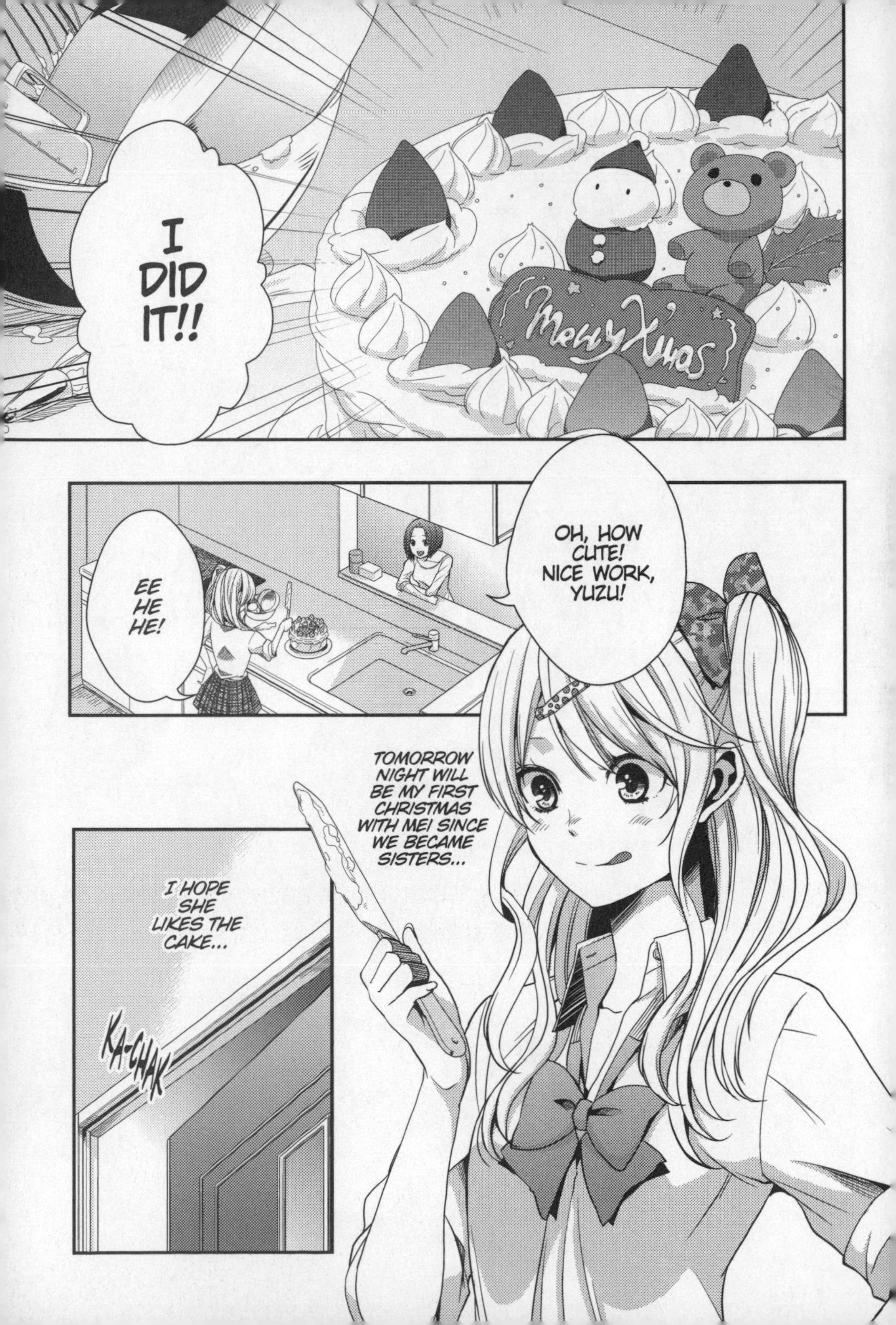

Merry X'mas
I DID IT!!
OH, HOW CUTE! NICE WORK, YUZU!
EE HE HE!
TOMORROW NIGHT WILL BE MY FIRST CHRISTMAS WITH MEI SINCE WE BECAME SISTERS...
I HOPE SHE LIKES THE CAKE...
KA-CHAK

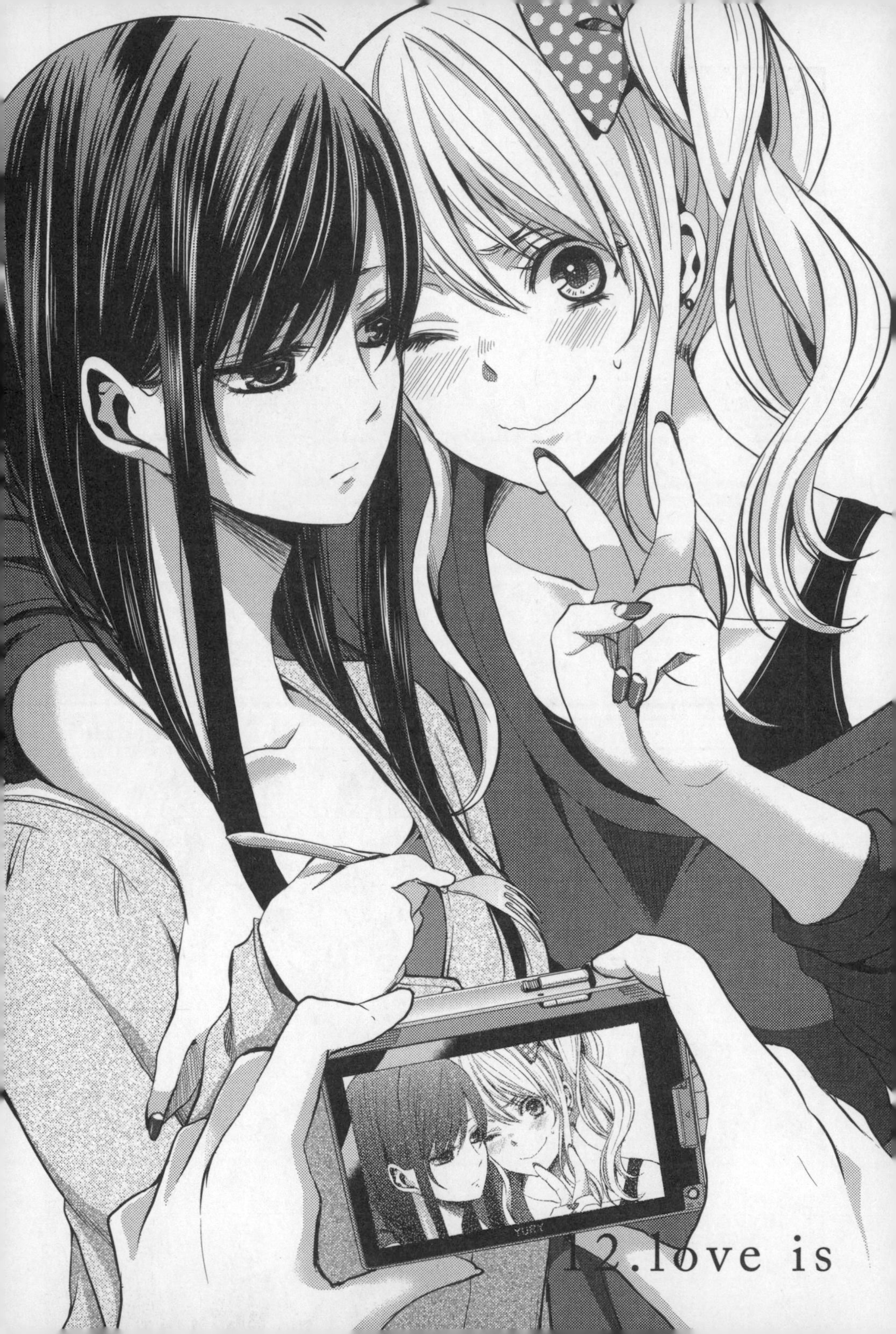
12.love is

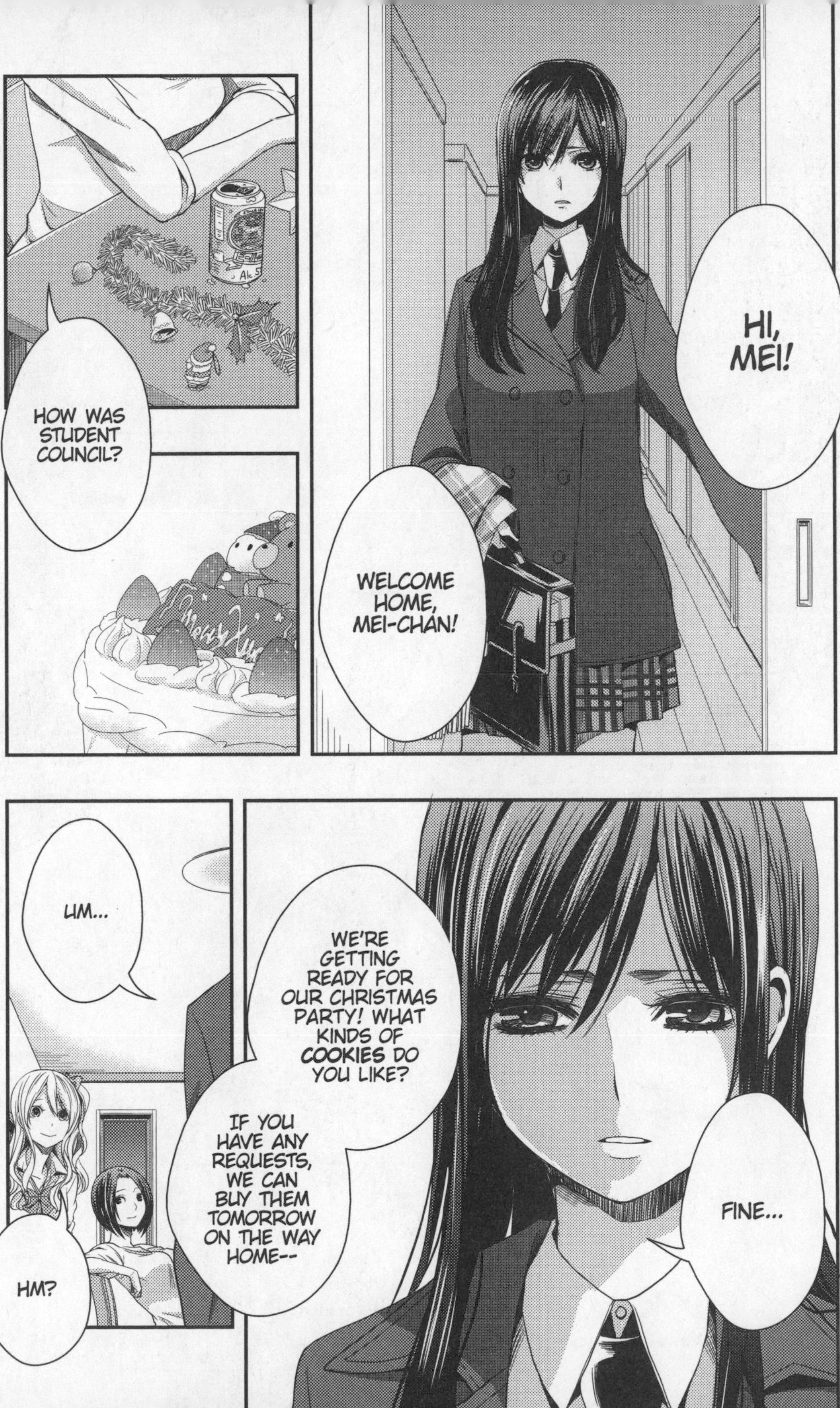
HI, MEI!
WELCOME HOME, MEI-CHAN!
HOW WAS STUDENT COUNCIL?
FINE...
WE'RE GETTING READY FOR OUR CHRISTMAS PARTY! WHAT KINDS OF COOKIES DO YOU LIKE?
IF YOU HAVE ANY REQUESTS, WE CAN BUY THEM TOMORROW ON THE WAY HOME--
UM...
HM?

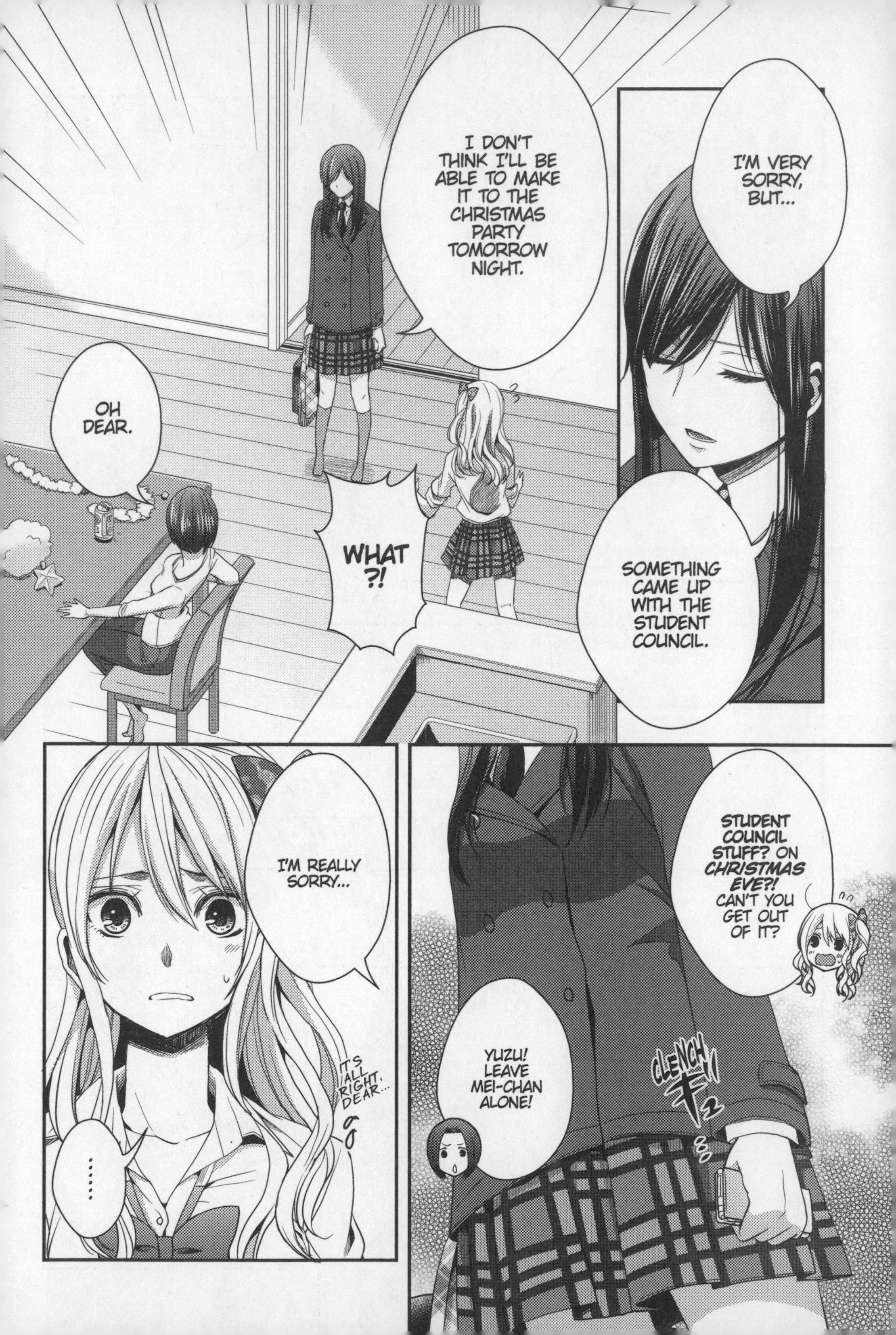
I'M VERY SORRY, BUT...
SOMETHING CAME UP WITH THE STUDENT COUNCIL.
I DON'T THINK I'LL BE ABLE TO MAKE IT TO THE CHRISTMAS PARTY TOMORROW NIGHT.
WHAT ?!
OH DEAR.
STUDENT COUNCIL STUFF? ON *CHRISTMAS EVE?!* CAN'T YOU GET OUT OF IT?
CLENCH
YUZU! LEAVE MEI-CHAN ALONE!
I'M REALLY SORRY...
IT'S ALL RIGHT, DEAR...
......

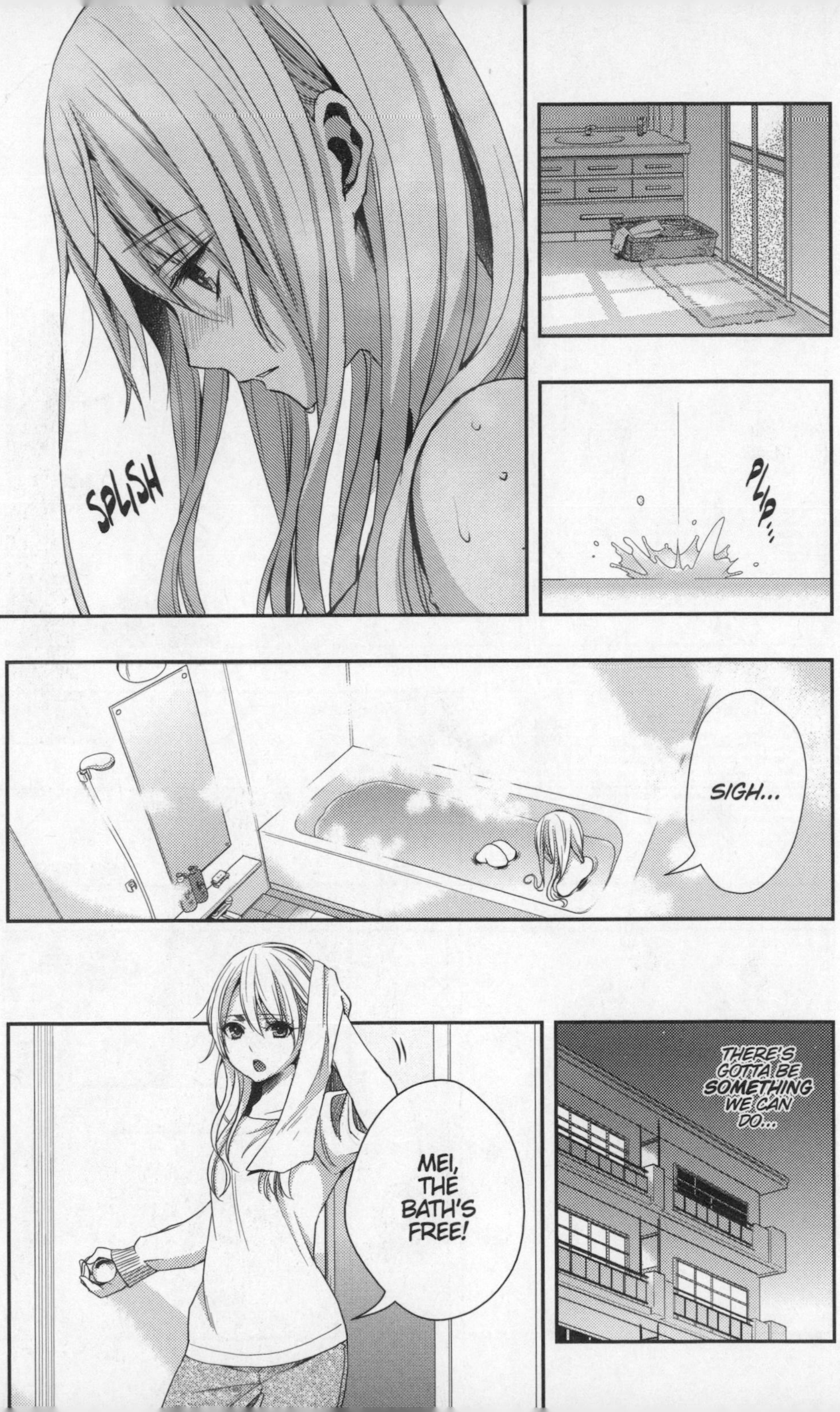
PLIP...
SPLISH
SIGH...
THERE'S GOTTA BE SOMETHING WE CAN DO...
MEI, THE BATH'S FREE!

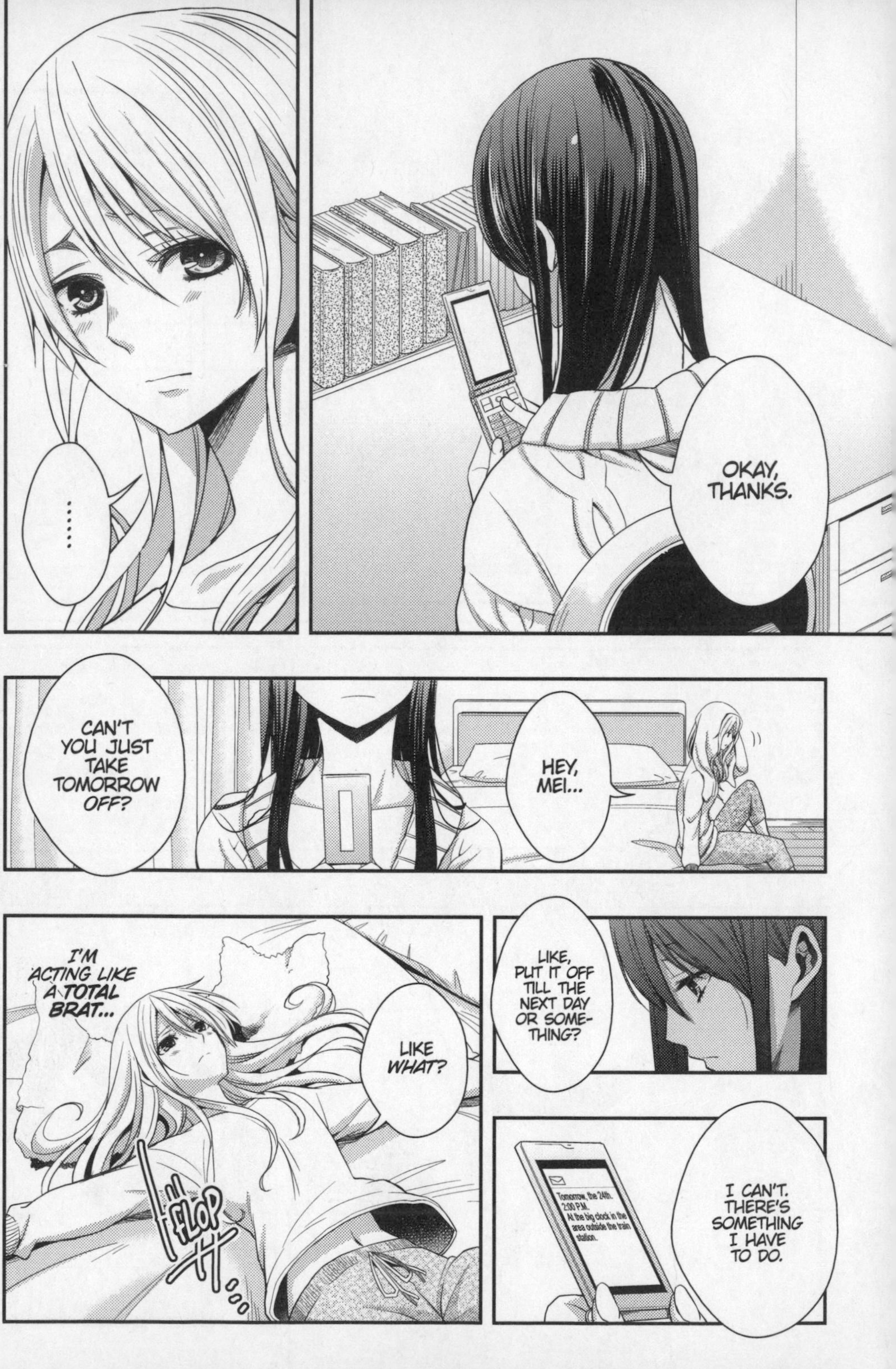
OKAY, THANKS.
......
HEY, MEI...
CAN'T YOU JUST TAKE TOMORROW OFF?
LIKE, PUT IT OFF TILL THE NEXT DAY OR SOME-THING?
Tomorrow, the 24th. 2:00 P.M. At the big clock in the area outside the train station.
I CAN'T. THERE'S SOMETHING I HAVE TO DO.
LIKE WHAT?
I'M ACTING LIKE A TOTAL BRAT...
FLOP

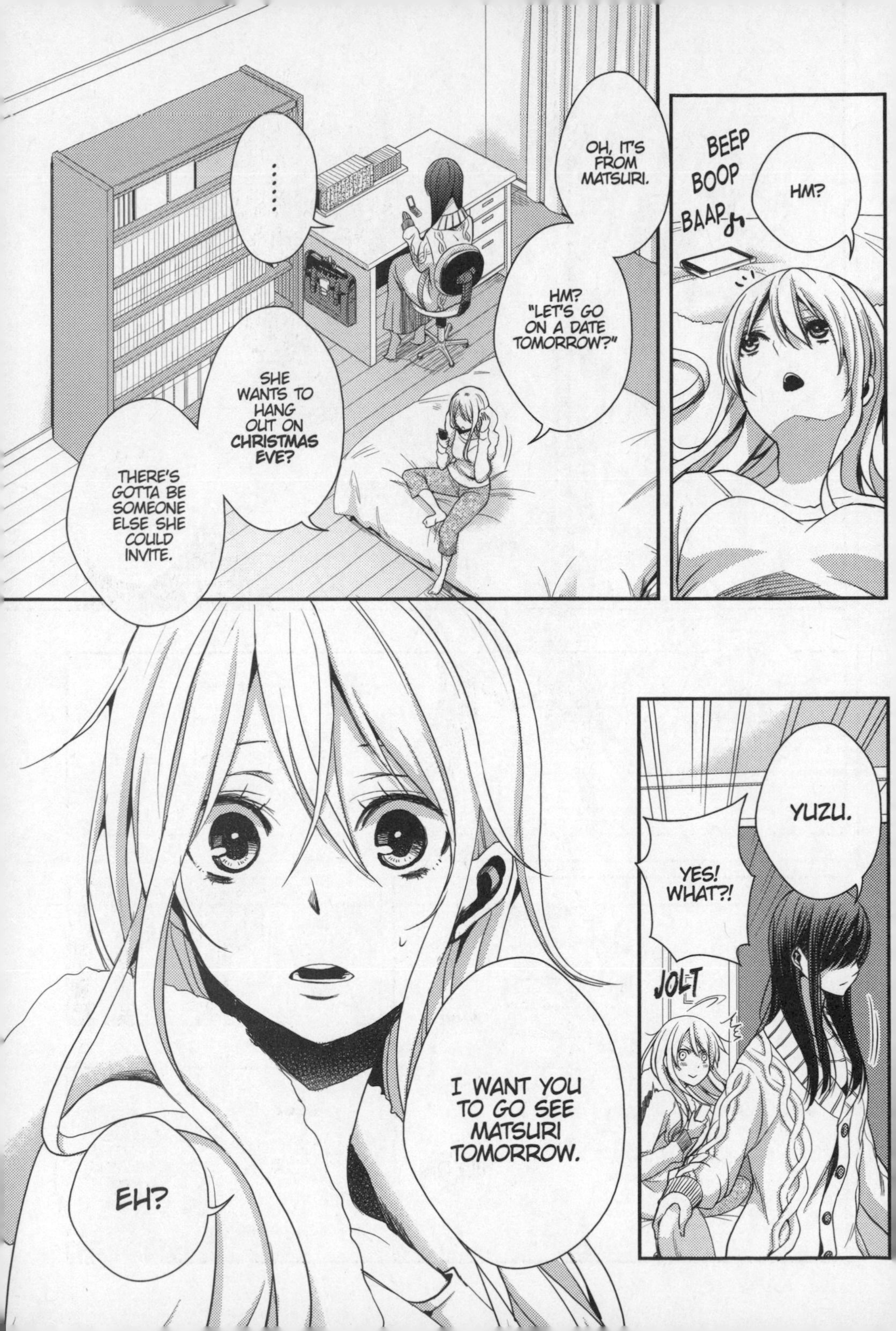
BEEP
BOOP
BAAP
HM?
OH, IT'S FROM MATSURI.
HM? "LET'S GO ON A DATE TOMORROW?"
......
SHE WANTS TO HANG OUT ON CHRISTMAS EVE?
THERE'S GOTTA BE SOMEONE ELSE SHE COULD INVITE.
YUZU.
YES! WHAT?!
JOLT
I WANT YOU TO GO SEE MATSURI TOMORROW.
EH?

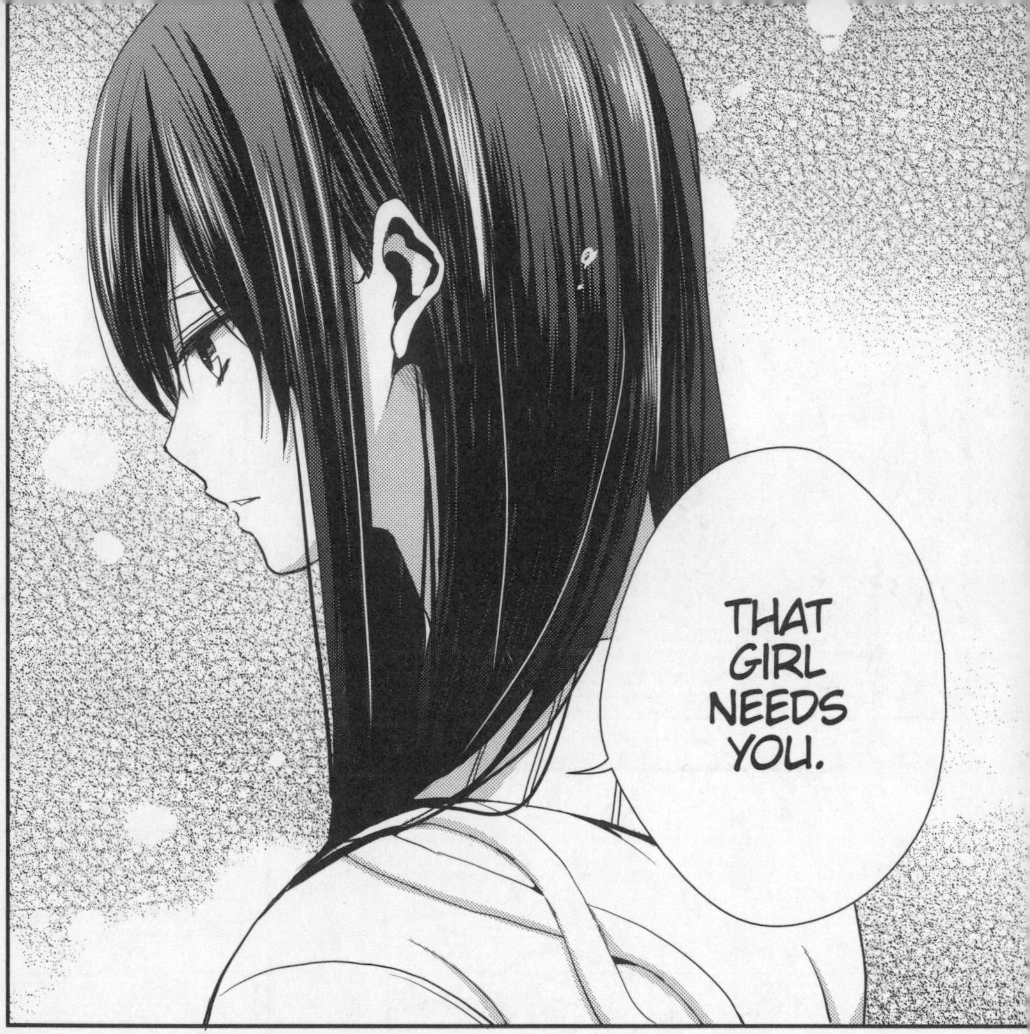
THAT GIRL NEEDS YOU.

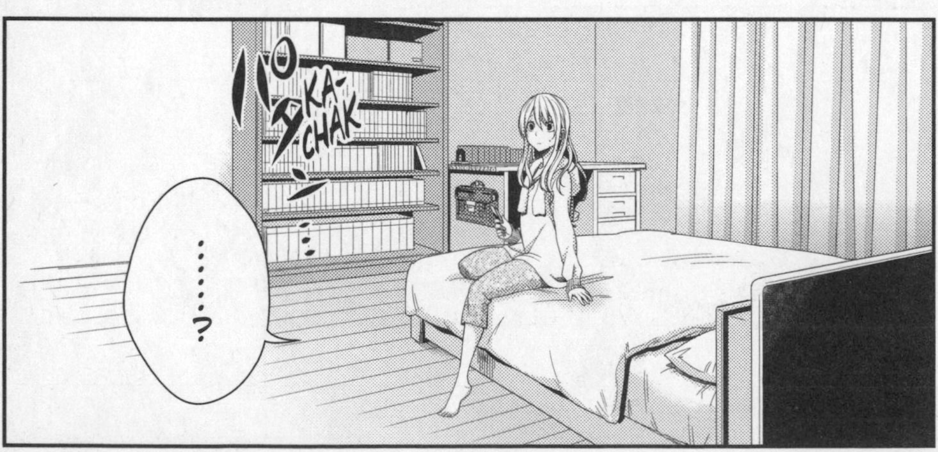
KA-CHAK
......?

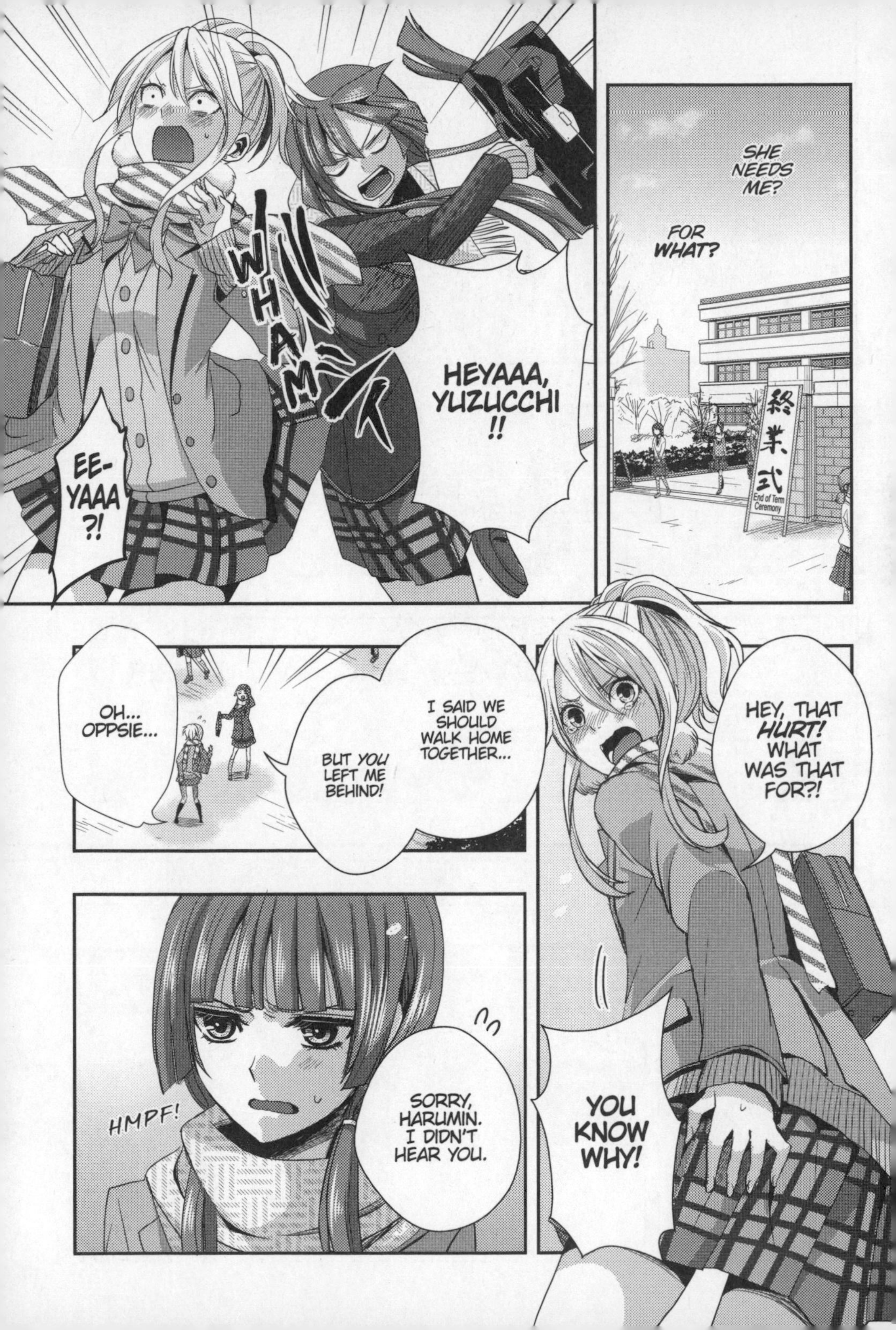
SHE NEEDS ME?
FOR WHAT?
終業式
End of Term Ceremony
HEYAAA, YUZUCCHI!!
WHAM
EE-YAAA?!
HEY, THAT HURT! WHAT WAS THAT FOR?!
YOU KNOW WHY!
I SAID WE SHOULD WALK HOME TOGETHER...
BUT YOU LEFT ME BEHIND!
OH... OPPSIE...
SORRY, HARUMIN. I DIDN'T HEAR YOU.
HMPF!

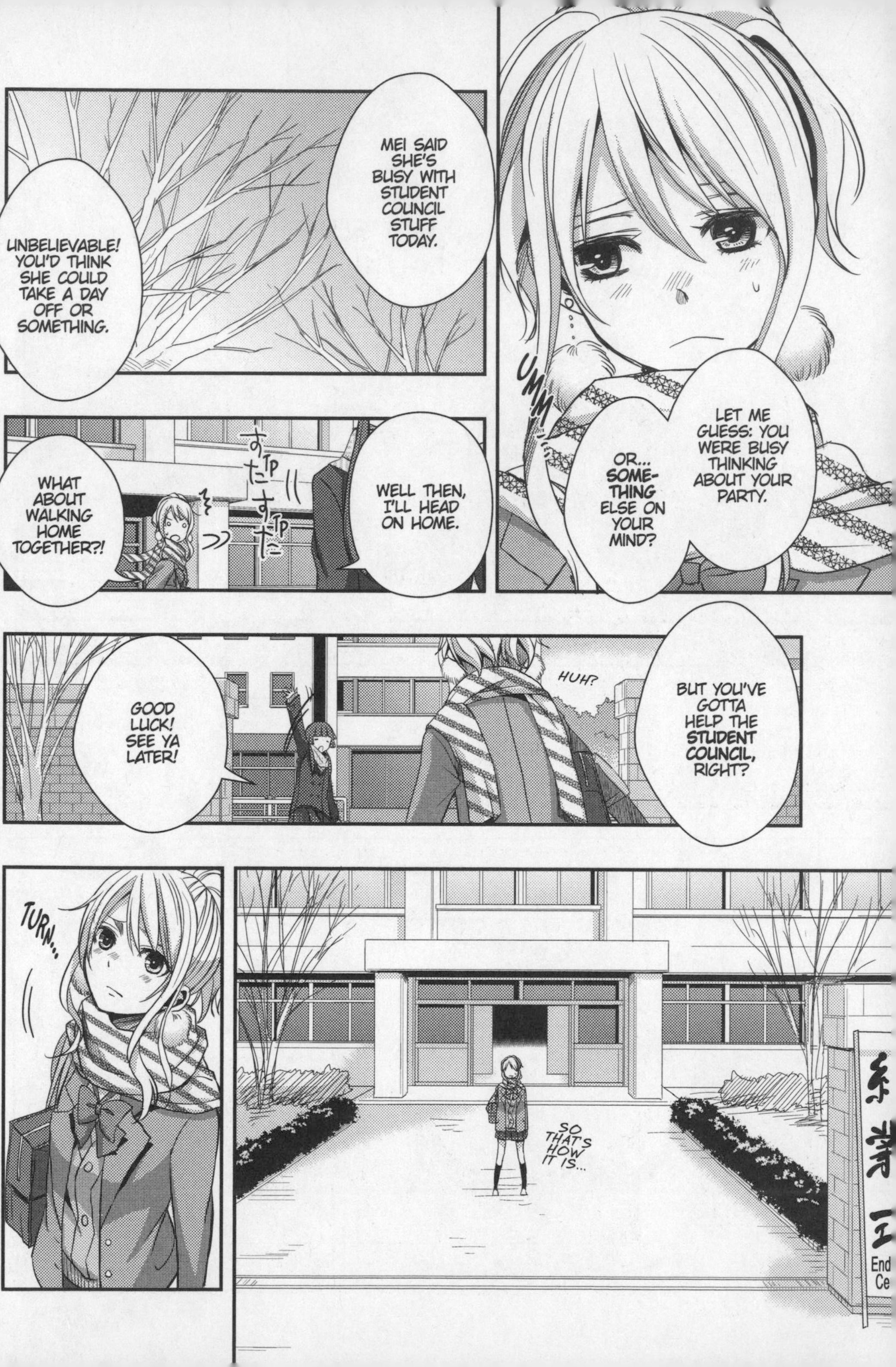

MEI SAID SHE'S BUSY WITH STUDENT COUNCIL STUFF TODAY.
UNBELIEVABLE! YOU'D THINK SHE COULD TAKE A DAY OFF OR SOMETHING.
LET ME GUESS: YOU WERE BUSY THINKING ABOUT YOUR PARTY.
OR... SOMETHING ELSE ON YOUR MIND?
UMMM...
WELL THEN, I'LL HEAD ON HOME.
TP TP
WHAT ABOUT WALKING HOME TOGETHER?!
BUT YOU'VE GOTTA HELP THE STUDENT COUNCIL, RIGHT?
HUH?
GOOD LUCK! SEE YA LATER!
TURN...
SO THAT'S HOW IT IS...
End
Ce

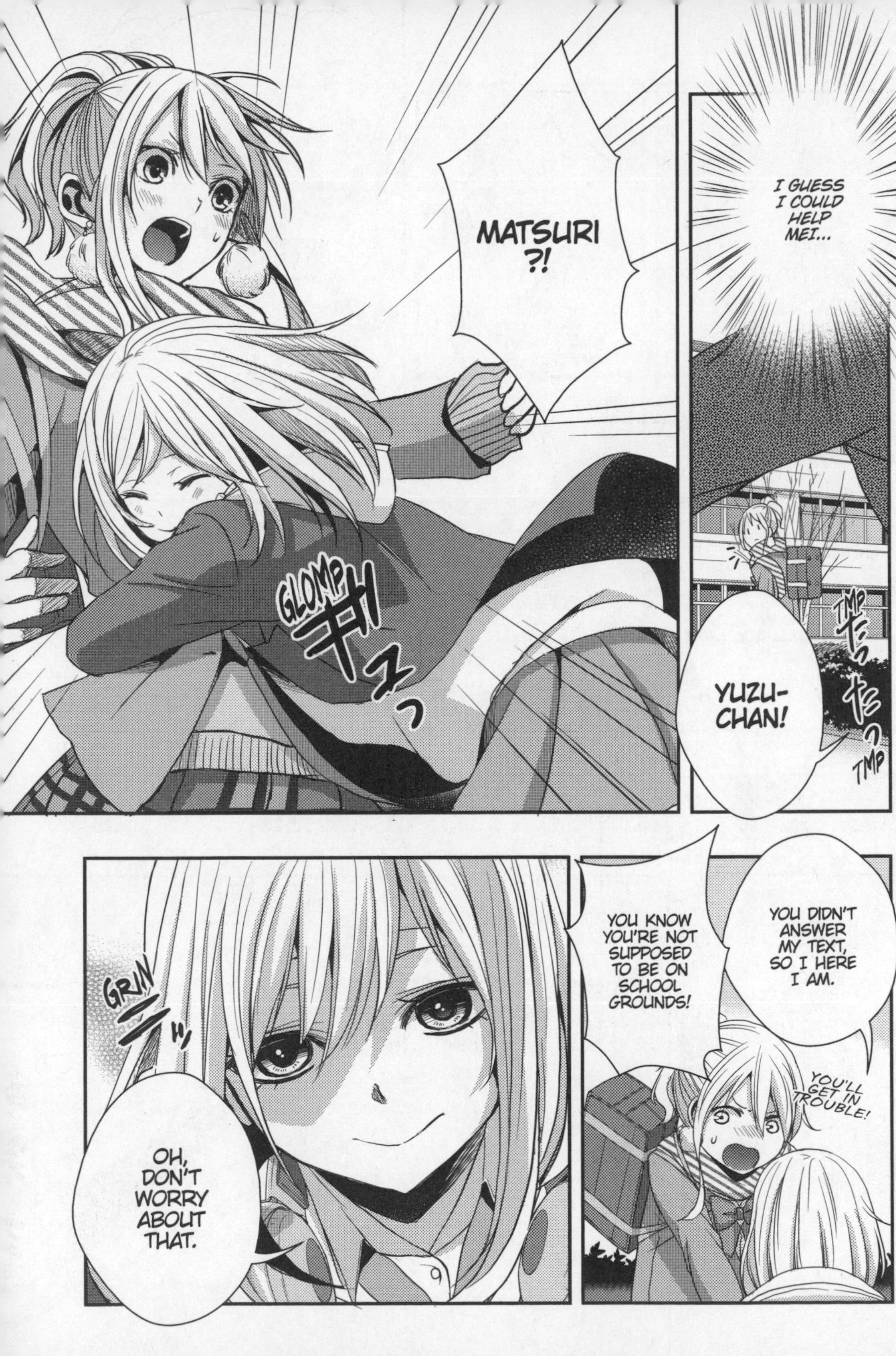
I GUESS I COULD HELP MEI...
YUZU-CHAN!
TMP
TMP
MATSURI ?!
GLOMP
YOU DIDN'T ANSWER MY TEXT, SO I HERE I AM.
YOU KNOW YOU'RE NOT SUPPOSED TO BE ON SCHOOL GROUNDS!
YOU'LL GET IN TROUBLE!
GRIN
OH, DON'T WORRY ABOUT THAT.

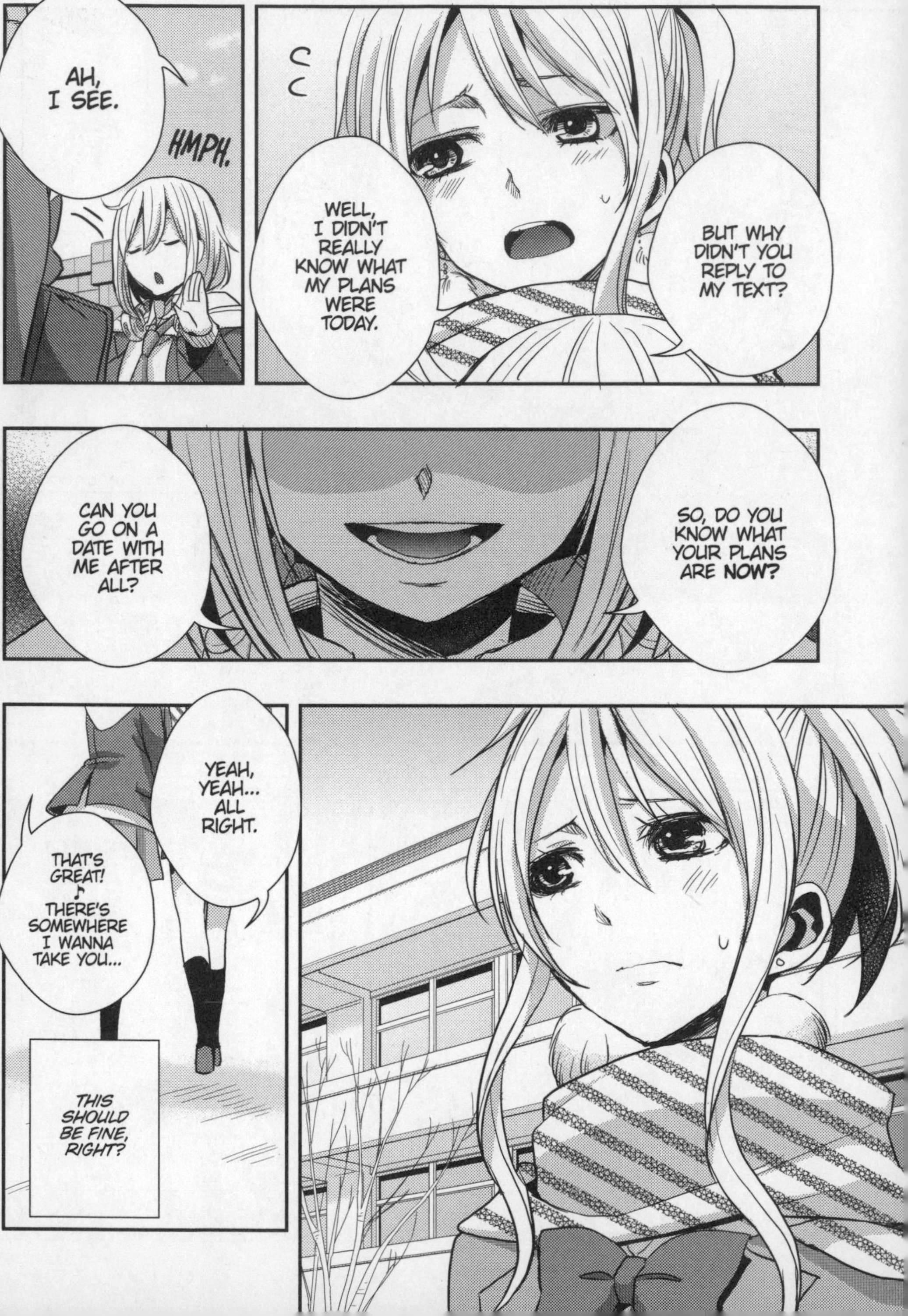
BUT WHY DIDN'T YOU REPLY TO MY TEXT?
WELL, I DIDN'T REALLY KNOW WHAT MY PLANS WERE TODAY.
HMPH.
AH, I SEE.
SO, DO YOU KNOW WHAT YOUR PLANS ARE NOW?
CAN YOU GO ON A DATE WITH ME AFTER ALL?
YEAH, YEAH... ALL RIGHT.
THAT'S GREAT! ♪ THERE'S SOMEWHERE I WANNA TAKE YOU...
THIS SHOULD BE FINE, RIGHT?

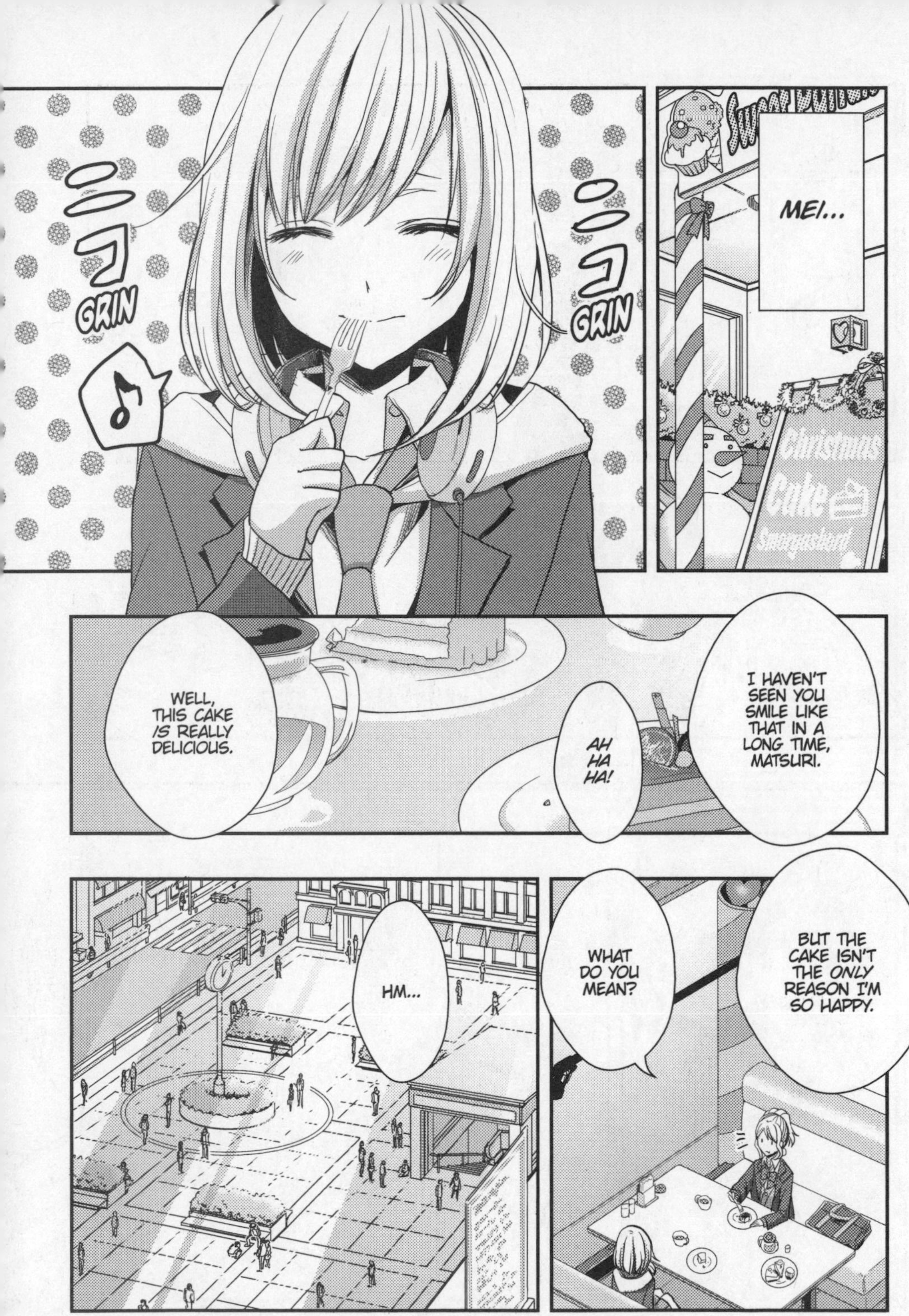
MEI...
Christmas
Cake
ニコ
GRIN
ニコ
GRIN
♪
I HAVEN'T SEEN YOU SMILE LIKE THAT IN A LONG TIME, MATSURI.
AH HA HA!
WELL, THIS CAKE *IS* REALLY DELICIOUS.
BUT THE CAKE ISN'T THE *ONLY* REASON I'M SO HAPPY.
WHAT DO YOU MEAN?
HM...

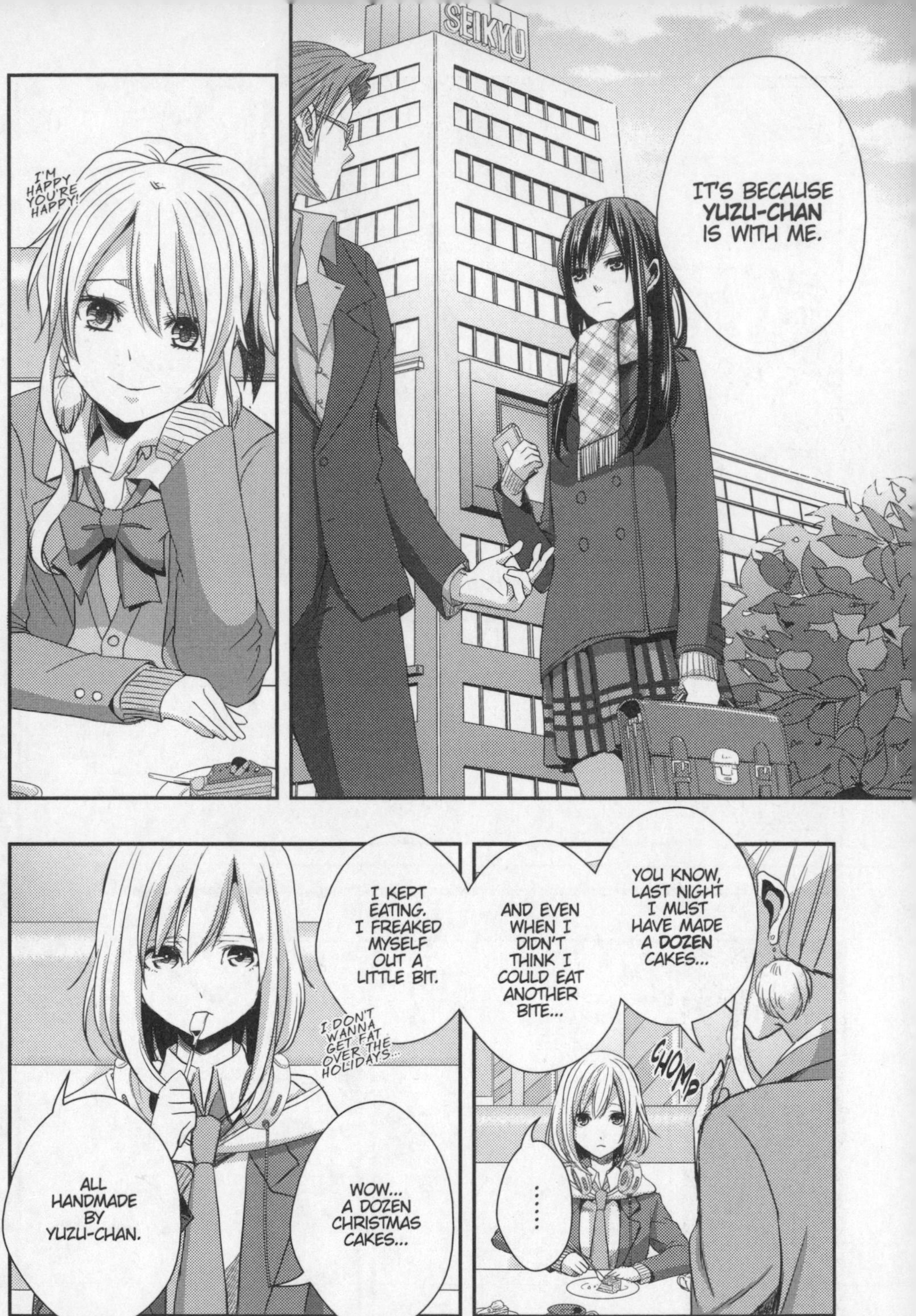
IT'S BECAUSE YUZU-CHAN IS WITH ME.
I'M HAPPY YOU'RE HAPPY!
YOU KNOW, LAST NIGHT I MUST HAVE MADE A DOZEN CAKES...
AND EVEN WHEN I DIDN'T THINK I COULD EAT ANOTHER BITE...
I KEPT EATING. I FREAKED MYSELF OUT A LITTLE BIT.
CHOMP
......
I DON'T WANNA GET FAT OVER THE HOLIDAYS...
WOW... A DOZEN CHRISTMAS CAKES...
ALL HANDMADE BY YUZU-CHAN.

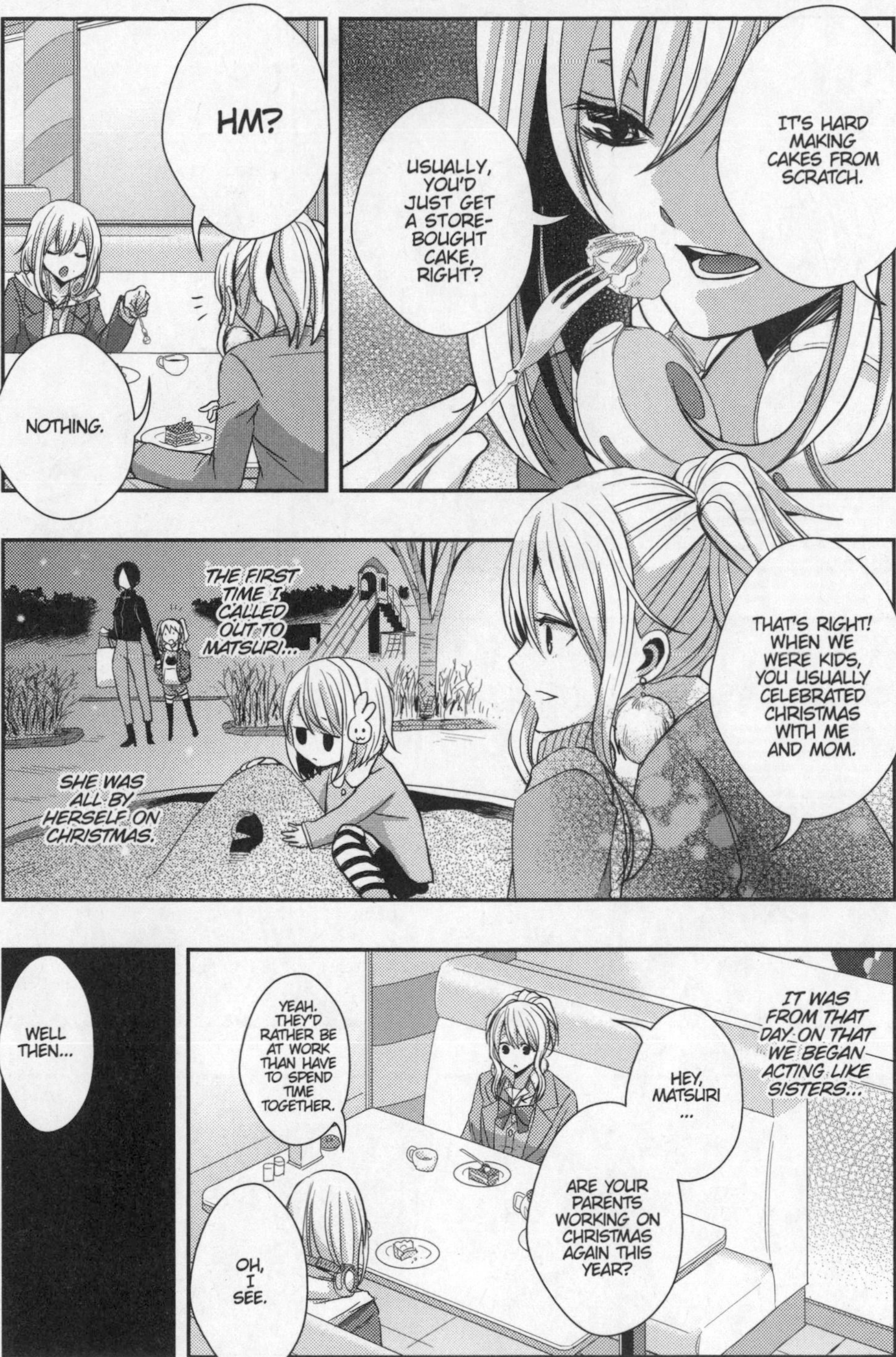
IT'S HARD MAKING CAKES FROM SCRATCH.
USUALLY, YOU'D JUST GET A STORE-BOUGHT CAKE, RIGHT?
HM?
NOTHING.
THAT'S RIGHT! WHEN WE WERE KIDS, YOU USUALLY CELEBRATED CHRISTMAS WITH ME AND MOM.
THE FIRST TIME I CALLED OUT TO MATSURI...
SHE WAS ALL BY HERSELF ON CHRISTMAS.
IT WAS FROM THAT DAY ON THAT WE BEGAN ACTING LIKE SISTERS...
HEY, MATSURI...
ARE YOUR PARENTS WORKING ON CHRISTMAS AGAIN THIS YEAR?
YEAH. THEY'D RATHER BE AT WORK THAN HAVE TO SPEND TIME TOGETHER.
OH, I SEE.
WELL THEN...

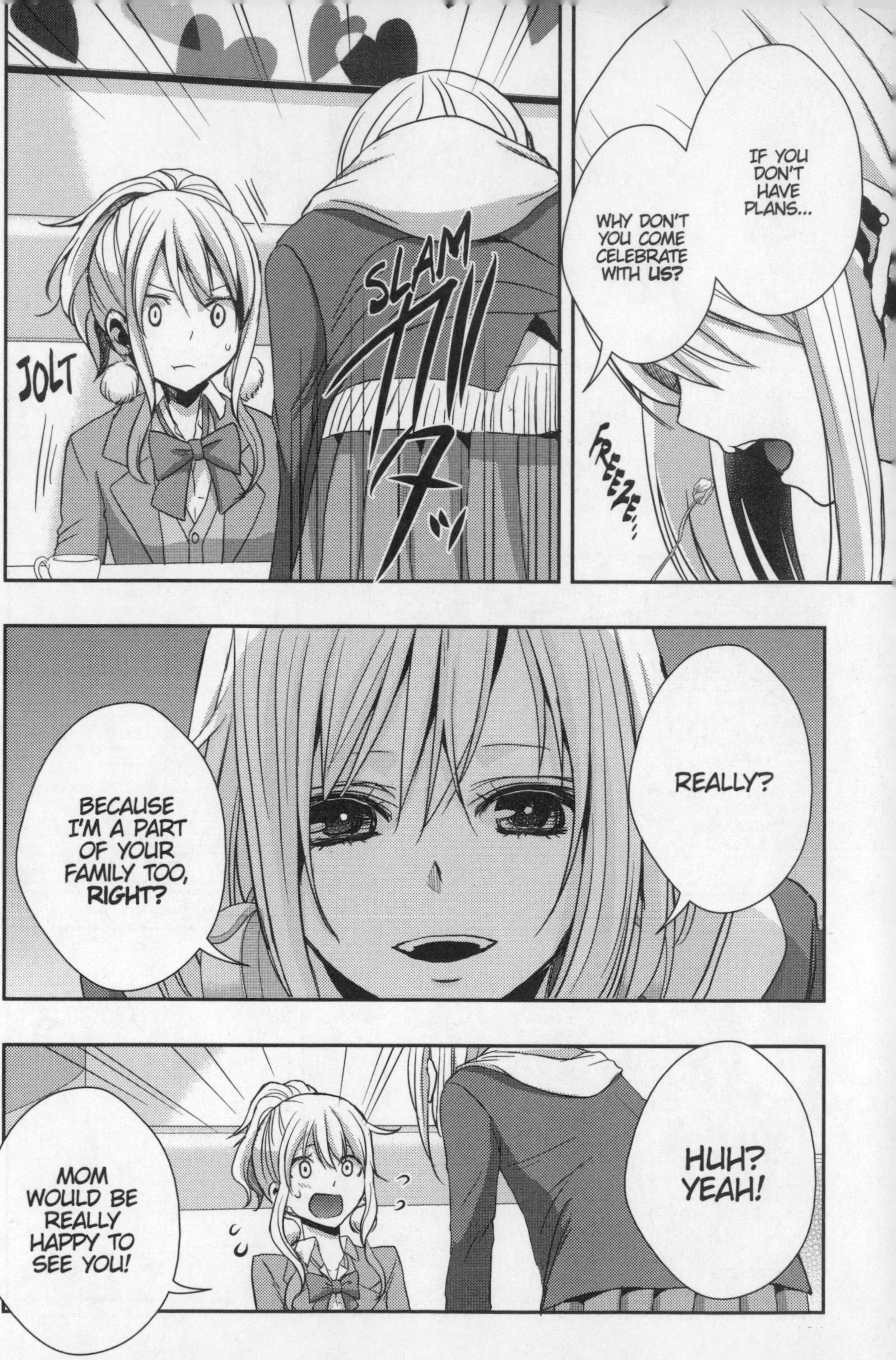
IF YOU DON'T HAVE PLANS...
WHY DON'T YOU COME CELEBRATE WITH US?
FREEZE...
SLAM
JOLT
REALLY?
BECAUSE I'M A PART OF YOUR FAMILY TOO, RIGHT?
HUH? YEAH!
MOM WOULD BE REALLY HAPPY TO SEE YOU!

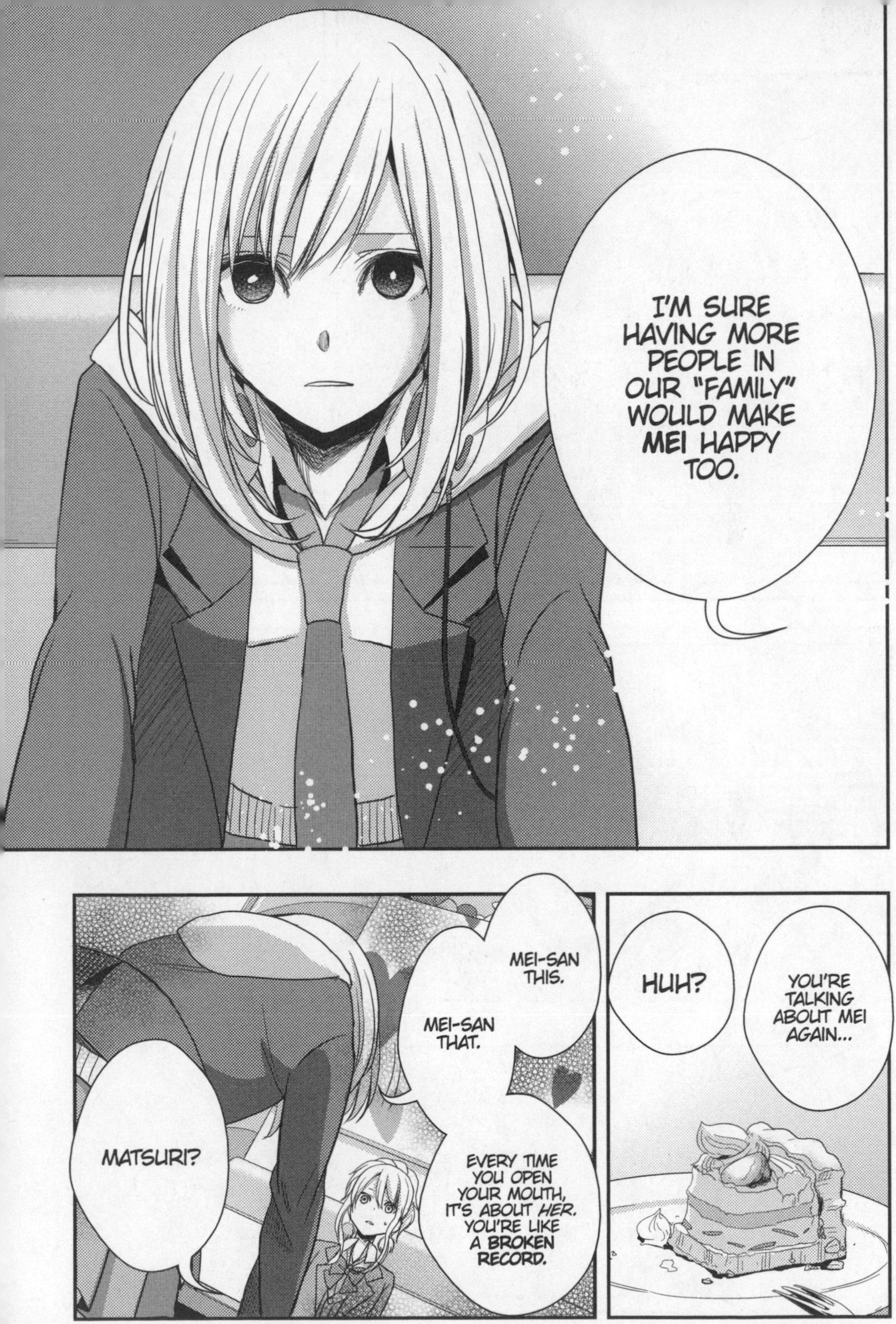
I'M SURE HAVING MORE PEOPLE IN OUR "FAMILY" WOULD MAKE MEI HAPPY TOO.
YOU'RE TALKING ABOUT MEI AGAIN...
HUH?
MEI-SAN THIS.
MEI-SAN THAT.
EVERY TIME YOU OPEN YOUR MOUTH, IT'S ABOUT *HER*. YOU'RE LIKE A BROKEN RECORD.
MATSURI?

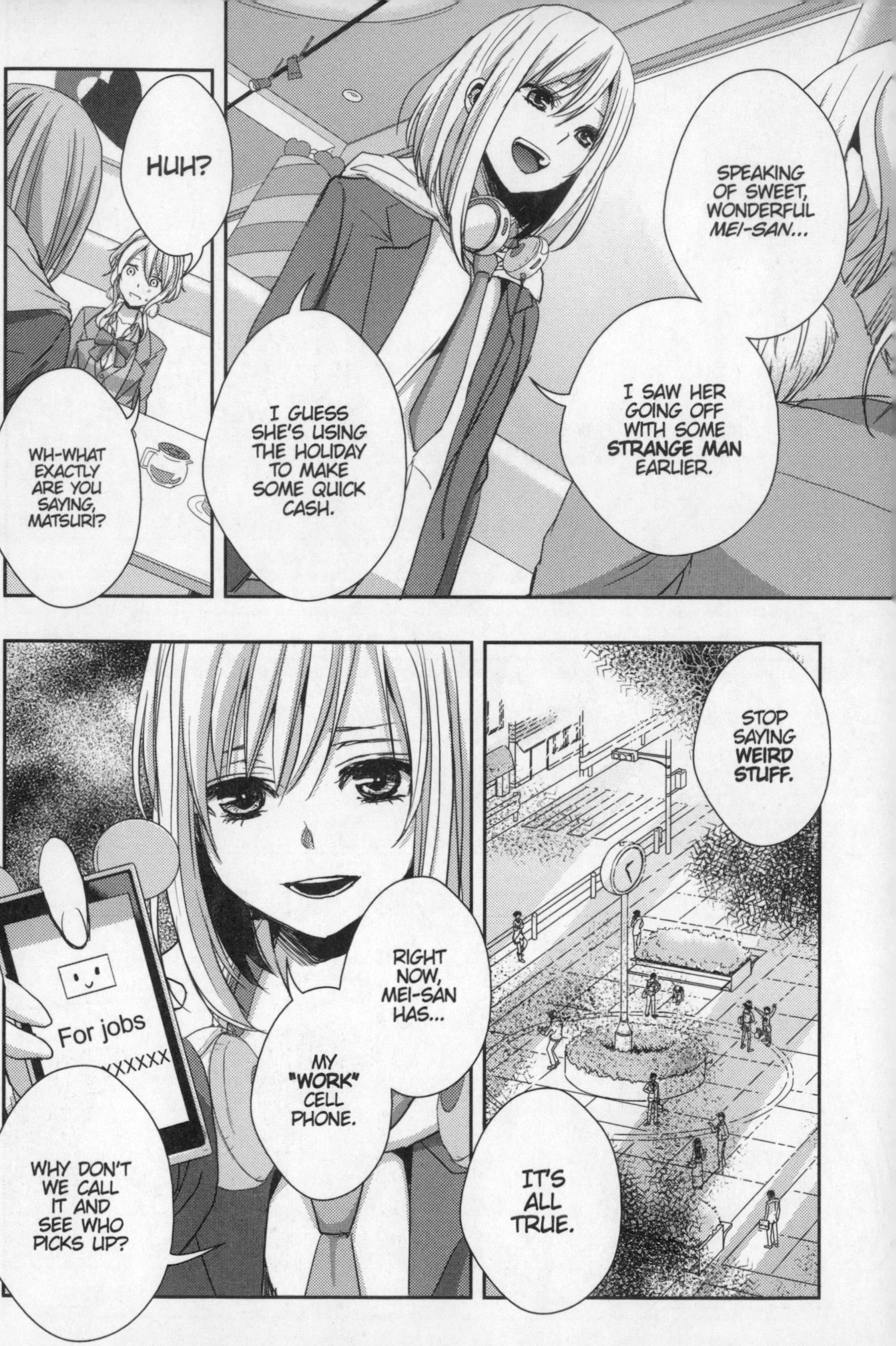
SPEAKING OF SWEET, WONDERFUL MEI-SAN...
I SAW HER GOING OFF WITH SOME STRANGE MAN EARLIER.
I GUESS SHE'S USING THE HOLIDAY TO MAKE SOME QUICK CASH.
HUH?
WH-WHAT EXACTLY ARE YOU SAYING, MATSURI?
STOP SAYING WEIRD STUFF.
IT'S ALL TRUE.
RIGHT NOW, MEI-SAN HAS...
MY "WORK" CELL PHONE.
For jobs
XXXXXX
WHY DON'T WE CALL IT AND SEE WHO PICKS UP?

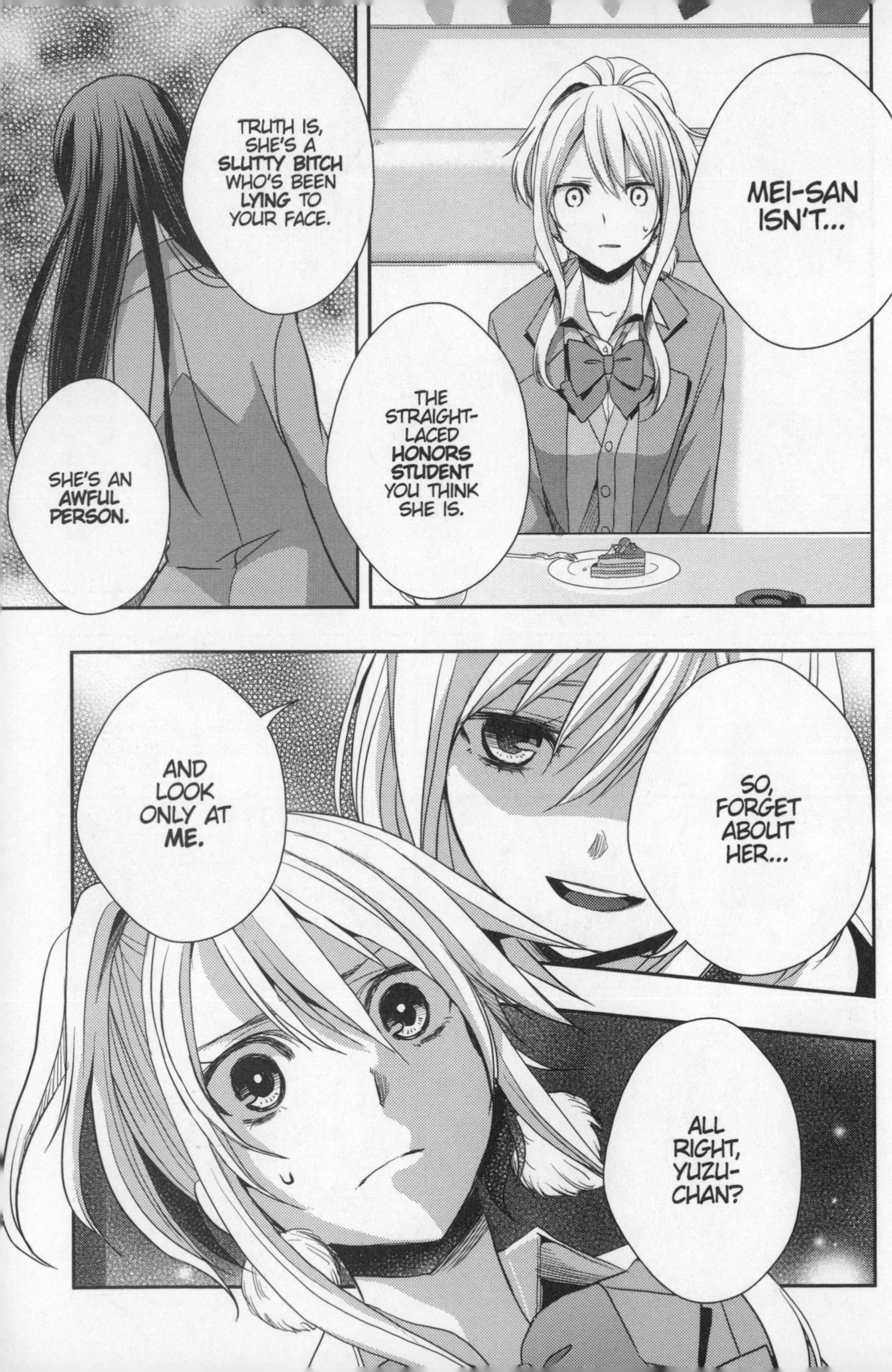
MEI-SAN ISN'T...
THE STRAIGHT-LACED HONORS STUDENT YOU THINK SHE IS.
TRUTH IS, SHE'S A SLUTTY BITCH WHO'S BEEN LYING TO YOUR FACE.
SHE'S AN AWFUL PERSON.
SO, FORGET ABOUT HER...
AND LOOK ONLY AT ME.
ALL RIGHT, YUZU-CHAN?

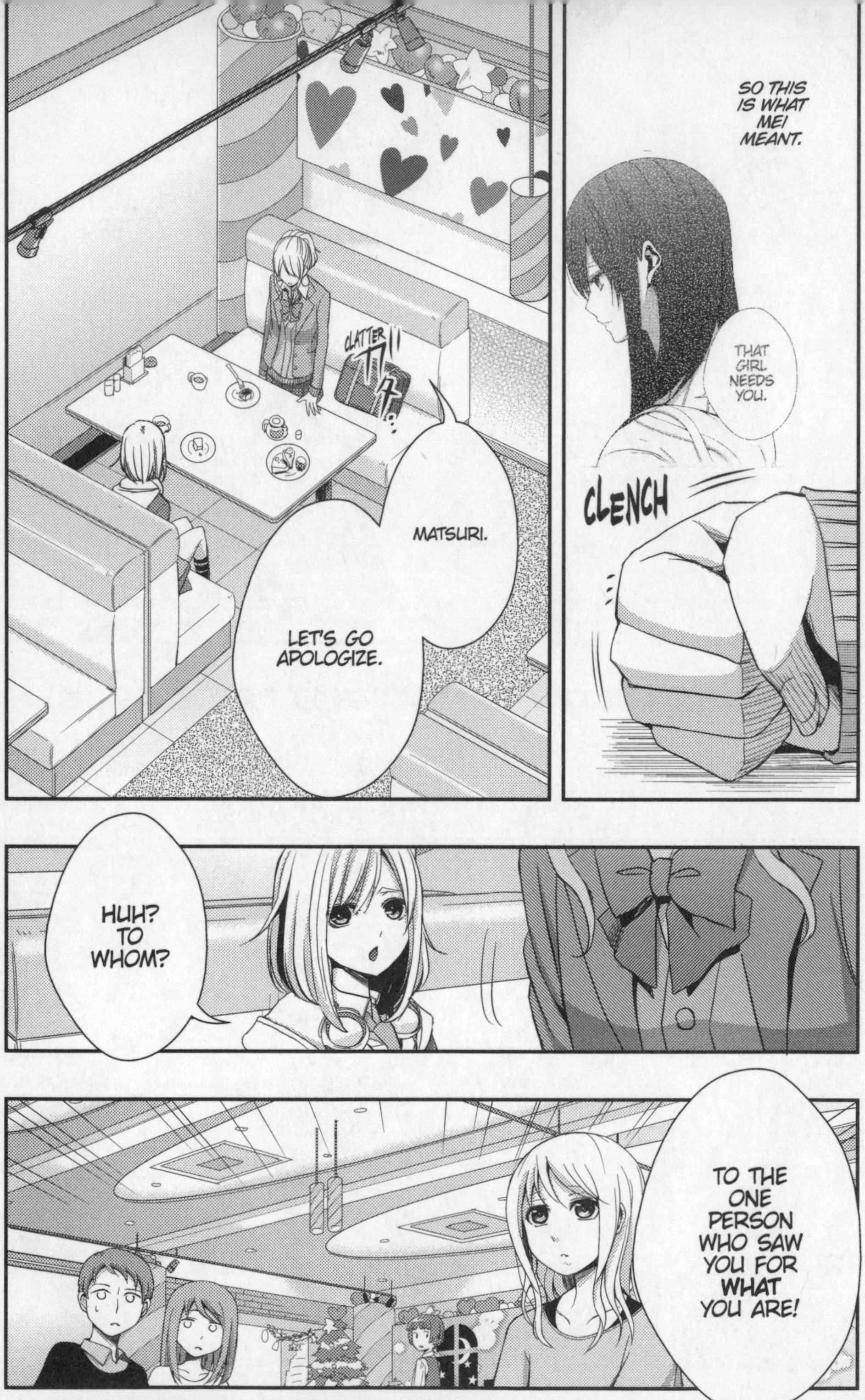
SO THIS IS WHAT MEI MEANT.
THAT GIRL NEEDS YOU.
CLENCH
CLATTER
MATSURI.
LET'S GO APOLOGIZE.
HUH? TO WHOM?
TO THE ONE PERSON WHO SAW YOU FOR WHAT YOU ARE!

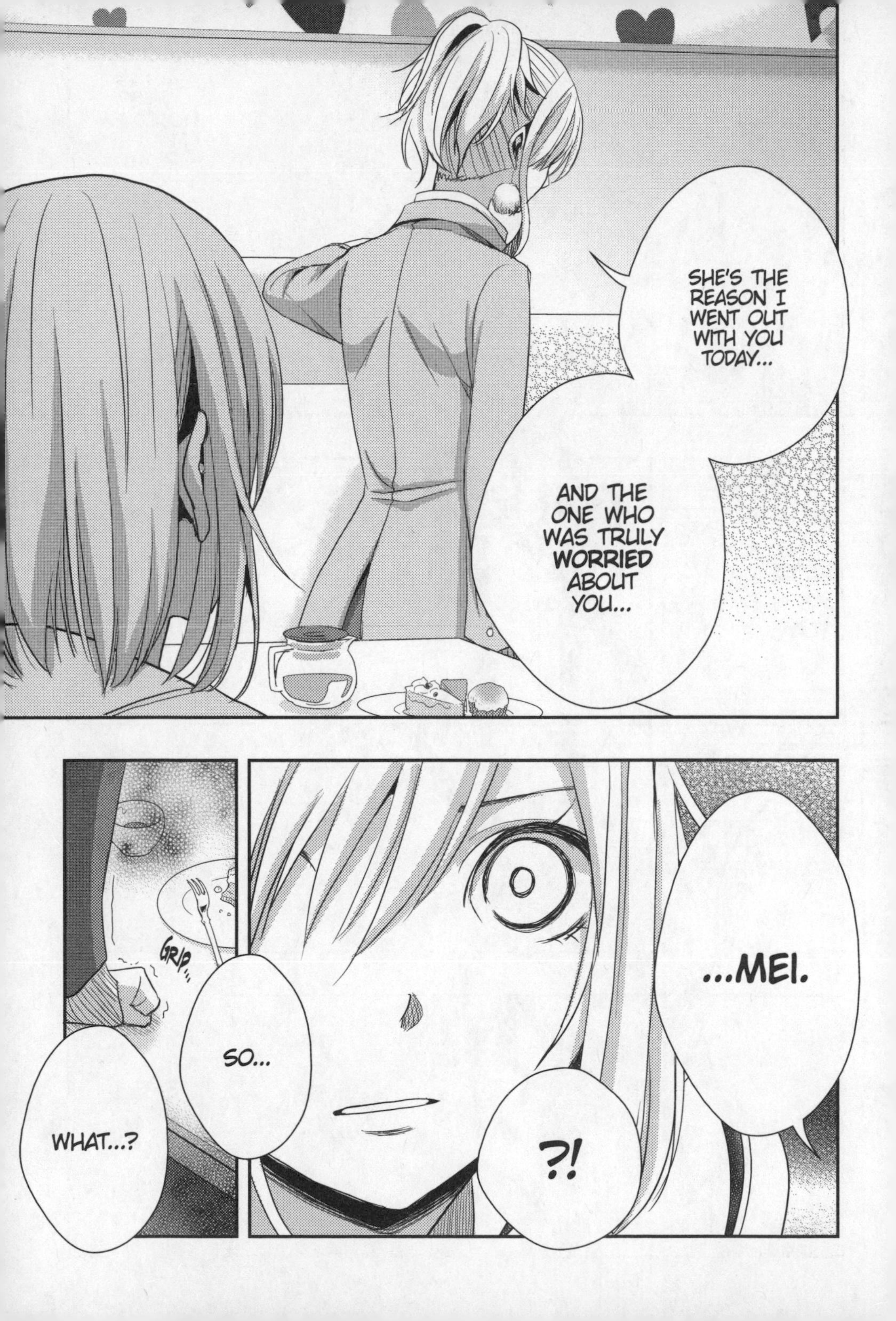
SHE'S THE REASON I WENT OUT WITH YOU TODAY...
AND THE ONE WHO WAS TRULY WORRIED ABOUT YOU...
...MEI.
?!
SO...
GRIP
WHAT...?

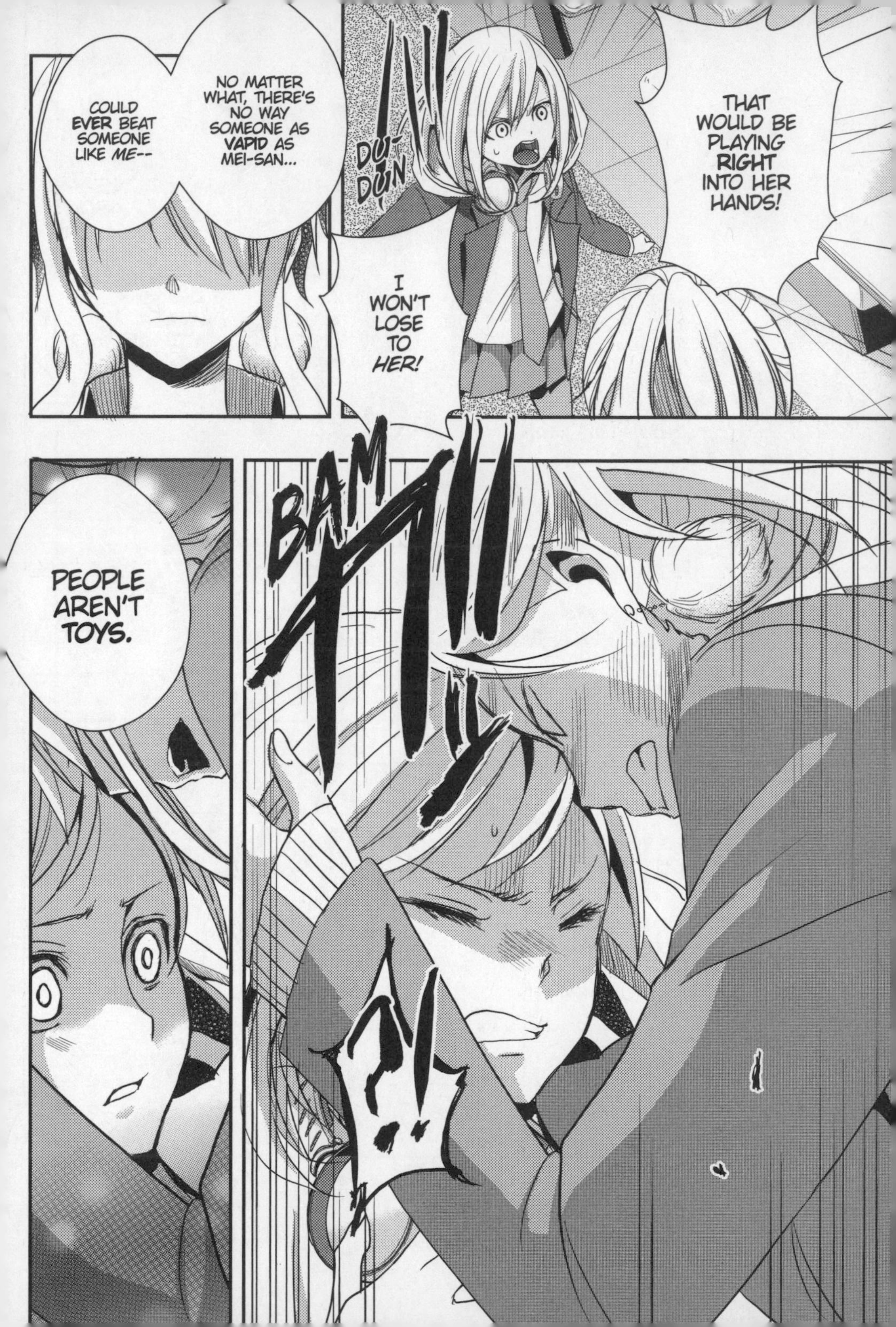
THAT WOULD BE PLAYING RIGHT INTO HER HANDS!
DU-DUN
NO MATTER WHAT, THERE'S NO WAY SOMEONE AS VAPID AS MEI-SAN...
I WON'T LOSE TO HER!
COULD EVER BEAT SOMEONE LIKE ME--
BAM
?!
PEOPLE AREN'T TOYS.

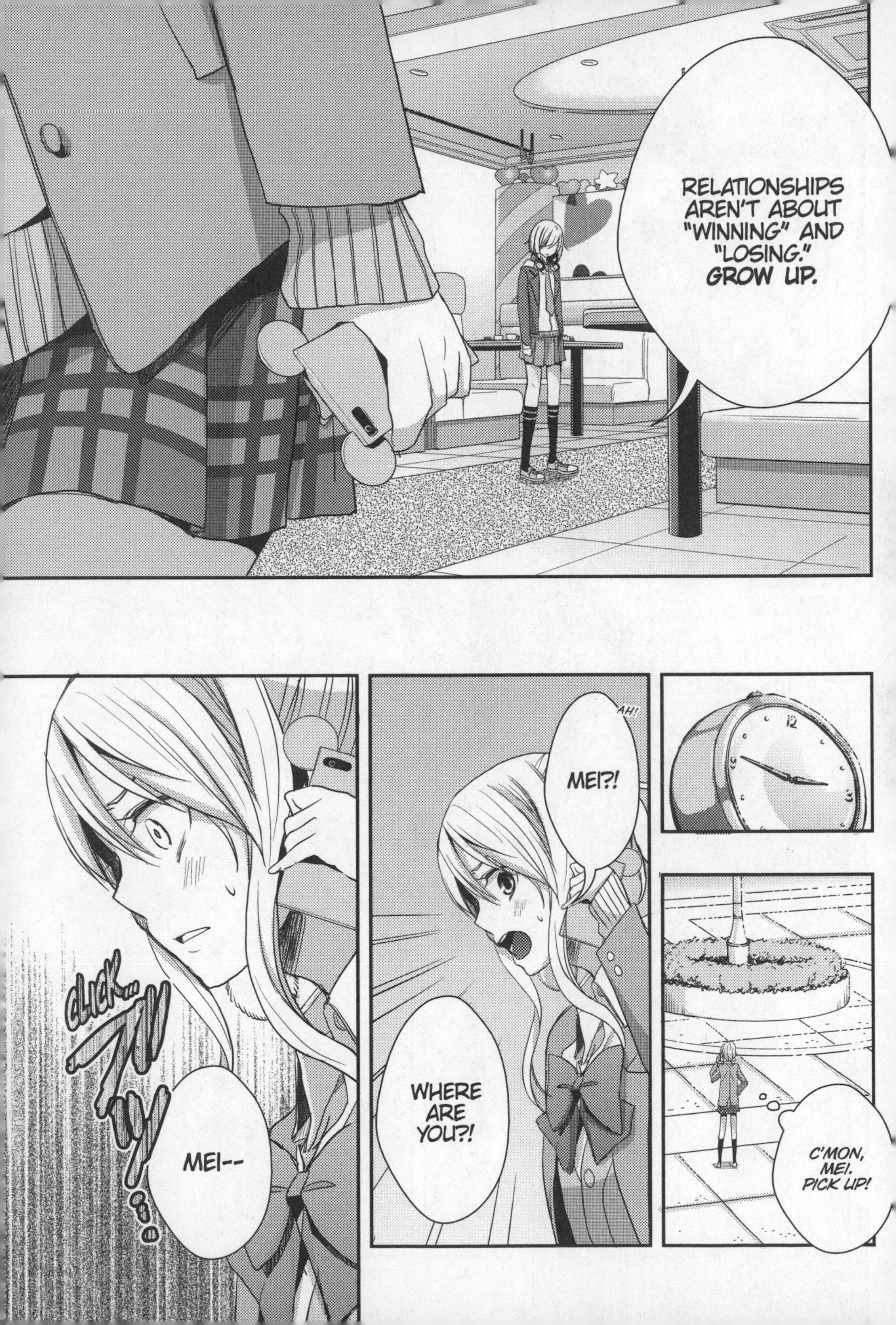
RELATIONSHIPS AREN'T ABOUT "WINNING" AND "LOSING." GROW UP.
C'MON, MEI. PICK UP!
AH!
MEI?!
WHERE ARE YOU?!
CLICK...
MEI--

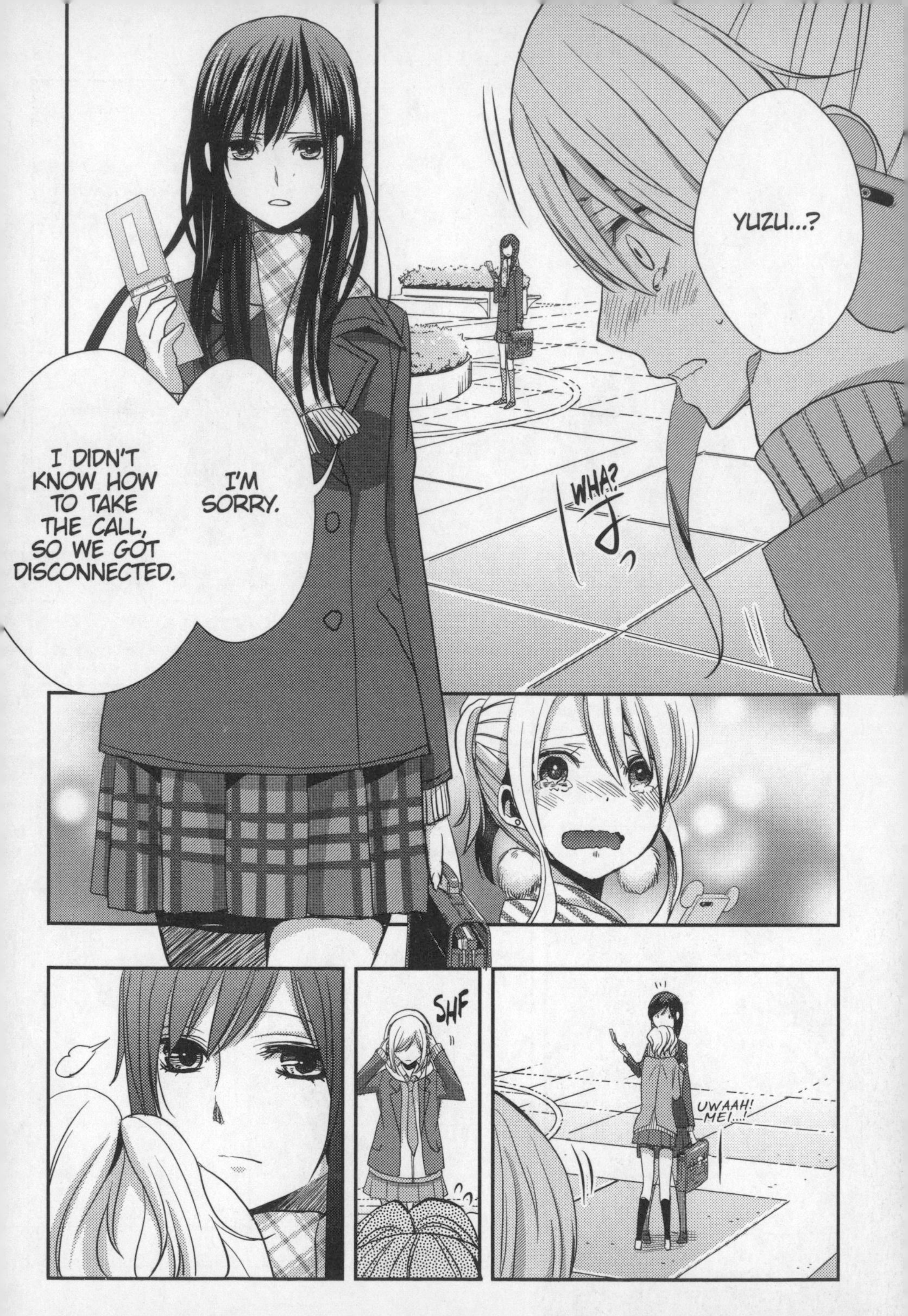
YUZU...?
WHA?
I'M SORRY.
I DIDN'T KNOW HOW TO TAKE THE CALL, SO WE GOT DISCONNECTED.
UWAAH! MEI...!
SHF

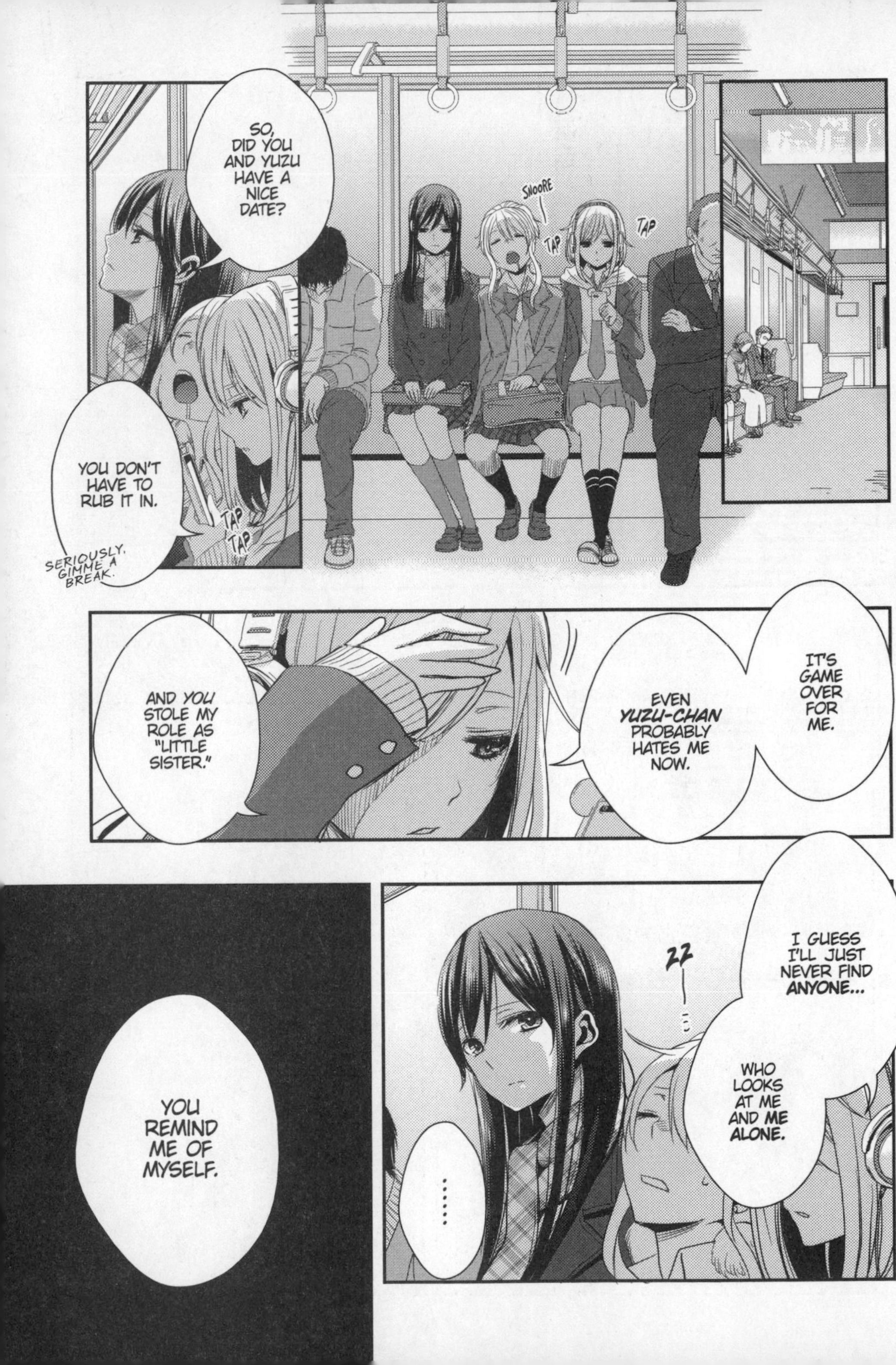
SNOORE
TAP
TAP
SO, DID YOU AND YUZU HAVE A NICE DATE?
YOU DON'T HAVE TO RUB IT IN.
TAP TAP
SERIOUSLY, GIMME A BREAK.
IT'S GAME OVER FOR ME.
EVEN YUZU-CHAN PROBABLY HATES ME NOW.
AND YOU STOLE MY ROLE AS "LITTLE SISTER."
I GUESS I'LL JUST NEVER FIND ANYONE...
WHO LOOKS AT ME AND ME ALONE.
ZZ
......
YOU REMIND ME OF MYSELF.

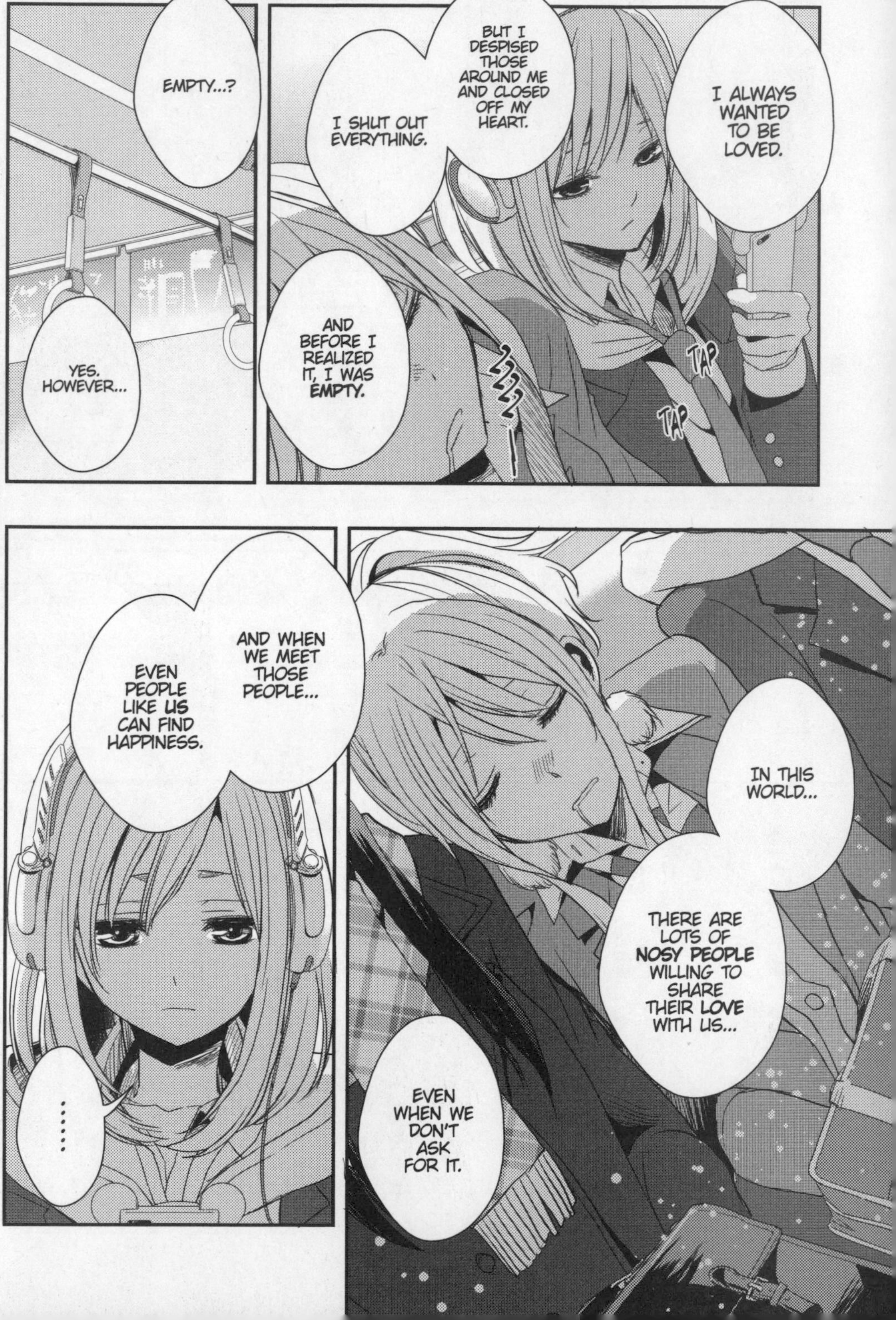
I ALWAYS WANTED TO BE LOVED.
BUT I DESPISED THOSE AROUND ME AND CLOSED OFF MY HEART.
I SHUT OUT EVERYTHING.
TAP
TAP
AND BEFORE I REALIZED IT, I WAS **EMPTY.**
EMPTY...?
YES. HOWEVER...
IN THIS WORLD...
THERE ARE LOTS OF **NOSY PEOPLE** WILLING TO SHARE THEIR **LOVE** WITH US...
EVEN WHEN WE DON'T ASK FOR IT.
AND WHEN WE MEET THOSE PEOPLE...
EVEN PEOPLE LIKE **US** CAN FIND HAPPINESS.
......

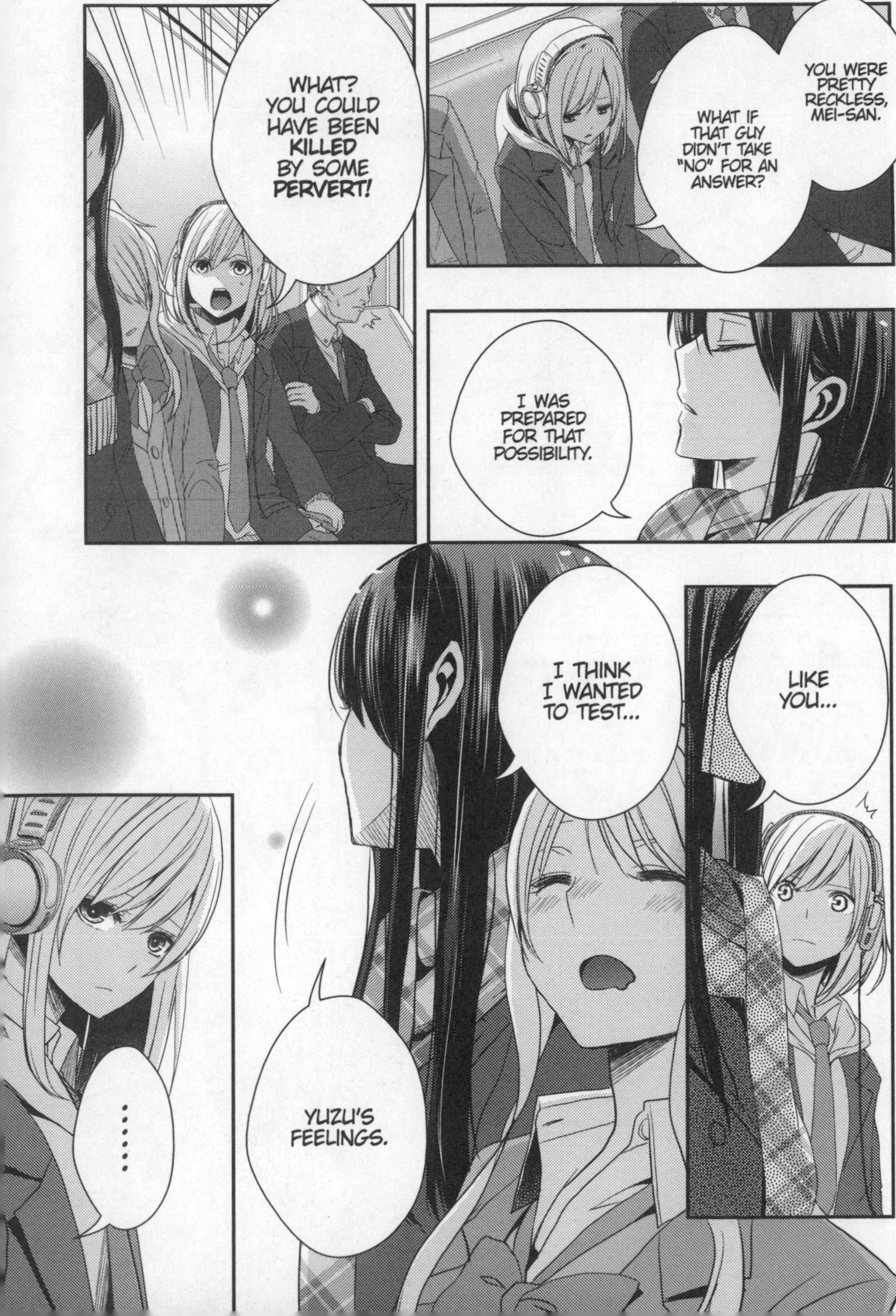
YOU WERE PRETTY RECKLESS, MEI-SAN.
WHAT IF THAT GUY DIDN'T TAKE "NO" FOR AN ANSWER?
I WAS PREPARED FOR THAT POSSIBILITY.
WHAT? YOU COULD HAVE BEEN KILLED BY SOME PERVERT!
LIKE YOU...
I THINK I WANTED TO TEST...
YUZU'S FEELINGS.
......

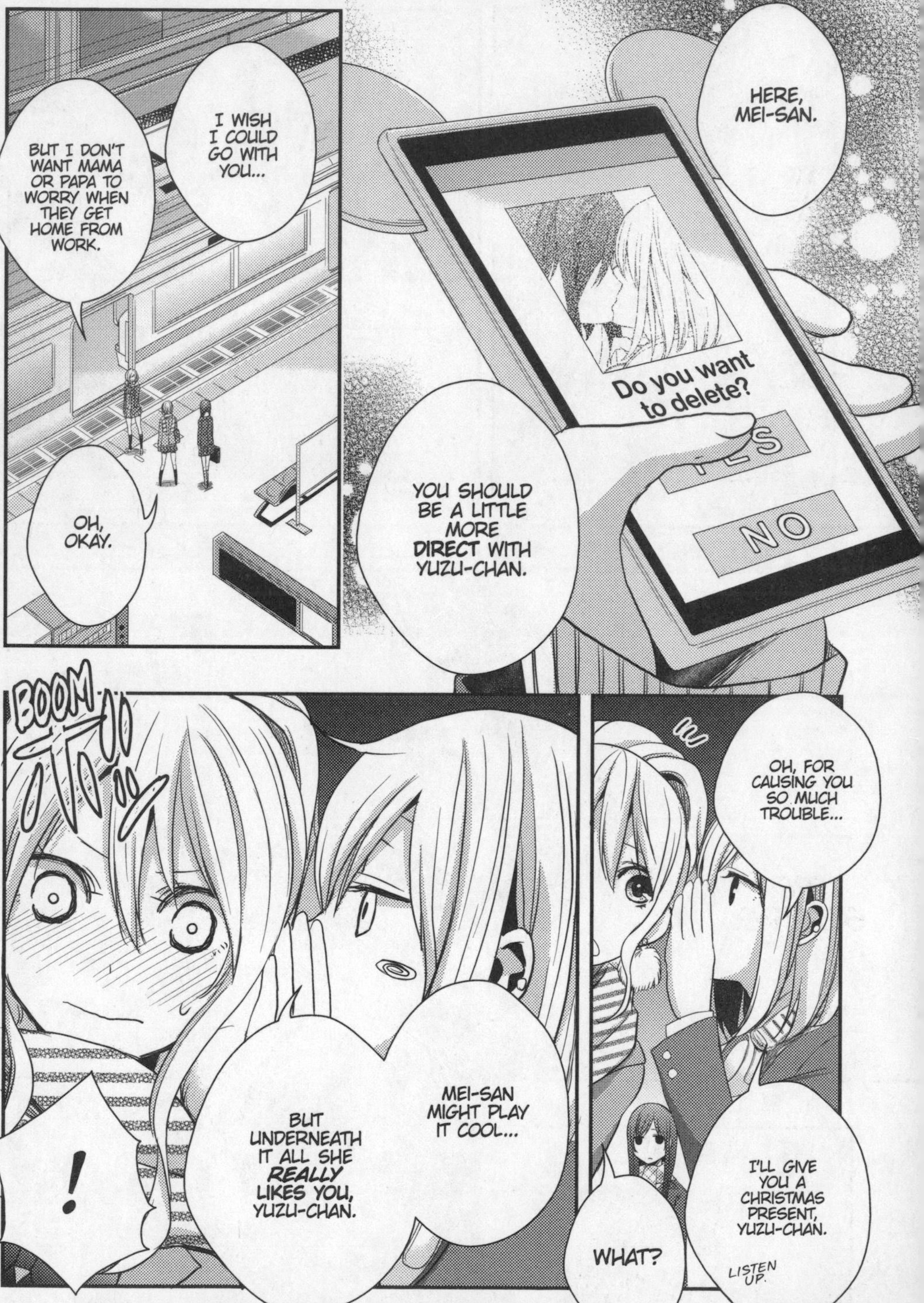
HERE, MEI-SAN.
Do you want to delete?
NO
YOU SHOULD BE A LITTLE MORE **DIRECT** WITH YUZU-CHAN.
I WISH I COULD GO WITH YOU...
BUT I DON'T WANT MAMA OR PAPA TO WORRY WHEN THEY GET HOME FROM WORK.
OH, OKAY.
OH, FOR CAUSING YOU SO MUCH TROUBLE...
I'LL GIVE YOU A CHRISTMAS PRESENT, YUZU-CHAN.
LISTEN UP.
WHAT?
MEI-SAN MIGHT PLAY IT COOL...
BUT UNDERNEATH IT ALL SHE ***REALLY*** LIKES YOU, YUZU-CHAN.
BOOM
!

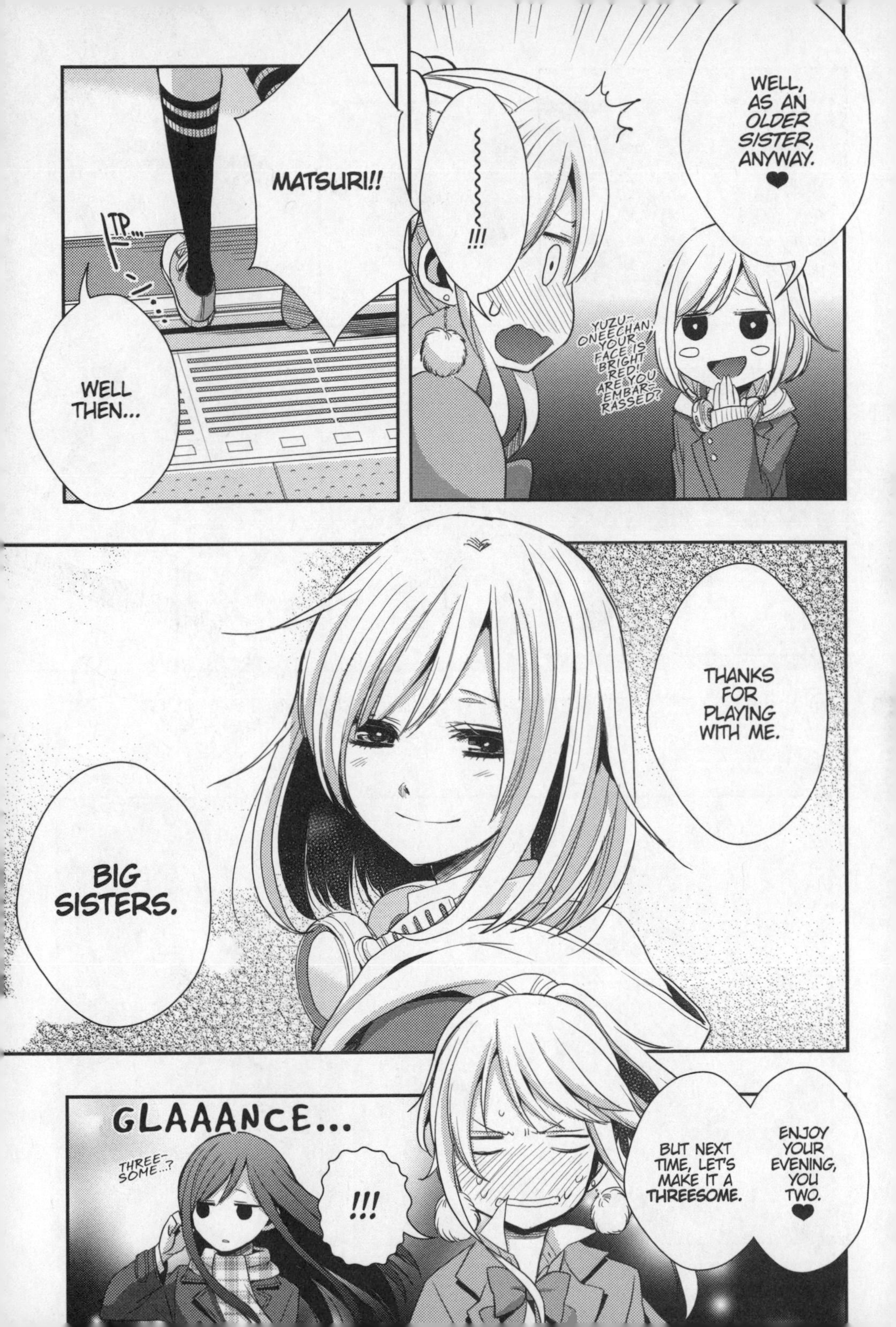
WELL, AS AN OLDER SISTER, ANYWAY. ❤
!!!
YUZU-ONEECHAN, YOUR FACE IS BRIGHT RED! ARE YOU EMBARRASSED?
MATSURI!!
TP...
WELL THEN...
THANKS FOR PLAYING WITH ME.
BIG SISTERS.
ENJOY YOUR EVENING, YOU TWO. ❤
BUT NEXT TIME, LET'S MAKE IT A THREESOME.
!!!
GLAAANCE...
THREE-SOME...?

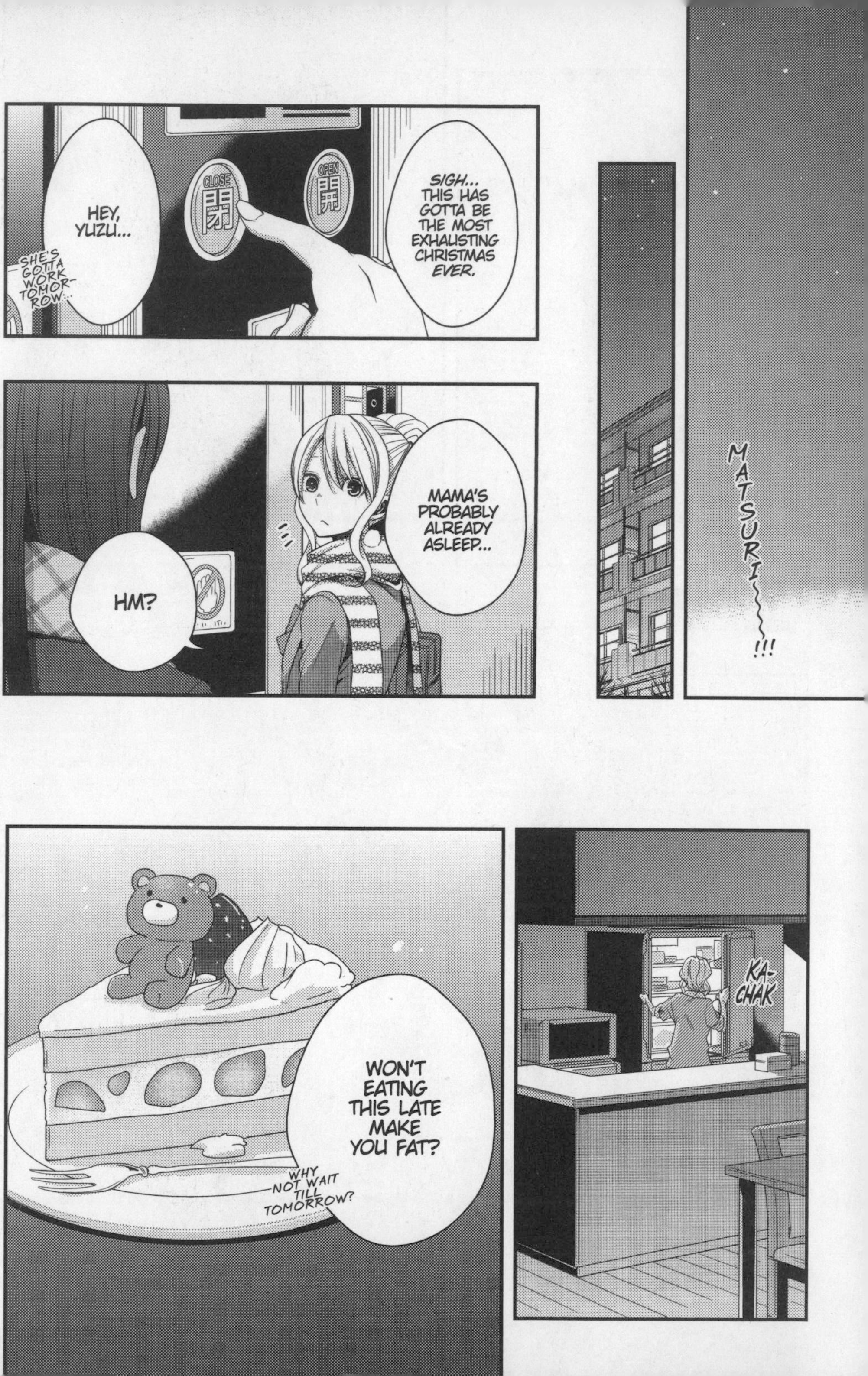

MATSURI~~~!!!
SIGH... THIS HAS GOTTA BE THE MOST EXHAUSTING CHRISTMAS EVER.
CLOSE 閉
OPEN 開
HEY, YUZU...
—SHE'S GOTTA WORK TOMOR-ROW...
MAMA'S PROBABLY ALREADY ASLEEP...
HM?
KA-CHAK
WON'T EATING THIS LATE MAKE YOU FAT?
WHY NOT WAIT TILL TOMORROW?

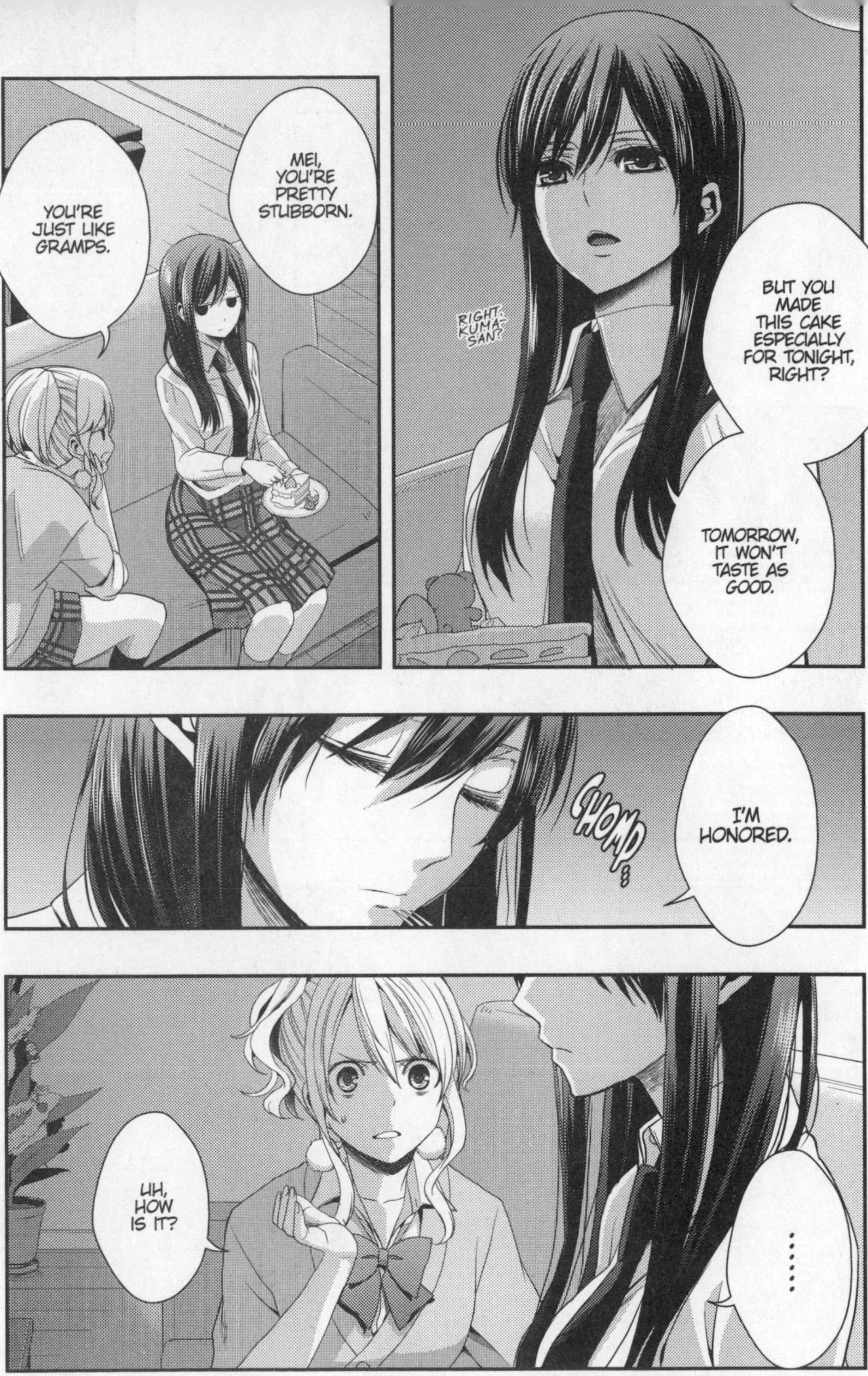
BUT YOU MADE THIS CAKE ESPECIALLY FOR TONIGHT, RIGHT?
RIGHT, KUMA-SAN?
TOMORROW, IT WON'T TASTE AS GOOD.
MEI, YOU'RE PRETTY STUBBORN.
YOU'RE JUST LIKE GRAMPS.
I'M HONORED.
CHOMP
......
UH, HOW IS IT?

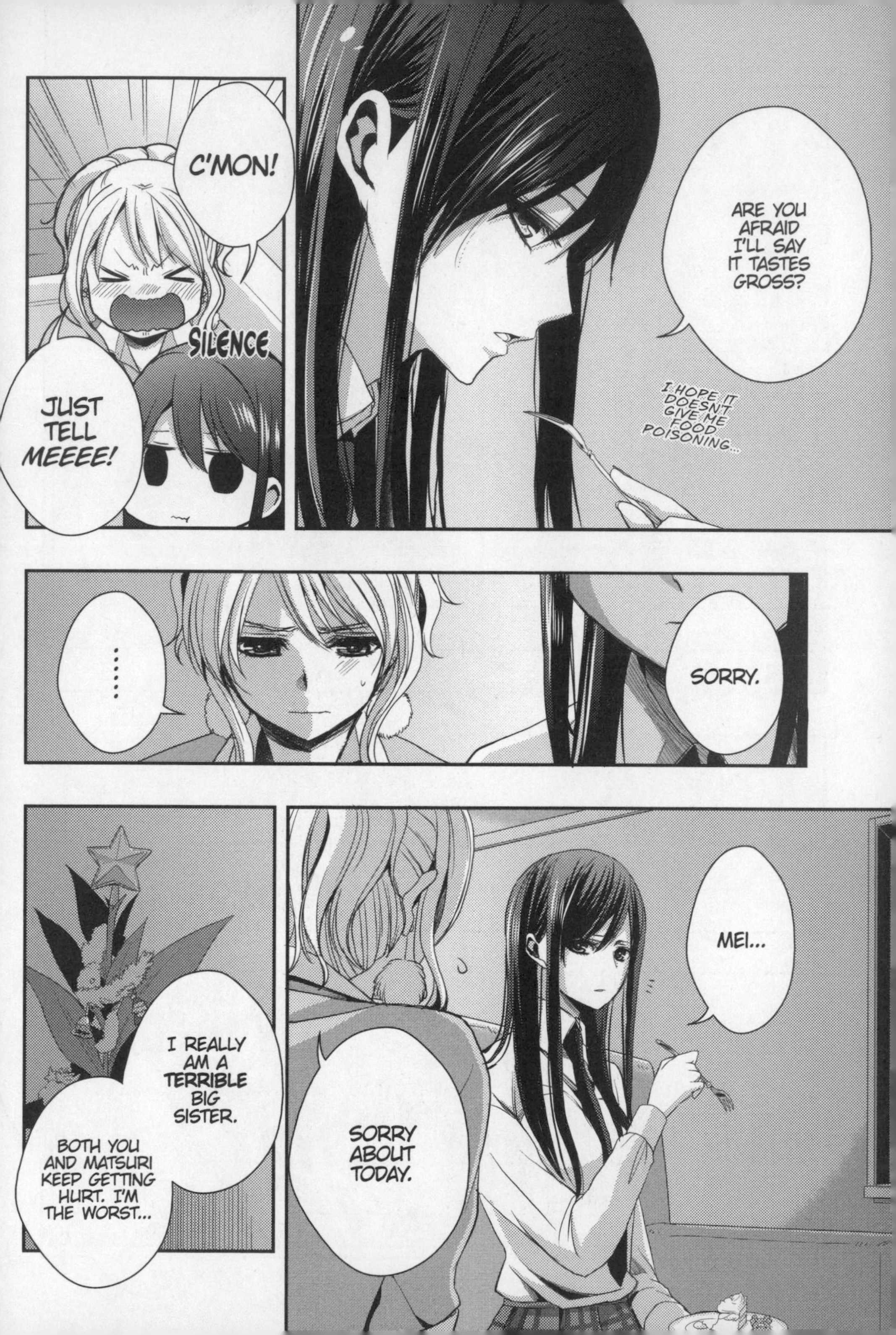
ARE YOU AFRAID I'LL SAY IT TASTES GROSS?
I HOPE IT DOESN'T GIVE ME FOOD POISONING...
C'MON!
SILENCE
JUST TELL MEEEE!
SORRY.
......
MEI...
SORRY ABOUT TODAY.
I REALLY AM A TERRIBLE BIG SISTER.
BOTH YOU AND MATSURI KEEP GETTING HURT. I'M THE WORST...

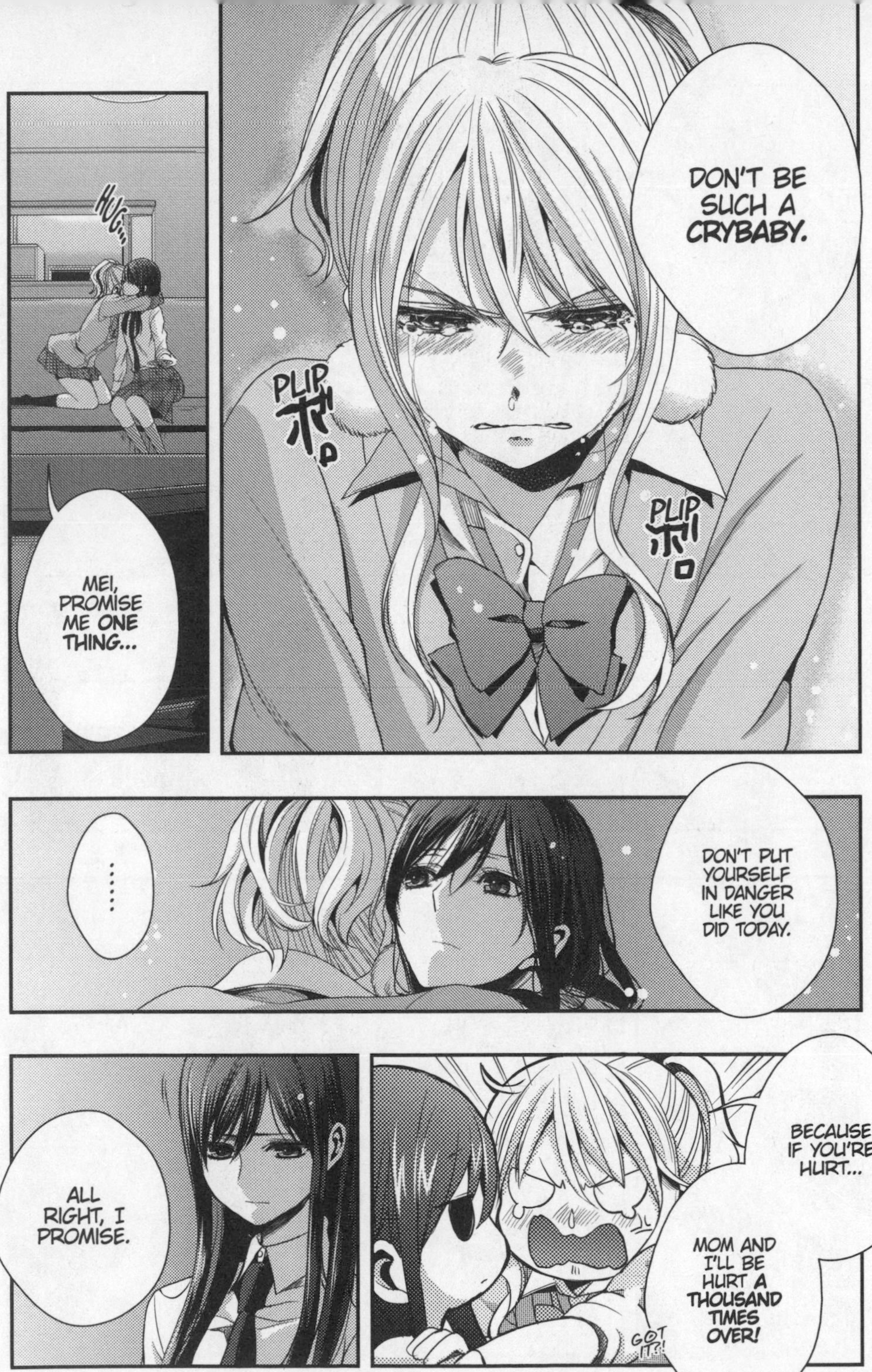
DON'T BE SUCH A CRYBABY.
PLIP ポロ
PLIP ポロ
HUG...
MEI, PROMISE ME ONE THING...
DON'T PUT YOURSELF IN DANGER LIKE YOU DID TODAY.
......
BECAUSE IF YOU'RE HURT...
MOM AND I'LL BE HURT A THOUSAND TIMES OVER!
GOT IT?!
ALL RIGHT, I PROMISE.

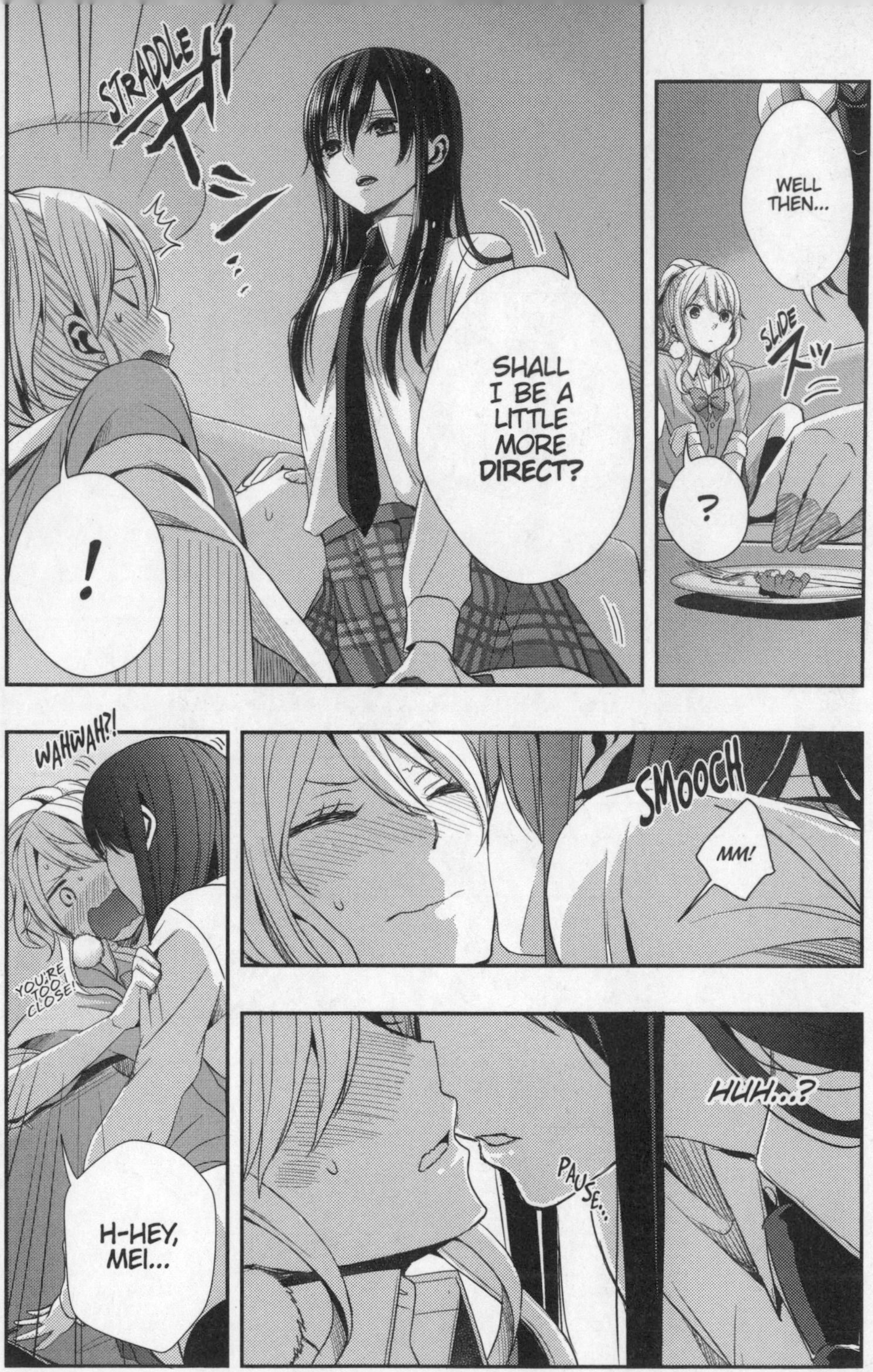
WELL THEN...
SLIDE
?
STRADDLE
SHALL I BE A LITTLE MORE DIRECT?
!
SMOOCH
MM!
HUH...?
PAUSE...
WAHWAH?!
YOU'RE TOO CLOSE!
H-HEY, MEI...

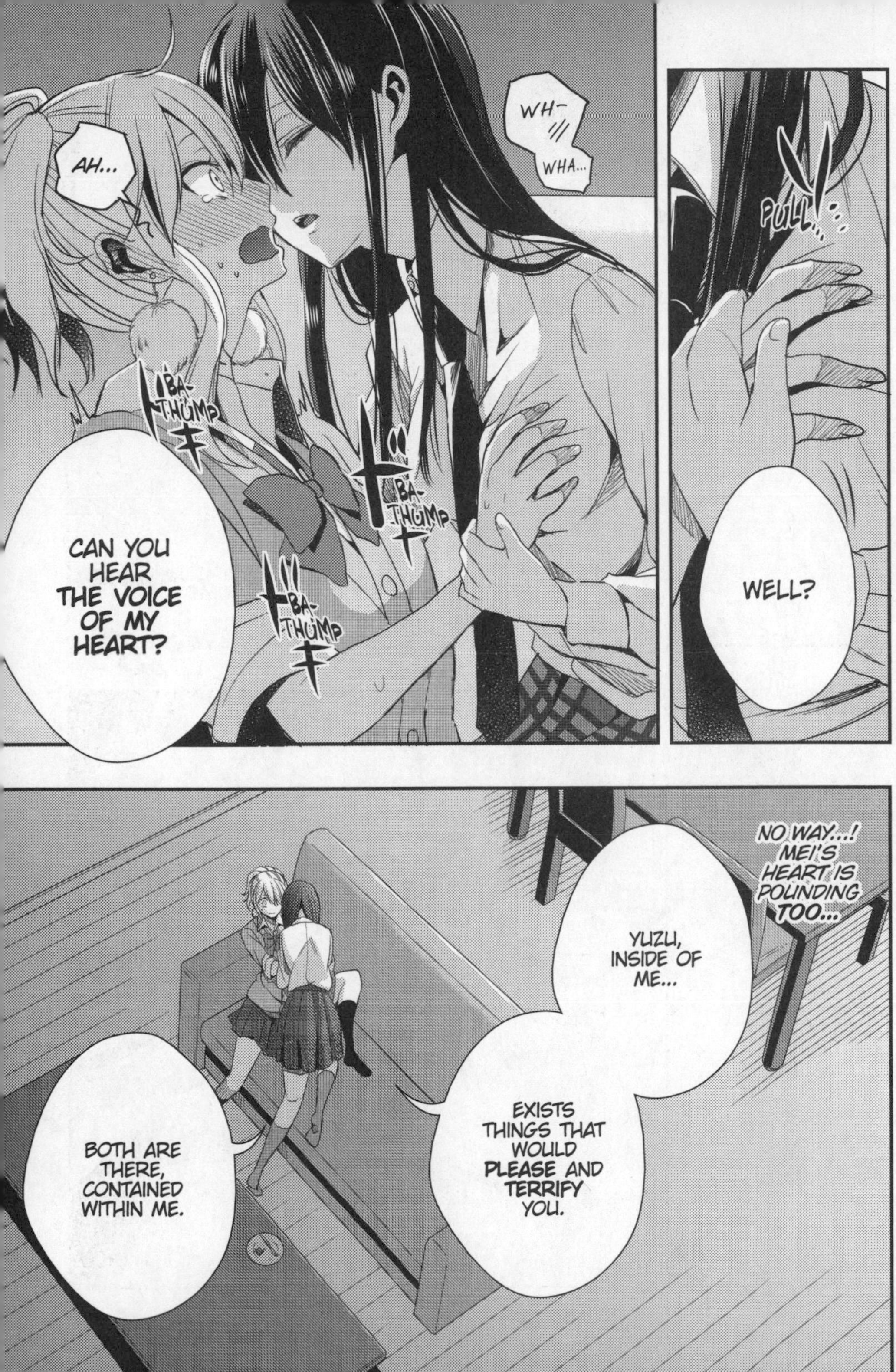
PULL...
WELL?
WH- WHA...
AH...
BA-THUMP
BA-THUMP
BA-THUMP
CAN YOU HEAR THE VOICE OF MY HEART?
NO WAY...! MEI'S HEART IS POUNDING TOO...
YUZU, INSIDE OF ME...
EXISTS THINGS THAT WOULD PLEASE AND TERRIFY YOU.
BOTH ARE THERE, CONTAINED WITHIN ME.

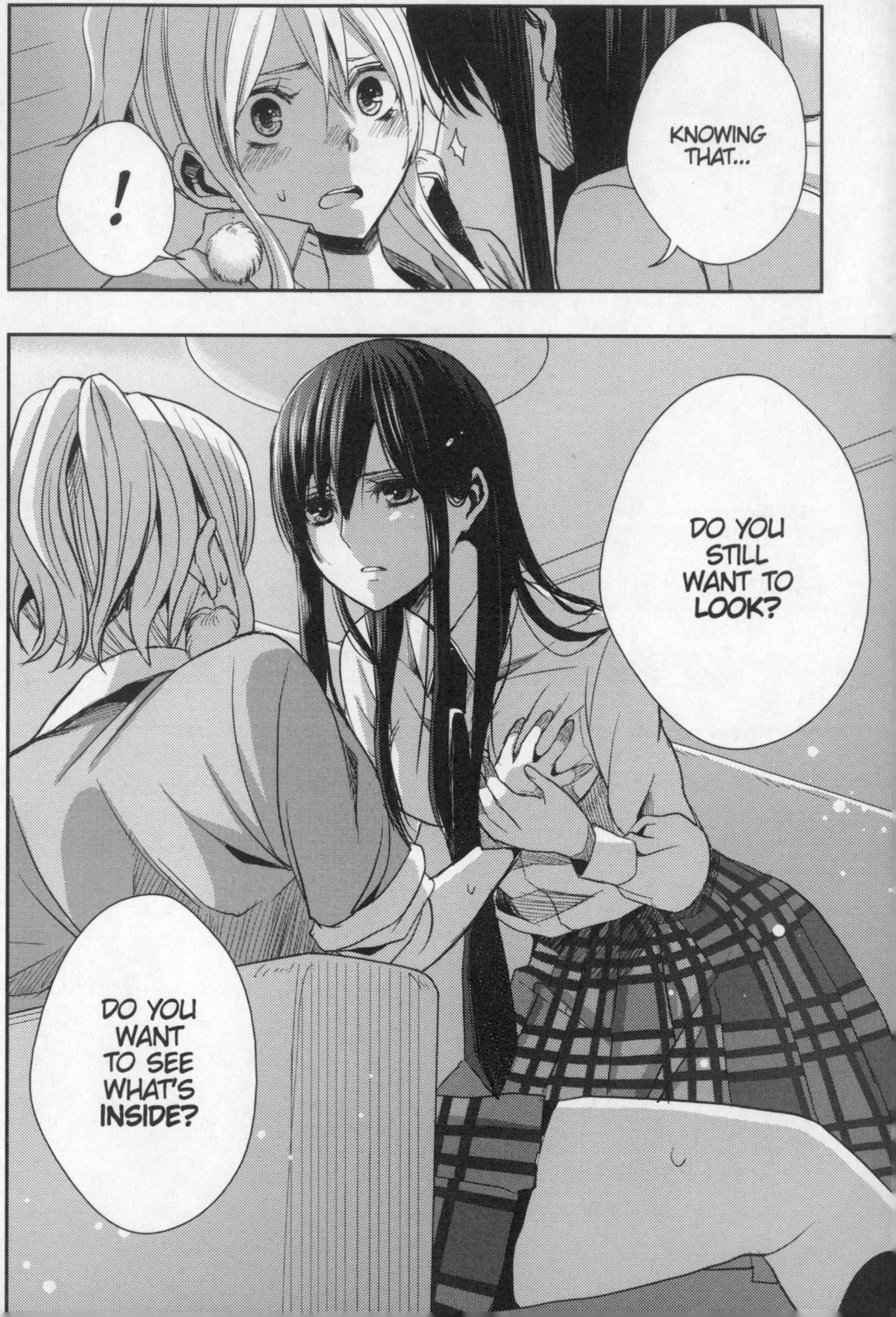
KNOWING THAT...
!
DO YOU STILL WANT TO LOOK?
DO YOU WANT TO SEE WHAT'S INSIDE?

To be continued...

citrus

SABUROUTA PRESENTS SECRET LOVE AFFAIR WITH SISTER

3

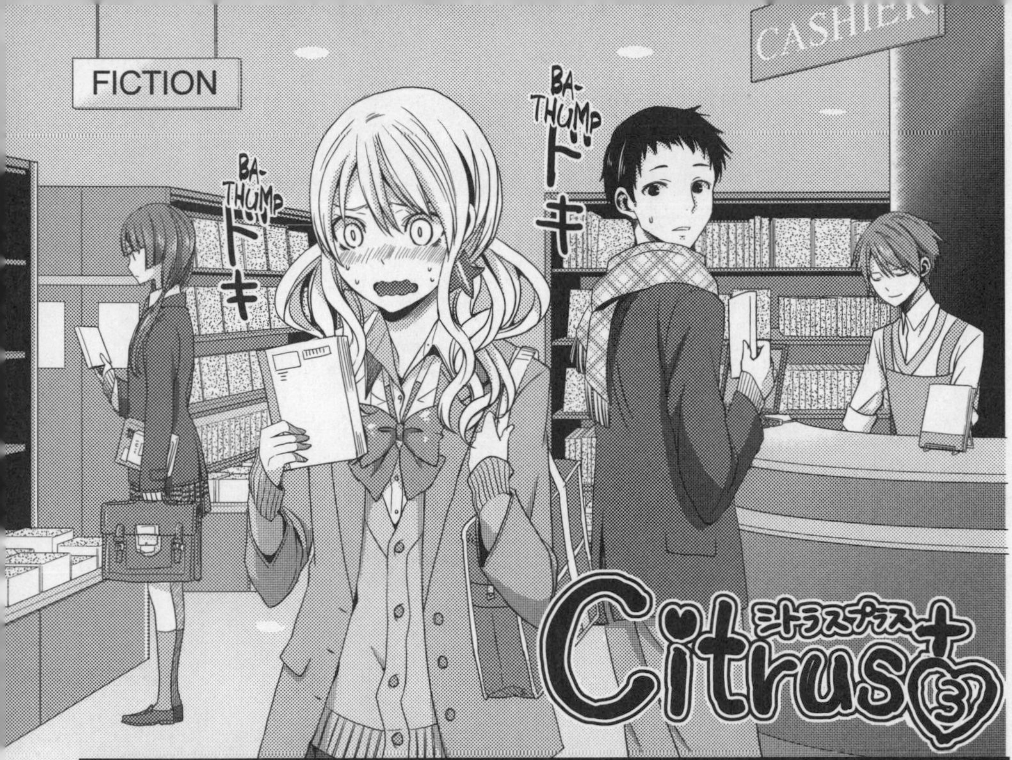
CASHIER
BA-THUMP
ドキ
BA-THUMP
ドキ
FICTION
Citrus+
シトラスプラス
3

THE OLDER SISTER HAS A SECRET

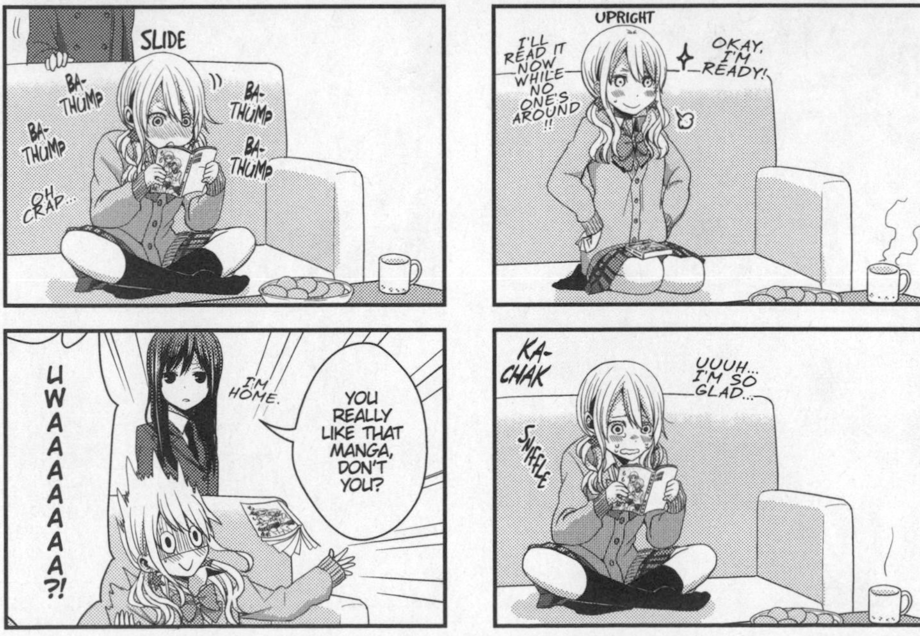
UPRIGHT
OKAY, I'M READY!
I'LL READ IT NOW WHILE NO ONE'S AROUND!!
SLIDE
BA-THUMP
BA-THUMP
BA-THUMP
BA-THUMP
OH CRAP...
KA-CHAK
UUUH... I'M SO GLAD...
SNIFFLE
I'M HOME.
YOU REALLY LIKE THAT MANGA, DON'T YOU?
UWAAAAAAAAAA?!

The Older Sister is Toyed With

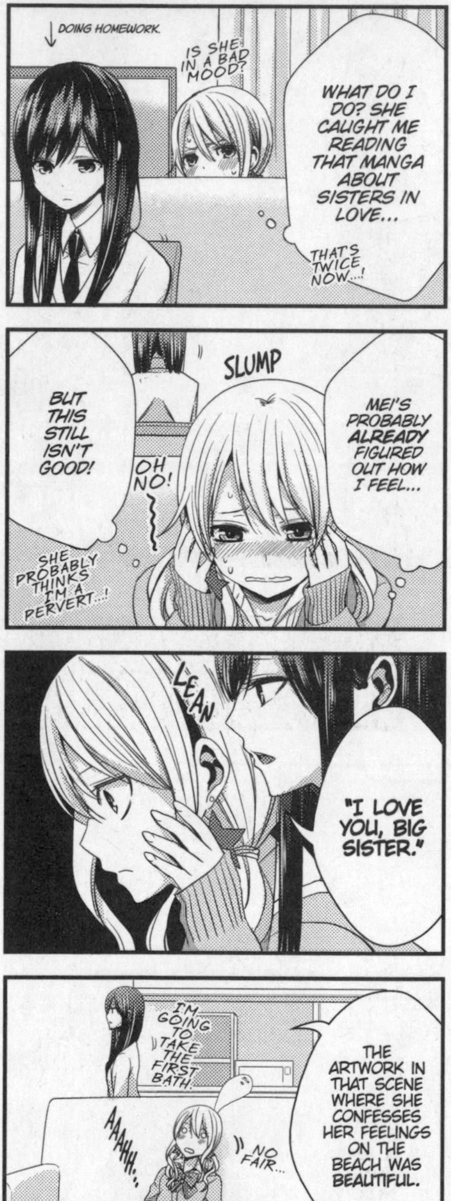
WHAT DO I DO? SHE CAUGHT ME READING THAT MANGA ABOUT SISTERS IN LOVE...
THAT'S TWICE NOW...!
IS SHE IN A BAD MOOD?
DOING HOMEWORK.
MEI'S PROBABLY ALREADY FIGURED OUT HOW I FEEL...
SLUMP
BUT THIS STILL ISN'T GOOD!
OH NO!
SHE PROBABLY THINKS I'M A PERVERT...!
"I LOVE YOU, BIG SISTER."
LEAN
THE ARTWORK IN THAT SCENE WHERE SHE CONFESSES HER FEELINGS ON THE BEACH WAS BEAUTIFUL.
I BELIEVE IT WAS PAGE 146 IN VOLUME 1...
I'M GOING TO TAKE THE FIRST BATH.
NO FAIR...
AAAHH...

The Older Sister is...

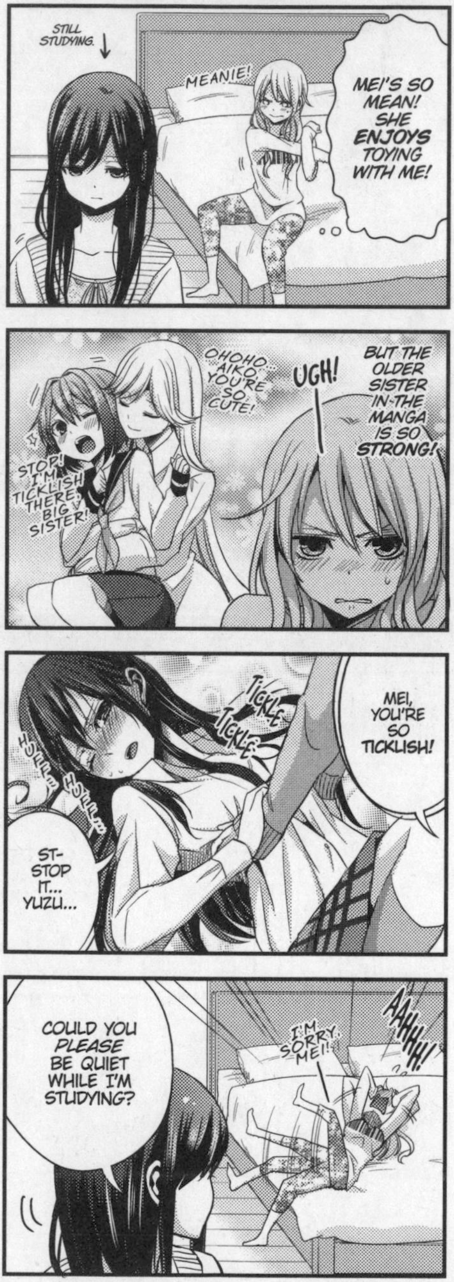
MEI'S SO MEAN! SHE ENJOYS TOYING WITH ME!
MEANIE!
STILL STUDYING.
BUT THE OLDER SISTER IN THE MANGA IS SO STRONG!
UGH!
OHOHO AIKO, YOU'RE SO CUTE!
STOP! I'M TICKLISH THERE, BIG SISTER!
MEI, YOU'RE SO TICKLISH!
TICKLE TICKLE
HUFF HUFF...
ST-STOP IT... YUZU...
AAAHH!
I'M SORRY, MEI!
COULD YOU PLEASE BE QUIET WHILE I'M STUDYING?

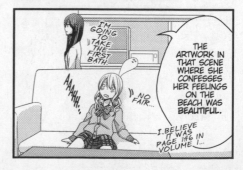

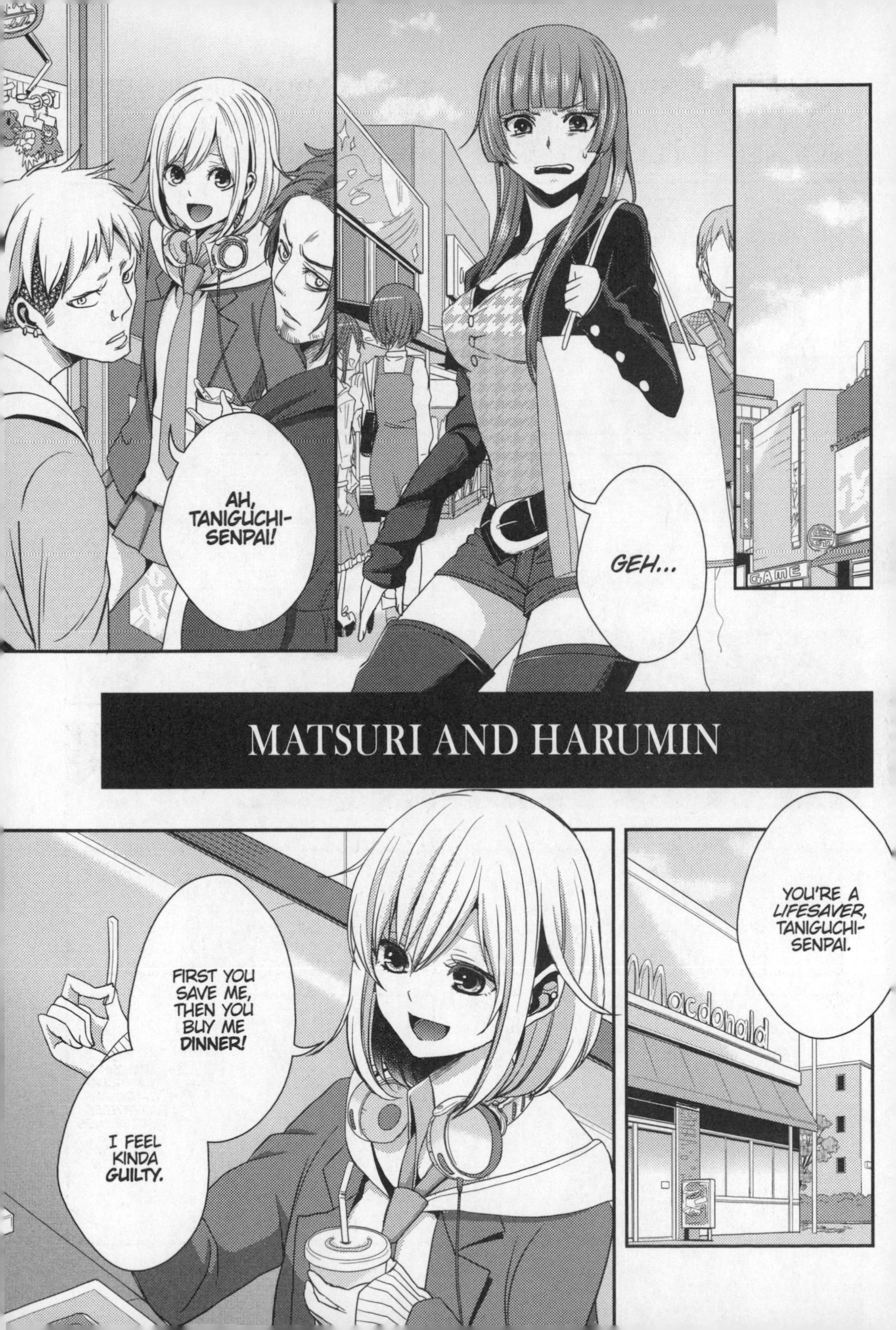
GAME
GEH...
AH, TANIGUCHI-SENPAI!
MATSURI AND HARUMIN
YOU'RE A LIFESAVER, TANIGUCHI-SENPAI.
Macdonald
FIRST YOU SAVE ME, THEN YOU BUY ME DINNER!
I FEEL KINDA GUILTY.

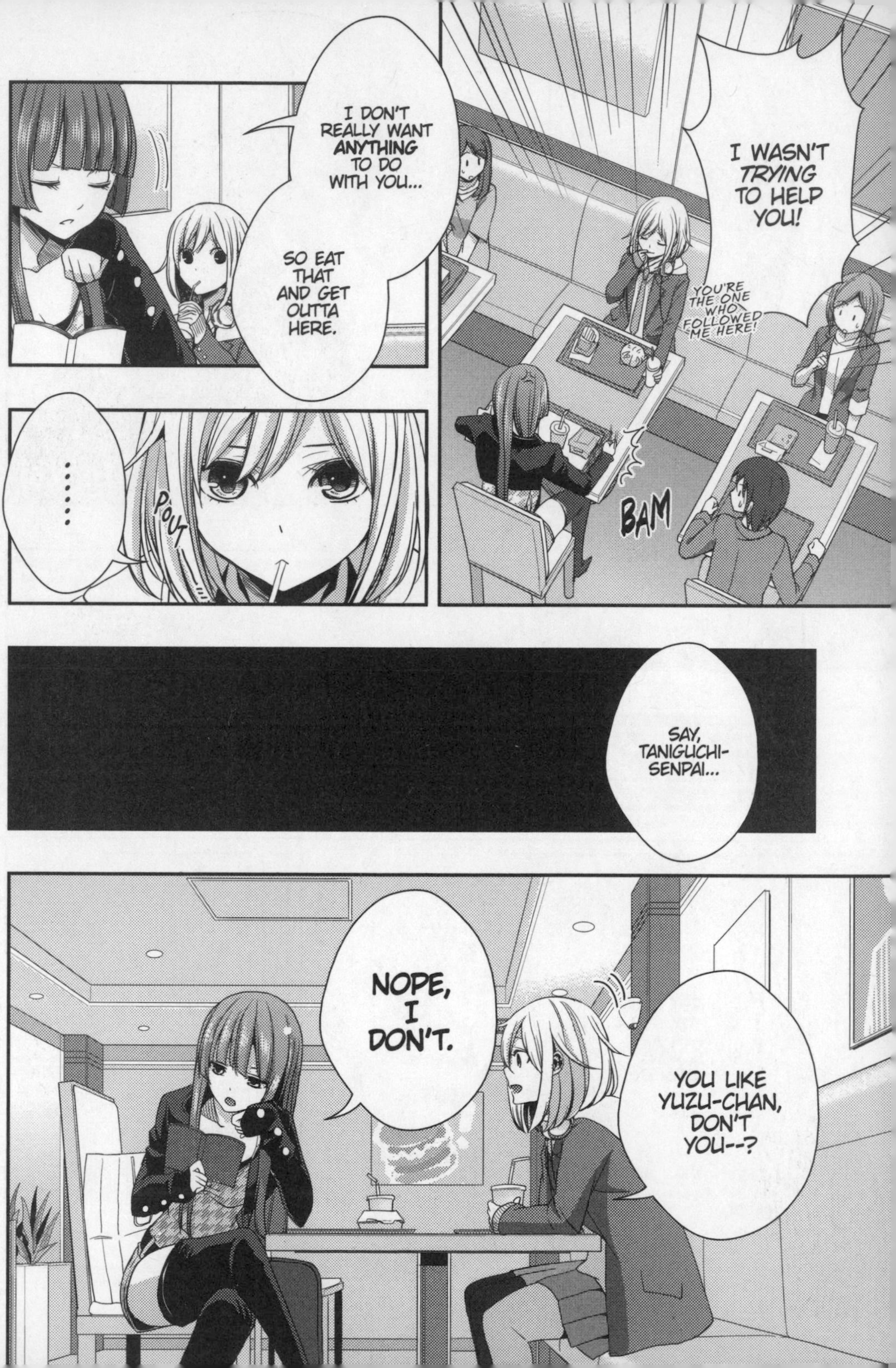
I WASN'T *TRYING* TO HELP YOU!
YOU'RE THE ONE WHO FOLLOWED ME HERE!
BAM
I DON'T REALLY WANT ANYTHING TO DO WITH YOU...
SO EAT THAT AND GET OUTTA HERE.
......
POUT
SAY, TANIGUCHI-SENPAI...
YOU LIKE YUZU-CHAN, DON'T YOU--?
NOPE, I DON'T.

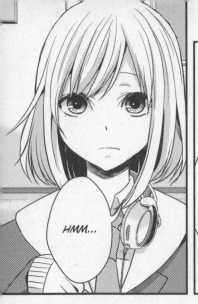

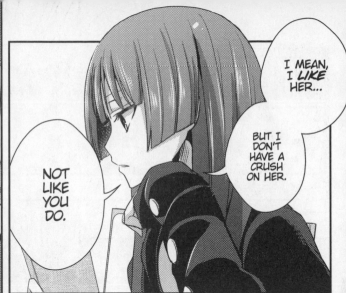

I MEAN, I LIKE HER...
BUT I DON'T HAVE A CRUSH ON HER.
NOT LIKE YOU DO.
HMM...
TANIGUCHI-SENPAI, YOU KEEP YOUR CARDS CLOSE TO YOUR CHEST, DON'TCHA?
HUH?
YOU WEIGH EVERY OPTION BEFORE MAKING A MOVE...
BECAUSE YOU'RE SO DETERMINED NOT TO GET HURT.
BUT THAT MEANS THAT YOU END UP RUNNING AWAY A LOT.

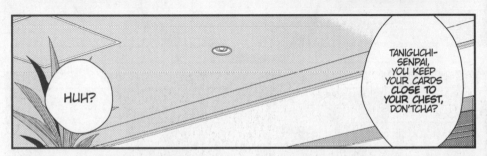

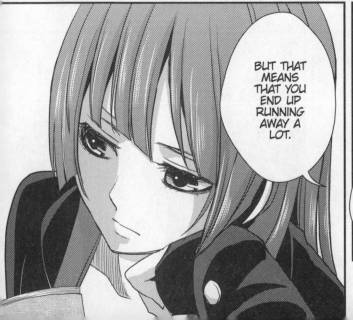

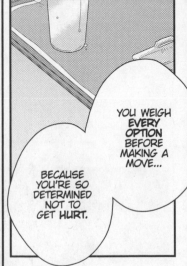

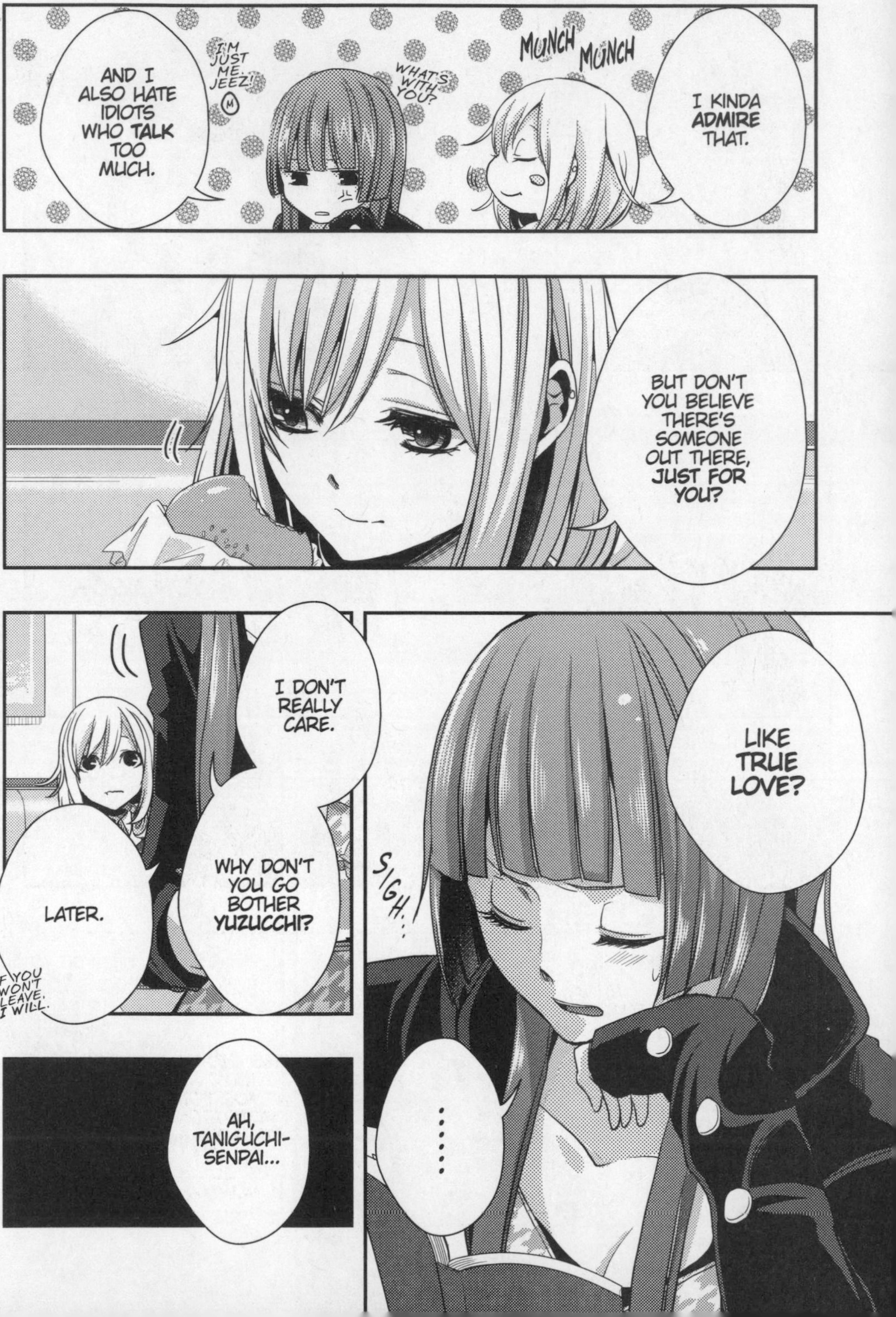
I KINDA ADMIRE THAT.
MUNCH MUNCH
WHAT'S WITH YOU?
I'M JUST ME. JEEZ!
AND I ALSO HATE IDIOTS WHO TALK TOO MUCH.
BUT DON'T YOU BELIEVE THERE'S SOMEONE OUT THERE, JUST FOR YOU?
LIKE TRUE LOVE?
SIGH...
......
I DON'T REALLY CARE.
WHY DON'T YOU GO BOTHER YUZUCCHI?
LATER.
IF YOU WON'T LEAVE, I WILL.
AH, TANIGUCHI-SENPAI...

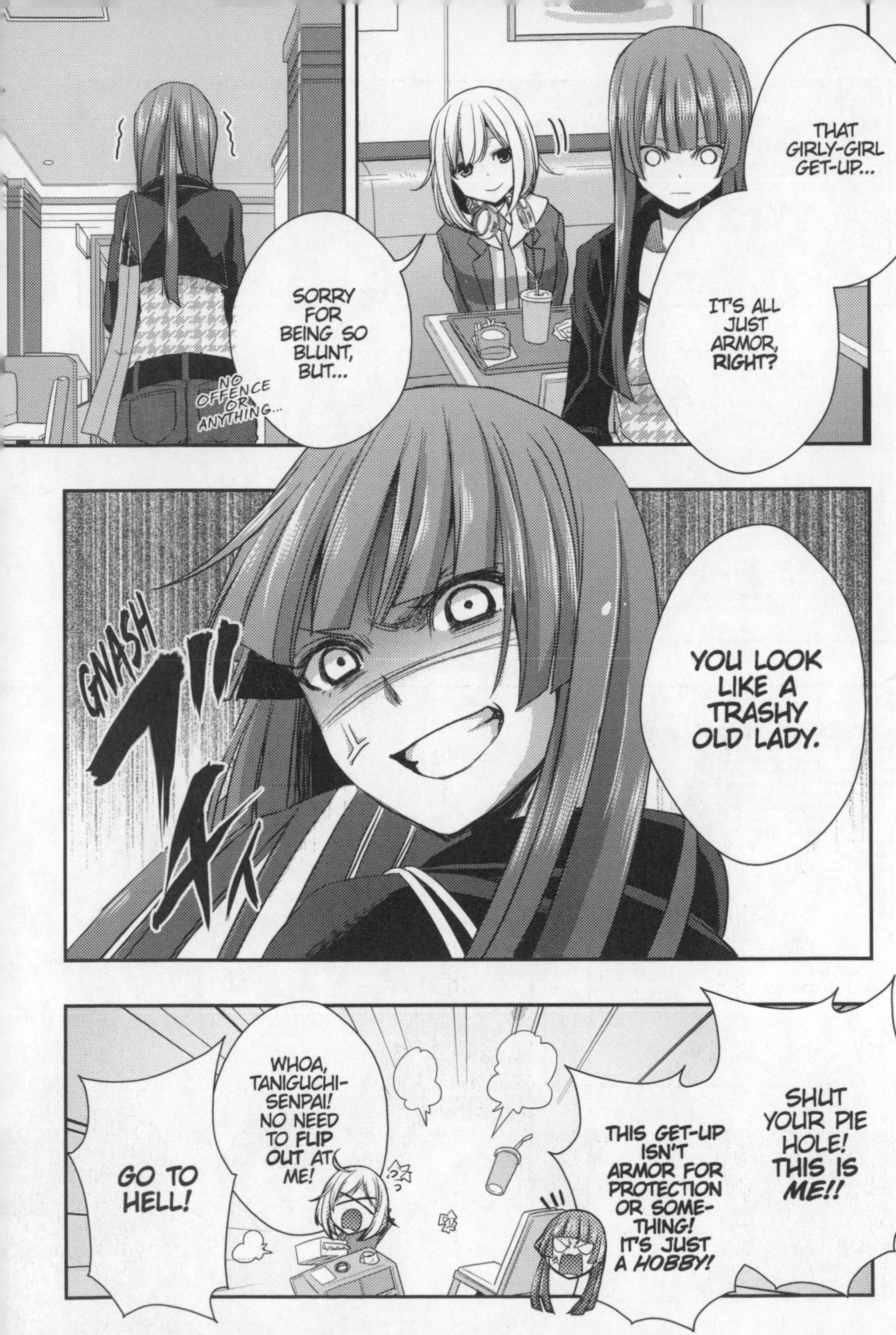
THAT GIRLY-GIRL GET-UP...
IT'S ALL JUST ARMOR, RIGHT?
SORRY FOR BEING SO BLUNT, BUT...
NO OFFENCE OR ANYTHING...
YOU LOOK LIKE A TRASHY OLD LADY.
GNASH
SHUT YOUR PIE HOLE! THIS IS *ME!!*
THIS GET-UP ISN'T ARMOR FOR PROTECTION OR SOME-THING! IT'S JUST A *HOBBY!*
WHOA, TANIGUCHI-SENPAI! NO NEED TO FLIP OUT AT ME!
GO TO HELL!

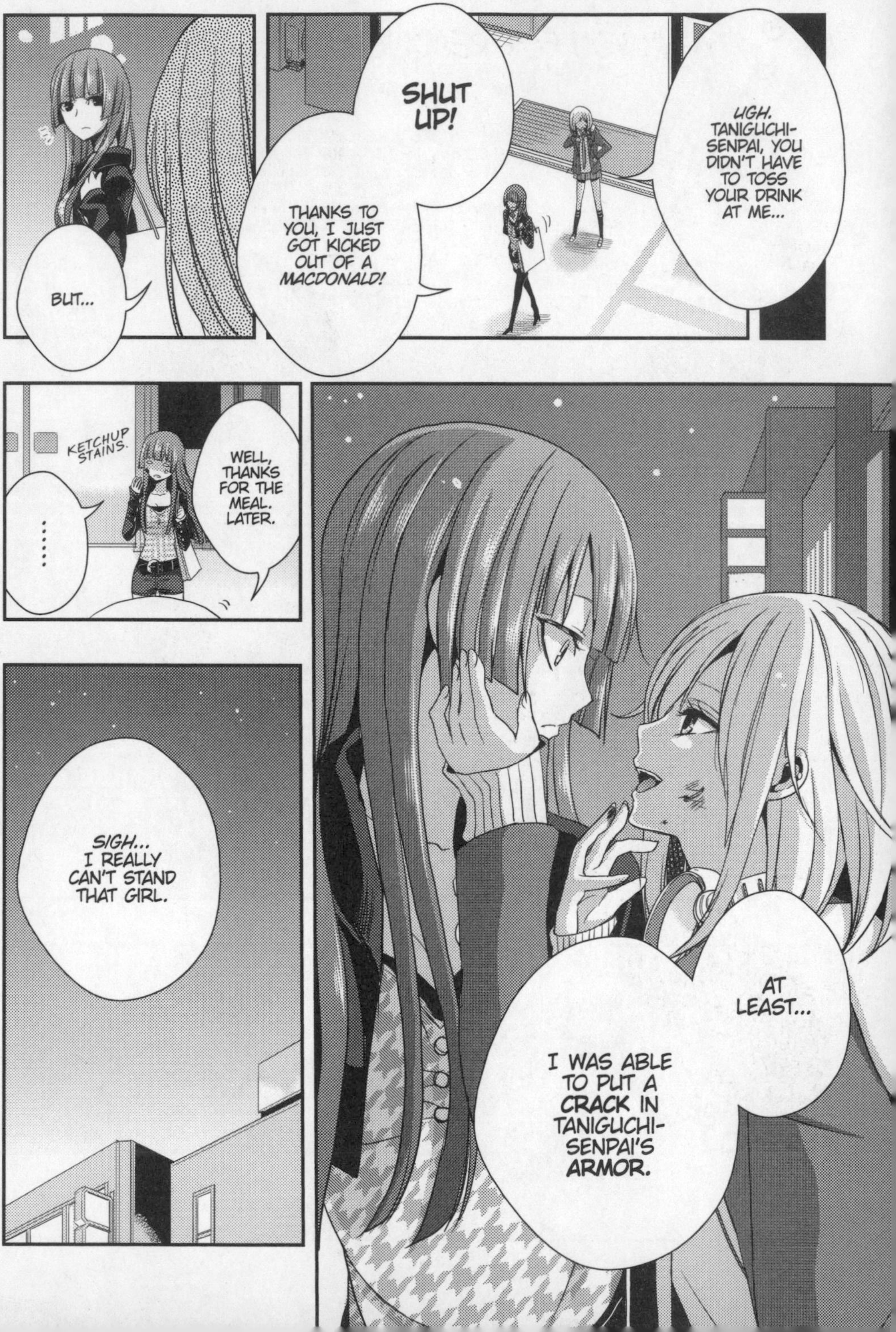
UGH. TANIGUCHI-SENPAI, YOU DIDN'T HAVE TO TOSS YOUR DRINK AT ME...
SHUT UP!
THANKS TO YOU, I JUST GOT KICKED OUT OF A MACDONALD!
BUT...
AT LEAST...
I WAS ABLE TO PUT A CRACK IN TANIGUCHI-SENPAI'S ARMOR.
WELL, THANKS FOR THE MEAL. LATER.
KETCHUP STAINS.
......
SIGH... I REALLY CAN'T STAND THAT GIRL.

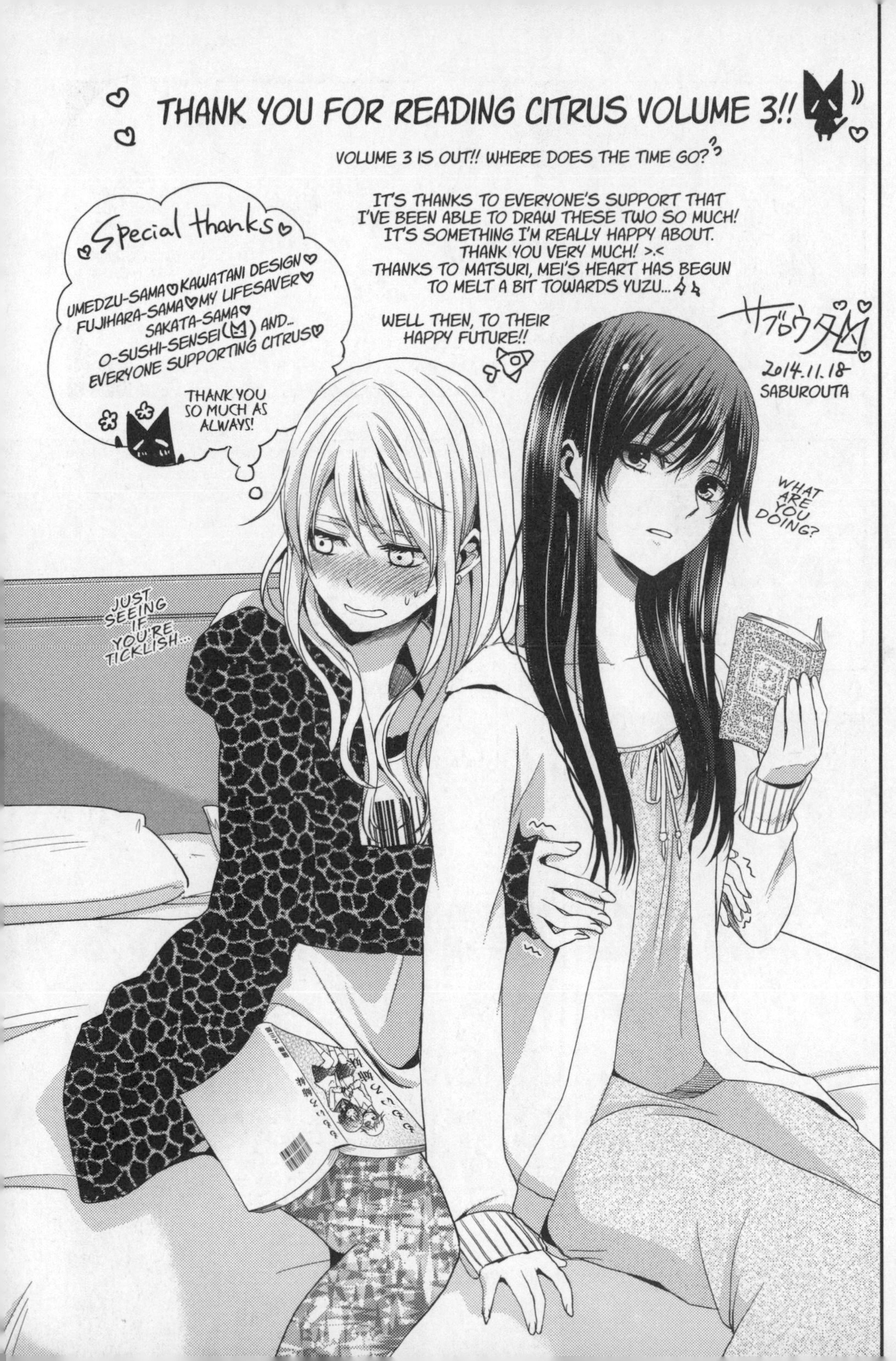
THANK YOU FOR READING CITRUS VOLUME 3!!
VOLUME 3 IS OUT!! WHERE DOES THE TIME GO?
IT'S THANKS TO EVERYONE'S SUPPORT THAT I'VE BEEN ABLE TO DRAW THESE TWO SO MUCH! IT'S SOMETHING I'M REALLY HAPPY ABOUT. THANK YOU VERY MUCH! >.< THANKS TO MATSURI, MEI'S HEART HAS BEGUN TO MELT A BIT TOWARDS YUZU...
WELL THEN, TO THEIR HAPPY FUTURE!!
サブロウタ
2014.11.18
SABUROUTA
Special thanks
UMEDZU-SAMA KAWATANI DESIGN FUJIHARA-SAMA MY LIFESAVER SAKATA-SAMA O-SUSHI-SENSEI AND... EVERYONE SUPPORTING CITRUS
THANK YOU SO MUCH AS ALWAYS!
WHAT ARE YOU DOING?
JUST SEEING IF YOU'RE TICKLISH...

SEVEN SEAS ENTERTAINMENT PRESENTS

citrus

story & art by SABUROUTA   VOLUME 3

TRANSLATION
Catherine Ross

ADAPTATION
Shannon Fay

LETTERING
Roland Amago

LAYOUT
Bambi Eloriaga-Amago

COVER DESIGN
Nicky Lim

PROOFREADER
Lee Otter

ASSISTANT EDITOR
Lissa Pattillo

MANAGING EDITOR
Adam Arnold

PUBLISHER
Jason DeAngelis

CITRUS VOLUME 3
© SABUROUTA 2014
First published in Japan in 2014 by ICHIJINSHA Inc., Tokyo.
English translation rights arranged with ICHIJINSHA Inc., Tokyo, Japan.

Seven Seas books may be purchased in bulk for educational, business, or promotional use. For information on bulk purchases, please contact Macmillan Corporate & Premium Sales Department at 1-800-221-7945 (ext 5442) or write specialmarkets@macmillan.com.

Seven Seas and the Seven Seas logo are trademarks of Seven Seas Entertainment, LLC. All rights reserved.

ISBN: 978-1-626921-64-1

Printed in Canada

First Printing: August 2015

10 9 8 7 6 5 4 3 2 1

FOLLOW US ONLINE: www.gomanga.com

READING DIRECTIONS

This book reads from **right to left**, Japanese style. If this is your first time reading manga, you start reading from the top right panel on each page and take it from there. If you get lost, just follow the numbered diagram here. It may seem backwards at first, but you☐ll get the hang of it! Have fun!!

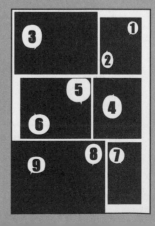

The best-selling *yuri* series heats up!

Even though outgoing and bubbly Yuzu doesn't always get along with her serious step-sister Mei, she still wants them to be a family. But when Mei kisses Yuzu, it makes their already complicated relationship that much more complex!

That's when Matsuri shows up, a childhood friend of Yuzu's who is determined to battle it out with Mei for the title of "Yuzu's little sister." What Yuzu doesn't realize is that Matsuri isn't the sweet little girl she used to be, and she's willing to use every dirty trick she can to break up Yuzu and Mei's relationship. Will Yuzu be able to protect Mei from this devious interloper?

OLDER TEEN (16+)
$13.99 USA
($15.99 CAN)
ISBN 978-1-626921-64-1
51399>
9 781626 921641

Seven Seas Entertainment, LLC.
www.gomanga.com
Distributed by Macmillan